MONEY AND OUTPATIENT PSYCHIATRY

More Advance Acclaim for
Money and Outpatient Psychiatry

"Establishing a practice alone or as part of a group is really opening a small business. Yet, as part of their training, few practitioners are exposed to the concepts and habits of successfully managing a business. Even if many of us would rather not think of the business side of psychiatric work, without a smoothly running office our practices will be besieged with distractions and the care of patients will suffer. Mikalac has addressed the needs of all those involved with outpatient psychiatry and has written a comprehensive text that defines criteria for physicians planning to open a practice and for its successful and ethical operation. Everyone looks for pearls of wisdom. This book is a gem—so pick it up, use the concepts, and refer to the references for additional help."
— Tracy Gordy, M.D., Distinguished Life Fellow of the ApA and Vice Chair, ApA Committee on RBRVS, Codes and Reimbursements

A Norton Professional Book

MONEY AND OUTPATIENT PSYCHIATRY

PRACTICAL GUIDELINES

FROM ACCOUNTING TO ETHICS

CECILIA M. MIKALAC, M. D.

W. W. Norton & Company
New York • London

Copyright © 2005 by Cecilia M. Mikalac

Production Manager: Leeann Graham
Manufacturing by R.R. Donnelley Harrisonburg

Library of Congress Cataloging-in-Publication Data

Mikalac, Cecilia M.
  Money and outpatient psychiatry : practical guidelines from
accounting to ethics / Cecilia M. Mikalac.
     p.   cm.
  "A Norton professional book."
  Includes bibliographical references and index.
  ISBN 0-393-70440-8
  1. Psychiatry—Practice.   2. Psychiatrists—Finance, Personal.
3. Psychiatry—Moral and ethical aspects.   I. Title.

RC455.2.P73 M55 2005
616.89'0068—dc22   2005040666

W. W. Norton & Company, Inc., 500 Fifth Avenue, New York, N.Y., 10110
www.wwnorton.com

W. W. Norton & Company Ltd., Castle House, 75/76 Wells St., London W1T 3QT

1 3 5 7 9 0 8 6 4 2

Contents

List of Acronyms

AMA	American Medical Association
ANA	American Nurses Association
A/P	accounts payable
APA	American Psychological Association
ApA	American Psychiatric Association
A/R	accounts receivable
CEO	chief executive officer
CEU	continuing education units
CME	continuing medical education
CMS	Center for Medicare and Medicaid Services
COBRA	Consolidated Omnibus Budget Reconciliation Act of 1985
CPT®	current procedural terminology
DBA	doing business as
DOS	date of service
DSM-IV™	*Diagnostic and Statistical Manual of Mental Disorders, Fourth Edition*
EAP	Employee Assistance Program
EIN	employee identification number
E/M	evaluation and management
EMT	emergency medical technician

EOB   explanation of benefits
ERISA   Employee Retirement Income Security Act
FLP   family limited partnership
FLSA   Fair Labor Standards Act
FUTA   federal unemployment tax assessment
GAAP   generally accepted accounting principles
GAF   global assessment of functioning
HCFA   Health Care Finance Administration
HIAA   Health Insurance Association of America
HIPAA   Health Insurance Portability and Accountability Act
HIPDB   Health Care Integrity and Protection Data Bank
HMO   health maintenance organization
ICD 9   *International Classification of Diseases*, Ninth Edition
ID   identification
IRS   Internal Revenue Service
LLC   limited liability corporation
LP   limited partnership
LLP   limited liability partnership
LLLP   limited limited liability partnership
MGMA   Medical Group Management Association
MMS   Massachusetts Medical Society
NASW   National Association of Social Workers
NOS   not otherwise specified
NP   nurse practitioner
OIG   Office of the Inspector General
PA   physician assistant
PAHCOM   Professional Association of Health Care Office Management
PC   professional corporation
PCP   primary care physician
PhRMA   Pharmaceutical Research and Manufacturers of America
POS   place of service

PPO	preferred provider organization
PSC	personal service corporation
PSRO	professional standard review organization
QA	quality assurance
RBRVS	resource-based relative value scale
RVU	relative value unit
SEP	simplified employee pension plan
SUTA	state unemployment tax assessment
TIN	taxpayer identification number
TOS	type of service
UPIN	unique provider identification number
UR	utilization review
USC	United States Congress

Acknowledgments

I would like to thank my editor, Deborah Malmud. This book would have met an untimely death without the initial hatchet job. Her surgical skills are topnotch. I would also like to thank Elizabeth Fitzpayne, Boston Medical Library's branch librarian for the Massachusetts Medical Society, for her efficient and tireless assistance with all my requests.

Despite years of experience with filing taxes, billing, and accounting, I continue to need the help and advice of trained accounting and billing professionals. Barbara Weinberg, owner of Healthcare Billing Services, provided invaluable information both as a professional psychiatric biller and an astute observer of provider billing behavior. I would like to say that my accountant of fifteen years, Carol Rice, has taught me everything I know about accounting and taxes. However I know she would require a disclaimer. Instead, I will say that she has taught me everything I *should* know; any errors herein being strictly my own. My sister, Dolores Peterson, comptroller and professor of accounting at Reading Area Community College, proofread, amended, and improved the chapter on accounting. Jan Zobel provided several last minute amendments and advice for the same chapter.

Finally, and most sincerely, I would like to thank the courageous colleagues and supervisors who were trusting enough over the years to tell me their actual financial practices and philosophies as well as their experiences, bad and good, in almost every aspect of psychiatric business. Among these I especially want to thank Mark Schlickman, M.D., Rachid Och, M.D., Carolyn Smith Ph.D., Barbara Wissner, M.D., and my long time supervisor, Richard Prager, Ph.D.

MONEY AND OUTPATIENT PSYCHIATRY

Introduction

So much is still to be written about money and psychiatry: the psychology of financial behavior, attitudes and beliefs about money, a compendium of money transferences, more on the gender, age, and race issues associated with money . . . the list goes on and on. But what I needed when I started my practice, and what many mental health professionals in outpatient psychiatric practice tell me they need today, was a simple how-to book covering the basic principles of money management. Why billing, accounting, and business management are not covered in professional mental health education is hard to understand, especially when health care costs are pressuring everyone. Good money management can be taught and learned in professional settings. It is not difficult to grasp, but it does take experience to implement. There is no better place to practice these techniques than the outpatient setting in which all trainees obtain experience. Obtaining insurance information, filling out claim forms, coding, and discussing affordability can and should be done at all levels of training, perhaps through an interface with the patient accounts department. For those out of training already, consultation with a supervisor or colleague or discussion in a peer supervision group is also efficient.

I've written this book for two large groups of people: psychiatric clinicians of every profession (psychologists, psychiatrists, social workers, nurses, and others) and psychiatric educators and their trainees. Those who want to start a practice quickly will find the first section the most useful. It contains all the basic information you need: setting up the practice, writing policies, legal and ethical issues, tax and accounting information, and how to bill and accept payment. The other chapters can wait until you are in the swim or simply interested. Clinicians who already have a practice might decide to skip the first section (although the chapter on legal and ethical issues may be of interest) and direct their reading to the topics they struggle with most.

Educators and trainees may decide to use the book in its entirety. I begin with issues related to hands-on money management in mental health practice because the principles are easy to apply and have the most relevance to everyday practice. Some may be tempted to skip the second section on external financial influences and jump right to the section on how to talk about money with patients, but I caution you against this. Patients constantly have those external influences in mind. Without a firm understanding of those influences, conversations with patients will be too superficial or bogged down with the weight of what has been left unsaid.

I did not include many case examples because I feel the use of one's own cases is more effective in converting theory to practice. I would encourage trainees and educators to present cases that illustrate the relevant points.

Let me also point out what is not covered in this book. It is not a reference on personal or business management, although it mentions elements of these. There are plenty of excellent books out there on how to manage your personal finances and run a business. Appendix C contains some references I have found useful. I do not present the Generally Accepted Accounting Principles (GAAP) in any formal sense. These principles are rapidly becoming the national and international business standard but are not usually necessary for starting out. If you want to learn how to apply them, I'd recommend a formal accounting course. I also do not address many of the issues specific to clinics, mainly because clinics have special licenses and must follow regulations that vary greatly by locale, which would be too cumbersome to include in a practical book like this. Finally and regrettably, I do not go into the many fascinating psychological aspects of money. I leave that work for others.

PART I

MANAGING MONEY
WITHIN
YOUR PRACTICE

CHAPTER 1
Before You Start

This chapter reviews the framework on which a practice is established. It is divided into three sections: establishing your goals, assessing your starting point, and taking the preliminary steps toward setting up the practice. The goals established in the first section and the starting points determined in the second section will be used to prepare the policies of the third section. The rest of the book delves into related financial topics, referring often to the goals and guidelines set up in this first chapter. When specific tasks are recommended, use the worksheet at the end of the chapter as a ready reference. Failing to set out a clear and adequate plan is one of the most common mistakes in starting a business (Duoba & Gada, 2003).

ESTABLISHING YOUR VISION AND GOALS

The vision of the practice is the aim, the ideal, the way you view the future practice in your mind. Do you want to start a comprehensive mental health center, a small group practice, or a solo psychotherapy practice? Your choice will shape the monetary policies and procedures you implement, have financial implications in terms of revenue and cash flow, and impact related issues such as tax payment, liability, and hiring employees. This vision will be your guide over years of practice, so it must have some permanency and detail to which you can refer. Talk to others about your idea to assess whether the image is coherent enough to explain. If you can easily explain your future practice to others you can be fairly sure you understand it yourself. If an image or vision for the practice does not come to you now, read on. Inspiration may strike later. My advice is not to begin practice until you have a vision clearly in mind. Without it, running the business end will be difficult.

A mission statement describes your vision. It should be short (this is not the business plan), describe the nature of your work, and be easily understood by others. The ability to explain your practice quickly and coherently is important for developing your referral base and patient caseload. When colleagues and patients ask about your practice, this statement is your consistent reply. The following are typical examples of mission statements for various types of psychiatric practices:

> I have a full-time private practice of mostly psychotherapy and some psychopharmacology patients. I accept all insurances but I am not on any HMO panels.
>
> We are a multidisciplinary psychiatric group accepting most insurances, including TUFTS HMO and HMO Blue [two local HMOs]. We do not provide emergency services but can usually arrange to see a new patient within the month.
>
> I'm an experienced couples and family therapist, but I also do some individual psychotherapy. I do not see children under eight unless it is in the context of family therapy.

Write your mission statement on the worksheet at the end of this chapter, and use it often. Craft it so that you can say it out loud easily.

Psychiatric practice is a profession, not a business (although it has some features of a business), and is subject to different legal and ethical standards. Now is the time to obtain your profession's code of ethics and put it in an accessible place. You will need it for setting up the initial policies of the practice and for resolving various financial dilemmas in the future. Appendix D contains a list of where to obtain your profession's code of ethics.

After you have envisioned your practice, written the mission statement, and obtained a copy of the ethical standards of your profession, it is time to reflect on your nonmonetary and monetary goals for the practice. Both will have an effect on the financial management of the practice.

Nonmonetary Goals

Nonmonetary goals have to do with personal work satisfaction. What do you want out of the practice? More control? A better schedule? Increased responsibility? An increased level of responsibility is inherent to solo practice. Pressman noted, "The private practitioner, having no intervening board or supervisor, is solely responsible for every aspect of service" (1979, p. 2). If an increased level of responsibility is not desirable, solo practice should be reconsidered.

Nonmonetary goals impact the revenue of the practice in several ways. Personal satisfaction lessens the monetary desires of professionals. For example, employee physicians earn less but set higher income goals than self-employed physicians, indicating that with increased control and responsibility come lower income objectives (Rizzo & Blumenthal, 1995). The lower the income goal, the easier it is to meet. The converse is also true. Physicians who are dissatisfied have higher income goals (Rizzo & Blumenthal, 1995), which of course are harder to meet.

Nonmonetary goals also influence a practitioner's schedule, intensity of work, and compensation. If the goal is to establish a successful freestanding multidisciplinary group, the hours of work in meetings will not be compensated by billing patients or insurance. If the goal is to have more time at home with the children, the hours available for work will be limited and income will be lower.

Monetary Goals

Monetary goals have to do with the desired income from the practice. Setting firm monetary goals can trigger anxiety. The process stirs up feelings related to survival and self-worth, as well as moral beliefs about accepting payment for psychiatric services. It requires concrete calculations involving expenses that some people would rather avoid. However, failure to set an income goal is the first step down the slippery slope of financial mismanagement. First, it sets a precedent for ignoring the monetary aspects of practice. Secondly, an inadequate or poorly defined income goal at the start can lead to confusion later when the practitioner feels dissatisfied or the practice is languishing financially without clear cause. Finally, an income goal forces you, as the owner, to establish hours, policies, and workloads that meet the goal and to set expense levels below the goal, making success and profit more likely.

At the simplest level, one monetary goal is to have incoming revenue exceed expenditures. The lower the expenses of the practice, the more easily this goal is met. (A list of typical psychiatric practice expenses is

TABLE 1.1
Typical Psychiatric Business Expenses

Accounting	Licenses
Advertising	Malpractice insurance
Billing service	Photocopying
Books and journals	Postal service
Computer service	Rent
Continuing education	Supervision
Disability insurance	Supplies
Electricity	Taxes, federal
Faxes	Taxes, state
Health insurance	Taxes, municipal
Internet access	Telephone

included in Table 1.1) The amount of money by which revenue exceeds expenses is commonly called a *profit* but for solo practitioners this amount is, in effect, their income from the practice. (A technical note: The money a sole proprietor takes home is not called a salary but a "draw" off the business.) Once incoming monies exceed expenses, other monetary goals then become possible, such as earning up to a certain amount per week, adding benefits, or saving for a new computer system.

While income goals should be set using financial standards, in truth many people try to use earnings to compensate for other difficulties. A study of physicians found that racial discrimination, job dissatisfaction, high levels of financial risk, and training costs all raise income targets (Rizzo & Blumenthal, 1995). No amount of money can compensate an individual for discrimination, dispel personal unhappiness, or improve money management. Professionals who set income targets to counteract the effects of these problems will find themselves frequently raising the income target while still remaining dissatisfied. The solution is to tackle the underlying problem and not attempt reparation through earnings.

The other problem with income targets is that they tend to escalate as income increases: the more money you have, the more you think you need to have (Niemann, 1999; Reich, 2001). For this reason, it is important to tie monetary goals directly to a list of expenses or a specific need *and then stick to it*, otherwise the goal will constantly edge higher. Reset a monetary goal higher only after the initial one has been met *and* if a compelling new need or desire arises. A concurrent assessment of the fiscal health of the practice and practitioner will assure that the new goal is realistic, as well as necessary. (If you have trouble separating income from personal satisfaction, I recommend reading Dominguez and Robin's *Your Money or Your Life* (1993).

ASSESSING YOUR CURRENT FINANCIAL SITUATION

You know where you want to go; now get a fix on your starting point. Assets and liabilities can be defined legally, as for disposal of property in a will; psychologically, in terms of personal strengths and weaknesses; and economically, in terms of whether they generate wealth or increase costs (Fox, 1995; Guilder, 1981). Your accountant or financial advisor may introduce other definitions that apply to your situation. Any asset, personal or economic, must be maintained over the life of the practice if you are to succeed (Covey, 1989). Maintenance usually involves some cost, whether it's for a home, office, or a professional license.

Practice Assets and Liabilities

The material goods in an office are not important for a successful psychiatric practice unless they are used to generate revenue in the practice. Your chairs, lamps, phone, office space, and billing equipment are used to generate revenue; your other furniture, artwork, plants, and water cooler are not. The latter become assets only when and if they are sold for money. Until then, their value is "unrealized." In the meantime, the latter goods incur costs to the practice both in acquisition and for maintenance.

Your professional license, reputation, knowledge base, and clinical skill are the most important assets you have, not your office furniture or car, because these are the resources that allow the generation of future income (Fox, 1995; Guilder, 1981; Kyosaki, 1998). Care must be taken to build and preserve these assets. Keep your license up to date. Continue your professional education and hone your skills. Attend to your reputation. Quality, reliability, and responsiveness (Kotler, Hayes, & Bloom, 2002) are the most important selling points for a service-based business. Each day brings an opportunity to augment your assets because every contact with a patient or colleague demonstrates your reliability, integrity, and skill. No matter how strapped for time and money you may be, don't neglect these areas; it is on these assets that your practice is built.

Personal assets are also important for psychiatric practice. First and foremost is your own mental and physical health. Many of the professional codes of ethics mention "attention to self" as an obligation (Code of Ethics of the National Association of Social Workers [1999], Section 4.05; Code of Ethics for Nurses [2001], Section 5; Ethics Primer of the ApA [2001], Preamble, p. 81). A license in mental health offers no protection from depression, substance abuse, obesity, or high blood pressure. If you have any psychiatric or medical disorder, seek help from a good practitioner who is in a position to maintain confidentiality (not someone at work). Likewise, if you feel you are at risk for boundary violations of any type, seek treatment or supervision before beginning practice.

Mental health work is sedentary and emotionally draining. It can also be isolating due to the confidential nature of the work and the stigma of mental health concerns. To remain healthy, psychiatric practitioners need to set aside time for exercise, relaxation, and socializing. A schedule that doesn't allow time for working out, eating well, or getting together with family and friends is not good for the practitioner and therefore not good for the practice. Skimping on free time may work for a year, but it will not work for 10 years. Block out the time you need for socializing, relaxing, and exercise first and then fill in practice hours around it (Walfish & Coovert, 1990).

The personal skills ("assets") essential for running a practice are organization, reliability, good communication, discipline, social awareness, and an ability to shoulder a high level of responsibility. While these assets do not generate wealth directly, they indirectly facilitate both the business and personal end of the practice. In terms of personal weaknesses ("liabilities"), procrastination spells death for any psychiatric practice (Fox, 1995) because of the extraordinarily detrimental effects on billing, record keeping, and referrals. Introversion, unhappiness, and money management problems are also likely to kill a practice but can be corrected with psychiatric treatment or good financial counseling prior to starting up.

Besides procrastination, the only other serious liability to successful practice is lack of commitment. Patients and referral sources quickly pick up on any signs of lack of commitment, causing a practice to limp along for years (Pressman, 1979). Note any limits on your personal commitment to the practice. How much time and energy are you really willing to spend at the office seeing patients, completing paperwork, and returning phone calls? How much time off will you take each year? How often are you likely to cancel office hours and for what reasons? Most importantly, what are your limits over the long term?

Most patients who enter psychiatric care expect a long-term, consistent relationship even when the treatment itself is not long. For patients who finally make the leap into psychiatric treatment, it is profoundly discouraging to have the practitioner close up shop one year later. Don't set clients up for failure. Ask yourself these questions: Will you be retiring or moving in the next 10 years? What other commitments do you have or will you have in the future that may interfere with or take priority over the practice and your patients? Having a child, taking in an aging parent, or starting another business are examples of life events that legitimately compete with work commitment. How high is your level of ambivalence about starting the practice? Do you see it as a hobby or a test to see if you like it? If so, you are probably still unsure about your ability to commit to a practice.

If your level of ambivalence is high, if you expect to relocate within five years, or if you have other commitments which are likely to interfere with office hours, I recommend waiting for a better time to start. To the public and the professional community, opening a practice implies a certain level of commitment to providing care. If you pull out by closing the practice after a short time, taking an extended leave, or canceling appointments often, your professional reputation will be damaged. This is not to say that it can't be done; the unexpected sometimes happens. Death, illness, or serious family problems may suddenly cut short what was meant to be a long-term commitment. However, take care not to open the practice with the likelihood of, or a plan for, closing down.

Your Current Financial Situation

I can't emphasize enough how important your fiscal health is to the health of your practice. A difficult financial situation can and will influence the practice in a negative way. This book will not address general financial management in detail, but I do want to mention three general principles of money management that apply not only to your personal situation but also to the financial situation of your psychiatric practice. These three principles are the reduction of debt, keeping track of expenses, and accumulating savings.

Debts cost money and increase expenses. Except in extraordinarily rare circumstances, debts should be paid off as soon as possible beginning with those that cost the most money over time. Because practice income varies from month to month while loan and mortgage payments stay the same (until the very end of the loan), your practice revenue has to be high enough to cover loan and mortgage payments even through slow times. Practitioners who have significant loans or credit card debt and are just starting out may need a second source of income to cover debt payments until the practice is well established.

Excessive personal debt is bad for the practice. Loan payments in excess of 10% of gross earnings create feelings of burden in the person who owes (Baurn, 1999). Under these circumstances, there is more temptation to deviate from the best financial practices in order to increase income for servicing the debt. This finding has been suggested by a study of cash flow in residents done by Heinreid, Binder, and Heinreid (1990), but hard data has not yet been obtained. The anxiety and pressure may result in complete avoidance of billing (the reaction formation defense) or may be transmitted to patients behaviorally by aggressive fee collection practices or preoccupation with payment. Patients, who often have their own debt problems, react in turn by resisting payment, leaving treatment, or accusing the practitioner of avarice. The trick is to manage debt well independent of the practice or securely within the confines of the minimum income the practice will generate. Substantial levels of debt are a good reason to seek consultation with an accountant or financial planner before starting a practice.

Detailed tracking of monthly expenses, including cash expenditures (the coffee you buy on the way to work) is critical to money management at home and in any business. You must know exactly what monthly

TABLE 1.2
List of Typical Home Expenses

Rent or mortgage	Cost of public transportation
Home or apartment insurance	Parking fees
Home maintenance and repair	Tolls
Household goods (furniture, supplies)	Gasoline
	Childcare
Home heating costs	Clothing
Electricity	Food and groceries
Water and sewage	Alcohol
Cable	Health insurance
Computer-related expenses	Disability insurance
Telephone	Doctor visits
Taxes (federal, state, local)	Labs and tests
Credit card payments	Medicines
Other loan payments (car, student loans)	Gifts
	Entertainment (include eating out)
Car payment	
Car insurance	Hobbies
Car maintenance and repair	Vacation expenses

expenses you will have in order to generate enough income to swing a profit. New computer programs like Quicken® make it easy to track expenses from year to year, both at home and within a practice, but a simple notebook method, like Dome®, may be best for those without a computer. The hardest tasks are keeping track of cash expenditures (best done by getting receipts for everything, no matter how small, or by recording cash purchases in a small notebook daily) and the spending of family members or other employees. (See Table 1.2.)

Knowing where your money goes now helps anticipate where it is likely to go in the future. Then consider what new expenses you might have soon. Will you need a new car? Will one of your children be starting college? Will you need to hire a biller when visit volume gets to a certain level? Anticipation of an upcoming expense allows you to save now and avoid loan or credit card payments in the future. This keeps expenses low and spares you the aggravation of carrying debt. Which brings us to the third point of basic financial management: building and maintaining adequate savings.

Savings includes retirement accounts as well as any personal emergency reserves and specific caches of money for college, down payment on a home, or a new computer. Most financial advisors recommend an emergency reserve of three to six months living expenses in liquid form (not tied up in mutual funds, certificates of deposit, or real estate) to guard against unemployment, economic downturns, and unexpected medical crises. Knowing your monthly expenses to the dollar again becomes important for calculating the amount of this reserve fund.

The most successful savings plans are "forced savings," where money destined for the savings account is taken automatically out of the paycheck or draw at the time of deposit. In effect, the money is never "seen" by the saver so the saver is not tempted to use it. This may be a predetermined dollar amount, let's say $200 a week, or a percentage of earnings, say 5% of all deposits. If the savings account will also be used for quarterly taxes and retirement, a large percentage of deposits may be siphoned off, perhaps 50%. The critical factor is to pay the savings account first, before the other bills are paid.

Adequate savings are critical to financial survival in business. They can be tapped for car emergencies, medical deductibles, and computer crises. Nest eggs also allow the saver to avoid interest, finance charges, and late payment fees when a big purchase is necessary. But perhaps most important, cash reserves give peace of mind when economic times are tough. If your budget does not seem to allow for the accumulation of savings, costs should be trimmed to provide a steady flow of money into the reserve account.

If you feel deficient in one of the three big financial management areas—minimizing debt, keeping track of expenses, or accumulating substantial savings—now is the time to get fiscally fit. You don't want the practice subsidizing bad financial habits, yours or your patients'. Take an honest and comprehensive look at your financial situation now, *before* you start or change your practice. There are a number of excellent self-help books on the market, available in libraries and bookstores in personal finance sections which give detailed steps for improving money management. Your accountant or a fee-for-service financial advisor can also help with both advice and setting up a plan specific to your needs and circumstances.

ASSESSING YOUR CURRENT
CLINICAL SITUATION

First, let's evaluate the financial aspects of your current practice or employment situation. What is your gross income (income before taxes, deductions, and expenses)? How many hours are you working per week and how much of this is direct versus indirect patient care? Direct patient care includes face-to-face time with patients and all the work related to actual treatment and payment for services, including billing, reading, and phone calls. Indirect patient care has to do with maintenance of the practice: continuing education hours, administrative meetings, ordering supplies, accounting, networking, and office housework.

The hours devoted to direct and indirect care may increase or decrease when you start a new practice. If your plan is to change from a solo practice to running a group practice, a substantial amount of time may be needed for meetings, accounting, and payroll, work hours that will not be reimbursed directly by either the patient or insurance companies (although they may be reimbursed indirectly through proceeds from practice profit or by an overhead fee charged to contracted workers). The opposite move, changing from an institutional practice to a solo psychotherapy practice without managed care, usually means that more hours can be spent in direct patient care and relatively few in meetings or administrative tasks. Whatever the change, be sure you are okay with it.

What benefits do you have in your current position and how much do you pay for them? Benefits include disability insurance, life insurance (if you need it), health insurance, malpractice insurance, and reimbursement for academic time. How much vacation, sick, and personal days do you take each year? Write all of this down on the worksheet at the end of this chapter for comparison with your future practice.

If you are an employee or part of a group, check your contract to see if you can take your current patients with you. Some contracts have a noncompete clause limiting the transfer of patients from your present practice into a new one. The presence of such a statement in the contract does not necessarily preclude taking patients with you. There are limits on the enforcement of such clauses, first, because the patient-treater relationship is usually considered paramount to the patient-institution relationship, and, secondly, because failure to allow patients to switch impinges on their right to choose both their provider and the setting in which they get care

(Macbeth et al., 1994). That said, contract law is important and the presence of such a statement, whether enforceable or not, creates complications. If your contract has clauses that limit or preclude taking patients with you, try to negotiate an arrangement with your employer that will work for both of you without adversely affecting the patients involved. If that fails, consult an attorney.

Make a list of all your current patients, if you have them. Next to each, write the name of their insurance plan and their current payment status (paid up or how far behind). If you work at an institution where practitioners are not at all involved with payment, some of this information may be obtained from the patient accounts department. Compilation may take some time, perhaps a few days, to generate, and may not be accurate depending on the quality and reliability of the billing department. The other option is to ask patients directly for the information when you talk to them about transferring to the new practice.

Mark *yes* next to those you'd like to take with you *regardless* of current insurance or payment status. Patients change insurances frequently and many will change again by the time you establish your new practice. Some patients will be able to change their insurance plan during the next open enrollment period at work in order to follow you. Or, if their care is not expensive (as with quarterly medication patients), they may opt to pay out of pocket to stay with you. Collection rates are typically lower for institutions than for private practice, probably because the fiscal relationship is indirect or because of the inefficiencies of large organizations. Patients delinquent with an institution may not be delinquent once transferred to a smaller group with more personal contact.

Talk to each patient you want to come with you about making the change. Allow several visits and plenty of time for discussion and decision making. Both insurance and payment issues should be discussed and resolved individually with each patient prior to making a formal decision to transfer. For patients with a less-than-stellar payment history, make explicit that they cannot fall behind on their bills should they choose to make the transition, because you will be ending treatment with patients in the new practice who do not pay their bills.

Try not to take it personally if a patient does not want to transfer to the new practice. Transportation, travel time, and cost all play a big role in patient decisions about where to get care. Sometimes the attachment to an institution is stronger than the personal attachment to you, especially if the patient has been in treatment a long time at one place or if the institution has a top-notch reputation that is important to the patient. Finally, there will be hidden issues preventing some patients from accepting your offer: desire to change providers, clandestine noncompliance, fear of dependency, or an undisclosed secret. Be prepared for patients to decline or accept your offer, and expect a few surprises.

Return to the patient list again. Mark *probably* next to all of those patients who commit to transferring to the new practice. (Not all the patients who say they will transfer will actually do it.) Glance over the list. Is the number of patients coming with you enough to start a practice less than half-time, half-time, or full-time? Full-time mental health practitioners book about 20 patient hours a week and half-time practitioners about 10 hours a week (Grodzki, 2000). This allows ample time for paperwork, billing, phone calls, and emergency visits (Pressman, 1979). If you will be starting with fewer than 10 hours a week, you may need another source of income until you can build the practice up.

Let's look at your current level of expertise and how this will affect the way you start off. If your level of expertise with patients is low because you just finished training, you will need to start slowly with a smaller number of patients who you are quite sure you can treat, making adjustments as you discover what you can and can not handle well at this point in your career. Inexperienced practitioners make more errors in diagnosis, implementation of treatment, and communication of policies, which require extra time for correction or lead to premature closure of treatment. This is all part of the learning process. Take the time to do things right and gain experience. New practitioners need more referrals since their caseload will be more unstable, and they need more unbooked hours per week to work out problems. If your level of experience with patients is high but your skill with billing is low, you will also have to start more slowly. Billing is something any practitioner can learn if he or she is not overwhelmed with too many patients or types of insurance from the start.

Assess your knowledge base and start where it is strong. If your area of strength is psychopharmacology, begin the practice there. If your area of expertise is with adults, begin with adults. Be prepared to expand your area of expertise as you grow. Not only will this prevent boredom, it will give the practice the kind of diversity that helps to protect it from economic ups and downs. Never practice outside your area of professional competence without proper supervision or training. To do so is unethical in all psychiatric professions (Code of Ethics of the National Association of Social Workers [1999], Section 1.04; Code of Ethics for Nurses [2001], Section 5.2; Ethical Principles of Psychologists and Code of Conduct [2002], Section 2.01; Ethics Primer of the ApA [2001], Preamble, Section 2, #3).

Now assess your current practice location. Does the community need what you want to provide? Get additional information from other providers and then assess the level of competition and the providers themselves. What is their level of expertise? What is the gender ratio? What race are they and what languages do they speak? Is there a minority market? Are any providers about to retire? What are their current time commitments and availability? What insurances do they take and can you fill a gap in the market there? If everyone is carrying a waiting list, there is certainly room for you. If no one works weekends, that creates an opportunity for someone who wants to work weekends. If no one is contracted with Medicare, the large over-65 market is untapped.

Pressman (1979) and I found that many practioners settle on a location without assessing actual need, overestimating the potential demand for their services (one of the most common mistakes in starting a small business; Duoba & Gada, 2003). And too few practitioners consider relocating to an area with less competition. Relocation by just a few miles can make a huge difference, especially if you can pinpoint a town just starting to grow. If you are early in your career, do not have children in school or family members who need local care, and if you intend to make your practice the mainstay of your career, relocating to an area with no competition can be a terrific idea. The less competition, the easier it is to build and maintain a practice.

Finally, how connected are you? Establishing and maintaining good professional connections is critical to generating consistent referrals over the years. A sound referral base boosts revenue and allows vacant hours to be filled quickly when a patient finishes treatment. Ideally, referral connections begin prior to starting practice and are maintained as an intrinsic part of your daily work through phone calls, letters, copies of reports, conversations at professional gatherings, and sometimes by meeting in person over a particularly difficult case.

Let's take a look at referrals from several sources: mental health professionals, non-mental health professionals, the phone book, patients, and social contacts. The mental health arena is a crowded one. Primary care doctors and gynecologists are adept at psychopharmacology and becoming more so. Psychotherapy is offered by many licensed professionals and some unlicensed ones. Alternative treatments like acupuncture, holistic medicine, self-help books, and herbal remedies abound and can be effective. Where, then, will your referrals come from?

Unless you are highly specialized, other mental health providers generally will not be your main source of referrals because they will be picking up and treating patients themselves. They may send you patients when their own practice is filled but if they are full you may be full too. Other mental health providers will refer the family members and friends of patients they are treating, but those numbers will not be high enough to sustain a practice alone.

Specialization generates more referrals from within the mental health profession. If you are the only group therapist, the only child psychologist, or have a niche practice like sex therapy, you may indeed get many or most of your referrals from other mental health professionals. However, most mental health providers are not specialists and specialization has its own financial hazards. Since specialists are needed by fewer patients, the total number of referrals will always be lower. And, in an economic downturn, specialty services are the first to go. Generalists far and away receive the most referrals (Adams, 1990).

To summarize, don't put the bulk of your energies into securing referrals from other mental health professionals even though these are the people who may know you and your work the best. The main source of referrals for most psychiatric practitioners will be non-mental health professionals: primary care physicians (Pressman, 1979), teachers (Pressman), lawyers, clergy, and other social service providers. They are not competitors (except for primary care physicians in the area of psychopharmacology) and they have the desire and often an obligation to refer people who need mental health treatment. Make it easy for them. Talk to these sources often. Go out of your way to facilitate their referrals and professional work. Consistent and prompt responses to calls go a long way toward making your name the one that comes to mind when a resource is needed.

Another significant referral source is the phone book. Due to the stigma of seeking mental health services, many people hesitate to ask someone for a referral and turn to the Yellow Pages in private. These potential clients are often new to treatment and may need guidance on their options. Many will not have the right insurance coverage when they call or will be unclear about the type of professional they can or need to see. It is important to take such calls as seriously as those from a professional referral source. These *self-referrals* are generally motivated and take personal responsibility for their problems, an excellent prognostic factor for any psychiatric treatment.

Your main social contacts should not be a source of referrals for your practice because providing quality care with attention to boundaries and confidentiality precludes treating your family and friends. However, don't underestimate the positive effect of a wide circle of acquaintances on your practice. The sheer number of people you know has an effect (Grodzki, 2000), even if, and perhaps especially if, those ties are superficial. Acquaintances operate outside your usual network and will know people you don't (Granovetter, 1974). Even if you don't solicit or accept referrals directly from social contacts, belonging to organizations and taking part in social activities can be useful professionally.

To build a strong referral network, try to meet with people in person (Woody, 1989), perhaps at work to talk about a patient or for lunch after a meeting. Be prepared to sum up the nature of your practice in one or two sentences (remember your mission statement?) and give them your card. The card may include a line about your type of practice: marital and family counselor, general adult psychiatry, psychotherapy, hospice counselor. If you give too many details or stress the limits of your practice ("I don't take insurance," or, "I only want good therapy cases"), people will err on the side of not referring and target a practitioner they feel is more likely to accept the patient. I am not a fan of mailing opening practice notices to all of the providers in an area to generate referrals. No conscientious practitioner will risk their reputation by sending a patient to a professional who is completely unknown to them. That said, if you are opening a practice in an area where there are no other psychiatric providers, reputation becomes a moot point; a simple mailing may be just the ticket.

Keep in contact with your referral sources over the years. Return every call by the end of the day, send out reports on time, and communicate about the outcome as soon as possible. If this means staying late 15 minutes one day or making some calls from home, so be it. Your referral sources must feel confident that you are professional, reliable, and communicative toward both them and their patients (Adams, 1990) if they are to continue sending you patients.

Some professionals cite former patients as a source of referrals (Chapman, 1990), but there are drawbacks to accepting patient referrals. The first problem is the term *former patient*. Many ex-patients will return to your practice years later either to do a different piece of work or for treatment of a recurring disorder. Many professionals, myself included, use the maxim "once a patient, always a patient" not to imply continued illness but to reflect potential continuation of the practitioner-patient relationship into the future. The second problem is that confidentiality issues emerge when seeing people from the same social network, whether they are former or current patients. I do not accept referrals for family members or friends of patients and refer them on to other colleagues. Ex-patients then remain free to return. They are not deterred because you have seen their ex-brother-in-law or best friend who may have conveyed some secrets, unsavory opinions, or contradictory observations.

Before ending this section on your current practice situation, I want to say a word about conflicts of interest that can arise if you continue to work at one setting while operating another practice. If you continue to work at a clinic while running a private practice, or if you continue an institutional academic position while running a group practice in the next town, referring from one practice into another (self-referring) can create ethical and legal problems (Pressman, 1979) or bad feelings between the two business entities. The presence of two practice settings is also somewhat confusing for patients and insurance companies. To be successful with a split or double practice there needs to be clear guidelines about referrals, coverage, and how to handle phone calls and emergencies from one site while the practitioner is at the other site (Pressman). Accounting, charting, and records for both practices need to be kept separate. Sometimes one site accepts an insurance plan the other site does not. Dual-practice situations should probably be mentioned to patients at the outset and again any time issues related to referrals, phone calls, coverage, or the visit site come up during the course of treatment. This way patients know what to expect.

SELECTING SERVICES AND SETTING FEES

The types of work a practitioner performs are called *services* or *procedures*. Typical psychiatric services are psychopharmacological management, individual psychotherapy, couples' therapy, emergency assessment, psychological testing, and disability evaluations, but there are many others, like home visits and phone consultations. New practitioners are often astounded by the variety of requests patients make for services and it is best to be prepared in advance.

List the various services you plan to offer and the duration of each using accepted insurance service code terminology. The gold standard is the current *CPT*® (Current Procedure Terminology) *Manual* published by the American Medical Association (2004), which contains a section specific to psychiatry, but similar descriptions can be obtained from any insurance company, your current psychiatric employer (you may fill out encounter forms that list the service codes and simple descriptors), and from colleagues. For procedures not listed in the *CPT Manual*, write your own simple description that includes the duration of the visit.

Try to use conventional descriptions even if you do not intend to accept insurance or if the service is not currently reimbursed by insurance. This will avoid confusion for patients who bill their own insurance and minimize inconsistencies between providers within a group. It will also facilitate change should you ever decide to accept insurance, use a professional billing service, or if insurance companies begin to cover a service that previously was not covered (this has happened often). Check Table 1.3 for examples.

The psychiatric services you provide will be listed and described on an introductory sheet given to patients at the beginning of treatment. This ensures that you and the patient are on the same page in terms of what can be offered for treatment. Agreement about the type of service being provided is part of the treater-client contract and is essential for informed consent.

TABLE 1.3
Sample Service Descriptions

DESCRIPTION
Psychiatric evaluation × 50 minutes
Individual psychotherapy × 50 minutes
Individual psychotherapy × 25 minutes
Brief medication visit × 15 minutes
Home visit × 30 minutes

Listing the services you offer also helps you as the practitioner remember that the payment is for a service, such as psychotherapy or advice based on expert knowledge (Morreim, 1995), not for health itself, which cannot be bought. In other words, the fee is paid even when the client remains ill. This is a frequent area of confusion for patients and practitioners.

Once you have a list of services, you must establish fees for each. Find out what others in your field charge by asking colleagues, looking at fee sheets posted in nearby clinics, and checking local insurance reimbursement schedules, but view the stated fees with some skepticism. Sometimes fee reductions occur for such a large portion of the practice that the listed fees are, in reality, only figurative (see Chapter 13 for more information on this topic). Institutions may inflate charges to bargain for better reimbursement from insurers or compensate for free care delivered. Many, if not most, practitioners slide their fees but will almost always quote the full fee as their asking price (Herron & Welt, 1992). To compensate for provider distortion when asking about fees, be sure to ask about the *range* of fees for specific services or the percentage of fee reductions.

Calling and asking what others charge is not a violation of the laws against price-fixing. Price-fixing occurs when practitioners agree to set their fees the same, thus eliminating any competition from lower charges. If you call up a local professional, ask him his fees, and decide to charge the same more or less, this is not price-fixing. However, if he recommends that you charge what he charges and you do, that *is* price-fixing and it is illegal. You have colluded with him to set your fee (more will be said about these rules in Chapter 2, "Legal and Ethical Considerations").

Remember that it is hard for practitioners to be open about their fees and their fee-reduction practices. They worry about competition from you and wonder what you will think of them and their practices. Be gentle, curious, open, and nonjudgmental when asking about others' fees. Try to be open about your own fees and policies when others ask.

Once you have a sense of the range of fees for different services, you must set your own fees. There are several things to consider. Pressman (1979) recommended that your fee be within the range of 90% of other practitioners' fees, because most Professional Standard Review Organizations (PSROs) and insurance companies consider a fee to be "usual and customary" if it is within this range. If you set your fees higher than this range, there will be unexpected limitations on the level of insurance reimbursement. Take the example of an insurance company policy that reimburses 80% of the "usual and customary" fee for psychiatric services. If the high end of the usual rate in your area (also called the "allowed amount") for a psychiatric evaluation is $200 and your fee is $300, the insurance will only reimburse 80% of the usual and customary rate of $200, or $160, not 80% of $300. The patient ends up paying not the $60 copayment they predicted (20% of $300), but the amount left after the $160 insurance payment, which is $140.

Determining where in the usual and customary range to put your own fees is up to you. Most people expect the fee to reflect the level of mastery (Grodzki, 2000). The Ethics Committee of the American Psychiatric Association recommends considering the skill, reputation, and experience of the provider, the difficulty of the services performed, and the quality of the service (ApA, 2001b). Some new practitioners are advised to use high fees as a marketing tool, the implication being that if the fee is high, the provider must be excellent. While it is true that the less clients know about a purchased service, the more likely they are to use the fee as an indicator of quality (Kotler, 2002), this is no longer the case with psychiatric and psychological services. Patients consult Web sites, books, professional organizations, friends, and family members to obtain information about who is qualified and what comprises good treatment, and are less likely to judge the quality of a provider by the height of the fee. As a rule, try not to set your fees at the high end of the local range if you are inexperienced. Patients who pay top dollar to someone just out of training are bound to be disappointed and may feel angry or misled. On the flip side, don't set your fee at the low end if you have 20 years of clinical experience. Too low a fee might cause others to question either your expertise or the quality of treatment (Grodzki, 2000; Kotler, 2003; Marcinko, 2000; Parvin & Anderson, 1995).

Market forces are also important to consider when setting fees (Fromm-Reichman, 1950; Grodzki, 2000). If there is a lot of competition for patients or the local economy is soft, patients are more likely to respond to small fee differences when selecting a treater. While established practitioners will not generally lower their fees in the face of a recession or increased competition, they may offer more or greater fee reductions during tough times. New practitioners who enter the market during a downturn or where competition is stiff are more likely to set their fees lower in order to fill the practice quickly. While market pressure exerted by new arrivals with lower fees may not immediately reduce the fees of experienced clinicians, it will prevent them from raising fees further so that, in effect, prices are controlled.

Let me mention a few other factors for fee-setting. Grodzki (2000) and Kotler (2002) both recommended also considering the goals of your practice before setting fees. Do you want it to be small and select or large and busy? Higher fees mean there will be less demand for services. How much money do you want or need to make? If income is less important, one has the choice of keeping fees low and volume high, or fees high and volume low. Just remember the one mandatory goal of having income exceed expenses. The charge per hour should be high enough so that you do not have to overextend yourself to cover expenses.

Leaving economic and mathematical rationales behind, remember that the charges should also reflect what the practitioner feels the services are worth, which may not be what the insurance company or the general public feels they are worth (Goldsmith, 2000). If you plan to accept fee discounts from managed care companies or allow a sliding scale, try not to take this into account. Making fees higher initially to compensate for fee reductions starts the practitioner down the slippery slope of fee distortion. Instead, set your initial fees as if there will be no fee reductions and then proceed from there as the practice grows.

There are now many studies documenting that one source of the income disparity between women and men is that women ask for lower salaries and fees (Burnside, 1986; Callahan-Levy & Meese, 1979; Heatherington, 1993; Holden, 2000; Leventhal & Anderson, 1970; Leventhal & Lane, 1970; Liss-Levinson, 1990; Lott, 1987; Mikula, 1974; Nadler & Nadler, 1987; Parvin & Anderson 1999). To protect against this, women psychiatric practitioners should take care to set their fees at least in the middle-range and be vigilant in keeping them there or higher.

Finally, fees need to be reasonable. You want to be as comfortable with your fee for patients who pay out of pocket as for patients who use insurance (Goldsmith, 2000). The Ethics Committee of the American Psychiatric Association is not in favor of "excessive fees" and defines an excessive fee as one which "a person knowledgeable as to current charges by physicians would be left with a definite and firm conviction that the fee is in excess of a reasonable fee" (ApA, 2001b). While this definition is not so useful in determining exactly how high is too high, it does convey the sense of a limit and reminds us that the public will be aware of it in a general sense. Kotler (2003) put the effort to set reasonable fees well: Try to generate enough profit to cover expenses and live comfortably while still maintaining a reputation for fairness and competency.

To a certain extent, fees will also determine the types of patients attracted to the practice (or, the *case mix*, which is discussed more fully below). Some practitioners set very high fees in order to generate a large profit from a small number of clients. Kotler (2003) stated that this strategy can be successful under the following conditions: if high fees are viewed by target patients as an indicator of quality, if the high fees won't attract competitors, and if high fees won't attract the scrutiny of any regulatory agency. Setting a low fee will pull for persons of lesser economic means, those who are underinsured or uninsured, and bargain-hunters. Take care to fully explore the market by examining the demographics of your practice location. How many people can pay your full fee and what percentage of them is likely to present to you for treatment?

Once the fees for each service are chosen, draft a fee sheet that can be posted in the waiting room or handed to each new patient as part of the introductory packet. The fee sheet makes the issue of payment for services explicit and allows the patient to fully understand and plan for any charges they incur. It also facilitates frank discussion about costs and insurance reimbursement, and ensures consistency of charges throughout the practice if more than one practitioner is involved. Fee disclosure and the patient's agreement to pay are both part of the treatment contract and necessary for informed consent. The fee sheet makes both these elements explicit rather than implicit and less susceptible to interpretation on the part of either party. As a consequence, both billing and payment will proceed more smoothly.

Case Mix: Choosing Patients and Insurances

Case mix refers to the diversity of clients (cases) that a practice carries. Case mix may vary by diagnosis, degree of difficulty, demographic factors, service code, or insurance status. A narrow case mix means the patients and their treatments are similar to one another and a wide case mix means there is great variety in patients and services. A private psychoanalytic practice which does not accept insurance payment will have a narrow case mix diagnostically, socioeconomically, and by service. A group practice that accepts many health insurance plans and offers psychopharmacological and psychotherapeutic treatment to adults and children will have a wide case mix.

Case mix impacts both the income and cash flow of the practice because it affects the volume of referrals and the type and extent of payment for the offered services. Screening out patients requiring medication treatment leaves psychotherapy as the remaining treatment modality. Because psychotherapy is more time-consuming than psychopharmacological management, this in turn limits the number of patients who can be seen in a day and the income that can be generated each week. For a second example, a geriatric practice will carry a large number of patients on Medicare with the contracted fee reduction. This will lower the income generated per hour but will also ensure steady referrals because the Medicare population will be growing for some time, ensuring high patient volume.

In general, a narrow case mix may be beneficial when serious limits on the practice are desired and when income or steady cash flow is less important. This might be the case for a solo practitioner who has another source of income and who does not want to see patients outside a set number of hours or deal with any complicated or potentially urgent cases. A wide case mix is preferable when steady or high income is important, as in a group practice where employees and payroll taxes have to be paid on time no matter what happens that week.

Specialists may have a narrow case mix in terms of diagnosis but a wide case mix otherwise. For example, a specialist in affective disorders will have a high proportion of patients with depression or mania, but all in various stages of recovery. Many will have been stable for years and only come in four times a year for medication refills. They work and have standard insurance. Other patients are hospitalized often, unemployed, or on disability. However, because many affective disorders are chronic, the practice will eventually become filled with the case mix narrowing first by chronicity and secondarily by insurance with more and more patients on Medicare and Medicaid.

In contrast, practitioners who specialize in couples' therapy rarely retain cases for long periods of time; turnover is good and case mix by diagnosis may be wide. However, the case mix by form of payment and socioeconimic status may be narrow since many insurances do not cover couples' work. If a practitioner only does couples' therapy, the narrow case mix by service type creates more risk during an economic downturn, when fewer couples' and families can afford to pay for treatment out of pocket. Couples' cases that do present during a recession are usually forced to do so by the seriousness of the situation. As a consequence, the percent of difficult cases will rise when the local economy is distressed.

Unless actions are taken to broaden it, the case mix of any practice will narrow over time either because healthier patients with treatable conditions will finish and leave while chronic or serious cases will stay with the practitioner, or because the provider's reputation has become built on the provision of a certain service or patient type. While this may sound desirable to the new, financially insecure practitioner, five or ten years of seeing essentially the same patients or providing the same service can be grueling. Action must be taken if the stimulation of a wider case mix is desired.

Once a certain number of slots are filled with patients who are more or less permanent, restrictions will be necessary to keep the remaining slots turning over. If the practice is already too full of chronic cases to allow admission of shorter-term patients, some stable patients may be transferred back to their primary care physicians. To prevent burnout, try to diversify case mix by including diagnoses or services that lend themselves to higher turnover, such as disability evaluations, family therapy, or educational seminars. Altering insurance contracts can also change case mix. Adding an HMO or dropping Medicaid may widen the case mix of many practices. Training in a new treatment modality is also an effective way to increase variety.

Case mix raises one common moral question: Is it ethical to pick and choose among patients who present for treatment? Psychiatrists, as physicians, are obligated to treat any patient who presents to them in an emergency (ApA, 2001a). In small private practices, they avoid most emergency presentations by only seeing patients with appointments who have been screened by telephone (no "walk-ins"). None of the mental health professional codes obligate a practitioner to treat every or all patients. When personal values compel a professional to "treat all comers," make sure the resources are there to provide adequate back-up. This may mean carrying a beeper or providing a home phone number. If these resources are not available, careful screening is the best policy.

WRITING THE FEES, POLICIES, AND PROCEDURES SHEET

I am a strong proponent of giving written introductory sheets to patients that contain statements about privacy and confidentiality, policies and procedures, billing, and fees. Talking about treatment, fees, guidelines, and policies initiates the contract between yourself and the patient, and lays the groundwork for informed consent (Morriem, 1995), yet patients are often too nervous or overwhelmed to recall much of what is conveyed about policies in the initial visits. A written sheet allows the patient to review what has been said in the quiet of their own space and many times over so that they are clear on their duties and your expectations. Outside the office they may become aware of questions or problems that they had not considered during the visit. The introductory sheet is also useful for the practitioner, since it obligates careful consideration of the policies presented and consistent application to all patients.

Although many practitioners do not list their services and fees on the introductory sheet, it is strongly recommended that you do so. Not only does this clarify the treatment contract and cost to the patient, it also confirms that the practitioner's fee policy is stable, which is an important boundary guideline (Simon, 2001). The *Scope and Standards of Psychiatric-Mental Health Nursing Practice* (American Nurses Association) specifically noted that the therapeutic contract must include the fees and payment schedule.

Policies regarding charges for missed appointments and late cancellations are also good to include in the introductory sheets (Green, 1993; Lifson & Simon, 1998; Woody, 1989). Since no insurance will pay for missed appointments, patients need to be made aware of this potential cost to them. Some professional codes give recommendations about billing for late cancellations and other policies (ApA, 2001a); read these sections prior to making a decision about your own policy. Medicare and Medicaid specifically prohibit charging patients for appointments not kept. Some states, like Arizona, do not allow charges at all for services not rendered (Kusserow, 1989).

A majority of mental health practitioners do charge for no shows and late cancellations, and the percentage approaches 75% in private practice (Smoller et al., 1998). The purpose is to provide a disincentive for canceling when the treatment gets difficult and to maintain the momentum of therapy. Analysts, who can only carry a few patients at a time, charge for the same reasons but also to protect their income (Fromm-Reichman, 1950;

Hofling, 1986), a tenth of which may be accounted for by one patient. The concept is one of leasing an hour (Fromm-Reichman, 1950), or paying for the analyst's time whether or not a professional service is performed. There is also the theory that even when the patient does not show up, the thera-peutic tie is maintained by the expectation that payment will nonetheless occur. This may indeed be the case. One study showed that practitioners who charge for missed appointments are eight times more likely to take steps to contact a patient who misses an appointment, demonstrating that such a policy does reinforce the treatment relationship, at least for the provider (Waitzkin, 1984).

There are many who rightly question the policy of requesting payment when no service has been provided and who never charge for missed ap-pointments. (About 40% of mental health professionals never charge for missed appointments [Waitzkin, 1984].) Other professionals charge a smaller amount for no-shows, reflecting that a service was not rendered but still providing a disincentive for canceling. Some do not charge for late cancellations or no shows if the patient reschedules within the week, thus demonstrating good faith in trying to come in and maintaining the flow of treatment. Some providers do not charge if the hour is filled by another patient, thus protecting the practitioner's income.

I do not charge for late cancellations due to snow or other bad driving conditions because I do not want patients risking their lives to get to my office in order to prevent being billed for the hour. I also give each patient one "free miss" each calendar year in recognition that "things happen" which are beyond anyone's control. If I miss an appointment with a pa-tient because of a scheduling error, I give that patient one more free miss for the year and note this in my patient accounts book. Occasionally I make individual agreements about late cancellations with a patient who has an unusual job requiring frequent changes of appointments, a serious medical condition requiring frequent hospitalization, or a large enough number of children that the patient is likely to have to cancel more than once due to an ill child. Needless to say, when any patient seems to be misusing a late-cancellation policy, even if they are following it *techni-cally*, this needs to be discussed.

While frivolous cancellations and no-shows are mitigated by charging for them, the goal is not to earn income this way. Frequent cancellations need to be addressed as a treatment issue even if you are being fully reimbursed for them. Regular no-shows or cancellations are usually a form of passive noncompliance or an expression of dissatisfaction with the treatment. Allowing missed appointments to continue without discussion because the patient willingly pays is a form of collusion and possibly financial exploitation as well.

Regardless of the type of policy you choose for no-shows and late cancellations, consistent implementation is critical. Documentation of the general policy (provided by the introductory sheet) and its application to each instance is also important for accounting and liability purposes, or in case there is a disagreement with the patient.

Other monetary practices and policies which can be included in the patient sheet are the billing cycle, patient and practitioner responsibilities regarding insurance, and ending treatment for nonpayment. These topics will be addressed in the relevent chapters on billing, insurance, and termination. A sample patient information sheet from my own practice is included in Appendix A.

Simply handing the sheet to the patient in the first or second session is not enough. Each point must be addressed verbally and specifically at the beginning of treatment with every patient to make sure he or she understand the expectations. Be prepared to reexamine these points again with the patient in the future; a single conversation is not enough. Patients are anxious and overwhelmed at the onset of treatment and often forget your policies. You will most likely have to go over them again if and when there is a problem.

After you have written up your patient information sheet listing fees, services, and policies, return to your initial mission statement and goals. Do they seem compatible? If not, what seems like it should or could be modified? Reread your code of ethics. Is there anything in your information sheet that runs counter to your professional guidelines? If so, you will need to change it to fit the standards of your profession.

SETTING A SCHEDULE

After you have drafted your fees and policies, pick a tentative schedule for seeing patients. Allow half an hour at the beginning of each day to open the office, arrange charts, retrieve messages, and return phone calls and deal with any obvious problems. More time may be needed to open the office and start patient flow on Monday mornings because of the backload of calls and problems from the weekend. For similar reasons, allow some time at the end of each day to close up the office and finish up any paperwork or phone calls. To keep up with notes and allow time to review the chart before each patient, it is better not to book more than three 15-minute visits in an hour or more than four hourly patients back to back without a break to catch up. While all this unbooked time does not generate revenue directly, it does so indirectly by aiding patient flow, so that patients are seen on time for their alloted time. This improves patient satisfaction. Happy patients don't cancel or show up late and generally pay their bills on time in full. And they'll do their best to stick with you through all their insurance changes and moves.

Become aware of how many patients you can really see in a day and still give good care. Time for paperwork and billing should be included in the weekly schedule and depends on the number of new patients seen each month. Initial evaluations require more time outside of the actual visit for gathering data and writing the report. If there isn't sufficient time to complete paperwork, phone calls, and accounting in a timely fashion, the practice may be overbooked.

Scheduling affects patient selection. The more days worked per week, the more symptomatic patients can be because twice-weekly visits are possible. Patients with difficult work hours like CEOs, EMTs, and physicians can also be accomodated more easily. Evening hours attract steady workers and married parents. Daytime hours are preferred by the elderly, disabled, single mothers with school-age children, and local workers with flexible lunch hours. If filling a practice is important, an adaptable schedule is key. In the beginning, a clinician may need to work less desirable hours to get and keep patients (Coonerty, 1990). Once the practice is consistently full, or nearly so, the schedule can be gradually changed to weed out inconvenient appointment times.

You should allow time for seeing patients on an emergency basis even if you don't specifically provide emergency services. Patients have crises, and crises are best handled by the provider who treats them. This means keeping some potentially open hours later in the week to squeeze in a patient with a crisis earlier in the week. Occasionally adding a patient to the end of the day Thursday or the beginning of the day Friday to ameliorate or prevent a crisis is usually not too inconvenient and will go a long way toward accomodating clients in need. That said, a patient in real distress is almost always willing to accept any appointment time you can give them within reason.

Let me make a note here about Monday and Friday appointments. In general, there is a higher cancellation rate for Monday mornings and Friday afternoons than for the rest of the week. To mitigate no-shows and cancellations, avoid booking appointments on Monday mornings and Friday afternoons. That time can be used more efficiently for crisis appointments, staff meetings, billing, and making phone calls. Calls to insurance companies, managed care companies, and colleagues are also difficult on Monday mornings and Friday afternoons because the call volume is high. Save time and aggravation by making those calls some time during the middle of the week.

For providers who want to work part-time, remember that it is hard to build and maintain a part-time practice seeing fewer than eight patients per week. Overhead costs do not vary much by caseload; you'll need an office, furniture, phone service, and supplies whether you are seeing two patients or two hundred, so the cost of operation per patient actually goes down as caseload goes up. It is harder to make money with a part-time practice, not only because fewer hours can be billed but also because fewer patients can be accomodated by a limited schedule (Duoba & Gada, 2003). Carrying too few patients conveys a lack of commitment (Pressman, 1979) and availability to referral sources, while patients read limited hours as inaccessability. As a result, obtaining and keeping new patients is more difficult.

Try to book at least eight to ten sessions per week and attend to the timing of office hours carefully. If you really don't want to see that many patients, at least increase the hours the practice is open, even if the hours remain unfilled, so you can be reached more easily. Spread office hours across the week rather than bunching them all into one or two days. The practitioner who works two days a week for five hours each seems more available than the one who works 10 hours one day a week.

The other risk of carrying too few patients is that the practice becomes more of a hobby than a business, leading to an erosion of professional practices and procedures. Grodzki (2000) used the following checklist to verify that a practice is not a hobby: having a business plan and effective billing, filing, and record-keeping systems, employing consultants for supervision, accounting and legal purposes, returning all phone calls promptly, having printed policy sheets, and spending 75% of office time seeing patients.

The fewer patients in the practice, the more financially dependent the practitioner is on each one and the more likely he will be to retain patients who ordinarily would be let go (Fromm-Reichman, 1950). The more patients in the practice, the less intensely the practitioner is psychologically or financially bound to any one, fostering a more neutral and less grasping position for the treater.

To summarize, a part-time practice can be done well but more attention must be paid to generating referrals, responding to patients when not in the office, accommodating crises, and demonstrating commitment to the practice. In addition, fiscal management has to be tighter because the cost of operating the office is higher for each patient and less revenue will be generated overall. Finally, care must be taken to guard against undue retention of patients because the provider will be more dependent on each.

While carrying too few patients creates special problems, carrying too many patients can also cause trouble, although perhaps not as much in the financial arena. Overbooking can result in delays for both initial and regular follow-up appointments. The former can result in referrals drying up and the latter in negligent care. When urgent cases have to be squeezed in, patients with scheduled appointments experience long waits, a prime cause of decreased patient satisfaction. Patients' time is valuable, too. Delays cause patients to drop out, change treaters (Kaplan et al., 1996), come late, cancel, or postpone payment, all of which decrease revenue, patient flow, and office efficiency. Secondly, an overscheduled provider is more likely to be rushed and forget certain aspects of care or documentation (Waitzkin, 1984) increasing risk of malpractice and inaccessability of the practitioner (ProMutual Risk Management Group, 2002–2003). Taragin (1992) stated that the lower malpractice risk of female physicians with comparable patient volumes is secondary to the fact that women physicians spend more time with each patient (see also Kaplan, 1995, and Kaplan, 1996). And overbooking may lead to professional dissatisfaction and burnout (Parvin & Anderson, 1995).

How does overbooking relate to the cash flow of the practice? Is the high caseload an attempt to correct a revenue problem? If so, perhaps something more effective and immediate will remedy the problem, such as reducing costs. Your accountant or financial advisor might be of help here. Medicolegally and psychologically, it is best to limit your practice to the number of patients you can treat well and then structure your finances accordingly.

After choosing a schedule that generates the right amount of revenue and allows time for paperwork and emergencies, estimate how many weeks you will be out for vacation each year and how many days you might miss due to sickness, family illness, or weather. Remember that patients will also take vacations, get sick, and cancel due to family illness. Between their cancellations and yours, forty visits a year (not fifty) is typical for weekly therapy patients and almost always adequate to keep the treatment moving forward at a good pace.

It is most cost-effective to take your vacation when most of your patients will be taking vacation, usually in the summer months of July and August. My opinion is that for mental health professionals, longer vacations of two to four weeks, are better than taking one week at a time. One-week vacations are too short to prevent burnout; by the time you relax enough not to think about the office the week is almost up. One week is also too short for patients to get used to your being away. Provider vacations are excellent opportunities to forward patient growth and decrease psychological dependency. They also allow patients to consider ideas about their illness and treatment without input of the provider. For patients easily influenced by the power of the treater, this freedom can result in a new understanding of the process and their level of commitment to treatment, the patients' presenting new insights or ideas in the initial visit after the provider's return. Tell current patients about any long vacation three months beforehand to be sure they are stable and prepared enough to manage it, even with coverage. Closing the practice to new patients for some period prior to any long vacation ensures that potentially unstable patients are not brought on board just as the provider is leaving. Needless to say, good coverage is essential for all practices regardless of the duration of the vacation and can usually be traded with another practitioner with similar needs.

The biggest problem with long vacations is managing the fiscal hole created by them, although four weeks off is fours week off, whether taken all together or separately. When you are an employee, it seems as if you are "paid" for vacation and sick time but in reality you are paid an income that the facility divides over the course of the whole year so that you receive a paycheck even when you are sick or on vacation. When you are sick or on vacation as an employee, you are not generating income for the business, but you don't care about that because the paycheck will come in regardless. When you are self-employed, you are more acutely aware that you are not generating income when you are out sick or on vacation.

There are two kinds of cash-flow holes created by long vacations. The first type, what I call the *bank hole*, occurs during the vacation and is an issue only for those in solo practice. The bank hole occurs because although checks come in while you are on vacation, you are not there to collect, post, and cash them. They sit in the mailbox until you come back. To compensate for this, you have to have enough money in your personal checking account ahead of time to draw on while you are away on vacation, since no checks will be going in while you are away.

The second money crunch, which I call the *payment hole*, comes after your long vacation as a consequence of not performing any services for which you can be paid during the time you were out. The timing of the payment hole depends on the practice's payment sources and billing cycle. Practices heavily dependent on patient payment, which generally occurs one to four weeks after the visit, will have a cash-flow problem mostly in the first month after a long vacation. Practices heavily dependent on insurance payment will experience low cash flow four to six weeks after the vacation because that is when payments would have come in for services performed at the time of the vacation. Payments for visits from the month *before* the vacation will still be coming in as you get back.

Overcoming the holes in cash flow created by vacations takes a little planning. Be sure to make your yearly income high enough to accommodate at least four weeks of vacation per year (summer vacation plus any winter holiday, spring break, or sick time). This means money is set aside and available not only to pay for the actual vacation itself (the bank hole) but also to cover office expenses during the time after vacation when revenue is down (the payment hole). If planning for this seems hard, make arrangements to pay yourself a salary (called a *draw* if you are a sole proprieter) every two weeks, just as you would have as an employee. An accountant can tell you more about this.

Return again to your mission statement and list of goals. Does the schedule you have laid out fit these goals? For example, if your goal is to provide long-term, insight-oriented psychotherapy, working one day a week will not be compatible with this purpose since transference crises and life events often require extra visits within the week. If your goal is to have more time with family and you only allowed for two weeks of vacation, perhaps that needs to be revisited.

CALCULATING FUTURE INCOME, EXPENSES, AND THE COST OF BENEFITS

You already set some monetary goals. Now we have to see if they are realistic and if you have room to set an income target that is higher. The first step is to set an income minimum, the absolute lowest income you need to make ends meet. It must at least cover the essential expenses of the practice and any expenses at home not covered by another source of income. (Use the lists in Tables 1.1 and 1.2 to generate this amount.) These two numbers, the income minimum and the income target, establish the limits between which you will operate the practice over the years as money cycles ebb and flow. Deviation above the target or under the minimum should prompt examination of the practice. Overshooting the income target is fine as long as it can be maintained and does not come at the cost of nonmonetary goals. Constantly skirting the income minimum means the practice is at risk of folding.

Now it's time to estimate your starting income and potential income based on your schedule, patient list (if you have a patient base to start with), and your fees. Starting income will be the revenue generated if you see all of your current patients at their usual visit frequency for their usual service type at the established fee. If you expect to render four hours a week of psychotherapy at $125 per visit and see six monthly psychopharmacology patients per week at about $65 each, that will bring in about $3,560 each month. Starting income will vary greatly depending on your current clinical situation. If you will be starting from scratch, with no patients at all, your starting income will be zero and your expenses will have to be covered by another source (hopefully personal savings or excess income from another source).

Potential income is the expected revenue generated if all your planned clinical hours are booked. Remember that not all scheduled appointments will occur. When calculating monthly income for a mixed practice of short or medium term therapy, subtract about 10% for cancellations. For a long-term psychotherapy practice, it's best to calculate weekly income assuming all patients show up and then multiply for 40 weeks instead of

52 weeks for the yearly income, since most reliable long-term weekly patients make about 40 visits a year. Short-term contracted therapy is different; 10 sessions will be 10 sessions. Since all cancellations will simply be rescheduled, there is no need to correct for lost visits.

Pressman (1979) offered another formula for calculating revenue lost through canceled appointments and uncollected debt. Although it is not based on hard data, I think it is an accurate guestimate. If you will be doing all the billing yourself and plan to stay on top of it, your collection rate should be close to 98%, especially after the first year. It is my belief, and also Pressman's (1979; although this has not yet been proved by research) that the less directly the biller is related to the provider of service, the lower the collection rate. Therefore, assume a less than 95% collection rate if you are using a billing service. In addition, you must subtract the billings service's payment, which is usually about 7% of collections. If you plan to use credit cards (most practitioner's do not) subtract 2–3% from your potential income for the service fee (see Chapter 5 for more information on credit card payments).

Below are some examples of starting and potential income calculations.

Example 1.1: *Mrs. Richardson is a newly licensed clinical social worker specializing in short-term individual psychotherapy. She doesn't want to work full-time and will be taking about four weeks of vacation each year, two in the summer, one at the winter holiday, and one during spring break. She does not accept insurance and does not give fee reductions.*

Starting income:	*Zero (no current patients)*
Planned schedule:	*Mondays, 3 hours @ $80/visit*
	Wednesdays, 5 hours @ $80/visit
	Fridays, 3 hours @ $80/visit
Potential income:	*$80 × 11 hours ($880) − 10% cancellation rate ($88) = $792/week or ~$3,150/month*
Potential yearly income	*($3,150 × 11 months because of vacation): ~$34,800*

Example 1.2: *Dr. Diaz just finished her psychiatric residency and is starting a private practice by taking 23 patients with her from her former clinic. Six of them are Medicare patients. She plans to work full-time and expects*

her practice to fill quickly because she is the only woman psychiatrist who can speak Spanish fluently in her area. She will be taking at least four weeks of vacation a year but probably more like six if she includes sick time and holidays.

> *Starting monthly income: ~ $4,220/month*
>
>> *8 weekly psychotherapy patients @ $125/visit = $4,000/month – 10% cancellations ($400) = $3,600/month*
>>
>> *OR 8 weekly patients × 40 weeks per year ($40,000) divided by 12 months = $3,333/month*
>>
>> *1 weekly psychotherapy patient at Medicare rate of $106/visit = ~$353/month*
>>
>> *4 half-hour psychotherapy/medication patients seen monthly @ $85/visit = $340/month (no cancellation rate because all appointments rescheduled)*
>>
>> *5 patients for quarterly brief medication visits @ $65/visit and 5 patients for quarterly brief medication visits @ Medicare rate of $51/visit = (20 visits per year @ $65) plus (20 visits per year @ $51/visit) = $1,300 + $1,020 = $2,320/year or $193/month*
>
> *Potential income:*
>
>> *Tuesdays, Wednesdays, and Thursdays she hopes to see five psychotherapy patients each day and three medication patients, and on Mondays and Fridays she hopes to see three psychotherapy patients and about 10 psychopharmacology patients with about 20% of her overall caseload being Medicare patients.*
>
> *Potential yearly income:*
>
>> *17 hours (80%) × $125/visit = $2,125 – 10% cancellation ($213) = $1,912/week*
>>
>> *4 hours (20%) × $106/visit = $424 – 10% ($42) = $382/week*
>>
>> *23 brief medication visits (80%) × $65/visit = $1,495/week*
>>
>> *6 brief medication visits (20%) × $51/visit = $306/week*
>>
>> *Total potential monthly income = $16,380/month*
>>
>> *Total potential yearly income (10.5 months per year) = ~ $172,000*

There is always an upper limit on the amount of income any practice can generate because each provider can only see a certain number of patients per day. Make sure that your income goal falls within that scope. If your income goals are beyond what can be reasonably generated in your practice, another source of revenue must be found outside the practice, perhaps in real estate or some other business venture. If you can accept the income limits of your practice, proceed. If not, see a financial planner about other income-generating ideas.

The most common mistakes in estimating potential income are forgetting the fee reductions for managed care, Medicare, or Medicaid contracts, overestimating the number of patients that can be seen in a day or a week, and forgetting the lag in insurance payment. Your first months in practice will be dry because insurance payments have a 4–6-week turnaround time. In addition, in the beginning you will make a lot of billing mistakes and although you will ultimately get that money, you may get it much later than expected due to having to resubmit a claim because of an error. Have some money in the bank to tide you over for the first few months.

You will also lose some patients early on because of inexperience in managing the practice, usually due to miscommunications about your policies, fees, or the nature of treatment. The learning curve may decrease your income stream below your first estimate, but it will recover with experience. In terms of how long it will take to reach your potential income, it is hard to anticipate the rate at which a practice will grow. Your starting referral base, the time you are willing to put into generating referrals, the level of local competition, and the general economic climate all play important roles.

Next, estimate your starting expenses for the practice. It is best to keep expenses low. The lower the overhead, the easier it will be to make a profit. The biggest business expense is usually office rental. For very part-time practices, subletting office space is less expensive than renting but may seriously limit appointment times because you have to work around the lessor's schedule. Subletting also limits privacy. Records must be locked up separately or taken with you. Answering machines must have a separate access code or run from a private site such as a cell phone or home. Patient-related paper waste must be shredded or taken with you for private disposal. However, if your practice will be limited to one day a week or fewer than 10 patients and you won't need to grow beyond that, subletting usually makes the most economic sense. If you are starting with more than 10 hours a week or if you intend to work hard to expand, then it is better to find an inexpensive full-time office where you are free to spend time billing, making phone calls, and can accommodate more patient requests.

The overhead costs for psychiatric practice are otherwise low. Besides the rent, you will need a few chairs, a desk, lighting, a locked filing cabinet, and a shredder. Nothing needs to be fancy or expensive (Grodzki, 2000; Woody, 1989) and you can always upgrade as the practice improves. You will need some office supplies, such as claim forms, appointment cards, letterhead stationery, and pens. Colleagues can provide you with the names of local suppliers or catalogs. With the cost of toner and ink, it is generally less expensive to have your stationery printed than to do it yourself on a computer. Likewise, fax machines and copy machines usually do not pay for themselves except in the largest of group practices. A twice-weekly stop at the copy center is all most practitioners need. There will also be monthly postal expenses for mailing claims, correspondence, and bills.

Whether you will need a typewriter or word processor depends on the legibility of your handwriting, the task at hand, and your typing skills. As long as the numbers and headings are legible, all your accounting records can be handwritten. Legible handwritten claim forms are still allowed but are discouraged by insurance companies because they can't be processed by optical scanners. Progress notes can be handwritten if your handwriting is legible to others, but the initial evaluations, reports, and consultations probably should be typed, since they are likely to go to subsequent or concurrent treaters. If you can type, an electric typewriter is a handy, inexpensive tool. Word processors are more expensive.

Every professional needs a phone and answering machine, and maybe a beeper or answering service depending on how you plan to cover emergencies after hours. Phone bills will be a monthly expense. Special plans by location can accommodate the towns where most of your patients reside. Long-distance calls are few, usually to insurance companies without 1-800 numbers.

There are a few other expenses. Postage, xeroxing, and faxing usually don't amount to much. You will need to pay your accountant and financial advisor yearly or quarterly, depending on how often you use them.

Supervision will be a monthly expense for those starting out or those with heavy psychotherapy practices. Paid advertising, except for the basic Yellow Pages listing, has limited utility (Grodzki, 2000). Don't bother with it.

A computer is definitely optional for most smaller practices at this time and may remain so as long as paper claims are still accepted by insurers, which is likely to be the case for many years. It may be best to forego the purchase of a computer until the practice is up and running to see to what extent you will need it (Scherer, 2000). Remember, the goal is to keep practice expenses low. Most practitioners already have a computer and new ones can be purchased fairly cheaply but then you will need to add a black-and-white printer with toner and basic software for word processing and accounting. These add to the expense, but in general the purchase of a simple computer system with accessories should run less than $1,500. If your handwriting is not legible, a computer becomes more essential for both word processing and accounting.

As we will see in the chapters on record keeping and billing, professional-level software is often unnecessary. Most simple accounting and word-processing packages work well for mental health practices. Since there is no need for fancy software, the bare bones of hardware is usually sufficient. Modems and faxes are unnecessary unless you plan to bill electronically or will need to obtain a lot of lab results. The use of modems and faxes also requires extra security and privacy work. You don't want faxes coming into an office where patients are being seen or have the incoming phone line tied up by a fax. Extra security features will also be needed if you intend to keep the computer online while working, but again this is usually unnecessary for most practitioners.

Supplies and business-related expenses are tax deductible. For tax rules related to furniture and computers, consult your accountant. Remember that you only save a small amount of money (just the tax rate) on tax-deductible purchases so it is better to avoid a purchase or to choose the least-expensive option, than to spend more and count on the tax deduction. Expensive equipment, clothing, or furnishings (Scherer, 2000) do not generate money for the practice, and such trappings work against you fiscally because they increase expenses and require more careful maintainance.

Figure out what you need to purchase for opening the practice, save up the money, and buy the supplies and necessary furnishings before you start without taking out a loan or purchasing anything on credit. Also save enough money to carry you for the first few months. Trying to start with too little money saved (Duoba & Gada, 2003) is a common business mistake. Pressman (1979) was not opposed to borrowing money or securing a loan for something large, like a computer, to start a practice, but this ultimately costs more money, sets a bad precedent for spending before money is earned, and puts more pressure on the practitioner to generate income right away. Most businesses are begun with no loans or debt at all (U.S. Small Business Association, 2002) and yours should be no exception. Delay opening the practice until you can afford it and keep expenses low.

Some practitioners (Grodzki, 2000) recommend hiring others to do menial or nonreimbursable labor, such as billing, office cleaning, and reception work, in order to free up time to earn money by seeing patients. This makes sense fiscally if you really will see patients during the time freed up *and* if the income thus generated is more than the cost of hiring out the work. Often this is not the case. If you want to hire an office cleaner because you hate to clean, that's okay. There's no need to rationalize that it will "save money" by allowing you to see more patients. In a full-time practice, some clinical hours will always remain unbooked and this usually provides sufficient time for office work and housekeeping. Booking appointments can be done by phone or during sessions, eliminating the need for a receptionist. The time needed for billing varies by practice. For more details on whether hiring a biller makes financial sense, see Chapter 4.

Malpractice insurance is relatively low for psychiatric practitioners, although it varies by location, level of experience, and professional degree and has been increasing of late. Psychiatrists in solo outpatient practice pay about $4,000 a year and all the other professions are considerably less. Payment is usually made monthly, quarterly, or yearly. If you intend to supervise or employ other practitioners, your malpractice costs will be higher. Malpractice can be obtained privately through an insurance carrier in your area or through a professional organization. If you plan to work part-time as an employee and part-time in your own practice, your employer may be happy to split malpractice costs with you.

After rent, the biggest expense of any practice is usually health insurance. Many practitioners limit their practice to part-time in order to obtain health insurance through their full-time job. Others have the option of obtaining health insurance through a working spouse. Regardless of the choices available to you, check out the cost of paying for health insurance yourself. Costs of $300 to $1,000 per month translate to 5–15 patient hours per month to cover health insurance, depending on your fees. Shop around for the least expensive plan but one that will fit your needs. You can obtain group rates by applying for health insurance through a local business association, professional organization, or sometimes through the state (as is done for the self-employed in Massachusetts). Remember that the premium paid for health insurance is 100% tax deductible for the self-employed. If you keep a lot of money in savings (and you should), choosing a high-deductible plan is a great way to cut monthly premium costs.

Disability insurance is a good idea but is becoming increasingly difficult and expensive to obtain for physicians (Guadagnino, 2002; Moody, 2004; Perilstein, 2001). It may or may not be necessary given your health, savings, other potential sources of income, and the status of your dependents. Life insurance is less costly to obtain but is also sometimes unnecessary, especially for practitioners with no dependents. Consult a financial planner about the necessity and value of both life and disability insurance. If you don't own your office, insurance is usually not worthwhile because the most valuable items (hopefully) are the records, which can't be replaced. Don't keep valuables at the office and don't rent an office that you think is likely to burn down or be subject to theft. Most material things can be replaced for less than the amount paid by insurance over the years. If you are in doubt about this, consult either an accountant or a financial planner. Also check with your landlord about his or her insurance. Liability insurance for the office may or may not be necessary, depending on the rental contract. Check with the owner and a financial advisor about whether additional insurance is needed.

If you are self-employed, you have to pay quarterly income taxes. Getting behind in paying quarterly taxes is a common cause of bankruptcy of small businesses (Holland, 1998). Set yourself up so that paying quarterly taxes is painless. This usually means setting aside a certain percentage of income, usually around 30% depending on your income bracket and state tax rate, at the time of deposit to fund this quarterly expenditure. At the same time, you can funnel another percentage (maybe 10%) into a retirement account (SEP for most self-employed persons) as well as simple savings (maybe another 5–10%). This means that of the money you collect each week, a significant portion will go to taxes, retirement, and savings, just like an employee paycheck. This may be as low as 30% or as high as 55%, depending on your income level, retirement goals, and other needs. An accountant and financial planner will help you make this estimate. The remainder is what you pay expenses with and live off. So, we see that health insurance, disability, retirement, and savings use up a substantial portion of practice income (Grodzki, 2000).

Let me say a word here about choosing your business consultants. Start with a fee-only financial advisor. Many financial advisors are paid by commission on the revenues generated by investments or the sale of financial products like insurance. This creates a conflict of interest when their desire for revenue does not fit with your financial needs. With a fee-only advisor, you pay an hourly fee for financial consultation and avoid the attendant conflicts of interest. A list of fee-only financial planners can be obtained through the National Association of Personal Financial Advisors (www.feeonly.org).

In terms of choosing an accountant, the needs of most practices are basic. Any certified public accountant with experience in small businesses can usually do the job, but referrals from colleagues in the same business can be useful. If your personal tax situation is complicated, for example, if your spouse owns another company, or if there are other investments, gravitate toward an accountant with experience in those areas. Should you decide to incorporate, form a group practice, or hire many employees, specialized accounting skills may be necessary. An initial interview to assess your needs and the accountant's level of experience with your type of business will help in making a choice.

PREPARING FOR THE UPS AND DOWNS

No matter how carefully you plan your practice, attend to your referral sources, or perform your work, there will be ups and downs in income over the course of time. Income rises and falls with economic cycles, sometimes unpredictably. While earnings generally fall during recessions, sometimes the high level of stress causes more people to present, especially where insurance covers most of the cost. If a slump is associated with layoffs and an associated loss of health insurance, then practice income will decline.

Local economic factors play a more important role than the national situation, not only in the general growth and increasing wealth of the population, but in the choice of health plans by local employers, company mergers, or changes in the local health care community. Personal factors may play a role as well. There may be years when you have to work less or find it easy to work more.

Because of the ups and downs in income, it is important for practices and practitioners to have a generous amount of savings in the bank to cover expenses. Most financial advisors recommend six months expenses in pure savings, not tied up in CDs or retirement funds. Savings will also help cover unexpected expenses like office-computer crashes, major car repairs, or meeting a high deductible for medical expenses. Pressman (1979) stated that it is acceptable for a practitioner to take out a short-term personal loan to tide one over during a rough period, but it is cheaper and less stressful not to have to take such action, and better to be prepared.

Even if you have substantial savings, dipping into savings should not be the first thought when revenue starts to fall off in the practice. Lowering expenses is more immediate and easily reversed. Cut-backs may be small and simple like canceling newspaper subscriptions, buying fewer professional books, or eating out less. Or they can be major such as trading in an expensive car for a less-expensive one or canceling the Club Med vacation in favor of camping. Good business management includes the willingness and ability to downscale lifestyle when indicated. Good personal management includes the same. No one should become so addicted to their current lifestyle that they can't tighten the belt when needed. This means that with the addition of any new expenditure in good times, there needs to be the question of how easy it will be to let go during bad times.

There are certain expenses you should *not* cut back on when income falls. Generally these items are necessary for the maintenance of your wealth-generating assets: your knowledge base and your license to practice. This means: Don't cut back on lunches with referral sources, continuing education seminars, supervision, physical maintenance of the office, or self-care (Grodzki, 2002).

After cutting expenses, think about how to increase income. "Beating the bushes" means making some calls to your primary referral sources to let them know you have openings. When times are hard, more patients present with depression and worries. Primary care givers and social services are anxious to refer. You can also change your telephone screening to accept patients you ordinarily would screen out but are not actually opposed to taking on. For example, I generally practice psychotherapy but will take on more medication patients if there is an economic downturn. Another option is to moonlight. Opportunities can usually be found locally through word of mouth but contacting a locum tenens recruiter may also work and has the advantage of being truly temporary. Ask others what they are doing to compensate. Duoba and Gada (2003) stated that resistance to asking for help from others is one of the most common mistakes made by new business owners.

Use the free time created by a downturn as an opportunity to generate future wealth. This may be the best time to pursue learning a new skill, writing a book, getting more active in your professional organization, or learning how to form a group practice. When patient volume is low these activities do not cut into the time used to generate income as much. Who knows when you will have such an opportunity again.

WORKSHEET

1. Explain your vision of the psychiatric practice to a couple of people. Do they understand it clearly?
2. Write a short mission statement here describing the basic nature of your practice. Be sure that you can say it easily and consistently. If you can't, the mission statement is either too long or you still have some ambivalence about the nature of the work you are going to do. Rework it.

   _____

   _____

   _____

3. Obtain and read a copy of your profession's guide to ethics in practice. Put it in an accessible place.
4. Write your nonmonetary goals for the practice here:
   a.
   b.

   c.
   d.

6. Write your monetary goals for the practice here:
   a. Income to exceed expenses (a mandatory goal)
   b.
   c.
   d.

7. Assessing commitment:
   a. What is your level of commitment to your future practice?
   b. List any limitations in terms of hours of work per week.
   c. List any long-term limitations.
   d. What commitments do you place ahead of your practice? (Hint: There
      should be at least three—your own health and a few relationships!)

   _____

   _____

   _____

   _____

   _____

8. Do you have a lot of debt? What are your monthly debt payments altogether?

9. Do you or can you track all your expenses by month? List all your monthly
   expenses by category if you can. Use Table 1.1 to help.

10. Are there any upcoming expenses?

11. Are you satisfied with your savings? Do you have adequate emergency re-
    serves and retirement savings?

12. What is your current gross income?

13. How many hours do you work per week in
    a. Direct patient care?
    b. Indirect patient care?

15. How much vacation and sick time do you get per year and how much of it do
    you actually use?

16. Benefits   Cost to you
    a. Retirement
    b. Health insurance
    c. Disability insurance
    d. Life insurance
    e. Academic reimbursement
    f. Other

15. Read your current employment contract.
    Is there any noncompete clause?
    Can you take patients with you to a new practice?

16. List your current patients with their insurance and payment status. Indicate who you'd like to bring to your new practice and then mark those you think will actually transfer. How many hours a week would seeing these patients use?
    a. <10 hours a week (start less than half-time)
    b. 10–16 hours a week (can start half-time)
    c. More than 17 hours a week (can probably start full-time or nearly so)

17. What is your level of experience with
    a. Patient care?
       1–5 years: Start slowly.
       5–10 years: Start right in.
    b. Billing
       a. 0–1 years: Start slowly with a substantial financial cushion.
       b. 2–5 years: Start right in but with a cushion.
       c. 5–10 years: Start right in.

18. Thoughts about your current location:
    a. How does it compare to your ideal location?
    b. Should you consider other locations? Which ones?

19. List the services you will offer and the fee you will charge for each.

20. Make an introductory sheet that includes any of the following:
    a. The services you offer and the fees for each
    b. No-show or late-cancellation policies
    c. Billing and insurance issues
    d. Coverage for emergencies
    e. Confidentiality and privacy
    f. Other nonmonetary information

21. Pick a tentative weekly schedule.
    a. Is it really feasible?
    b. Does it allow time for emergency visits?
    c. Does it allow time for phone calls and progress notes?
    d. Is there time for billing?
    e. Is there time for longer paperwork like reports or consultations with other practitioners?

23. Pick a tentative holiday and vacation schedule.

24. How much money will you earn if you continue to see all your current patients at the new office? How much money will you earn if you fill most or all of the hours you have planned?

25. Estimate how much money it will take to buy your furnishings and supplies. Do you have enough money to start now or do you need to save a little more?

26. Have you consulted an accountant or financial planner? What did they advise?

27. Do you have enough money in the bank to accommodate an economic downturn?

CHAPTER 2
Legal and Ethical Issues

W hile both legal and ethical codes deal with aspects of professional financial conduct, the practices they describe and proscribe are not the same. Laws address specific behaviors prohibited or allowed by citizens, businesses, or corporations. By extension they also apply to practitioners. Ethical codes for licensed professionals outline standards of conduct that go well beyond what is described in law. *Although professional codes of ethics are not law they may be incorporated into state regulations, thus becoming law,* or may be adopted by state boards of licensure that then allow appropriate sanctioning by the state for infractions (Behnke & Hilliard, 1998). For this reason it is important for all practitioners to read and understand their professional code of ethics as well as the applicable laws and regulations of the states in which they are licensed to practice. Some laws and regulations are written specifically for the professions, but many business laws are also relevant. These will be discussed in some detail below.

Ethical requirements conceivably might conflict with the law, and the professional codes differ in their treatment of any potential disagreement. Although Section 3 of the *Principles of Medical Ethics* (ApA, 2001c) clearly states that physicians must respect the law, the *Annotations with Regard to Psychiatry* (ApA, 2001c, Section 3.1) imply that there might be situations in which illegal conduct is ethical, for example, when protesting social injustices. (We will return to this idea in the section on *gaming* the insurance system.) In addition, Section 3 states that physicians have an obligation to seek changes to laws that oppose the interests of patients, reflecting a long tradition of advocacy for the individual.

Section 1.02 of the *Ethical Principles for Psychologists* (APA, 2002) also addresses potential conflicts between the law and ethical codes, recommending that "psychologists make known their commitment to this Ethics Code and take steps to resolve the conflict in a responsible manner. If the conflict is unresolvable via such means, psychologists may adhere to the requirements of the law, regulations or other governing legal authority." This implies that adherence to the law instead of the code will not necessarily be considered unethical. Unlike the psychiatric code, the psychology code does not suggest political action when regulations or law conflict with ethical treatment of patients.

The *Code of Ethics of the National Association of Social Workers* (1999) also specifically addresses conflicts between the law and professional ethics. "Social workers must make a responsible effort to resolve the conflict in a manner that is consistent with the values, principles, and standards expressed in this Code." Section 6.04 addresses the need for political action to address policies that conflict with the ethical principles of social work, reflecting this particular profession's long-standing and unique role in promoting social justice. Like the psychiatric code, simple adherence to the law is not enough.

The nursing codes do not address legal issues in general or cite any obligation for action to address conflicts between the law and ethics codes.

LEGAL BASICS

There are four types of laws all citizens (and professionals) must follow (Behnke & Hilliard, 1998). One set of laws is defined by the federal constitution and the constitution of the state in which the provider practices (constitutional law). A second set of laws is formed by statutes enacted by legislatures at the state and federal levels (statutory law). Regulations comprise the third set. Regulations are the rules drafted by specific governmental bodies at the state and federal level, such as the Department of Mental Health, Licensing Boards, or the Food and Drug Administration, which enable them to fulfill their mandates. Finally, there is the body of case law, drawn from court proceedings or trials. An example is the famous

Tarasoff case.* For the most part, state laws are the most relevant to professional and business financial practices.

Some Definitions

When a professional or other citizen violates established law, that action is said to be illegal. When an illegal act is prosecuted in *criminal* court, a punishment is given to the offender, such as a fine or prison term, but no compensation is provided to the victim. If a victim desires compensation, action must be pursued in *civil* courts. Financial wrongdoing may be pursued civilly, criminally, or both, depending on the nature of the act, whether compensation is sought, and the specifics of the law in question.

Fraud is the false representation of a matter of fact with an intention to deceive another (West's Encyclopedia of American law, 1998). Fraud can be civil or criminal (Appelbaum & Gutheil, 1991; West's, 1998). All states have statutes criminalizing certain types of fraud but not all cases of fraud will rise to the level of criminality (West's).

Torts are those wrongs for which compensation may be provided to a victim for damages and are addressed in civil, not criminal, courts (Behnke & Hilliard, 1998). Torts are divided into two types, intentional torts and unintentional torts. Intent becomes important in determining civil liability (West's, 1998). *Malpractice* refers only to unintentional torts (Macbeth et al., 1994). *Intentional torts*, such as billing fraud, are not malpractice and are generally excluded from coverage by malpractice insurance.

UNFAIR TRADE PRACTICES

The same anti-competition and anti-trust laws that govern businesses and corporations also apply to health care practitioners (West's, 1998; Woody, 1989). These laws are designed to keep markets free, open, and amenable to supply and demand. The idea is that when healthcare providers supply similar services, fees are influenced by competition and are determined fairly (Marcinko & Hetico, 2000).

---

* *Tarasoff v. Regents of the University of California*, 1976, established the duty of all mental health professionals to warn a known third party and/or the police of potential harm when a threat is communicated to a clinician by a patient during treatment.

The Sherman Anti-Trust Act of 1890 (a federal law, although most states have similar laws) prohibits conspiracies in restraint of trade (West's, 1998). In psychiatric practice, this act is violated by *price-fixing*. Price-fixing is when practitioners agree among themselves what they will charge the public, thus eliminating competition by fee between providers. Note that a conspiracy is necessary for the law to be violated (West's). In other words, it is not a violation of the law to find out what other practitioners charge in order to decide how to set one's own fee. It is also not a violation of the law for practitioners to change their fees at the same time in response to market forces, as long as they do not organize to do so.

The Stark Laws (also federal) restrict physician *self-referral*. Stark I (The Stark Amendment to the Omnibus Budget Reconciliation Act of 1989 [42 USC 1395nn]) prohibits physicians from referring Medicare and Medicaid patients to laboratories in which they or a family member have a financial interest. Exceptions are made for rural providers or if the physician is one of many investors in a large publicly traded company like a mutual fund. Stark II (1993) extended Stark I by prohibiting referral to other health care enterprises where the physician might have a financial interest. Exceptions are made for referrals to members of a physician's group practice or within a place of employment. Most states have laws that supplement the Starks Laws, and many require disclosure of any financial interest to the patient prior to referral (Kusserow, 1989). Note that while the federal Stark Laws refer only to physicians, many state laws use the term *provider* to include all professionals within the law.

There are other ways to interfere with competition and free trade in mental health practice. Excluding psychologists or any specific group of professionals from a referral list (ApA, 2001b), advising a local facility not to allow employees to moonlight (ApA), and agreeing to shut out a new colleague from referrals all violate federal law. However, excluding someone from referrals because they are known to be incompetent or unethical is allowed.

A *kickback* is money given to a source for providing a referral. *Fee-splitting* is a form of kickback in which the fee for the service is split between the provider of the service and the person who referred the patient. For example, a social worker who gives a percentage of her $80 fee to the psychiatrist who sent her the patient is fee-splitting. Under federal law, kickbacks involving government officials or funds provided by the government are illegal (West's, 1998). Because Medicare is a government program, kickbacks and fee-splitting are prohibited. "Soliciting, offering, or receiving a kickback, bribe, or rebate, e.g., paying for a referral of patients in exchange for . . . services . . ." is a violation of Medicare regulations and is prosecuted as fraud (Centers for Medicare & Medicaid Services, 2003c, Section 14002.2B). Kickbacks between a mental health service provider and the government, say to obtain a contract at a facility, are also illegal and are prosecuted under the Federal Bribery Statutes (West's, 1998).

Not all kickbacks are illegal. Most states have statutes prohibiting certain types of kickbacks (West's, 1998) but allowable kickbacks vary from state to state. If a kickback, rebate, or incentive does not specifically violate a state or federal law, and is the standard practice in an industry or profession, a kickback may be legal and even tax-deductible as a business expense (West's). While charging kickback fees may sometimes be legal, this is not to say it is good for health care or the professions. The codes of ethics for psychiatrists, psychologists, and social workers all specifically prohibit kickbacks or fee-splitting. (For more information on legal kickbacks, see Chapter 9, "Monetary Incentives and Conflicts of Interest.")

Insider information refers to special knowledge gained about the financial status of a company from company officials or an insider before it is made public. In mental health practice this may occur when a patient who is an insider reveals such information to the therapist during a session, not usually as an intentional tip but as part of a discussion about problems at work. "The use of such information in the purchase or sale of stock violates federal securities law. It is also a violation to pass on the information to family for their use" (West's, 1998, p. 163). A mental health professional who uses insider information for financial gain or passes it on to a family member for their use is committing a crime. (The use of such information is also a violation of the ethical principles of confidentiality and nonexploitation of the patient (ApA, 2001a).)

All states have trade laws, and they vary considerably from state to state (Behnke & Hilliard, 1998; Kusserow, 1989; Leiter, 1993). Be sure to consult your own state laws or an attorney if you have questions regarding any actions that might be questionable in terms of their restraint on free trade. Your local reference librarian can lead you to relevant legal codes and reliable Internet sources. Most state professional societies have legal consultants who are happy to answer questions about local mental health and business law.

FRAUD

Fraud is the intentional misrepresentation of fact with an intent to deceive. Misrepresenting the duration of a mental health visit on a claim form is one example. Fraud may also occur through concealment of a fact that should have been disclosed, such as ownership in a company to which the professional refers. Fraud has three other components besides misrepresentation or concealment of a fact: the professional must know that the statement is false, the victim must rely on the false information, and the victim must suffer harm as a consequence of the fraud (West's, 1998). Note that in mental health practice, the victim may be the insurance company, the government (in the case of Medicare or Medicaid), or the patient. The fiduciary relationship between a mental health provider and a patient makes any misleading statement more likely to qualify as fraudulent because the criteria about reliance on the information and injury to the patient (in terms of the therapeutic relationship) are almost always met (West's).

Fraud may be actionable in either civil or criminal courts (Appelbaum & Gutheil, 1991) depending on the nature of the act and whether compensation is sought. Billing fraud is usually prosecuted criminally (Pope, 1988). It is important to note that in criminal and fraud investigations, the psychiatric records of the provider are not privileged, although the specifics may vary from state to state (Appelbaum & Gutheil). While there are many areas of fraud in mental health, such as misrepresenting competency, I am addressing only those areas of fraud that have to do with money.

Insurance and Billing Fraud

Pope (1988) reported that in 1988 fraudulent billing was the second most prevalent cause of adverse licensure actions against psychologists, but data for all of the professions is hard to come by and inconsistent. Post (1991), in 1984, reported that 24% of disciplinary actions against physicians in New York State in the 1980s were for fraud, while Morrison's (1998) study in California found only 9%. Many professional boards do not keep records, and since fraudulent actions are generally excluded from malpractice coverage, the professional insurers no longer keep data. In 1996, the Office of the Inspector General (OIG) created the Health Care Integrity and Protection Data Bank (HIPDB), which is attempting to flag, collect, and report on health care fraud (Granville & Oshel, 2003). In 2000 the Data Bank estimated that about 10% of health care expenditures were overpaid due to fraudulent billing (Granville & Oshel).

There are many types of insurance and billing fraud: misrepresenting the diagnosis, altering claims, billing for services not rendered, duplicate billing, unbundling charges, misrepresenting the services rendered (*upcoding*), billing *gang visits*, certifying that you have actually seen the patient when you have not, billing families or groups as individual visits, and routinely waiving copayments. Let's look at some of these in more detail.

Before the era of managed care and cost containment, downgrading the diagnosis (making it less severe) was a more common misrepresentation than upgrading (making the diagnosis more severe) because the specific diagnosis did not affect payment or cost. Minimizing the diagnosis was justified as protecting patient privacy (Appelbaum & Gutheil, 1991) or patients from the despair of knowing they had a more serious form of illness. Sometimes depression codes were changed to anxiety codes to avoid problems obtaining life insurance. Nowadays it is more common to upgrade than downgrade the diagnosis in order to obtain more visits or to qualify for parity. This increases costs.

Misrepresentation of the diagnostic code accounted for 43% of cases of fraud in a 1993 survey by the Health Insurance Association of America (HIAA; Granville & Oshel, 2003), making it the most common type of fraud. While upgrading the diagnostic code in psychiatric practice does not increase the fee, it may increase the total number of visits paid for by the insurance company. This is especially true if a parity law is in place for biological conditions like schizophrenia but not for psychological conditions like borderline personality disorder. For example, upgrading obsessive-compulsive personality disorder to obsessive-compulsive disorder might result in more insurance coverage due to the clear biological cause.

Upgrading, downgrading, or distorting the diagnosis is fraudulent in other ways. Many patients want and need to know their diagnosis; telling them one diagnosis in the session and then writing another diagnosis on a form confuses the patient and in some ways makes them an accomplice. Distorting diagnoses makes it difficult for governments and insurers to obtain accurate information for calculating current and future health care costs and skews statistics collected from claims about prevalence of psychiatric illness. Upgrading diagnoses increases the total cost of psychiatric health care, which affects all practitioners and patients by triggering higher premiums for health insurance.

Altering claims is a catchall phrase for billing services and staff changing claims data after the provider has signed the form. However, it does not appear to be a common form of fraud.

Billing for services not rendered was the second most common type of fraud (34%) reported in the 1993 HIAA survey (Granville & Oshel, 2003). This not only means billing for visits that did not take place, but misrepresenting the service given; for example, billing a 90805 (25-minute medication and therapy visit) when it was really only a 90862 (brief medication visit). Insurance companies cannot be billed for no-shows or late cancellations, since no service was rendered. Medicare and Medicaid also prohibit billing the patient for late cancellations and no-shows (Centers for Medicare & Medicaid Services, 2003a), even if the provider has this as a general policy. In some states (Arizona, Kansas, Kentucky), billing for no-shows and late cancellations for *any* patient is a violation of state laws that prohibit charging customers when no service is rendered (Kusserow, 1989). Billing for late cancellations and no-shows is legal in other states, like New Jersey, only if such a policy is stated to the patient beforehand. A less clear issue is charging patients for a full session when they come late or leave early. Many Medicaid programs can be billed only for the time actually spent with the patient face-to-face. Private insurers have not yet included such stipulations in their contracts.

Duplicate billing, either of the insurance company alone or of the insurance and the patient, is also fraudulent (CMS, 2003a). While it may seem laughable that an insurance will pay twice on the same claim, this can happen if there has been a longer than usual turnaround time on the claim and the provider submits a second claim thinking the first did not go through. When a claim has been paid twice, it is the responsibility of the provider to return the overpayment promptly. Although it can be tempting to hold onto overpayments when an insurance company has tortured you in the past with delayed or unpaid claims, rude service, or intrusive authorization procedures, and it may seem like justified revenge, it is still fraud. Use your professional integrity to do the right thing and return the money, then file formal complaints about the other problems. (See Chapter 6, "Understanding Insurance," for how to do this.)

It is also illegal to bill the patient for money the insurance company has already paid, thus getting more than is justified by either the contract or your fee schedule. This can happen if the insurer initially denies the claim and the patient pays, but later the insurer does pay. In this case, the overcharged amount must be returned to the patient promptly. Another example of fraud is *balance billing* the patient on the full amount when the provider has contracted for a smaller fee, as is commonly the case with Medicare or Blue Cross. If you ever feel tempted to bill for the balance of the full fee, then the contracted fee is too low and you should end or renegotiate the contract.

The fraudulent practice of *unbundling charges* refers to splitting up services for individual payment when they are included in one procedure code. For example, billing for a medication visit and a separate therapy session when both were accomplished in the same day by the same provider, or charging for routine phone calls or paperwork included under the relevant code (there will be more about codes in Chapter 4 on billing) is considered *unbundling*. Billing couples, families, or groups as individual visits (Pope, 1988) is another form of unbundling.

Billing for *gang visits* occurs when a provider visits a group home or nursing home and bills for every patient in the home when only three were serviced directly and the rest were just viewed from a distance. Practitioners feel safe doing this knowing that if the nursing staff did not pick out the patient to be seen, there is probably no problem to report and a pro forma note on an "eyeballed" patient can be written. Other providers feel entitled to compensation for all residents in a group home since they see themselves as "on-call" or "covering" the entire home, even if only a few patients are seen. However, this is not how the insurance companies see it, nor are these rationalizations likely to fair well before a jury. Claims can be submitted only for the patients actually examined or treated in a group setting.

A related practice is certifying that you have actually seen the patient when you have not in order to obtain insurance coverage, as in the case of supervision of trainees. There are very specific rules about billing for patients seen by trainees, which must be followed to the letter. Billing under the name of a family member who was not actually present (even if the family member gave permission) in order to extend coverage is similar because the person on the claim form was not the person seen (Pope, 1988). Note that in all these cases, other parties are often complicit (the institution, family member, or patient) in the billing fraud, so it is unlikely to be reported. It remains fraud nonetheless.

Changing the date of onset of illness used to affect insurance coverage because of "pre-existing condition" clauses that denied insurance payment for a specified period of time for a condition known to exist prior to joining the insurance plan. When those clauses were eliminated as part of insurance reform, the incentive to commit fraud in this way was also eliminated. However, motivation to change the date of onset of an illness in certain workman's compensation or accident cases remains.

Routine waivers of co-payments or deductibles (CMS, 2003a; Goldsmith, 2000; Pope, 1988) occurs when practitioners tell all, most, or many patients that they do not have to pay the co-payment or deductible. It was the third most common (21%) type of fraud in the HIAA study (Granville & Osher, 2003). The purpose of the waiver is to make the provider more attractive by being cheaper. The practitioner makes up the lost revenue with increased volume or by charging higher fees. This practice is illegal, and for good reason. Waiving the patient deductible and co-payment eliminates all motivation for the patient to hold down costs, thus increasing health care costs overall. It also misleads insurance companies who believe they are paying a percentage of treatment costs when in reality they are paying 100%. If such agreements are made with the knowledge and acceptance of the patient, or at the suggestion of the patient, then charges may not only include fraud, but collusion (West's, 1998). For indigent patients, the waiver of a significant co-payment is allowed if there is documentation of need.

Much has been made of Medicare's ability to investigate and prosecute fraudulent billing practices, but the protest, mostly from physicians, is overblown. Honest mistakes in billing do not constitute fraud and, in the case of a mistake, Medicare is generally only seeking the money due back them (recoupment) just as you might refund a patient or another insurance company when you have accidentally been overpaid. In Medicare's own words, "We recognize that honest mistakes can happen. Physicians making unintentional coding errors do not commit fraud, and CMS [Centers for Medicare Services] does not impose fines for coding errors. When we identify overpayments, we are required to recover them. Most are handled administratively. Only in rare circumstances does CMS refer providers to law enforcement agencies for further investigation" (CMS, 2002). There is no sudden lawsuit. Medicare first requests a review of records, usually in the form of a letter addressed to the practitioner. Such a request is an opportunity for the practitioner to review the involved claims, make the refund if the request is justified, or write a letter of explanation if there is a misunderstanding. If there is a serious disagreement or if fraud has been committed, an attorney can and should be consulted (Fenton, 2000).

False Advertising

Most states have laws against false advertising (Leiter, 1993). For mental health professionals, advertising fraud usually involves exaggerated or distorted credentials, expertise, or treatment cures. Appelbaum and Gutheil (1991) noted that fraud in advertising may not just occur in the public arena but in the privacy of an office visit, such as when a practitioner promises a result that is unrealistic.

THE PATIENT CONTRACT

The provider-patient contract is not a business contract but a fiduciary (from the word *fidelity*) contract (Morreim, 1995). Fiduciary relationships have four general components: trust, privacy, vulnerability of the client, and special knowledge on the part of the provider. Trust is critical and forms the foundation of all fiduciary relationships because of the private nature of the communication and the potential vulnerability of the patient. The patient is exposed on two counts: the revelation of private behavior and thoughts that might be used for exploitation, and complete reliance on the knowledge of the professional. The more specialized the knowledge, the more dependent the patient is on the accuracy of that knowledge (Morreim). In fiduciary relationships, the patient is protected from exploitation by the requirement that the interests of the patient be held above the interests, including financial interests, of the practitioner (Morreim). This requirement makes provider-patient contracts different from ordinary business contracts, where business owners are expected to pursue profits as best they can and "let the buyer beware."

If the patient is a member of an HMO (health maintenance organization) and the provider is an employee or contractor of the same HMO, there may be limitations on the ability of the provider to act without regard to the financial interests of the HMO. In theory, patients understand and agree to this when they become members of an HMO, but in reality most patients do not consider what these limitations might mean for them prior to signing for an HMO plan. More will be said about the fiduciary limitations caused by insurance companies in Chapter 6, "Understanding Insurance," but in HMOs the fiduciary contract still stands with all its component parts: trust, patient dependence on the superior knowledge of the provider, and placement of the patient's needs above the needs of the provider (Mercado, 2000).

Breaking a fiduciary contract is different from breaking a business contract. While the patient may withdraw from the treatment relationship at any time for any reason, generally the provider may withdraw only if the patient is not in crisis, if alternative treatment can be provided, and if the patient is given fair warning about the termination. We will revisit these requirements in Chapter 14, when we discuss the termination of non-paying patients.

Violations of fiduciary contracts are generally covered through malpractice insurance as unintentional torts, while violations of business contracts or insurance contracts by providers are not usually covered by malpractice. Typical fiduciary contract violations in mental health practice include abandonment, exploitation of the patient, or undue influence. Violations of insurance and employment agreements are part of regular business law and are not generally covered as part of malpractice. This is because they do not arise out of negligent practice but from actions in a contract (Behnke & Hilliard, 1998). This area has become such an important part of psychiatric practice that a section on insurance and managed care contracts is included in Chapter 6.

TAX AND BUSINESS LAW

Violations of general business laws and tax laws are not covered by malpractice. Business and accounting records for tax and insurance purposes are subject to specific laws. Generally all accounting, tax, and business expense information related to psychiatric practice must be kept for at least seven years. Other areas of business law apply to psychiatric practices with employees. These include workmen's compensation and insurance regulations, discrimination policies, payment of family members, and general tax law. Practices that use employees are responsible for knowing and implementing these laws. Details about implementation are covered in the next chapter.

MALPRACTICE

Fraud, violation of contracts, business regulation infringement, and tax evasion all fall outside the areas covered by malpractice insurance. So what is malpractice, and what does it cover in the financial arena?

Malpractice is a type of civil tort, a wrong committed by a provider that is noncriminal, unintentional, not based on the breach of a contract, and that has led to damage to a second party. Four elements must be proven to sustain a charge of malpractice: fiduciary duty to the patient, negligence or deviation from the standard of care, harm to the patient, and causation, meaning that the wrongful or negligent act caused the harm (Appelbaum & Gutheil, 1991). While most providers are quite familiar with claims arising from treatment, few are aware of claims that result from the financial practices of the practitioner (Rappaport, 2000). Most malpractice insurers specifically exclude coverage for fee disputes with patients (Pope, 1988; ProMutual, 2002) as well as mishandling of the transference and sexual misconduct, both of which are often accompanied by negligent financial practices. Malpractice does cover claims against a practitioner for inadequate informed consent or failure to adhere to the standard of care, both of which may involve money.

INFORMED CONSENT AND
COST OF TREATMENT

Informed consent overlaps with the financial aspects of practice through disclosure of fees and cost of treatment. Fee disclosure is an inherent and necessary component of informed consent (American Nurses Association, 2002; Behnke & Hilliard, 1998; Gigerenzer, 2002; Green, 1993; Lifson & Simon, 1998; Macbeth, 1994; APA, 2002; Morreim, 1995; Pope, 1988) and must be discussed early in treatment (Behnke & Hilliard, 1998). Most practitioners are careful to provide written documentation of their fees in the first or second session. However, discussions about the total cost of a treatment are still not standard, although they should be, since high costs potentially harm the patient (Beahrs & Gutheil, 2001). There is no way for a patient to know how many sessions are likely to be needed, so it is up to the practitioner to provide an initial estimate of the expected cost of treatment (Morreim, 1995; American Nurses Association, 2001). Granted, this is often difficult since the duration of treatment varies with the severity of the condition, which often is not known at the outset, and with factors that may only be discovered later, such as comorbidities, compliance problems, or simple failure to respond to conventional treatment.

This being said, I think it is best to provide a "guestimate" to patients at the beginning of treatment, especially if the patient asks, with fair warning that this estimate is based only on what is currently known. If the patient fails to respond in the expected number of sessions or duration of time, then both patient and practitioner can review the treatment and illness to see if some other factor can account for the delay or lack of response. If new information is gleaned over the course of time that alters the prognosis, the kind of treatment needed, or the expected duration of care, then this can be discussed with the patient and the estimated cost of treatment revised.

Example 2.1. *Let's say a 40-year-old woman presents to a social worker for treatment of complicated bereavement. The therapist estimates that the course of treatment will be about 10 50-minute sessions over the course of six months. At a cost of $80 a session, she estimates the total cost of treatment will be about $800, of which a certain portion will be covered by the patient's insurance. The total cost of treatment and the portion the patient will pay are discussed upfront based on information the patient provides about her insurance coverage for mental health benefits, and the patient consents to treatment. During the treatment, the social worker discovers that what had seemed like complicated bereavement is actually a major depressive episode that would likely benefit from pharmacological intervention. The prognosis now becomes less certain and the duration of treatment is increased based on the usual recovery time for major depression. The social worker discusses her findings and recommendations with the patient and refers her to a psychiatrist. The psychiatrist concurs and informs the patient about the nature of antidepressant treatment, the estimated frequency of medication visits and the likely duration of treatment, as well as the fees for each visit. The patient and the social worker revise the treatment plan and the patient understands that the intensity of treatment is now increased, as is the cost. She has enough information to plan accordingly and consents to continue.*

Example 2.2. The treatment of a typical major depression with medication and individual therapy in combination might last 12 to 18 months, but when serious character pathology is discovered during the course of treatment, the likelihood of response to conventional treatment decreases. Psychotherapy might have to be intensified to once a week and the duration of therapy might be increased to 3 to 5 years. Such a finding can be discussed with the patient by saying, "I now believe there is more here than simple depression . . . ," and the provider goes on to explain the relevant symptomatology in interpersonal relationships or defenses. The content and nature of the therapy is changed to facilitate treatment of the personality disorder, so informed consent is obtained again, as if a new treatment were beginning.

Once the new diagnosis and treatment plan change are discussed with the patient, she can prepare accordingly. Given the increased demands on her time and budget, she may decide to go to a therapist within her insurance plan as opposed to outside the plan. She may choose to see a specialist in order to allow her the best chance at recovery, even if it costs more. Or she may choose not to seek treatment for the character pathology at this time. The important point is that she is fully informed of her diagnosis, the options for treatment (including no treatment), the cost of treatment, and can then decide how to proceed based on her own values.

Providing an estimate of the costs of other treatment is also an important part of informed consent (ApA, 2001a; Morreim, 1995) but in practice it is rarely applied. This means, for example, telling patients with depression that while the combination of therapy and psychopharmacology has the best recovery rate, treatment by medication alone is the cheapest and, for some people, actually all they need. Few therapists provide this advice since it is not in their own financial interest. This problem is compounded for analysts, whose service is the most time-consuming and expensive. Gruenberg (1995) rightly asked, "Does it exploit a patient to recommend psychoanalysis to a patient when another form of treatment might be equally (or more) effective, quicker, cheaper, or easier on the patient?" He goes on to support full disclosure of alternatives with their costs and potential efficacy or lack thereof.

Providing informed consent and discussing costs with patients requires a longer than 15-minute visit if the patient is to be allowed time for thought and asking questions. Short visits may be used in sequence, perhaps one to explain the findings and recommendations and then another short visit to ask questions, and perhaps a third to make the final decision. In other words, for truly informed consent to occur, there must be ample time for back and forth between the provider of mental health services and the patient. Higher volume practices have less participatory decision-making (Kaplan et al., 1996) probably because time constraints limit in-depth conversation (Davis, 2000). This has major implications for psychiatrists who book a lot of patients for 15-minute medication visits or who shorten the initial evaluation to 30 minutes in order to accommodate a lot of patients or increase practice revenue. Care must be taken that the desire to generate income does not cut into the time needed for truly informed consent.

Informed consent also has implications for treatment efficacy, since patients who are fully informed and allowed to participate in making decisions about treatment have more favorable outcomes (Kaplan et al., 1995). Better outcomes enhance your reputation as a practitioner. Don't hold back on providing the actual recommendations or costs out of fear the patient won't like it or will leave the practice. Information, the transfer of specialized knowledge, is what the patient is paying you for (Morreim, 1995). There is no "failure" if accurate information is given and the patient chooses to go elsewhere or forgo treatment altogether, either because of cost or for other reasons.

Gag clauses in managed care contracts used to prohibit providers from mentioning other (usually more costly) forms of treatment for a condition. In psychiatry, this usually meant not revealing that individual therapy was either an option for treatment or the recommended form of treatment. Most gag clauses have since been eliminated from contracts since they violated the principles of informed consent (Davis, 2000; Massachusetts Medical Society, 1996).

Disclosure of conflicts of interest is also part of informed consent (Gigerenzer, 2002) and will be discussed more fully in Chapter 9.

THE INFLUENCE OF MONEY ON THE STANDARD OF CARE

The law allows a provider to turn away or screen out patients who can't pay, but once a patient is accepted the duty to care for the patient becomes primary and the provider may not modify standards of care downward based on patient's ability or inability to pay (Mercado, 2000; Morreim, 1995). Therefore, the content of the informed consent discussion may not vary with the patient's resources. All treatments and their costs must be disclosed to all patients, regardless of insurance or financial status. This also applies to patients seen at reduced fees (Pope, 1988). Poor patients can not be steered into group or medication treatment while upper-income patients with the identical diagnosis are steered toward individual therapy or analysis. Interestingly, while the ethical codes for the psychiatric professions specifically mention duties to treat the indigent, none specifies that the same standard of care must be applied to those indigent clients. This is one case in which the legal code is more comprehensive than the professional code.*

ETHICAL BASICS

For a long time, organized medicine seems to have placed protection of income above moral virtue (Davis, 2000; Light, 1993; Stone, 2000), modifying ethical standards only in response to public outcry, market forces, or legislation. Psychologists, after the initial debate about whether private practice could be ethical at all, seemed to follow suit. Only nursing and social work, probably as a consequence of their long history as public-health professions, have legitimately been spared accusations of placing income above the public's need for care. Ethical complaints against professionals often involve the financial realm. Hall and Hare-Mustin (1983) noted that 20–25% of ethical complaints against psychologists involved fraudulent claims, exorbitant fees, sensational advertising, and failures to correct misrepresentations. Similarly, Strom-Gottfried (2003) reported that for social workers, dual relationships, fraudulent behavior, and failure to discuss policies as part of informed consent were among the top violations resulting in complaint.

Yet it can also be said that no professionals, including psychiatrists, think of income as a positive moral issue (Morreim, 1995) whereby practices exist not only for public service but for their own good as well. For a practice to continue to serve, it must remain solvent; for a practitioner to be sane and happy, he or she must be in decent financial straits. Thus, ethical issues with money management concern not only patient care but self-care of both the business and the provider.

---

* Addendum 1 to the *Principles of Medical Ethics with Annotations Specific to Psychiatry* (p. 92) addresses some issues of informed consent and standard of care, but the wording stops short of recommending that the same information be disclosed to all patients.

WRITTEN PROFESSIONAL CODES
AND STANDARDS

Let me say a word about the ethical standards of the four major psychiatric professions: psychiatry (medicine), psychology, nursing, and social work. There are only two principles that are consistent from professional code to professional code: prohibitions against sex with patients and the duty to care for patients. The rest varies considerably, especially when it comes to money matters. These differences reflect the length of time each profession has been in private practice (psychiatric nurses are still awaiting a comprehensive code for outpatient practice), the history and development of the profession, as well as philosophical differences between the professions. Recognition of those differences becomes important in managing the business end of a multidisciplinary practice.

The code of ethics for nursing is the least comprehensive in terms of financial guidelines for practice, a serious limitation for psychiatric nurses in outpatient settings or private practice. Psychiatric nurses in outpatient care must glean what they can from the very general *Scope and Standards of Psychiatric-Mental Health Nursing Practice* and the *Code of Ethics for Nurses* (American Nurses Association, 2002/2001) and then apply their own moral standards for the rest. Psychiatrists have perhaps a less general code of ethics that, while it makes some ethical principles clear, leaves a lot of room for interpretation. Their code does not address important issues regarding financial practices such as fee disclosure and contract adherence. Occasionally the *Opinions of the Ethics Committee* of the American Psychiatric Association (2001b) are published. These booklets provide answers to specific questions posed to the ethics committee in the recent past, but do not in any way expand on the code of ethics. In addition, few psychiatrists are aware of this publication, so the opinions are not well circulated.

In contrast, the *Ethical Principles of Psychologists and Code of Conduct* (APA, 2002) is wonderfully comprehensive. It is more contract oriented and sometimes reads like a legal text, but these attributes are a reflection of psychology's long history of consultation with business (organizational psychology) and the legal system (forensic psychology). The *Code of Ethics of the National Association of Social Workers* (1999) is probably the most complete, modern, and useful, covering not only matters of law but issues related to the private good verses the public good. Perhaps because social work's traditional purpose was in the area of the public good, ethics seems to be a natural component of their professional writing. The financial aspects are less complete than the psychology code, but certainly more complete than either nursing or psychiatry.

ETHICAL PRINCIPLES REGARDING FEES AND BILLING

Although professional practices regarding fees and billing may vary widely depending on local standards and circumstances specific to the nature of the practice, a few ethical principles are universal: clarity of communication, establishing reasonable and consistent fees, addressing how charges for missed sessions will be handled, and managing nonpayment therapeutically. Disclosure of nonpayment to subsequent treaters is more controversial.

Clarity of Communication

A unifying ethical principle for billing and fees is clarity of communication to the patient (Pope, 1988; American Nurses Association, 2002; APA, 2002). Written policies, fee sheets, bills, and statements must be accurate and clear (Lifson & Simon, 1998; APA, 2002; NASW, 1999), but simple presentation of written material is not enough. Important points should be discussed verbally to assess patient comprehension, facilitate discussion, and set a precedent for resolving problems or conflicts. In addition, providers often have to revisit these issues later in treatment, since things that had seemed clear on initial intake sometimes seem less clear later on. Insurance companies have come a long way in terms of making their Explanation of Benefits (EOB) clear to both the patient and the provider. Practitioners should follow suit. Not only does this facilitate payment, it is evidence of clarity, honesty, and integrity, and mitigates errors because the patient can easily compare the bill to their own records and help to correct mistakes. Brodsky notes that for psychologists, complaints alleging professional misconduct regarding fees are common "but rarely seen in a context in which fees are straightforwardly structured or are dealt with as important data in the professional relationship" (Brodsky & Schumacher, 1990).

Fees Should Be Reasonable

Psychiatric fees should be reasonable (Goldsmith, 2000; Morreim, 1995; NASW, 1999) but how does a professional determine if a fee is reasonable? One test might be the ease by which self-pay patients can pay for treatment at your full rate. If costs can not be paid out-of-pocket by middle-income patients with common psychiatric disorders needing conventional treatment, then the fee is probably too high. Another test is the percentage of discounted fees. If fee discounts have to be given to a majority of patients in the practice, then the stated fee is probably not reasonable.

Charging what other professionals charge is not necessarily a good test for reasonableness, although it is probably the one practitioners use most. When status is such an important element of professional practice and the fees a practitioner charges are presumed to be a measure of competence, there is psychological pressure to raise the fee beyond what any patient can afford. Professionals then compensate for inaffordability by reducing fees for almost every patient once the insurance is maxed out. The resulting fee distortion makes it hard for patients, insurers, and practitioners to know what a reasonable fee actually is.

Fees Must Be Consistent

The fee charged must be consistent (Goldsmith, 2000), meaning the same fee is charged to all patients and insurers. Exceptions can be made for patients with financial need if there is proper documentation in the chart and for insurance-contracted fee reductions as long as these remain exceptions and not the rule. Once a discounted fee becomes the rule, the original fee loses legitimacy and is no longer a proper representation of value. A written fee sheet can and should be given to all insurance companies with which there is a contract, as well as to all patients whether or not they will be paying those fees. This accomplishes many ethical goals. Patients with a contracted insurance discount or a fee reduction based on financial need are clear about what they would pay if their insurance or income changed. This allows them to plan properly for when the fee reduction no longer applies, and informs them about the actual value of the services in the general market. Secondly, a written fee sheet assures patients and insurance companies that there is a consistent fee policy in place, a sign of a person who sets limits professionally and personally, and a testament to the boundaries (ApA, 2001a; Lifson & Simon, 1998) so important to appropriate handling of transference and countertransference issues.

Charging for Late Cancellations, No Shows, Shortened Sessions, or Aborted Sessions

Most professional codes are either supportive or mum on the practice of charging for late cancellations and no shows (ApA, 2001a), but those that support such a policy agree that the patient must be clearly notified in advance (Behnke & Hilliard, 1998; APA, 2002; Lifson & Simon, 1998; ApA, 2001b). Usually communication of a no-show policy occurs at the onset of treatment and again at the first incident. As with all policy matters, it is unethical *not* to enforce such a policy once it is in place *and* it must be applied equally to all patients (ApA, 2001b). However, it is also a mistake to apply your policy rigidly without any consideration of patient circumstances (ApA, 2001b). For example, charging for all missed cancellations can be seen as unfair to persons with serious medical conditions who need to cancel more often due to illness, or to mothers of small children who need to cancel at the last minute due to illness of a child. A balance has to be reached where the policy is applied consistently but not rigidly. Supervision or consultation with colleagues about exceptions to a policy is helpful.

Drafting a comfortable policy is also critical. Policies with which a practitioner feels uncomfortable are more susceptible to inconsistent use. If you do not believe it is ethical to charge for services not rendered, then you should not charge for late cancellations and no-shows even if your ethical code allows it and all the other professionals in your location do it. Instead, you may deal with the matter another way, perhaps through rigorous discussion followed by termination if the patient continues to no-show.

Charging for appointments canceled after a patient quits prematurely is unethical (ApA, 2001b), since the nature of a fiduciary relationship allows the patient to end it for any reason, at any time, without penalty.

Remember that the goal of charging for late cancellations and no-shows is not to provide income but to discourage patients from missing appointments. Simply collecting payment for no-shows without exploring the underlying dynamic is unethical.

Nonpayment, Accumulation of Large Balances Due, and Termination

All of the professions recognize nonpayment as an ethical and just cause for termination of psychiatric treatment (American Nurses Association, 2002; Behnke & Hilliard, 1998; NASW, 1999) because payment for services is an integral component of the provider-patient contract (Behnke & Hilliard, 1998). However, certain obligations must be fulfilled before the patient is "fired." It is standard practice to inform patients during treatment when they are at risk for being terminated for any legitimate reason such as threats, noncompliance, frequent cancellation, or failure to pay the bill. It is also useful to mention behaviors that lead to termination in the policy sheets provided at the beginning of treatment. (The process for termination is discussed fully in Chapter 14, "Managing Nonpayment.")

Allowing patients to accumulate a large debt to the provider is probably unethical (Pope, 1988; APA, 2002). The bigger the balance, the harder it becomes to pay. The patient may feel unable to quit because of the debt, or compelled to quit for fear of creating a larger obligation to the treater. Debt skews the treatment by creating a second relationship, that of creditor-debtor, which then exerts an influence on the thoughts and behaviors of the parties involved. Limits on the amount of money patients are allowed to owe the provider should be low. Typical debt limits for middle-income patients are $400, one month's worth of services, or 10% of the patient's monthly income. The key requirement is that the debt can be easily repaid within several months time. If the patient can't afford treatment without accumulating a debt, another solution to the problem of affordability needs to be found such as lowering the fee, decreasing the frequency of visits, or transferring the patient to a less-expensive provider.

Revealing Nonpayment to Subsequent Treaters

A final issue, which I have not seen addressed in the literature, is whether to reveal a patient's nonpayment history to subsequent treaters. People opposed to such revelations cite issues of privacy as well as stigma, since awareness of the patient's poor payment record might discourage subsequent providers from accepting the patient. I think it is better to disclose nonpayment to subsequent treaters so it does not cause the next treatment to fail as well. Disclosure allows the next treater to take measures to prevent their treatment from ending prematurely. From a psychological point of view, nonpayment is a destructive relationship behavior. Disclosure allows it to be addressed in therapy so that it does not affect relationships outside of the office. Nonpayment may also be a symptom of an underlying psychiatric disorder, such as pathological gambling, sociopathy, or depression. Notifying subsequent treaters makes it more likely that hidden psychiatric causes of nonpayment will be identified and addressed. Ideally, revealing the problem of nonpayment to subsequent treaters should be discussed with the patient at the time consent is obtained, along with the reasons it needs to be revealed. If the patient refuses (this has never happened to me, but I could see it happening), the treater needs to point out that failure to address this issue may lead to another premature termination, and that hiding relevant information will start any new treatment off on the wrong foot.

ETHICAL ISSUES REGARDING CONTRACTS

All contracts should be adhered to (ApA, 2001a; Morreim, 1995). For mental health providers, there are usually three kinds of contracts: the treatment contract (unwritten), insurance and employment contracts (usually written), and civil contracts with society (also unwritten). The treatment contract is unwritten but may be supplemented by written policies and guidelines. As part of the contract, these policies must be enforced. If the patient and provider agree to make an exception, the discussion and plan of action are clearly documented in the notes. "Policy as promise" is a useful motto here (Sommers, 1999).

Employment and insurance contracts are written contracts enforced by law, but there are ethical issues as well. Just because a contract is legal, it may not be ethical. Many of the professional codes of ethics recommend not participating in contracts that conflict with the principles of the profession. Chapter 3 will address specific problems to look for in insurance and employment contracts.

Mental health professionals, like other citizens, also have social contracts, including the responsibility to fulfill civil obligations such as jury duty, child support, and payment of taxes. Fulfillment of these obligations may have negative financial ramifications, small or large, but failure to fulfill them can erode professional integrity at best and result in legal charges at worst.

ETHICAL ISSUES REGARDING INSURANCE

Insurance raises many ethical issues for psychiatric professionals, some of which are addressed in the codes of ethics and others in publications for the professionals. The insurance system is now an integral part of psychiatric care, for better or for worse, and every practitioner who accepts insurance payment has specific obligations associated with insurance. These include completing the necessary paperwork (Durham & Bros, Hardin, 1986; ApA, 2001b), helping patients appeal denials (Behnke & Hilliard, 1998; MMS, 1996), advocacy for the patient (American Nurses Association, 2002; ApA, 2001a; Mercado, 2000; MMS, 1996; Morreim, 1995; NASW, 1999), and scrutiny of the insurance company for adherence to ethical principles of health care (Morreim, 1995; NASW, 1999). Less clearly an obligation in the literature, but I think still important for informed consent about cost, is an explanation about any potential limits on coverage for psychiatric care (Behnke & Hilliard; Morreim, 1995). Because the patient cannot be abandoned when insurance stops paying, addressing what will be done at that time is a concern of the practitioner. Frank discussion of the limits of insurance coverage early on eases discussion later when insurance coverage runs out, because both you and the patient have been thinking about this as the treatment moves along.

I provide an insurance information sheet to patients who will be using insurance to pay for their treatment. It contains basic information patients can use to decifer their coverage limitations and anticipate problems. I find that it not only empowers patients to take responsibility for their coverage, but also educates them to make informed decisions about insurance coverage in the future. (A copy of my insurance information sheet is included in Appendix B.)

Gaming the System: Is It Ever Ethical?

Gaming the system in mental health usually refers to deliberately distorting information in the record, claim form, or authorization request in order to extend what the practitioner feels are unfair insurance limitations. Haavy Morreim has covered this topic extensively in his book, *Balancing Act: The New Medical Ethics of Medicine's New Economics* (Morreim, 1995). Morreim noted, and I strongly agree, that gaming the system becomes tempting to practitioners when a patient has no legal or economic entitlement to care, meaning no insurance or very limited coverage, yet still has a moral entitlement to care because they are ill, suffering, or in need of treatment. For these cases, some practitioners feel it may be ethical to "game" (cheat, trick) the insurance company in order to get what they feel is the patient's moral right to treatment. Common examples are upgrading the diagnosis on claim forms or exaggerating the symptoms on an authorization. The rationalization used is that the ends justify the means.

The American Psychiatric Association's *Principles of Medical Ethics with Annotations Especially Applicable to Psychiatry*, Section 3, deals with respecting the law, and adherence to contracts. The first paragraph states, "While no committee or board could offer prior assurance that any illegal activity would not be considered unethical, it is conceivable that an individual could violate a law *without being guilty of professionally unethical behavior* (my italics)." Whether it was the board's intent or not, providers in favor of cheating insurance companies to assure patients coverage for treatment can read support in this line. Insurance companies may see the board condoning fraud in this statement.

Both Morreim and I agree that this type of manipulation of insurance companies, even when it appears to serve the patient's interest, is unethical. Gaming is a clear violation of the contract agreement (Morreim, 1995) and promises are an essential component of civilized society. If mental health providers do not adhere to the spirit or the rules of the insurance contracts they sign, what is the point of having them at all? Do insurance companies then have the right to restrict contract offerings to those providers who will clearly uphold them?

Gaming can also affect the treatment relationship. Patients may wonder: If the practitioner is comfortable with cheating or manipulation insurers, might the practitioner be comfortable cheating or manipulating them? Including the patient in the manipulation is especially damaging to the treatment relationship. This could occur when a practitioner says to a patient directly, "I am going to put the diagnosis of bipolar disorder on the claim form in order to increase your coverage, but between us you only have a reactive depression." Collusion puts the patient in an uncomfortable moral position because the treater and patient have become partners in a crime or deception. Resolution of the dilemma for the patient can only occur by refusing the collusion or leaving treatment.

Gaming the system can have other negative consequences. Seeing a different diagnosis on the Explanation of Benefits than the one a patient was told in the office can make him feel frightened, diminished, or inadequate. Did the professional minimize the diagnosis to protect him from something he could not handle? For patients who are ambivalent about psychiatric treatment in general or in the throws of a negative transference, diagnostic inconsistencies may reinforce beliefs that the mental health field is unscientific or that the provider is disingenuous. Termination or noncompliance may follow.

To summarize my own and Morreim's view, gaming the insurance system causes harm to patients (malfeasance; Morreim, 1995), and it is unethical. There are plenty of other ways to manage nonpayment by insurances that are constructive. These are covered in Chapter 4.

I have not discussed gaming the insurance system for personal financial gain. Obviously, this is an exploitation of the patient and goes beyond any possibility of being ethical. Greed is no justification for gaming (Morreim, 1995). Money can be obtained in more principled ways.

OTHER MONEY-DRIVEN
ETHICAL VIOLATIONS

There are other financial behaviors that technically do not violate regulations, ethical codes, or laws, but which still exploit either the patient or the insurance carrier. While these practices can spur formal complaints, more often they are ignored or tolerated until the practitioner is brought up on more obvious ethical violations, like sex with a patient or fraud. Retrospective review then uncovers a long pattern of questionable behaviors having to do with boundaries and money management, including the following:

Hiring Patients

Hiring patients (ApA, 2001a) to do work within the office (for example, as a receptionist) or outside the office (housekeeping) is unethical because of the problems of dual relationships. As mentioned earlier, fiduciary relationships are characterized by an inherent power differential as a result of the patient's dependence on the provider. Such relationships are potentially easy to exploit and carry special obligations that protect the patient, including the ability of the patient to leave the relationship at will. Hiring a patient exaggerates the power differential by adding a second power differential, that of employer to employee. The second relationship binds the two individuals further, limits the patient's freedom to act, and biases the provider's ability to neutrally act on the patient's behalf. For example, if the patient is dependent on the provider for work, such as housekeeping, she may not feel free to leave treatment because she might lose the job as well. Likewise, a provider whose house is being painted by a patient will not feel comfortable suggesting hospitalization while the house-painting job is underway. (The related issue of barter for services will be addressed in Chapter 5.)

Not Billing the Patient

Not billing a patient, say in the case when a treatment went badly or as a courtesy to the patient, is also unethical. Payment is part of the treatment contract, a necessary weight in the balance of the fiduciary power. Payment gives the patient substance and a voice. The existence of a treatment contract or professional relationship becomes less clear when no billing or payment is occurring. Providers who engage in a sexual relationship with a client usually stop billing the client, perhaps as an unconscious attempt to deny the treatment relationship. Failure to bill raises the question of whether the treater is adhering to any professional boundaries in the relationship, boundaries we know are essential for successful treatment. Not billing also violates the principle of equal treatment for all. Policies are meant to be applied consistently to all patients and patients expect professionals to adhere to them. When providers don't bill, patients wonder why and seeds of doubt are sown.

Misuse of Financial Information
Provided by Patients

Misuse of financial information given by patients to the provider is considered unethical (ApA, 2001a; Gruenberg, 1995). The confidential relationship with the patient places the treater in a position where such information can easily be obtained and used for financial gain. Telling a friend that a patient's house might be up for sale soon, informing a charity that a patient is a likely prospect for donation, or encouraging a family member to invest in a patient's business are all examples of misuse of confidential patient information. It is the provider's duty to refrain from such use.

Requesting Money or Professional Advice
From Patients

Requesting donations for charity from patients (ApA, 2001a) is unethical because patients do not feel free to refuse when the requester is their mental health provider. Such requests set up the dual relationship problem mentioned above. Soliciting professional advice from a patient is unethical for the same reason. Practitioners should not ask legal advice from a lawyer-patient or building advice from a contractor-patient. The reason professionals sometimes feel tempted to do this is that the experience of the treatment relationship provides a level of trust about a patient's practices, values, and competencies. As a result, the provider feels more comfortable going to a patient than to someone they don't know or who might be less competent. However, the level of trust is not reciprocal or equal between the two parties. While the provider knows enough about the patient to increase her confidence that the work will be well done, the patient does not have the same level of knowledge about the practitioner. His experience with the provider is only in the area of mental health treatment, and he knows nothing about her behavior as a customer. That the inside knowledge of the patient is gained from a private, trusting, one-way connection underscores the special nature of the treatment relationship, a specialness that should not be used for the mental health provider's personal gain.

Practicing Outside Your Areas of Competency

Providing services that are outside one's area of competence is prohibited in all professional codes of ethics. Performing psychotherapy without proper training, as if it is "just talking," or providing advice about pharmacological issues without the requisite background are examples. The temptation to venture beyond the bailiwick of proficiency without obtaining the necessary instruction or schooling may occur when practice revenue seems too low to support additional training costs. The trick is to fix the revenue problem first, make it primary, so that training costs can be supported. Once the revenue problem is rectified, the idea of retraining may seem less compelling, or if it still seems like a good idea there is now money to pursue it.

We all need to train and expand our horizons into new areas of competence as time goes on, either to accommodate changes in the mental health field or to enhance interest in our practices. It is certainly ethical to practice new techniques on patients as long as the patient is aware that you are in training or obtaining supervision.

Overtreating or Failure to Terminate

Providing excessive treatment is also a violation of ethical principles. In some cases it may constitute fraud, as in cases of Medicare and Medicaid clients. Beyond the law, however, it is the duty of the professional to propose a halt to treatment when it is over or when little benefit will be gained by continuing. Most often providers are spared this task because patients bring up ending treatment when they are either well or not improving. The expense of treatment motivates them to end it when they can do so.

However, certain patients are at risk for never ending treatment. These include patients with dependent, narcissistic, or borderline features who feel they need the treatment relationship, anxious patients who are fearful of being out of treatment, and patients who obtain their care free of charge and enjoy coming in for the visits. If the amount of time spent or the amount of money paid is insignificant, the tendency to remain in treatment will be more pronounced. In these cases, it is the duty of the provider to bring up the issue of termination.

For the provider, termination ends the money stream from that case. If the practice is slow due to the economy, if a number of patients are ending at the same time, or if the patient is of high status, any tendency to collude with the patient in not leaving treatment will be exaggerated. Although the financial interests of the practitioner directly conflict with the financial interests of the patient when it comes to termination, the fiduciary nature of the treatment relationship dictates that the end of treatment occurs when indicated for the patient, not when it is best for the practitioner.

ETHICAL GREY AREAS

By *ethical grey areas* I mean topics which are not clearly unethical but for which valid ethical arguments can be made on both sides. The jury is still out on these issues: advertising for psychiatric clients, duties to treat the indigent, healthcare resource allocation, and whether it is ethical to be in private practice. Let's take a look at all of these areas.

Advertising and Marketing

Advertising and marketing are difficult areas because the ethics of business practice (duty to earn, duty to inform people of availability of services, duty to foster free competition) seem to conflict with fiduciary duties protecting relationships (interests of client above the provider, no undue influence, informed consent). This area of ethics has been changing rapidly and will likely change more in the future. In her analysis of ethics complaints against psychologists in the 1980s, Hall notes that 8–10% of complaints had to do with misrepresentation or sensationalization in advertising and that professional sanctions often followed poor advertising practices (Hall & Hare-Mustin, 1983).

The social work and psychology ethical codes both contain information on advertising (APA, 2002; NASW, 1999). The *Principles of Medical Ethics with Annotations for Psychiatry* makes no statement about advertising, and the *International Code of Medical Ethics* contains this unhelpful statement: "The following practices are deemed to be unethical conduct: 1) Self-advertising by physicians, except as permitted by the laws of the country and the Code of Ethics of the National Medical Association." The published opinions of the Ethics Committee regarding advertising are ambiguous (ApA, 2001b) except to say that "it is unethical for the psychiatrist to misrepresent himself or to make fraudulant claims. Deception of the public by misleading, inflated, and self-laudatory claims is to be avoided" (ApA, 2001b).

For those opposed to advertising for psychiatric services, active solicitation of clients off the street is felt to be unethical. This practice may pull for patients with nonsignificant symptoms, thus driving up health care costs and eliminating slots for patients who need and actively seek treatment. While the choice about whether to seek treatment based on an advertisement seems to be wholly within the client's control, some argue that the presentation of professional credentials in an advertisement is so compelling as to preclude any healthy skepticism on the part of a potential customer. For example, if a psychologist with a Ph.D. publishes an advertisement listing symptoms that suggest a need for treatment, would a lay person question the veracity of the advertisement? Furthermore, the use of testimonials from former patients is considered unethical for the same reason and for one other: namely, the undue influence of the professional on the patient who is making the testimonial. In other words, the professional would be using former or current patients for advertising purposes.

But can it also be ethical to advertise for patients? Prohibitions against advertising may limit access to valuable treatment. They may also limit competition in an area dominated by one or two well-known providers, thus violating the principles of choice and open competition. In 1977 the Supreme Court ruled that professional organizations may not restrict members from advertising either their availability or their fees and the Federal Trade Commission, in 1979, stated that such restrictions deprived consumers of information about the availability of services (Woody, 1989). Advertising may increase access, lower costs by improving competition, and fight the stigma associated with psychiatric illness. Advertisements can also provide much-needed public education, if they are done correctly (Sullivan & Viglione, 1990).

Whether one feels that advertising is or is not ethical, all can agree that any advertising done must be truthful and not mislead consumers. New York State's Education Law 6530, which provides definitions of professional misconduct, goes into some detail about what New York Law considers to be inappropriate and appropriate advertising for professionals. Many of the recommendations are useful.

Inappropriate advertising or soliciting includes that which:
- is not in the public interest
- is false, fraudulent, deceptive, misleading, sensational, or flamboyant
- represents intimidation or undue pressure
- uses testimonials

- guarantees any service
- makes a claim related to services, costs, or price, or superiority that cannot be substantiated (and the burden of proof is on the professional)
- offers bonuses or inducements in any form other than a discount
- demonstrations, dramatizations, or portrayals of practice in advertising on radio or TV

Appropriate advertising includes:
- none of the above
- advertising in newspapers, periodicals, radio, and professional directories of fixed prices, with full disclosure of any additional fees and the duration of time for any discounts (as in any other business solicitation)
- maintaining a copy of the advertisement for one year after its last appearance
- not compensating the press, radio, TV, or other media for publicity in a news item

Many other states have specific laws about truth in advertising and what practices are allowed or disallowed.

Section 5 of the *Ethical Principles of Psychologists and Code of Conduct* (APA, 2002) addresses advertising, is comprehensive and useful, and quite similar to the New York State requirements. It covers the use of fraudulent or deceptive statements, statements made by others on the psychologist's behalf, descriptions of workshops and courses, media presentations, prohibition of the use of patient testimonials (also because of undue influence), and prohibitions on direct solicitation of patients.

Advertising is not addressed in the *Principles of Medical Ethics with Annotations for Psychiatry* (ApA, 2001c). Answers to questions about advertising published in the 2001 edition of the *Opinions of the Ethics Committee* (ApA, 2001b) under Sections 1 and 2 are vague and not generally useful. For example, the practice of producing and selling an infomercial is deemed ethical by the committee "provided that the psychiatrists do not violate the ethical code, do not violate state or federal laws, and there is no fee-splitting. We caution that ethical problems may arise, but are unable to anticipate these." Yet the ethical code to which they refer (*Principles of*

Medical Ethics of the American Medical Association) has no content that relates to advertising other than a general request for honesty in dealing with clients.

In Question 2-M, the Ethics Committee recommends seeking guidance from local medical societies on all matters related to advertising. Whether local medical societies are equipped for this is unclear. The committee does state that misrepresentation of self and making fraudulent claims are definitely unethical and that deception of the public by misleading, inflated, or self-laudatory claims should be avoided. Sending notices out to other professionals asking for referrals (Question 2-WW) is allowed as long as the notices are not deceptive, misleading, or false: "Claims of unusual or special competence would be improper."

Duty to Treat the Indigent

Many wonder whether it is ethical to refuse to treat the indigent (Morreim, 1995) by screening them out over the phone, not allowing fee reductions, or not accepting Medicaid. The ethical codes vary on this issue to a certain degree. The code of ethics for medicine makes no statement about a duty to treat the needy despite a public perception that physicians have an obligation to treat those who are impoverished. In fact, Section 6 of the *Principles of Medical Ethics* highlights the importance of physicians being able to choose freely whom to serve, thus allowing restrictions based on financial resources. The only limitation on psychiatrists is that they can't refuse treatment if a patient presents in person in an emergency (ApA, 2001a; Marcinko 2000).

The code of ethics for psychology states, in Principle B, that "psychologists must strive to contribute a portion of their professional time for little or no compensation or personal advantage," thus conferring an obligation to treat at least some patients who can't pay. The code of ethics for nursing specifically mentions, in Article One, that "The nurse . . . practices . . . unrestricted by considerations of social or economic status," implying an obligation to the indigent. The social work ethical code, while not specifically requiring acceptance of indigent patients, places such strong emphasis on the commitment to those living in poverty in its preamble that an obligation to treat those in poverty is implied. Many clinicians' personal or religious beliefs require them to provide some care of the indigent or uninsured. How they choose to fulfill this obligation varies.

Outka (1976) argued that because so much professional training and research is funded by public tax dollars, all professionals owe it to the government to provide care to the indigent. Some could argue that this obligates treaters to provide free or reduced-fee services for those who pay taxes, but not for those who don't work or don't pay taxes, i.e., those surviving on government subsidies. They complain that people on Medicaid or Medicare get more treatment and have greater access to psychiatric treatment than those who are working but have no health insurance. This raises the interesting question of who is an indigent patient. Before Medicaid and the widespread adoption of health insurance, the indigent and the uninsured were the same people. Now, because of Medicaid and Medicare, the very poor often have some kind of health insurance while many low-income earners have no insurance at all. This can create a strange situation in terms of professional charitable work. A clinician working in a public institution drawing a salary may treat many poor patients without any personal financial sacrifice at all, while a private practitioner who accepts three sliding-scale patients per week may take a financial loss in doing so.

While professionals may or may not agree that there is an obligation to treat the poor, there is certainly an ethical obligation on the part of the provider to generate an adequate income for themselves and their dependents (Morreim, 1995). This means that providing treatment to the indigent in such a way as to compromise the financial integrity of the practice and all who work within it is both unethical and immoral. Insolvent or unstable practices help few people and may injure many. Yet the moral questions related to income are rarely discussed: What is an adequate income and how can it be determined? What level of cushion is reasonable to allow the practice to carry on during hard economic times? What sacrifices can and should be required of practitioners and their dependents if there are problems providing reduced-fee care to patients during periods of recession or job loss?

The Ethics of Resource Allocation

The conflict between maintaining good financial health while providing care to patients of all economic stations leads to one more issue. Is it is the duty of the practitioner to hold down the costs of health care to society, and to what degree do the psychiatric needs of society as a whole trump the mental health needs of our individual patients?

All the codes of ethics note a duty to society as well as to individual patients (ApA, 2001c; APA, 2002; NASW, 1990; ANA, 2001) but the relative importance of the two varies by profession. The medical code of ethics does not address conflicts between duties to patients and duties to society. Most American patients assume, usually correctly, that within the physician's office their individual needs will be seen as primary to society's needs and that the physician will advocate for them against all other interests. The profession of psychology notes duties not only to patients and society but also to organizations that hire the psychologist (ApA, 2001c). Conflicts between these three obligations must be dealt with so that there is no harm (Principle A) to any one party, but no ranking is provided. In contrast, the nursing code (ANA, 2001) clearly states that when duties to society and patient conflict, the duty to the patient must be primary if the conflict can be resolved no other way.

The conflict between the needs of the individual and the needs of the society is becoming more important as health care costs rise and the resource of money becomes a limiting factor in the provision of psychiatric care and medicine. This leads to the ethics of resource allocation, an area of monetary ethics that professionals simply cannot avoid. Professionals should visit these issues and make an attempt to reconcile personal views about access to care and the right to treatment with their actual practices regarding insurance, payment, and fees. Without such preparation, it will be difficult to field questions from patients during discussions about money, income, and the cost of treatment.

There are many opinions about what constitutes a fair or just distribution of health resources (Davis, 2000; Outka, 1976). One proposal is allocation of resources based on laws, regulations, or rules, otherwise known as *distributive justice* (Marcinko, 2000). Some rules, such as cultural rules, may not be written or part of a specific contract. An example of a cultural rule in health care is "similar treatment for similar cases" (Outka, 1976). Under the distributive justice model, the allocation of psychiatric services and the financial practices of professionals are considered fair and ethical as long as they follow the rules set up by contracts, insurers, and governments. Patients, however, may not consider "following the rules" as ethical or just if they are not well served by them. Yet to change those rules often requires changing the law. The biggest flaw of the distributive justice system is that the people who set the rules (well-to-do legislators and CEOs) are young, healthy, and have excellent health insurance. They are not representative of the majority of the population and may not understand the problems of access well enough or care enough about the people at the bottom to craft apt rules.

Another ethical system is "the greatest good for the greatest number of people," often called *utilitarianism*. Since most psychiatric illnesses are treated outside the hospital, this model argues that financial resources are better directed to outpatient rather than inpatient services. The hospitalization costs of one seriously psychotic patient could be used to treat many less seriously ill patients. The HMO (health maintenance organization) operates under the utilitarian model, trying to treat as many as possible by limiting the upper ends of coverage or perhaps by screening out the more seriously ill. This idea was initially accepted by the public as good for the whole, but as each individual came up against the limits, personal enthusiasm for the system waned. So, while the greatest good for the greatest number sounds good in theory, individuals oppose it when it is no longer in their personal best interest.

Two other ethical systems, *the social contribution model* (Outka, 1976) and the *free-market approach* (libertarianism; Marcinko, 2000), have this in common: more is given to the most productive members of society. The problem comes with how productivity is measured (Outka, 1976). Libertarians and conservatives in America usually consider income to be a more-or-less accurate measure of social contribution. "What you make is what you're worth," so those not earning much money are entitled to less. Yet many feel income does not measure productivity well, citing the uncompensated work most women provide in the home and the low wages paid to workers in essential services like sanitation, housekeeping, and maintenance.

These two systems distribute access to health care based not on need, but on a grading system (that is, income). Like the rule-based justice model mentioned earlier, the proponents and beneficiaries of this system are said to be "the establishment," or white middle-aged males. Non-establishment groups may oppose the system because it does not benefit them. In a mental health practice, a white male psychiatrist might experience resistance in payment from non-majority patients who consider him part and parcel of a biased health care delivery system. The ability to talk about this built-in bias, whether you agree with it or not, can facilitate hard discussions with patients about payment.

Another system, often called *egalitarianism*, favors the distribution of resources to those with the greatest need (Outka, 1976). By this system, the most seriously mentally ill, such as those with schizophrenia or patients requiring hospitalization, would be given priority, while those with less-serious illnesses, like marital problems or anxiety, might be placed on a waiting list or have their services reimbursed at a lesser rate by insurance companies. Because the occurrence of serious illness is random and devastating to anyone, rich, middle-class, or poor, medical care is reimbursed at the same rate for all patients, regardless of their ability to pay. This model places treatment of disease over preventive care, and treatment of emergencies over less-serious but perhaps more common illnesses. While our current health care system does not have enough money to treat everyone exactly alike (Outka, 1976), advocates of a national health care system see this model as an improvement.

The problem with all of these systems is that they allocate resources by some ranking system and foster competition for resources among citizens (Outka, 1976). They pit workers against nonworkers, young against old, rich against poor, or ill against healthy. The rivalry thwarts cooperation, contributes to inefficiency and inconsistency, and stifles creative innovation.

The point here is not to advocate for one system over another, but to familiarize the practitioner with some of the philosophical and ethical arguments patients bring up when they are reluctant to pay their bill, engage in treatment that is poorly covered by their insurance, or are despondent over their insurance coverage or access to psychiatric care in general. The practitioner who is unable to understand and discuss patients' legitimate concerns and views about the distribution of health care in America will have a hard time refraining from a defensive position and, as a result, will have trouble retaining patients when the discussion turns to payment, money, or fair compensation.

Is It Ethical to Be in Private Practice?

Given the compelling need for treatment when patients are ill, some have argued that private practice is inherently unethical because it denies access to patients who can't pay, commits the treater to patients who can pay, and pits the financial interests of the practitioner against the health and financial needs of the patient. Both nursing (ANA, 2002) and psychology (Pope,

1988) have seriously debated the ethics of private practice. While both professional organizations now consider private practice to be ethical, the limitations of organized nursing's support can still be seen in the scant attention paid to issues of private practice in their standards and codes. On the other side, advocates of private practice argue that it increases access by providing privacy, supports the free-market economy by increasing employment and generating wealth, lowers costs and improves quality by fostering competition.

For those professionals who feel private practice is unethical, the solution is to work for an organization or in public service on salary, thus placing the financial incentives of the practitioner one step away from the patient. For a while, things seemed to be moving in that direction as more mental health practitioners left private practice and began working in institutions that provided benefits as well as more regular hours. However, it soon became clear that the financial incentives were only made less direct. Institutions do not have the moral obligations of fiduciaries, so there is no check on their pursuit of financial gain. In addition, as productivity measures on individuals or departments were instituted, providers' financial interests again came into play. The lack of accountability, efficiency, and personal commitment to the patient by institutions and health care organizations is now driving things back the other way as more practitioners consider striking out on their own again.

Patients want a provider with a vested interest in a good outcome. The patient and provider share this interest and can discuss it openly. The financial interests of the practitioner in private practice are clearly visible to all patients and up for discussion every time the patient pays the bill. The financial incentives within health care organizations and government are largely invisible or hidden from the patient and, since payment proceeds out of view of the patient, are not an obvious topic of conversation and discussion. Patients who are suspicious of "systems" and government often feel more in control and less a potential target of exploitation if they can see someone in private practice.

Duty to Report Unethical Financial
Conduct in Colleagues

The duty to report colleagues is clearly spelled out in the *Ethics Primer* (ApA, 2001a) for psychiatrists but not in any of the other professional codes of ethics. However, enforcement of this duty is problematic because most of the information comes through privileged channels in sessions with patients, limiting the provider's ability to report. Licensing and disciplinary boards are then hampered because few patients are willing to follow up on their complaints by calling the relevant licensing board. On top of this, there is fear and hope on the part of providers that the complaints are hearsay, trumped up, or simple communication errors over policy. There is a need for anonymous surveys about financial practices in outpatient psychiatry to gauge the baseline occurrence of various practices, both ethical and unethical. Such surveys might provide a clue about where we are now in terms of standards of care. Publication of the results would allow patients and treaters to compare financial practices, making it more clear what to change or report. The data would also provide useful information for committees in a position to clarify ethical practices through formal statements, opinions, and guidelines.

CONCLUSION

How is a practitioner to proceed with all the legal, ethical, professional, and personal codes of conduct when it comes to financial matters? My advice is the following.

First, strictly adhere to the ethical guidelines of your profession, since they are usually the minimum necessary. Secondly, adhere to any personal moral standards that extend beyond those covered by your professional code. For example, if your profession's code does not mention a duty to care for the indigent but you believe you should do so, then you should be seeing some indigent patients.

Be aware that guidelines and legal requirements are rapidly changing and, in general, professional codes of ethics *trail behind* the rising ethical standards of public society. Pay attention to public sentiment and local professional practice. Listen carefully to patients and colleagues on matters of financial practice and health care. Do not hesitate to change your policies and procedures over time to conform more closely with your personal standards, as well as those of the public and the profession.

When you choose to practice in a certain way, be sure to truly understand why, rather than "because the guidelines say I should." Failure to understand the principles will necessitate a "rule for everything" practice without the coherent structure by which the morality of new situations can be assessed.

Remember that in psychiatric practice you are not only bound to uphold ethical professional principles but business principles as well. Rare are the cases in which business and professional ethics clash. Honesty, clarity of communication, adherence to policies, quality of service, proper exchange of money for service, accurate accounting, lack of discrimination, and not running at a financial loss apply equally to business and psychiatric practices. Your reputation is one of your greatest assets. Adherence to ethical principles can only enhance your work, even when it seems to cut into profits in the short term.

Finally, proper mentoring, supervision, and education of all psychiatric professionals should include discussion of ethical and unethical financial practices, as well as those practices for which the ethics are still undefined. This means going over current guidelines as well as discussing actual practices with examples. To discuss their own practices openly, teachers and colleagues must be at ease with their actions. While reluctance to discuss actual practices may sometimes indicate unethical or quasi-unethical behavior, more often it signals either a simple lack of adherence to policies ("Do as I say, not as I do") or a failure to understand the rationale behind the set policies. I have met many a practitioner loath to divulge a certain practice for fear it sounded unethical, when careful exploration revealed there were ethical underpinnings that could easily be supported and explained to others.

CHAPTER 3

Accounting and Taxes

K eeping good financial and accounting records is important. It permits easy resolution of billing disputes (Macbeth et al., 1994), allows
monitoring of any improvement or falling off of business (Duoba & Gada,
2003), and provides income data for running the practice. When records
are well kept, tax preparation is easy and less expensive; any audits or reviews are short. If you have employees for which payroll taxes must be deducted or a partnership or S-corporation (Duoba & Gada) that requires
distribution of profits, good records are critical.

In the chapter that follows, the business form the practice will take
(sole proprietor, partnership, or corporation) will be reviewed first because the methods of accounting and tax payment vary by business type.
Afterward, the basics of accounting and tax payment will be reviewed. Because state laws vary and tax laws change, the advice and principles below
are only general ones. Although there are many excellent books on accounting, tax preparation, and running a business, none can cover all the
details for every state. Seek consultation with a local accountant about tax
preparation, payroll deductions, and accounting records before beginning your practice.

CHOOSING THE BUSINESS FORM: SOLE PROPRIETOR, PARTNERSHIP, CORPORATION

The business form has tax and liability implications. The type of tax report, the calculation of taxes, and the distribution of profits and taxes

among partners are all dictated by the form your business takes. Relationships between owners and employees affect liability and are, in part, defined by the business form. Federal and state governments require every business to choose a business form and stick to it. If you don't choose one, or if you choose one that does not really match the operational structure of your practice, your business will be dealt with by the IRS and the court system in the form that most closely matches how the practice actually operates (Duoba & Gada, 2003), perhaps an unintended partnership or corporation. For example, in the case of a tax complaint against a mental health practitioner, a court could construe an office shared by psychiatrists as a partnership arrangement (Macbeth et al., 1994) if their individual business operations do not carefully follow the rules required for sole proprietors.

Remember that professions are different from other businesses. Professionals are not shielded from malpractice claims by forming a corporation (Macbeth et al., 1994). Forming a corporation limits *business* liabilities like corporate debts, not professional liabilities (malpractice). Most states specifically exempt malpractice claims from the liability limits or shields formed by incorporation. In addition, certain corporate forms may be allowed or disallowed for professionals depending on the state laws that govern professional businesses.

When growing a practice, one choice is to start as a sole proprietor, then progress to a partnership and further as the practice expands (Duoba & Gada, 2003). Each step would be accompanied by the accounting and tax changes recommended by a consulting lawyer and accountant. A second method is to join a small group where the proper practices are already in place, and then grow from that point. Both of these methods follow the natural course of business development and allow time for learning and incorporating the complexities of accounting and tax preparation. With small steps, the practice remains firmly anchored in reality and financial fantasies are minimized. Changes in the market can also be accommodated.

It is not easy to get out of a registered business type once it has been formed (Zobel, 2005). Dissolution of a corporation can result in large capital gains taxes and transfers of assets from a dissolved business might be assessed to individual owners (double taxation; Duoba & Gada, 2003). Always consult a local business attorney and accountant before making a decision (Duoba & Gada; Zobel) about the business form of your future practice. The consultation will usually include an assessment of your personal financial situation as well so liability issues can be identified and money management problems corrected before they affect the management of the business. Be prepared to present everything.

Sole Proprietorship

A sole proprietorship is a business owned by one person; a spouse is the only allowable co-owner (Pressman, 1979; Zobel, 2005). As a sole proprietor, "you and your business are one" (Zobel). You can't borrow money from the business because you would be borrowing from yourself. The business can't buy you a car because you are buying the car yourself. A sole proprietor is not an employee but an owner. As such, you can't collect unemployment if your business fails. Technically you do not get a salary either. Any money you take for personal use from the business as income is called a *draw*. In terms of income taxes, couples are considered one unit if they file jointly. In addition, the assets of each partner are considered the assets of both, often called *community property* in state statutes. As a result, the spouse of a sole proprietor can be held liable for income taxes not paid by the sole proprietor's business.

The big advantage of a sole proprietorship is that it is the fastest, easiest, and cheapest business to set up and run (Duoba & Gada, 2003; Zobel, 2000). No formal documents are needed unless you set up the practice in a name different than your own, the so-called DBA ("doing business as . . .") form of sole proprietorship (Pressman, 1979). To use a name different than your own, such as Suburban Mental Health Associates, you must file a form locally to document the business name and obtain a separate tax identification number. As a sole proprietor using your own name, you can use your social security number as your tax identification number (TIN), or you can request a different federal tax identification number from the IRS. The other big advantage of a sole proprietorship is that you have total control over all aspects of the business; there's no need to compromise with anyone else. You can set up and run the business however you want, within the confines of the law and the standards of care for your profession, of course.

There are several forms of sole proprietorship for mental health practitioners. One is a solo practice with no staff or associates. Another is a solo practice with support staff (receptionist, biller) or colleagues hired either as employees or as independent contractors. Solo practitioners can share overhead, like billing services or rent, with other solo practitioners (Chapman, 1990), although this practice carries some risk of being construed as a partnership if the financial documentation of any of the parties is poor.

As a sole proprietor, there is no double taxation on the money earned (Duoba & Gada, 2003). Business income is reported on the proprietor's income tax return on Schedule C; the business (practice) does not file a return or pay taxes separately.

The biggest disadvantage of a sole proprietorship is that the owner carries all of the financial risk of the business and there is no limit on business liability (Duoba & Gada, 2003; Zobel, 2005). Since you and your business are one, personal assets can be at risk, which then places family assets at risk. The rules about whether and how the assets of children and spouses can be protected from claims against the business vary from state to state. There are also restrictions on whether immediate family members can draw a salary from the business, perhaps as a biller or receptionist (Pressman, 1979). Be sure to consult an attorney or your state business tax bureau about using an immediate family member as an employee. A smaller disadvantage to sole proprietorship is that it is hard to borrow money in the name of the business alone (Zobel). But since, as a rule, you don't want to be borrowing money, this hurdle might not be such a bad thing. If a loan is needed, personal assets like a house must be put up as collateral.

Ownership in a sole proprietorship is limited to one person except for a spouse (Duoba & Gada, 2003), so family members and friends cannot join the business as owners. If you add another owner, the sole proprietorship instantly ends and a partnership forms, one example of an unintended business form. (Note that this is not the best way to form a partnership, see below.) Sole owners have to pay a self-employment tax for Medicare and Social Security. In a normal employer/employee situation, the employee pays half of this tax and the employer pays the other half. A sole proprietor pays both halves, about 15.3% on net business income less than $87,000 and a lower rate at higher net income levels. However, paying the self-employment tax makes you and your dependents eligible for Medicare and Social Security benefits should you retire, die, or become disabled, just like other workers.

Partnerships

Partnerships occur when two or more people are in business together and neither of them is an employee (Duoba & Gada, 2003; Zobel, 2005). Unlike the sole proprietorship, a partnership is an entity separate from either individual (see Figure 3.1; Zobel). A partnership can be formed by an oral agreement but it should be written. Unwritten agreements imply that profits and losses will be divided equally among partners. Partnerships usually require a certificate from the jurisdiction in which the partnership is doing business and state and federal tax identification numbers (obtained from the Internal Revenue Service via Form SS-4; Duoba & Gada; Zobel). The partnership files a tax return showing the business's profit or loss on Form 1065 but pays no taxes itself. Instead, the profit or loss is dispersed to each partner as described on Schedule K-1 of the partnership tax return. Each partner then pays taxes on the amount dispersed to them on their personal income tax (Duoba & Gada; Pressman, 1979; Zobel).

The obvious advantage of a partnership is that it allows for multiple owners of various types. One owner may have clinical skills but no capital, and the other may have business savvy but no clinical skills. Partners can be individuals, but they can also be other partnerships, businesses, or trusts. Profits and losses can also be allocated unevenly among the owners to reduce each one's tax liability and accommodate business needs (Duoba & Gada, 2003; Zobel, 2000), although no one can take a loss

FIGURE 3.1
The Partnership Business Form

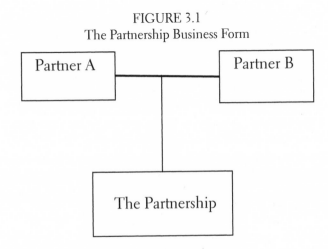

greater than the amount they contributed and a business purpose other than tax avoidance must be shown (Duoba & Gada, 2003).

Partnerships have several disadvantages. Each partner is responsible for all of the liabilities and debts of the partnership (called *joint and several liability*; Duoba & Gada, 2003; Zobel, 2005). Any contract entered into by one partner binds all the partners (Duoba & Gada, 2003), whether they agreed to it or not. All the income from the business must be reported as distributed, whether or not it is actually given to a partner or kept within the business for future development or purchases. Partnerships are dissolved by the death or withdrawal of any partner unless safeguards are in place. This does not mean that the business has to stop operation, but that a new partnership is formed. As a result, partnerships are hard to sell. If there are only two partners and one withdraws, the partnership automatically converts to a sole proprietorship with all business liabilities going to the remaining partner, while the assets may revert to a spouse. For protection, the partnership may need to purchase life insurance on key partners whose death or disability would seriously compromise income generation. Partnership agreements can include a system for buying or selling each partner's interest in the partnership, usually called the *buy/sell clause* (Duoba & Gada, 2003). This prevents ownership from passing accidentally to a spouse or dependent who is not a clinician or who does not want to assume the liability of the practice. Another solution is to include a paragraph about the process of adding partners as the business expands, particularly if there are only two partners (Pressman, 1979). Adding a third partner greatly reduces the risk of a halt in operations should one member die or withdraw.

The other disadvantage of partnerships comes not with the business or financial arrangements but with the necessary clinical and personal interactions. By definition, decisions must be shared and all final resolutions become compromises of sorts, which may or may not cause tensions down the road. Problems can also occur when one partner works harder, draws more business than the other, or wants to spend more (Pressman, 1979). The larger the number of partners, the harder it is to compromise and make decisions that all can agree to.

Partnership agreements are complicated documents that should be drafted by an experienced attorney, because state laws regarding partnership requirements vary (Duoba & Gada, 2003). Agreements should include the following: the monetary contributions made by each partner, who will manage and control the partnership, how profits and losses will be allocated to each partner, when cash distributions (called *partner draws*) will be made, the activities and responsibilities of each partner, and how shares will be valued if a partner withdraws or dies (Duoba & Gada, 2003). The partnership agreement may also include the process for admitting new partners, identify who will have the chance to buy the shares of a withdrawing partner (*right of first refusal*), and specify the duration of the partnership. A list of events that might cause it to end prematurely along with the criteria that would enable the partnership to continue if any of the events occurs is also helpful in preventing dissolution of the practice (Duoba & Gada, 2003).

There are several types of partnerships. General partnerships are the simplest to form. They are more complicated than sole proprietorships but less complicated than corporations. In general partnerships, the partners share management of the business, personal responsibility, and all legal obligations. General partnerships are not used as much anymore because each partner has to assume liability not only for him- or herself but for all the other partners (Duoba & Gada, 2003). (Remember that liability in this case refers to business liability, not malpractice liability.) To protect each partner from the liabilities incurred by the other partners, various forms of "limited partnerships" can be used.

Limited partnerships (LPs) allow for "limited" partners (Duoba & Gada, 2003). General partners manage the partnership and are personally responsible for all its obligations, while limited partners are like shareholders: they can't participate in management but their losses are limited to their contributions, so their liability is limited. Every limited partnership must have at least one general partner who assumes full liability. The organization of limited partnerships is determined by state statute and a limited partnership cannot exist until all the state requirements are met. Usually the business needs a certificate of limited partnership filed with the secretary of state's office that identifies the partners and gives other information about the business (Duoba & Gada).

Limited liability partnerships (LLPs) are existing general partnerships that are allowed by state law to convert to an LLP to reduce the business liability of the partners (Duoba & Gada, 2003). In some states this business

form is restricted to professionals. In other states, a family member, typically the spouse, is allowed to be a limited partner (FLP, or family limited
partnership), thus protecting the spouse should the professional be sued
(Rappaport, 2000). "Limited shield" states do not allow shielding of personal assets in limited partnerships, so the formation of an LLP may not be
useful. Limited limited liability partnerships (LLLPs) are a form of LLP
used in states that allow forced liquidation of the business to pay creditors
(Duoba & Gada). An LLLP prevents dissolution of the practice to pay outstanding debts.

While all this sounds very complicated, a partnership is relatively easy
to form with the assistance of a knowledgeable attorney and some awareness of the liability risks. What options will be available to you as a professional will be dictated fairly narrowly by state law. I bring up the various
options here only to show the range of options that might be available and
the motivation for states to allow different types.

Corporations

A corporation (sometimes called a *C-corporation* to distinguish it from a
subtype called an *S-corporation*) is a business entity that exists separately
from the people who own it (see Figure 3.2; Zobel, 2005). The types of
corporations that mental health professionals are allowed to form vary

FIGURE 3.2
The Corporate Business Form

| Owner 1 | Owner 2 | Owner 3 |

**Mental Health
Corporation**

from state to state (Benedict, 1990; Steingold, 2002), but they are fairly easy to form following state rules (Duoba & Gada, 2003). Corporations must register with the IRS and all the states in which the business is operating (Zobel, 2005). The articles of incorporation must be filed with the secretary of state (Duoba & Gada). Drafting the articles of incorporation usually requires the help of an attorney. Like a partnership, a buy/sell option within the agreement is important to allow continuation of the corporation if any member dies or withdraws (Duoba & Gada). Corporations pay taxes as separate entities using the accrual method (this will be discussed more later in the chapter), assume their own liability, and can hire owners as employees. Let's look at some of the advantages of the corporate form of business.

The main advantage of incorporation is that the owners (shareholders) are protected from personal liability if someone sues the corporation.[*] However, this protection ceases if corporate rules have not been carefully followed (it's not a corporation if it doesn't act like a corporation), if the corporation has no assets or if the owners have used corporate assets, perhaps a car or a computer, as if they were personal assets (Duoba & Gada, 2003). Incorporation may give a sense of legitimacy (Zobel, 2005) to a business, but if there are a limited number of shareholders, lenders and contractors will often require those owners to personally guarantee corporate loans or contracts, lowering the shield of liability protection (Duoba & Gada).

As a separate entity, ownership in a corporation can be more easily transferred or sold (Zobel, 2005), thus providing a potential source of cash in the future. Corporate owners can also be hired as employees and so have benefits, unemployment insurance, and half their Social Security tax paid by the corporation (Benedict, 1990; Duoba & Gada, 2003). Corporations can also retain earnings for future; they don't have to pay out all the profits to the owners, unlike partnerships (Duoba & Gada). This makes it easier to save money for computer systems or future expansion.

However, there are serious disadvantages to incorporation. Profits from a corporation are, in effect, taxed twice. The corporation pays taxes on all profits, usually at a flat rate of 35% (Steingold, 2001). When after-tax

---

[*] Zobel (2000, p. 7) and Duoba and Gada (2003, p. 101) said this is the main advantage. Also see Benedict (1990, p. 379).

income is passed on to the owners in the form of dividends it is taxed again as part of their personal income (Duoba & Gada, 2003; Zobel, 2005). This effect can sometimes be minimized by paying owner-employees a salary, but the tax rules are so complex that a tax attorney should be consulted to see if it is worthwhile financially (Benedict, 1990; Duoba & Gada; Zobel). In addition, corporations have to adhere strictly to the requirements of corporations (Duoba & Gada; Zobel), like electing officers, adopting by-laws, holding meetings with recorded minutes, and submitting various reports. Annual corporate fees, which may be considerable (Benedict, 1990; Duoba & Gada), have to be paid to all the states in which the corporation is registered (Zobel) regardless of whether the business makes a profit or loss. As a rule, the administration and taxation of corporations is complicated (Duoba & Gada), especially if the practice is doing business in more than one state, so accounting and legal fees are not insignificant. In terms of liability, malpractice liability for other professionals in the corporation may not be limited at all (Pressman, 1979), so incorporation does not provide any advantage (but see the professional corporation or PC status discussed below).

S-corporations are a special form of corporation. Like a partnership, an S-corporation files a tax return showing the profit or loss for the practice and the disbursement of that money to the owners, but does not pay taxes. Instead, the owners (shareholders) pay taxes on their portion of the disbursement when they file individually. Like a corporation, an S-corporation needs a federal tax identification number, corporate officers, and must fulfill all the administrative requirements of a corporation (some of which vary from the C-corporation). The profit of an S-corporation is calculated after the salaries are given to the owner-employees, but employee benefits are *not* allowed for any owner-employee with more than a 2% interest in the corporation, which is usually the case for the clinician-owners of an incorporated psychiatric practice. Like other corporations, S-corporations provide some protection from business liability of the corporation for the owners (Duoba & Gada, 2003; Zobel, 2005) and can passively accumulate income. Unlike C-corporations, S-corporations can use the cash method of accounting (discussed later in the chapter; Duoba & Gada), which is easier to master.

Limited liability companies (LLCs) are not available in all states (Duoba & Gada, 2003). They are similar to partnerships and file tax reports on Form 1065, the U.S. Partnership Return of Income, with Schedule K-1 showing the profit or loss distributions to members. Since the profit is dispersed to owners who declare it as income and pay tax on it, it is only taxed once (Duoba & Gada; Zobel). There must be at least two owners (Zobel), but membership is more flexible and anyone can manage the business (unlike a corporation that has to have designated officers; Duoba & Gada). Articles of organization must be filed with the secretary of state's office. In LLCs, all owners have limited liability for the business. The disadvantages of LLCs are that state laws may require multiple members and assets are not freely transferable to the owners. Formation and annual fees have to be paid to the state (Duoba & Gada), regardless of profit or loss.

Personal service corporations (PSCs) or professional corporations (PCs; Duoba & Gada, 2003; Zobel, 2005) are a corporate form usually reserved for licensed health professionals. PCs are taxed at a higher rate, but the business pays the tax, not the owner, and the salaries of working owners can be adjusted so that there is no profit. However, the working owners still pay personal income tax on their salaries. Business liability may not be limited (Zobel), but malpractice liability is limited. Each owner is liable only for his or her own acts (Benedict, 1990; Duoba & Gada; Steingold, 2001). Membership in PCs is usually restricted to licensed professionals, and often only one type of service can be provided. Consult an attorney and accountant if this corporate form seems like something you might want to consider for your practice (Benedict; Duoba & Gada).

GROUP PRACTICE VERSUS INDIVIDUAL PRACTICE

Group practices can take any business form and have no clear definition. A loose affiliation can exist of mental health providers all in solo practice within the same building, perhaps chipping in for utilities or a phone system. A solo practitioner may hire other clinicians as independent contractors, resulting in a group practice. Likewise, two partners can hire any number of employees or independently contracting professionals. Finally, a group practice corporation or company can be formed with all of the required layers of staff and professionals. In others words, the existence of a group of mental health practitioners does not in any way imply a certain business form. As a result, tax and liability issues are determined by the nature of the professional relationships involved.

In general, group practices are more complex and difficult to maintain (Pressman, 1979). Regular communication between the parties is critical. Establishment of rules and boundaries smoothes the way, but the process of forming and enforcing those rules requires compromise. The more people in the group, the greater the need for compromise and the less likely all members of the group will be satisfied with any given decision or arrangement. Finally, within a group practice, referrals are spread out among many parties. There may not be enough referrals to allow all clinicians to function at full capacity (Pressman).

Despite the complexities, group practices have some advantages. For beginners, joining a group can give a sense of "safety in numbers" (Pressman, 1979), reducing the anxiety of starting out solo. Collaboration and consultation are easy and may form part of the group practice contract, facilitating the clinical and business education of the individual provider. For more experienced practitioners, group practice is stimulating and less isolating than solo practice. For owners, group practice may increase income (Pressman). If you think you eventually would like to own or run a group practice, you would be well advised to join one first to learn the ropes. Once experienced, you may be admitted as a partner or owner (ask about this possibility periodically), or you may strike out on your own.

Clarifying Supervisory, Consultative, and Collaborative Relationships

Since group practices can come in any form, liability issues are determined by the nature of the professional relationship. Non-employee professional mental health relationships come in three types: supervisory, consultative, and collaborative. In supervisory relationships, the supervisor retains direct responsibility for the patient and gives the supervisee professional direction and active guidance (Lifson & Simon, 1998; Meyer & Simon, 1999; Weaver, 2003). The supervisor is usually paid by the institution providing the supervisee's training, not by the trainee. The patient is (and should be) fully informed that the treating provider is being supervised and what that means. If a lawsuit pertaining to the patient's care arises, the supervisor will almost always be named as potentially liable (Lifson & Simon; Macbeth et al., 1994; Weaver).

In consultative relationships the consultant is asked only for a professional opinion and may or may not examine the patient directly (Lifson & Simon,

1998; Macbeth et al., 1994; Meyer & Simon, 1999; Weaver, 2003). In mental health practice, the term *supervisor* is often applied to a senior consultant paid directly by the provider for consultation regarding cases. The patient is never examined directly and the advice of the so-called supervisor is given on a strictly take-it-or-leave-it basis. If an examination of the patient does take place, it is often limited to the facts needed to answer the question posed. Consultants do not control the case and liability is limited because the role in treatment is limited (Lifson).

Collaborative relationships are those in which two providers provide care simultaneously to a patient. The collaborators may have the same professional degree, as is the case when psychiatrists and primary care physicians see a patient with somatoform disorder, or the professional degrees may be different, as in the case of "split treatment," where a psychiatrist sees the patient for medication and a non-M.D. sees the patient for psychotherapy. Split-treatment relationships place the collaborating psychiatrist at increased risk for malpractice (Meyer & Simon). While in theory the M.D.'s liability should be limited to the psychopharmacological aspect of a split treatment, in practice a judge or jury may see the psychiatrist as more responsible for the patient or consider the therapist an agent of the psychiatrist (Macbeth et al.). To keep the relationship strictly collaborative and minimize liability, psychiatrists should avoid exerting control over or providing even the appearance of supervision to a non-M.D. therapist (Macbeth et al.). Be sure the patient understands the roles of each provider and that the psychiatrist is not supervising the therapist. For additional protection, make sure the therapist has a good reputation, is licensed, and has malpractice coverage (Macbeth et al.; Meyer & Simon).

Hiring Employees versus Independent Contractors

Another potentially murky area in group practice is the hiring of employees versus independent contractors. As a rule, employers are held responsible for the actions of their employees (Macbeth et al., 1994; Weaver, 2003), so liability is markedly increased when a mental health professional is hired as an employee. To reduce that risk, many try to hire clinicians as independent contractors. When clinicians must be hired as employees, psychiatric employers often do all the initial evaluations and assign the case to an appropriate clinician to reduce liability (Pressman, 1979).

Supervision by the employer may also be required. One hour per month for each six hours per week of patient contact is typical (Pressman). Remember that liability is reduced but not eliminated when hiring providers as independent contractors. It may be wise to obtain malpractice coverage for hired independent contractors under your own plan, even if the people you hire have their own (Macbeth et al.).

The choice about whether to hire another professional as an employee or an independent contractor also has important accounting, tax, and labor law implications. An employer must withhold and pay income taxes, unemployment taxes, and half the Social Security and Medicare taxes (Gilkerson & Paauwe, 2003; Zobel, 2005). A simple paper payroll system (see Figure 3.3) makes this easy to do, but the costs can be considerable. Employers hiring independent contractors do not have to pay these taxes because independent contractors pay their own income, Social Security, and Medicare taxes (Gilkerson & Paauwe; Zobel), and do not qualify for unemployment insurance. Employees enjoy certain labor protections and benefits that do not apply to independent contractors. They usually get disability insurance, although this requirement and who pays for it varies by state, and they are entitled to workman's compensation insurance. Most states require employers to purchase unemployment insurance for employees, but again, who pays how much varies by state (Zobel). Usually the cost is between 1–6% of gross wages.

Employees are divided into two groups, *exempt employees* and *nonexempt employees*, in reference to whether the requirements of the Fair Labor Standards Act (FLSA) apply to them. The FLSA worker protections include minimum wage and overtime pay for working more than 40 hours in a week (Duoba & Gada, 2003). In general, nonexempt workers are those who are paid an hourly wage, although some may be salaried. Exempt workers include executives, administrative staff, professionals (including physicians), and anyone who spends more than 50% of their time in some kind of management function (Duoba & Gada). If you plan to have employees, be sure to obtain consultation from an attorney, accountant, or your state's business tax or labor department to clarify which, if any, employees will be exempted and not exempted from relevant federal and state labor laws.

Although employers can't simply declare a worker an employee or independent contractor, the rules for determining whether a worker should be regarded as an employee or independent contractor (Macbeth et al., 1994)

FIGURE 3.3
Sample Payroll Book

WEEK ENDING

NAME	PERMANENT NON-RESIDENT	MARRIED SINGLE	EXEMPTIONS	SUN.	MON.	TUE.	WED.	THU.	FRI.	SAT.	REG	O.T.	REG	O.T.	REGULAR	OVERTIME	OTHER
1 Cynthia Yost	R	S	1		7	7	7	7	7	3	38		6.00		228 00		
2 Deborah A. Orr	R	S	2		8	8	8	8	8	4	40	4	6.00	9.00	240 00	36 00	
3 Lorna L. Winsor	R	S	2		8	8	8	8	8		40		6.00		240 00		
4 Nancy T. Daley	R	M	2		7	8	8	8	8	4	40	3	7.00	10.50	280 00	31 50	
5 Glenn E. Baldwin	R	S	1		6	6	6	6	6		30		7.00		210 00		
6 Joseph E. DeCesare	R	M	3		6	7	7	7	8		35		6.50		227 50		
7 Nicholas Vassar	R	S	1		8	8	8	8	8	2	40	2	7.00	10.50	280 00	21 00	
8																	
9																	
10																	
11																	
12																	
13																	
14																	
15																	
TOTALS															1705 50	88 50	

_January 31 20___

	WAGES	SOC. SEC.	MEDICARE	U.S. WITH. TAX	STATE WITH. TAX			NET PAY	WAGES	SOC. SEC.	MEDICARE	U.S. WITH. TAX	STATE WITH. TAX		
											CUMULATIVE TOTALS				
1	228 00	14 14	3 31	24 00	6 00			180 55	912 00	56 56	13 24	96 00	24 00		
2	276 00	17 11	4 00	25 00	6 25			223 64	1104 00	68 44	16 00	100 00	25 00		
3	240 00	14 88	3 48	21 00	5 25			195 39	960 00	59 52	13 92	84 00	21 00		
4	311 50	19 31	4 52	25 00	6 25			256 42	1246 00	77 24	18 08	100 00	25 00		
5	210 00	13 02	3 05	22 00	5 50			166 43	840 00	52 08	12 20	88 00	22 00		
6	227 50	14 11	3 30	5 00	1 25			203 84	910 00	56 44	13 20	20 00	5 00		
7	301 00	18 66	4 36	36 00	9 00			232 98	1204 00	74 64	17 44	144 00	36 00		
8															
9															
10															
11															
12															
13															
14															
15															
	1794 00	111 23	26 02	158 00	39 50			1459 25	7176 00	444 92	104 08	632 00	158 00		

Reproduced by permission of Dome Publishing Co., Inc. Warwick, R.I.

are not clearly defined. The IRS has a list of more than 30 checkpoints to evaluate the status of an employee. In general, the main considerations are the level of behavioral control the employer has over the work itself and the nature of the financial and business relationships between the two parties, but there are many other factors as well (Zobel, 2005). Let's review a few of these and how they might be manifest in a group practice setting.

Employers usually provide instructions or training to employees (Gilkerson & Paauwe, 2003; Macbeth et al., 1994; Zobel, 2005) and dictate when, where, and how the work will be done. So, if the owner of a mental health practice tells the other therapists what hours they will work and what kind of work they will be doing, or provides training or supervision for them, they would more likely be considered employees. If a worker's services are an integral part of the business (Gilkerson & Paauwe; Macbeth et al.; Zobel), such as when the owner of the practice does little clinical work so that the main income of the practice is dependent on the services of hired professionals, those workers will be considered employees. When a therapist works full-time and has only one employer, she looks like an employee (Macbeth et al.). If the employer hires the therapist's ancillary staff, like a biller, receptionist, or nurse, this again makes the therapist look more like an employee. Paid benefits, set hours, and continuous employment are all characteristics of employees, not independent contractors. Payment by the hour or week (Gilkerson & Paauwe; Macbeth et al.; Zobel) is typical of employees, while payment in various lump sums is typical for independent contractors.

The business role of the hired professional is also important. If the worker has no financial interest in the business and can't make a profit or sustain a loss individually (Gilkerson & Paauwe, 2003; Macbeth et al., 1994; Zobel, 2005), they don't qualify as an independent contractor. This means that the income of a mental health professional who is hired as an independent contractor should rise and fall depending on the amount of work done and their own paid business expenses. Administrative and lease arrangements may also be used to determine whether a group member is an independent contractor or an employee, especially when the mental health employer is also the office landlord or provides other services, such as reception, billing, and phone coverage.

The IRS prefers to construe most workers as employees (Macbeth et al., 1994), and penalties are severe for any employer caught hiring someone as an independent contractor when they should have been hired as an employee. In state or federal courts, if it is determined that a therapist hired as an independent contractor by the practice owner is actually an employee, the owner suddenly becomes liable for all back payroll taxes, in addition to interest and various penalties (Macbeth et al.). Form SS-8 (obtained from the IRS) can be used by a worker or an employer to ask if a particular worker should be classified as employee or independent contractor, but this often results in an investigation so should not be a first step. Instead, review the IRS guidelines in Figure 3.4 and make an attempt to categorize the worker (Macbeth et al.; Zobel). If you find, as many mental health business proprietors do, that your hires fall somewhere in between, consult a tax attorney or your accountant.

Because of the extra costs and liability, the addition of an employee or independent contractor for either clinical or nonclinical work should occur only when the practice is financially, professionally, and clinically stable (Pressman, 1979). In addition, wait until demand warrants the addition of another clinician. This means the practice or the other clinicians are consistently running 20–25% over their desired caseload (Pressman).

Vacation Coverage: Partner, Employee, or Collaborator

If you pay the colleague who covers your practice while you are away, that payment determines the business relationship. If you pay the person a fixed stipend, an employee relationship is established (Simon, 2001). If you split billed payments, then a partnership is inferred (Simon). If the covering person's only compensation is for services directly rendered to patients while you are away, then you remain as independent collaborators.

Office-Sharing Arrangements

Another instance in which professional relationships can become confused is when psychiatric professionals share office space or staff. In general, the risk is greatest to the professional holding the highest degree, usually a psychiatrist or psychologist, or to the party who owns the building if he or she is also a clinician. A collaboration may be inferred or patients may assume supervision or consultation is occurring between the professionals when this is not the case. Take the following steps to ensure that a simple office-sharing arrangement is not mistaken for a professional business arrangement:

FIGURE 3.4

 Internal Revenue Service IRS.gov

DEPARTMENT OF THE TREASURY

Topic 762 - Independent Contractor vs. Employee

To determine whether a worker is an independent contractor or an employee under common law, you must examine the relationship between the worker and the business. All evidence of control and independence in this relationship should be considered. The facts that provide this evidence fall into three categories – Behavioral Control, Financial Control, and the Type of Relationship itself.

Behavioral Control covers facts that show whether the business has a right to direct and control how the work is done through instructions, training, or other means.

Financial Control covers facts that show whether the business has a right to control the financial and business aspects of the worker's job. This includes:
● The extent to which the worker has unreimbursed business expenses,
● The extent of the worker's investment in the facilities used in performing services,
● The extent to which the worker makes his or her services available to the relevant market,
● How the business pays the worker, and
● The extent to which the worker can realize a profit or incur a loss.

Type of Relationship includes:

● Written contracts describing the relationship the parties intended to create,
● The extent to which the worker is available to perform services for other, similar businesses,
● Whether the business provides the worker with employee–type benefits, such as insurance, a pension plan, vacation pay, or sick pay,
● The permanency of the relationship, and
● The extent to which services performed by the worker are a key aspect of the regular business of the company.

For more information, refer to Publication 15-A (PDF), *Employer's Supplementa Tax Guide*. If you want the IRS to determine whether a specific individual is an independent contractor or an employee, file Form SS-8 (PDF), *Determination of Worker Status for Purposes of Federal Employment Taxes and Income Tax Withholding*.

Form available at http://www.irs.gov/taxtopics/tc762.html

1. Avoid any appearance of supervision or control over the other therapists.
2. Make no contract with a tenant that could be construed as an employment contract.
3. Do not share profits.
4. Do not include the other tenants' names on office stationery or signage. (For example, establishing a name for the group like "Professional Associates of Cedar St." may imply a business relationship.)
5. Keep all patient and financial records separate.
6. Make sure patients understand that all of the professionals in the office building practice independently and are not affiliated with one another.
7. Make sure all professional tenants are licensed, in good standing with their boards, and have malpractice insurance (Macbeth et al., 1994).

ACCOUNTING AND PAYROLL

Good accounting procedures allow anticipation of cash flow, proper payment of taxes, and accurate management of business information (Gilkerson & Paauwe, 2003). There are many acceptable accounting methods, from manual paper systems to high-tech computer programs. Consult your accountant before you start practice and adopt the accounting method they recommend. Make sure the system is simple enough that you can keep up with it and that it can accommodate the growth of the practice.

Good accounting practice requires keeping business and personal accounts completely separate in order to avoid potential difficulties in the event of an audit. This means not only separate records but also separate savings and checking accounts (Gilkerson & Paauwe). It also allows clear analysis of the financial status of the business, promoting better management decisions. On the downside, separating accounts increases bank fees and requires that sole proprietors transfer their draw (salary) from the business account to the personal account on a regular basis. Writing a check off a business account is not sufficient to verify that the expense was business-related. The business purpose of the transaction must still be clearly labeled. Get in the habit of labeling every transaction as it is recorded so there is never any confusion about which expenses are business-related and which are personal. The memo space on checks and the categories space on computer accounting programs greatly aid this type of accounting and data collection.

Cash expenditures can be tough because typically practitioners don't ask for or keep cash receipts for small items. This makes it hard to remember to record the expense and impossible to document it should the IRS or another entity request an audit. For this reason, some businesses avoid cash purchases altogether (Gilkerson & Paauwe, 2003). In my experience, it is hard to avoid paying cash for small business items like faxes and paperclips. It is better to get in the habit of asking for a receipt for every cash purchase, no matter how small, whether personal or for business, and then enter those receipts in the register just like any other transaction. Alternatively, your bookkeeper or accountant can show you how to set up a petty-cash fund, which can be reconciled monthly, rather than entering all small cash receipts individually. Remember that you must keep the receipts for all business-related cash purchases with the tax return to document the transaction.

Let's review some accounting terms before we get into the logistics of keeping accounts. You may not use these terms, but the companies and professionals you work with are likely to. If your eyes start to glaze over, skip this section and refer back to it when you need to. *Accounts payable* (often called A/P) refers to money that you owe others. A refund due to a patient or an insurance company for an overpayment and an invoice for mail-ordered envelopes are both accounts payable transactions. The stack of bills on your desk waiting to be paid along with the files of statements for the bills you have already paid is, in effect, your personal accounts payable file. *Open accounts payable* is money you still need to pay and *closed accounts payable* are the bills you have paid in full. Needless to say, you want your open accounts payable (the stack of unpaid bills) to approach zero. *Accounts receivable* (often called A/R) is all the money owed to you from insurance companies, patients, or tenants (if you rent out your office). *Open accounts receivable* is money still owed to you and *closed accounts receivable* are accounts for which full payment has been received. The term *cash receipts* includes the receipt of checks, money orders, credit and debit card transactions, and all wired or electronic funds, not just cash. *Cash flow* refers to the flow of money in and out of the practice. Because of the long turnaround time for payment from insurance companies, positive cash flow can be low while open accounts receivable (the amount you expect to receive) may be high (this problem will be discussed at greater length later in the chapter.) A *transaction* is any event that affects the financial records of the business, such as making a payment or accepting the receipt of a computer in exchange for services. *Ledgers* are collections of transactions grouped by type. In many businesses, there is one ledger for accounts receivable and another for accounts payable, but for psychiatric practice the most common ledger is called "patient accounts." *Journals* record all business transactions, including incoming revenues and outgoing expenses, in chronological order (Duoba & Gada, 2003).

There are two basic methods of accounting for businesses: the *cash method* and the *accrual method*. Most small practitioners and businesses use the cash method (Marcinko, 2000), checking the box labeled "cash basis" at the top of the tax form. The cash method shows income as it is received and expenses as they are paid. It is easy and speeds tax calculation because taxes are paid on a cash basis (you are taxed only on the money you have actually received and get deductions only for the money you have actually paid out; Marcinko). The accrual method records expenses when they are incurred and revenue when it is earned (the date of service), regardless of when the cash is paid or received. The accrual method more accurately reflects the nature of a business and is required for many corporations. However, it is more complicated to use (Marcinko; Robbins, 1990) and the extra time and effort do not usually make it worthwhile for small businesses. I will not be reviewing the accrual method at all in this book, since most practitioners will not be using it.

Now let's get back to the logistics, the how-to-keep-accounts section of this chapter. I am going to explain the most simplistic, cheap, and basic method. If your accountant recommends another method, use the one your accountant recommends, not mine. You will need the following: a locked filing cabinet for storing insurance payment stubs (called EOBs, or Explanations of Benefits), receipts, and the account books; a three-ring binder labeled *patient accounts*, accounting paper scored with at least six columns (available at any office-supply store); and either a spiral-bound business journal, like the ones put out by Dome® (available in any office-supply store) or a basic personal computer program, such as Quicken®.

First assemble the patient accounts ledger. In the three-ring binder, place a page of accounting paper for each patient you are seeing. Write the name of each patient and the relevant insurance information at the top. The left side is used to record the date the bill or claim was sent and the various dates of service, with the fee included on the bill or claim. The right columns are used to record the dates and payments received from the various parties. For example, column one will show the date and the amount received from the primary insurance company. The second column will show the amount that remains and the date the bill was sent to the secondary insurer or the patient. The third will show the payment with the date, and so on. The last column on the page shows the balance or credit on the account. Sample pages are reproduced below.

Example 3.1. A Self-Pay Patient

Date Billed	Dates of Service and Fee	Patient Paid	x	x	x	Balance or Credit
02/01/04	Jan 4 (eval) $170					
	Jan 11 (90807) $125					
	Jan 18 (90807) $125					
	Jan 25 (90807) $125	3/12/04 $545.00				3/12/04 0.00
3/01/04	Feb 2 (90807) $125					
	Feb 9 (90807) $125					
	Feb 16 (90807) $125	3/5/04 $375.00				3/5/04 0.00

Example 3.2. A Patient (Pt) with Blue Cross (BC)

Date Billed	Dates of Service	BC Paid	Pt Billed	Pt Paid	Balance
2/01/04	Jan 4 (90862) $65	3/10/04 $36.00	3/10/04 $29	3/29/04 $29	0.00
3/2/04	Feb 6 (90862) $65	4/10/04 $36.00	4/10/04 $29	4/30/04 $29	0.00

Example 3.3. A Patient (Pt) with Two Insurances, Medicare and Blue Cross (BC)

Date Billed	Dates of Service	Medicare Paid	BC Billed	BC Paid	Pt Billed	Pt Paid	Balance
01/31/04	Jan 15 90801 $170	3/1/04 $55	3/1/04 $115	3/24/04 $57.50	3/24/04 $57.50	4/12/04 57.50	0.00

Obviously, you can arrange the information anyway you wish, but the entries must be clear enough that neither you nor an auditor would have any trouble following the schedule of bills and payments for any patient account. Always enter ("post") patient payments to their account on the same day you receive the payment, preferably as soon as it is received. Calls to insurance companies about problem payments can also be noted on the patient account page.

Let's move on to the general journal for the practice. This will either be a paper business journal like the one shown in Figure 3.5, or the main register for the business in a computer software program, shown in Figure 3.6. Both income and expenses are recorded in the register on the date the transaction occurs. From this register, it is easy to total expenses and compare them from month to month and year to year. It is also easy to generate reports for taxes. Paper bookkeeping systems allow you to fold over the previous week's transactions to copy into the next week's, so that by the last week there is a tabulation for the year.

Computerized software programs generally look just like check registers and are easy to use. These programs strongly encourage the use of categories for every transaction, which makes data collection and expense management simpler. Computer programs also allow you to generate all kinds of reports with any date. For the computer phobic, I recommend starting with a paper system and then transferring to a computerized program when you have become proficient and can afford a computer.

Although I love using the computer for accounting, there are limitations to computerized accounting systems. Specialized bookkeeping software programs are very expensive and not worth the cost unless the business is large and has multiple earners. They are also hard to use without previous accounting experience. Quickbooks Basic® has no function for third party or multiple payers and so is not useful for mental health providers. It is also not HIPAA compliant, so it can't be used for electronic billing. In my opinion, for small practices, it is best to use an easy personal finances program like Quicken®.

To complete your accounting system, you will need files labeled with insurance company names to store the EOBs they send you. In general, payments for several patients will be made on one EOB, so storing them in the patient chart is not an option. Place EOBs in the proper insurance file in order of payment date, with the most recent at the front. Easy access and

FIGURE 3.5

Paper Business Journal Page. Courtesy Credit Dome® Bookkeeping

WEEK OF THE YEAR *13 th*   **WEEK ENDED** *March 31,* , 20___

TOTAL RECEIPTS FROM BUSINESS OR PROFESSION				EXPENDITURES				
DAY.			AMOUNT	ACCT. NO.	ACCOUNT	TOTAL THIS WEEK	TOTAL UP TO THIS WEEK	TOTAL TO DATE
SUN.					**DEDUCTIBLE**			
				1	MDSE.-MATERIALS	1,277 86	16,365 47	17,643 33
MON.			204 97	2	ACCOUNTING		150 -	150 -
TUES.			162 02	3	ADVERTISING	27 50	140 80	168 30
				4	AUTO EXPENSE	25 55	167 94	193 49
WED.			182 24	5	CARTONS, ETC.			
THUR.			263 53	6	CONTRIBUTIONS		20 -	20 -
				7	DELIVERY EXP.	24 08	388 30	412 38
FRI.			405 18	8	ELECTRICITY		81 60	81 60
SAT.			851 14	9	ENTERTAINMENT		87 70	87 70
TOTAL THIS WEEK			2,069 08	10	FREIGHT & EXPR.	22 78	213 74	236 52
				11	HEAT	13 81	165 19	179 -
TOTAL UP TO THIS WEEK			24,259 98	12	INSURANCE	40 -	136 32	176 32
				13	INTEREST	2 56	29 84	32 40
TOTAL TO DATE			26,329 06	14	LAUNDRY			
				15	LEGAL EXPENSE	30 -	70 -	100 -
MEMO				16	LICENSES			
				17	MISC. EXP.	24 91	115 65	140 56
				18	OFFICE EXP.	11 59	210 80	222 39
				19	POSTAGE		63 61	63 61
				20	RENT		450 -	450 -
				21	REPAIRS	16 50	4 93	21 43
				22	TAX – SALES		221 28	221 28
				23	TAX – SOC. SEC./MED.		83 10	83 10
				24	TAX – STATE U. I.		26 03	26 03
				25	TAX – OTHER		58 06	58 06
				26	SELLING EXP.		25 -	25 -
				27	SUPPLIES	12 74	57 23	69 97
				28	TELEPHONE		143 21	143 21
				29	TRADE DUES, ETC.		20 -	20 -
				30	TRAVELING EXP.		50 -	50 -
				31	WAGES & COMM.	333 57	2,418 43	2,752 -
PAYROLL				32	WATER			
				33				

MEMO section handwriting:

2,069.08
−1,863.45
2,069.08

Profit this week 205.63

26,329.06
− 23,827.68
Profit to date 2,501.38

EMPLOYEE	TOTAL WAGES	DEDUCTIONS				NET PAID
		SOC. SEC.	MED.	FED. INC. TAX	STATE INC. TAX	
Jody Smith	200 00	12.40	2.90	21.00	9.85	153 85
Joshua Brown	240 00	14.88	3.48	27.00	14.92	179 72
	440 00	27.28	6.38	48.00	24.77	333 57

ACCT NO.	ACCOUNT	TOTAL THIS WEEK	TOTAL UP TO THIS WEEK	TOTAL TO DATE
	SUB-TOTAL	1,863 45	21,964 23	23,827 68
	NON-DEDUCTIBLE			
51	NOTES PAYABLE			
52	FEDERAL INC. TAX		200 -	200 -
53	LOANS PAYABLE	50 -	400 -	450 -
54	LOANS RECEIV.			
55	PERSONAL	100 -	1,200 -	1,300 -
56	FIXED ASSETS			
57				
	TOTAL THIS WEEK	2,013 45		
	TOTAL UP TO THIS WEEK		23,764 23	
	TOTAL TO DATE			25,777 68

PLEASE NOTE

The difference between the gross payroll $440.00 and the net amount paid $333.57 is adjusted when withheld taxes are paid to the government. See instruction # 23.

(side text) COPYRIGHT · DOME ENTERPRISES

Reproduced with permission of Dome Publishing Co., Inc., Warwick, R.I.

FIGURE 3.6

Screen Shot of Typical Entries in Quicken® Basic Used as a Business Journal

Book

2004
7/21/2004   Page 1

Date	Num	Transaction		Payment	C	Deposit	Balance
4/20/2004		DES				95.40	1,004.32
		cat:	DES evals				
		memo:	0876079				
4/20/2004		Commonwealth Of MA				204.36	1,208.68
		cat:	Medicaid				
		memo:	0002115394 JF, JL, NV				
4/20/2004		CMS Medicare				214.96	1,423.64
		cat:	Medicare				
		memo:	09504902 JF, GS				
4/20/2004	EFT	Staples		11.31			1,412.33
		cat:	Office:Supplies				
4/21/2004	EFT	Staples		157.49			1,254.84
		cat:	Office:furniture				
		memo:	filing cabinet				
4/22/2004		BCBS Of MA				387.50	1,642.34
		cat:	Private Ins				
		memo:	53498087 JP, LZS				

Reprinted with permission from Intuit®.

ordering by date is critical when you have to pull stubs to check payments or copy an EOB to send to a secondary payer.

Finally, you will need a system that signals to you when to send out bills. I keep an index card for every patient in a box on my desk. Each day I pull the index cards and charts of the patients to be seen. After each appointment I record the date and type of service on the index card. No shows or late cancellations are also noted. At the end of the month, when I do most of the billing, I simply pull up the cards, transfer the information to the patient accounts ledger and do the bill for that patient. Because I like to do as much billing as I can before the end of the month, once a patient has had their last visit for the month I mark the card with a colored paperclip sticking up a bit. If I have a free hour, I glance at the index card box to see which bills I can send, pull a paperclipped card and whip that bill off. I also mark with clips those patients' accounts that have problems that need to be resolved.

Another easy method is to simply enter each visit directly into the Patient Accounts ledger as it occurs, including late cancellations and no-shows, and reserve one to three hours late in the week to review all the accounts.

The most critical aspect of bookkeeping is not to delay making entries (Gilkerson & Paauwe, 2003). Make accounting part of the daily routine of practice. Record all the payments received as you get them or before you leave the office. Record checks in the check register as they are written. Enter cash payments the day they are made and file the receipt immediately. If the practice is primarily psychotherapy (so fewer patients are carried) or if the practice is small, accounting shouldn't take much more than 15–30 minutes a day. If you are using a computer program, back up computerized financial records daily and create more than one backup disk.

The second most important aspect of bookkeeping is labeling every transaction. Good expense labeling aids accurate budgeting (Duoba & Gada, 2003) and allows practitioners to track expense trends, like rising malpractice premiums or phone bills. New expense categories can be added and unnecessary expenses, such as unprofitable advertising, can be dropped. When expenses are known in detail and tracked over time, the incorporation of rising costs into the fee structure can be done when it is really necessary, not just when others do it or haphazardly when financial pressures mount.

Many practitioners note the categories of expenses, but few categorize the source of incoming checks. Typical income source categories are *self-pay, private insurance, Medicare and Medicaid,* and *HMO.* Tracking income by source is critical for compiling data about where the practice is getting its money. At the end of the year, the practitioner can see how much income came from self-pay patients, how much from private insurance, and how much from government-sponsored insurance programs like Medicare. Transferring yearly data to a spreadsheet allows income data to be tracked over many years so practitioners can spot trends like decreasing reliance on HMO payments or increasing reliance on Medicare payments. This data also allows providers to assess whether contracted fee discounts from insurance companies are worthwhile enough to continue.

In terms of payroll accounting, it is quite easy to do once the deductions and labor requirements of your state are known. Your accountant can show you the simple calculations needed (the basics are included in the section on computing taxes below.) Since payroll work is highly repetitive, spiral-bound payroll books are easy to use, as are the computer functions included in any personal-accounting software package. For larger groups, or if you just don't want to be bothered keeping up with all the rules and requirements, the use of an outside human-resource administrative service is generally inexpensive and efficient (Galtress, 2000). It may also reduce the liability associated with worker complaints and employee-payroll fraud. Consult other large practice groups or your local professional organization for a recommendation. The cost is generally a low percentage of payroll but may vary depending on the options you choose. Options can include payroll processing, management of labor and liability issues including sexual harassment and employee termination, workers' compensation coverage, workplace safety compliance, and administration of benefits. Remember that you still have to collect and supply the data from each employee, which is often the most time-consuming part of the process.

Setting the wages of hourly employees, especially clinicians or staff who have to deal with patients, can be tricky. For nonexempt employees, you must start at the minimum wage for your state. To prevent the appearance of a kickback, set hourly wages based on the number of contact hours alone, not a percentage of collections (Pressman, 1979). You want the wages to be low enough that you can easily make a profit after paying employer taxes and benefits, but high enough that you can retain good employees. You can check the major national job surveys to keep track of the prevailing rate (Picker, 2003), but often local rates are more relevant. Two groups whose surveys are considered reliable and which are available online are the Medical Group Management Association (MGMA) and the Professional Association of Health Care Office Management (PAHCOM; Picker). The reference section of your library may have published information on local wage rates and the reference librarian may be able to lead you to local online surveys.

As skills or training increase, the hourly wage will have to increase (Pressman, 1979), but be sure the pay scale remains consistent throughout your organization. Equity is critical in preventing employee complaints (Picker, 2003). Clear, concise job descriptions, along with a system of performance evaluations, can help legitimize differences in compensation. If one employee requests a raise and research shows it to be indicated, consider applying it to other employees with the same workload and credentials. Be especially careful with bonuses and nonmonetary compensation like benefits. Many states require that all full-time employees be offered the same benefit package. Pay-equity issues apply to all forms of compensation, not just wages. A letter to all employees showing how bonuses are to be earned ensures fair application (Picker).

Store all accounting records together in a locked filing cabinet or a place with restricted access. For old records, clearly label the boxes or containers. Never store records, especially active ones, at home.

EMPLOYEE EMBEZZLEMENT

Employee embezzlement and fraud are not uncommon in physician practices, and small practices have the highest incidence (Haddrill, 2003). In practices with more than one member, accounting functions should be divided among several members so that no one person manages all the finances. Ideally, at least three persons need to be involved. One person, probably the front-desk person, will collect the fees and post them to the patient's account. A second person, perhaps the office manager, writes out the checks for the practice. A third person, the business manager, accountant, or owner, will review the bank statements and compare them to the patient accounts and bills. When accounting functions are divided up this way, a dishonest employee is obligated to involve at least one other person in the theft in order to escape detection, something that is hard to do. For further security, an outside party might perform an internal audit every quarter or so, where transactions are randomly picked and followed through the accounting system all the way to the bank statement. In a practice with just one owner and one staff member who functions as receptionist, billing clerk, and bookkeeper, it is imperative that the owner routinely monitor the bank statement, including a visual review of cancelled checks. It is also wise to contact patients with long-overdue accounts to make sure cash payments were not "misapplied."

If accounts are kept on a computer, limit access and be sure every computer is turned off and locked when leaving the office. Lock up financial records and the cash box at the end of every day and limit key distribution. If your practice will be large, there are other steps you can take to minimize employee fraud, such as encouraging credit card payment from patients, using a lock-box service so that cash receipts (remember that this term includes checks) go directly to the bank without being handled by an employee, and using a payroll service (Haddrill, 2003).

Other effective control measures include keeping a thorough system of documentation (recording receipts, packing slips, EOBs) and rotating duties. While employees are on vacation, another employee or the owner should perform all of the financial duties (for example paying the bills or billing patients) of the employee who is on leave. This helps prevent fraud and also uncovers errors or inefficiencies that can then be corrected.

UNDERSTANDING CASH FLOW

Having money is not the same as being profitable (Gilkerson & Paauwe, 2003). A practitioner can have a lot of money in the bank but still operate the practice at a loss. At times a practitioner may have little money in the bank even though the practice is making a profit. Cash flow is a matter of the timing between when money is earned, deposited, and paid out. Anticipating periods of heavy or light cash flow is important not only for the management of the practitioner's finances, but also for peace of mind.

There are several typical low-cash-flow periods in any psychiatric practice. One occurs upon starting the practice because of the six-week turnaround time for insurance payments and the two-to-four-week turnaround time for patient payments (if they are not paying in full each session). At the beginning of practice, inexperience with billing prolongs payment from insurance companies even further, since erroneous claims have to be resubmitted. Inexperience may also cause providers to forget to bill or send claims on time.

Other periods of low cash flow are six to eight weeks after any vacation (because no money is earned during that time), six to eight weeks after the winter holiday season (because patients and providers often cancel or take time off), and in the early fall if summertime hours were light due to patient vacations. Of course how low these cash flow periods are varies depending on the practice and the reigning economy. Although providers can use records to track cash flow over the years, often there seems to be no consistent pattern, except for the hole after prolonged vacations.

In order to manage low-cash-flow periods without stress, be sure to have cash reserves that allow payment of bills and the purchase of supplies during these periods. Most advisors recommend having enough cash reserves to cover three to six months of expenses (Duoba & Gada, 2003). This covers low-cash-flow periods and other crises, like hospitalization of the provider or computer meltdowns. Remember that wages, malpractice insurance, phone bills, rent, supervision, postage, supplies, taxes, health insurance premiums, and home expenses not covered by other income must all be paid regardless of cash flow.

Be sure to start your practice with an adequate level of cash reserves. Sometimes this means delaying the opening of the practice for the time needed to accumulate the reserves, but the delay is well worth it in the long run. Try to time payments for major purchases to avoid periods of low cash flow. For example, it might be tempting to buy a computer during summer vacation when you have plenty of time to learn to use it, but a credit card purchase might put the payment due at the very time cash flow is low because of summer vacations.

PAYING TAXES

Our tax system is basically "pay-as-you-go" (Zobel, 2005). Providers who are self-employed must send payments to the IRS and state treasury at the end of each quarter if at least $400 was earned (Duoba & Gada, 2003), unless your total tax liability for the year will be less than $1,000 (Zobel). Corporations also have to pay quarterly and so do all the partners in a partnership (Zobel). The dates quarterly tax payments are due are as follows:

First quarter: April 15 (three months)

Second quarter: June 15 (two months)

Third quarter: Sept 15 (three months)

Fourth quarter: Jan 15 (four months)

The different quarter lengths mean that the amount of taxes paid quarterly will vary a great deal. There is a penalty for late payment of quarterly taxes.

Payroll Taxes

For employees, the employer withholds income taxes from each paycheck and remits them quarterly to the state and IRS for employees. Earned income taxes for Social Security and Medicare are also withheld by the employer and submitted to the appropriate agencies on behalf of the employee. The amount withheld for Social Security is 7.65% of the workers wages, which the employer has to match. (Actually, the Social Security tax (7.65%) is two taxes: 6.20% for Social Security and 1.45% for Medicare, Zobel, 2000.) The FUTA (Federal Unemployment Tax

Assessment) is 0.8% of first $7,000 earned by each employee (Zobel) and is paid on Form 940. SUTA (State Unemployment Tax Assessment) may also have to be paid, with a corresponding decrease in the FUTA. Check with your local labor department or tax bureau about any SUTA that must be applied. Both FUTA and SUTA are only paid by the employer. Depending on which state you do business in, disability and health insurance premiums might have to be withheld and submitted as well (Zobel).

At the end of each quarter, employers fill out federal and state quarterly payroll tax reports. If you will have employees in your practice, your accountant can show you how to withhold these payroll taxes. The IRS also offers classes showing business owners how to do it (Zobel, 2005). If you want to spend more money, you can hire a payroll service to do it. The IRS has zero tolerance for incorrectly paid or unpaid payroll taxes (Zobel). Since the money technically belongs to the employee, problems with payroll may be treated as if they were monies stolen from the worker.

Calculating Quarterly Taxes

Quarterly tax calculations are based on income earned from all sources, not just self-employment income (Zobel, 2005). An accountant will often do the calculations at minimal cost, especially if your records are well kept, but you can do it yourself. I recommend getting your accountant to show you how to do it first, and then have them review it with you until you become fairly proficient. I'll outline the basics here only to give you the gist of the operations involved. For those of you who will be subtracting out SEP (self-employment retirement) or other retirement contributions, definitely consult your accountant first. The amount allowed for SEP contributions has been changing often and whether the retirement contributions are deducted pre-tax (as for SEPs) or post-tax varies with the type of retirement fund. These stipulations then affect quarterly tax calculation. Your state tax board and the IRS also offer publications that show how to calculate quarterly taxes.

First, gather all your income data for the quarter, including the income from other jobs and your spouse's income, if you file jointly. Separate these into two amounts: (A) self-employment income that has not had any taxes withheld (like from your private practice) and (B) income that has already had taxes withheld (perhaps from wages at your place of employment.

Based on the quarterly income so far, estimate your projected *untaxed* income for the year and the projected *total* income for the year.

To calculate the self-employment tax, multiply the yearly projected *untaxed* income by 92.35% (you don't have to pay self-employment tax on the first 7%; Zobel, 2005), then multiply that number by 15.3%. The result is the yearly self-employment tax.

Return to your *total* projected income for the year and subtract out one half of the self-employment tax calculated above as a deduction. Then subtract out the standard deduction (published in the information the IRS sends you each year), or your itemized deductions if they amount to more than the standard deduction. What's left is an estimate of your taxable income for the year. Calculate your estimated tax using this year's tax table (available from the IRS). From your estimated tax for the year, subtract out what will be withheld by any other employer, based on what has already been withheld. Add the balance to the self-employment tax calculated above for the estimate of your total tax liability for the year. Divide this by four for the quarterly estimate and send that amount in with Form 1040ES to the IRS. Calculation of state quarterly taxes varies from state to state but is basically similar (Zobel, 2005).

Once you've made quarterly payments for a while, there is an easier method that your accountant may recommend. Simply pay the same amount as last year each quarter or one quarter of what you paid last year in full. Although easier, these methods run a small risk of being inaccurate, especially if income varies greatly from year to year or quarter to quarter. Never use the easy method unless your accountant says it's safe.

In order to make quarterly tax payments on time without penalties, it is best to set aside a percentage of all incoming money for payment of taxes. Your accountant can give you a good estimate but generally it's about 30% of net income. In general, try to pay everything you owe for that quarter at the end of that quarter because eventually you will have to pay it all. The IRS does allow payment by installment, but there is a fee (Zobel, 2005).

Once you send in your quarterly taxes, you won't get any confirmation even if it's late or not the right amount. Penalties and charges for late or no payment will accrue *daily* by a percentage interest rate (about 8%, although it varies), so always send in as much as possible as soon as possible. Don't wait for the next due date! Send in the final return on time, even if there is no payment attached, because there are *other* penalties for filing the forms late. In other words, never delay *filing* your taxes because you don't have enough money to pay them (Zobel).

IRS Form 4868 is an extension to *file* returns late, not to pay late (Zobel, 2000). Pay as much as possible when the extension is filed so interest and penalties will apply only to the amount outstanding. Set aside more money for taxes next quarter so that the same thing doesn't happen. There are a few other ways to avoid penalties if you can't quite pay the full amount due (Zobel):

1. Make sure you owe less than $1,000 when you file the year-end tax return on April 15.
2. Each quarter, send in one quarter of the total you owed last year. Or,
3. For each quarter, send in 90% of what you owe.

These are only temporizing measures. Remember that at some point you will have to catch up and pay the full amount due for the year.

HOW LONG TO KEEP RECORDS

Practitioners often wonder how long they have to keep accounting records. In part, the answer depends on whether the financial records relating to the patient are considered an aspect of the patient's psychiatric record. My own opinion is that the record of a patient's appointments, bills, insurance claims, and payments bears witness to the nature of the relationship, reflects some of the behaviors of the patient, and may also indicate either progress or problems with the treatment. For this reason, I consider it part of the medical record and keep it at least as long as I keep the psychiatric record.

Financial records also need to be kept for tax purposes: old tax returns, all business-related receipts, cancelled checks, expense logs, payroll records, and any IRS correspondence. The recommended number of years to keep these records varies depending on several factors. The IRS has three years to examine records, but that three years begins either on the date the tax return is filed or two years from when the tax is paid, whichever is later (Gilkerson & Paauwe, 2003). If there is a change in accounting methods, keep records for a longer time to support the change. Employee-related records must be kept at least four years after the last tax was paid (Gilkerson & Paauwe). The IRS has up to six years to check your tax records if they think you've underestimated your income by more than 25% and there is no statute of limitations if you don't file a return at all (Zobel, 2005). Most state statutes of limitations for tax review are longer than the federal ones (Zobel).

Follow your accountant's advice in terms of how long to keep financial records for tax purposes but many will tell you to keep completed tax returns forever (Zobel, 2005). Keep everything else for at least five years from the date taxes were filed or paid, whichever is later (Zobel). If you are subject to audits by insurance companies or contracted agencies, check their record retention requirements before disposing of old records. Practically speaking, seven years is a good rule.

CHAPTER 4
Principles of Billing

I love to do my own billing. You might too. Nothing boosts the mood faster than a slew of checks in the mail. Those checks are a tangible reminder that your work has value. Billing can be a welcome break from patient care on a rough day. It's repetitious, easy, and the results are clear. There's no threat to life or limb, no noise except the clicking of the keyboard, and precious little ambiguity. Billing is productive work for free hours when patients unexpectedly cancel or don't show. There are intellectual benefits, too. You'll get information and insight about the financial state of health care directly from insurance companies and patients so that you can spot trends and modify your policies and practices to accommodate them. You can freely discuss the financial aspects of practice with colleagues, trainees, and patients because you know how things actually work, not just how they are supposed to work.

Personally reviewing patient accounts provides a quick and easy entrée to discussing money issues with patients. There's no need to wait for an institution or billing service to tell you about an accumulated balance. You can simply say, "I noticed you are a little behind on your bill. Is money tight at home?" The ability to address nonpayment directly with patients facilitates compliance with treatment and improves collections. A provider who bills (a "provider-biller") has an acknowledged business relationship with the patient, as opposed to a hidden business relationship. Complaints about payment, cost, and billing go directly to you. Any changes in either the treatment plan or payment plan can be modified to suit the treatment and the patient so that compliance is enhanced.

But doing the billing yourself is not without its frustrations. The biggest problem is that you absolutely have to stay on top of it even when the practice is busy. This means setting aside office hours for billing, occasionally staying late or going in early, and completing the week's work even when you're tired and would rather be home. Dealing with managed care and insurance companies can be tough. Phone calls can take time because of complicated menus, long intervals on hold, and repetitive information gathering. Sometimes you'll get transferred to the supervisor or have to wait for a call back. The good news is that most insurance companies don't make many mistakes, provider services are better than they used to be, and payment errors are almost always corrected. In my opinion, the whole billing field is markedly improving; there's no better time to jump in.

As a provider-biller, it's sometimes hard to deal with your own fallibility. The vast majority of denied claims will occur because of your (usually stupid) mistakes. Everyone loves to blame the insurance company, the billing service, or managed care, but in reality most payment errors are made by the practitioner. If acknowledging your blunders isn't hard enough, injury is added to insult when payment is delayed. But with time and experience, the number of delayed or erroneous claims will drop to a low level.

BILLING TERMINOLOGY

Let's review some common billing terms before learning how to bill. *Claims* are your requests for payment from the insurance company. *Claim forms* are the billing forms sent to insurance companies. The *HCFA 1500* (pronounced "hick-fah fifteen-hundred," for Health Care Finance Administration Form 1500) is the only claim form most providers will ever need. Private insurance companies and state Medicaid companies once had their own forms, but with the trend toward computerization, claims have become standardized. Order HCFA 1500 forms from a medical office-supply company, local Blue Cross carrier, or from your professional organization.

The insured is the person in whose name the health insurance policy was taken out. The Insured may be the patient or the patient's spouse, parent, or ex-spouse. The insurance card carries the name of the insured but often doesn't mention the relationship to the patient. Sometimes the card also carries the name of the family members covered by the policy, such as the spouse or children. People who are covered by the policy but who are not the insured are called *Beneficiaries*. The distinction between the *Beneficiary* and the *Insured* is disappearing. It used to be that the insured's identification number ended in "01," and the beneficiaries numbers were the same but followed by "02," "03," and so on, depending on the number of family members on the policy. Now many insurance companies simply register each beneficiary as an insured under their own social security number. The HCFA 1500 does require you to distinguish between the patient and the insured if they are different people.

The individual *insurance identification number* was most often the person's social security number. For privacy reasons, more insurance companies are assigning another number. As mentioned above, beneficiary ID numbers may either be their own number or the Insured's number with a two-digit code after it. The insurance card will indicate which is applicable.

A *provider number* (UPIN, unique provider identification number) is assigned to each provider by every insurance company. Years ago each insurer assigned a different provider number but things have been simplified since then. Although some HMOs and state Medicaid programs still assign their own provider numbers, most insurance companies now use the provider's Blue Cross or Medicare provider number. Eventually a universal provider identification number will be required and no companies will be allowed to assign their own. Ask to have your provider number preprinted on your HCFA 1500s in the appropriate space. For the few insurances companies who assign their own number, the preprinted one can be crossed out and the special provider number added.

Provider numbers come in two types: group and individual. Solo practitioners and independent contractors use individual provider numbers on claims so payments are made directly to them. Providers who are employees or part of a group use a group identification number on the claim form so the money is sent to the group while an individual number in another space shows who provided the service. A provider who is an employee at one practice but has a private practice on the side will use two identification numbers, a group number for visits done at the group site and an individual number for services at the private site. Providers moving from a group setting to a private setting must obtain individual provider numbers before billing insurances companies, otherwise payments will be sent to the former group site. Allow four to six weeks for the assignation of an individual provider number. Obtain it from the Medicare Web site, or call your local Blue Cross carrier.

A provider's *tax identification number* (TIN) is used to track payments and must be included on every claim form. At the end of every year, insurance companies send the Internal Revenue Service W-9 forms showing their total payment to you for the past year. They include your tax identification number so the IRS knows approximately how much you've been paid. Most sole proprietors and independent contractors use their social security numbers, but you can apply to the IRS for a special TIN if you want. Incorporated entities, partnerships, and other forms of business must have special tax identification numbers requested from the state and IRS.

The *date of service* (DOS) is the date on which the psychiatric service was rendered. When calling to correct an error, the representative will always request the date of service for the claim in question. Explanations of benefits (EOBs) sent to providers and patients always list the dates of service individually. For psychiatric services, every date of service must be entered on a separate line on the claim form.

Type of service (TOS) codes are used to categorize various services, for example, laboratory, X-ray, psychiatric, medical, or physical therapy services. Since most procedure codes are now category specific and since the mental health parity laws have restricted differential pay for psychiatric services, type of service codes are used less often. In my region, only the local Medicaid carrier still requires a TOS code. If a claim is denied for lack of a type of service code, simply call the company and ask for the TOS code for mental health or psychiatric services. They are not universal.

Procedure codes (CPT® or Current Procedural Terminology codes)* are numbers that specify the exact service provided. The American Medical Association has held the copyright on CPT codes since the first *CPT Manual* was published in 1966. There are about 50 psychiatric procedure codes, but only half of these are for outpatient services and most mental health providers will only use five or six. The psychiatric procedure codes run from 90801 to 90899 and are included in the Medicine section of the

---

* *Current Procedural Terminology* (CPT) is copyright 2004 American Medical Association. All Rights Reserved. No fee schedules, basic units, relative values, or related listings are included in CPT. The AMA assumes no liability for the data contained herein. Applicable FARS/DFARS restrictions apply to governmental use.

CPT Manual (AMA, 2003). From year to year, there may be modifications or deletions of procedure codes, but most of the psychiatric procedure codes have been stable for some time. *Modifiers* are two-digit numbers added to procedure codes to boost payment for unusual services or explain the modification of a service type. The psychiatric coding handbooks list the modifiers still being used in mental health, and the *CPT Manual* lists modifiers for all services in the front (most are for surgery). The use of modifiers in psychiatry (and in general) has markedly declined. If a modifier is required, you will be notified when the claim is denied. Most outpatient mental health providers will never need to use a modifier.

It is absolutely essential to purchase and read the current CPT Manual *before starting practice,* whether you will be doing your own billing or not. It can be purchased directly from the AMA but also through professional medical-supply or book catalogs. There are also excellent coding books specific to mental health that describe the relevant codes and show how they are applied and documented. I like the *CPT® Handbook for Psychiatrists* by Schmidt, Yowell, and Jaffe (ApA, 2004). It's short, easy to read, and useful for all psychiatric professions. All of the mental health professional organizations have CPT resource teams that can answer specific coding questions. To make things easy on yourself, make a short list of the five or six procedure codes you will use with any documentation requirements. Keep it on an index card and refer to it when writing patient notes and billing. In a short period of time, you will have it memorized.

In cases where a patient is covered by two health insurance policies, the term *primary insurer* refers to the insurance company that should be billed first. *Secondary insurers* are billed for the remainder after the primary insurer has paid. Primary and secondary insurers are common among the elderly, who often have Medicare and some kind of "Medigap" health insurance policy to cover the deductibles, co-payments, and services not covered by Medicare. Primary and secondary insurances used to be common in marriages where both partners worked, but with the high cost of premiums few couples buy into both plans now.

It can be difficult to figure out which insurance is primary and which is secondary. When Medicare is *not* involved, the primary insurance is always the one provided by the patient's employer and the secondary insurer is the one available through the spouse. If the patient gets a Blue

Cross HMO through work and Aetna through the spouse, the provider bills the HMO first and the remainder is billed to Aetna. The reverse order is used for the spouse.

When one of the two insurances is Medicare, things can get tricky. I strongly urge you to order Medicare's excellent free booklet called "Medicare and Other Health Benefits: Your Guide to Who Pays First" (CMS, 2003b; publication number CMS-02179). The main points are:

1. For retirees, Medicare is always primary to a Medigap policy like Medex and any retiree health insurance. Sometimes members of a couple have different secondary insurance plans provided with their pensions. These retirement plans may or may not include the other spouse. In this case, Medicare would be billed first, the patient's retirement health plan second, and any policy available through the spouse's retirement plan third. As pension benefits are squeezed and premiums rise, this kind of triple coverage is waning.

2. When a Medicare patient is 65 and has private insurance through his own employer (because he is still working) or his spouse's employer (because she is still working), Medicare is primary if the employer has fewer than 20 employees and secondary if the employer has more than 20 employees or is part of a multi-employer plan. If the Medicare patient is disabled (under 65) and has private coverage through work or through a spouse's work, the private plan pays first if it has 100 or more employees or is part of a multi-employer plan. If the employer has less than 100 employees, the Medicare is billed first (CMS, 2003b).

3. Medicaid is always the payer of last resort. It is the secondary payer when two plans are available and the third payer when three plans are involved.

The *explanation of benefits,* or EOB, is the insurance company's statement of payment or denial. It is sent to both the provider and the patient and explains how much was paid to the provider for which services on what days. It also contains information about the deductible, co-payments, and lists any reasons for discounts or denials of payment. The EOB is the only written record of claims receipt, payment, or denial, and it should be saved indefinitely. The relevant EOB must be by your side whenever you call to inquire about a payment problem, and a copy of it must be sent with corrected claims and to secondary insurers. File EOBs carefully so you can pull them quickly and easily. Copies of lost EOBs can be obtained by phoning the insurance company.

The *allowed amount* is the upper limit on charges that an insurance company will reimburse. Usually it is determined by a market analysis of the "usual and customary" fees for similarly licensed providers. When insurance companies state that they will pay 80% of the fee, they do not mean 80% of any fee charged but only those fees within a reasonable range. The term *allowed amount* is also used to designate a contracted fee reduction. The fees "allowed" by Medicare or an HMO are lower than the fee the provider usually charges. The EOB will first list the charged fee and then the allowed amount, or contracted fee.

Clean claims are those submitted without errors by the provider. It is a good idea to keep copies of all submitted claims so that if there is a mistake, it is immediately apparent who made it. (When ordering your HCFA 1500s, consider getting the carbon-copy version that automatically generates a copy.) Failure of an insurance company to make payment on a clean claim within a certain time period allows the provider to petition for interest due on the late payment. *Dirty claims* are those claims submitted by the provider with errors, such as lack of signature or incorrect codes.

UNDERSTANDING PSYCHIATRIC BILLING CODES

There are two kinds of codes used in billing: diagnostic codes and procedure codes. Diagnostic codes are required on all claim forms to document the disorder for which services are being provided. Most insurers require use of the *ICD 9 CM* (*International Classification of Diseases, Ninth Revision, Clinical Modification*) codes, which are virtually the same as the psychiatric diagnostic codes in *DSM IV* (*Diagnostic and Statistical Manual IV*). When consulting the *DSM-IV*, note any *x*s appearing in the code. They tell you how many digits must be present in the code. *An x appearing in the code means that a specific number must be included in that space when writing the code.* Failure to do so will result in denial of the claim. For example, 311 is the diagnostic code for depression NOS (not otherwise specified); it only has three digits. The diagnostic code for major depression is 296.xx, meaning that the final two spaces must be filled out using the specifiers for the disorder shown in the *DSM-IV*. A diagnosis of 296 for major depression will not be accepted on a claim form, but 296.20 will be. Keep a copy of the *DSM-IV* code sheet nearby for easy access when writing notes and filling out claim forms.

A conversion to *ICD 10* diagnostic codes, which are completely different, has been placed on permanent hold. Appendix H of the *DSM-IV* lists the new diagnostic codes, which will be fully compatible with *ICD 10*, should the conversion ever take place.

The American Medical Association's *Physician's Current Procedural Terminology Manual* (*CPT Manual*; AMA, 2003) contains the definitions and guidelines for each procedure code. These service codes are nearly universal and eventually will be required. Psychiatric procedure codes (908xx) are listed in the medical section (90000) of the manual, along with descriptions and restrictions on use. Every psychiatric provider must become familiar with the CPT® system,* even if no insurance companies will be billed, because patients seeking reimbursement from insurance will need this information from you. It's not hard to learn because there are so few psychiatric codes.

The patient's chart must provide evidence that the billed service was provided to the patient in the case of an audit or review. Basically, the insurance company wants to verify that the patient got the services, that the services were medically necessary, and that the services described are part of the insurance plan package of covered services (Schmidt et al., 2004). The date of service, duration of visit, presence of the patient, and details about the symptoms, illness, and treatment are all required. The *CPT Manual* does not provide guidelines for documentation but many insurance companies do, including Medicare. Be sure you follow them. As a rule, the documentation requirements of psychiatric procedure codes are minimal compared to the requirements of the general medical evaluation and management (E/M) codes because there are no national guidelines yet (this will be discussed in more detail later in the chapter).

Let me review some of the most basic psychiatric procedure codes. Psychiatric diagnostic evaluations are billed under code 90801 (or 90802 if play therapy or some other nonverbal method is used) for all licensed mental health professionals. Most insurance companies allow one 90801 for each episode of illness or treatment. Although it is not a timed code, the expectation is that the interview will take about 45–60 minutes (Schmidt et al., 2004). Psychiatric evaluations require documentation of

---

* *Current Procedural Terminology* © 2004 American Medical Association. All rights reserved.

the date, chief complaint, referral source, history of present illness, past psychiatric history, past medical history, social and family history, mental status exam, treatment plan, diagnoses on all five axes, and a legible signature (Schmidt et al.).

Procedure codes 90804 through 90809 are all codes for outpatient psychotherapy. They vary by duration of the visit and whether the visit included any medical component. Medical components include medication management, writing orders, reviewing labs or tests, and evaluating the implications of concurrent medical illnesses. Psychotherapy codes that include a medical component (90805, 90807, and 90809) can only be used by physicians, physician assistants, and nurse practitioners, and are reimbursed at a slightly higher rate. Other clinicians must use the nonmedical codes for psychotherapy (90804, 90806, and 90808). If there is no medical component to the visit, as might be the case for a therapy patient in excellent health on no medication, nonmedical codes must be used, even by psychiatrists, nurses, and physician assistants.

Child therapists or mental health providers to nonverbal clients often have to use the interactive therapy codes (90810 through 90815). Psychoanalysis visits have their own code, 90845, but since the reimbursement is usually less and medical necessity requirements harder to meet, it is not often used. Family or couples' therapy without the patient present is 90846, and with the patient present, 90847. Many insurance companies will not pay for visits in which the patient is not present.

Licensed medical professionals (MDs, NPs, and PAs) have some other procedure code options, most notably 90862 for pharmacological management, often called the brief medication visit. Although it has no time parameters, as a general rule it should take at least 10 minutes, and probably 15 or 20. If the visit is much shorter, let's say five minutes for a long-term stable patient in for a quick refill, the medical code M0064 is better. Note that M0064 is reimbursed at a lesser rate because less work is involved, but more patients can be seen per hour.

Another option for medical professionals is to use the general medical procedure codes (commonly called the E/M codes) rather than the psychiatric codes. For example, an initial evaluation of a new patient can be coded 90801 using the psychiatric codes or 99201 using the evaluation and management codes. In general, the E/M codes for outpatient services do not result in significantly higher reimbursement, and have such stringent and difficult guidelines for documentation that I do not recommend using them. However, high-volume multi-specialty groups that provide services to group homes or who see patients with unusually complex disorders sometimes benefit from repetitive use of these codes. Schmidt and colleagues' *CPT Handbook* (2004) gives an excellent overview of how and when to use E/M codes.

Not all services have procedure codes. Psychotherapy by phone and phone consultation with family members and other service providers are coded using 90899, which is the code for all unlisted services. An explanation must be attached to the claim explaining the service. And not all procedure codes are reimbursed by insurance. Reports for agencies or lawyers (90889) and evaluations of past records (90885) can be coded but are not usually reimbursed by insurance companies. This presents a problem for practices seeing children or disabled patients under the care of multiple providers, because much of the work needed is not reimbursed. Patients can be billed for these services as long as they are told so upfront, but many patients cannot afford to pay for such services when they are extensive, as they often are for psychiatrically ill children or adults with multiple disabilities.

On the subject of reimbursement for services, let me say only the briefest word about the RBRVS (Resource-Based Relative Value Scale) and RVUs (Relative Value Units.) The Resource-Based Relative Value Scale estimates the actual work required for each service and adds in the practice expense and liability risks inherent to each. The weight of each service is given in RVUs or Relative Value Units. Using this scale, we see that service code 90806 (50-minute psychotherapy) has an RVU rating of 2.61, while 90807 (50-minute psychotherapy with medical evaluation and management) has an RVU of 2.78 because of the additional work and increased liability. Medicare fees are computed with a simple conversion factor using the RVUs for each service. Codes with more RVUs are reimbursed at a higher rate. RVUs are interesting to look at but are unnecessary to know for billing purposes. For more information, consult Schmidt and colleagues' *CPT Handbook* or the various AMA publications on the RBRVS, which are updated each year.

You don't have to use CPT®* codes when billing patients (Goldsmith, 2000) unless the patient is submitting claims to the insurance company,

---

* *Current Procedural Terminology* © 2004 American Medical Association. All rights reserved.

but including the procedure code next to the description of the service on all bills helps patients translate their EOBs.

You cannot bill separately for the time spent reviewing the chart before the patient arrives or the time spent writing the note after the patient leaves. This work is already counted as part of the RVUs for each service (Schmidt et al., 2004).

PROVIDER BILLING RESPONSIBILITIES

These are the billing responsibilities of the provider:

1. Be clear and consistent about your fees.
2. Ask for payment in a timely fashion. Be clear about when payment is due.
3. Be fair. Accommodate problems reasonably and consistently.
4. Provide accurate data to billing services and insurance companies.
5. Record payments immediately.
6. Be scrupulously honest.

Clarity and consistency of charges is the provider's responsibility (Woody, 1989). As mentioned in Chapter 1, it is highly recommended that you use a fee sheet. Fees should be the same for every patient and insurance company (Goldsmith, 2000). If there is a negotiated discount for a patient, the reason for the reduction is documented in the chart. Fee sheets should be presented to contracted insurers. Discounts to insurance companies are noted in the specific contract and are presumed to be exceptions based on volume. Don't allow so many patient or insurance discounts that the actual fee becomes a sham. Presenting the fee sheet is not enough; be prepared to verbally state the cost for any service when and if you are asked, and include the fee for the service on every bill.

It may seem strange to say, but it is the provider's obligation to ask for payment from patients and insurance companies. If you don't ask for payment, you will not receive it. Asking means billing; billing for money and asking for money are the same thing. Not only do you have to ask, you have to ask in a timely fashion. Timeliness is critical to billing. This means insurance claims need to be sent out on time, usually within 30 days of the date of service, although many insurances allow up to 90 days.

If you use a billing service, the processors need the information for billing even sooner. Patient bills should be sent right away, either at the end of the month for a series of service dates or immediately following the service if it is infrequent. Speedy billing allows patients to plan, budget, and pay on time. It also eliminates confusion about what services have and have not been paid for. If there are any problems, they come up right away for resolution. A regular billing cycle demonstrates consistency to patients and provides regular cash flow to the practice (Woody, 1989).

When you are asking for payment, be clear about when the payment is due. Insurance companies know they only have two to six weeks (depending on whether you submit electronically or on paper), but patients don't know unless you tell them. Include a note at the bottom of each bill, or tell them when payments are due when they begin treatment. Tell your billing service when the due date is as well. Remember that the due date determines when a payment is considered "late," which in turn determines when an account goes into the nonpayment category.

Be consistent but fair in your billing practices; accommodate problems reasonably. Demanding payment on a short time frame from a patient in a genuine fiscal crisis is not responsible. Try to work out a payment plan or set a new due date, documenting the reason for the change in the chart. In addition, don't penalize patients for the payment problems of their managed care or insurance companies. This is not to say they can't take part in resolving the problem (see Chapter 5), only that they should not be punished or made to pay when the insurance company will be paying. Likewise, the patient can't be penalized if the payment problem is your own fault. This means that if you forgot to tell a patient that interest will be charged on late payments, you can't charge interest on the late payment. If you forgot to tell them that you bill for no-shows, you have to let that no-show payment go. If you don't submit the insurance claim in time to get paid, the patient should not be penalized for that.

Insurance companies and billing services can only be as helpful as the data you give them allows them to be. Include all the information they ask for in the format they desire. Don't skip steps you think are unnecessary, repetitive, or trivial. Believe me, the businesses involved have their reasons for the requirements, mostly having to do with industry standards, software requirements, and the trend toward standardization. You will only hurt yourself by being sloppy or purposefully skipping steps. Your claim will be denied and you will have to resubmit. Be good and follow the instructions.

Record (post) payments by insurers, patients, and second parties on the same day received for accuracy. Cash checks within the month so patients and insurance companies can quickly catch errors and theft. Record keeping is the responsibility of the provider (Woody, 1989).

Be scrupulously honest in billing. Never lie, cheat, or distort the truth when billing a patient or insurance company. In my opinion, this is not so much a matter of willpower or moral rectitude but one of understanding the temptation to cheat. The more experience you have with billing, the easier it is to defraud patients and insurance companies. Most providers never do it, but the lure arises when money is tight or when the provider simply wants more (more money, more stuff, or more prestige). Sometimes there is an urge to trick an insurance company who is causing the provider a lot of headaches.

Resist fraud by keeping yourself in a good place with money. Make sure you are satisfied personally, have enough money, and that your "wants" are in check. Drop troublesome insurers and managed care companies. They are not worth the frustration they cause over the long haul. Try to improve your billing system too or consider using a billing service if you think the temptation to bilk insurers is high. Remember that fraud, cheating, and distortion will damage the practice, destroy your reputation, and undermine your sense of self-worth.

BILLING INSURANCE COMPANIES

These are the steps for submitting claims to insurance companies:

1. Obtain the HCFA 1500 forms, the CPT® coding book, and the *DSM IV* diagnostic codes.
2. Get the insurance information from the patient's insurance card and have them sign the HCFA 1500 form on the initial visit.
3. Fill out the claim form accurately as soon as the service(s) for the month have been completed. (Or, submit your data to the billing service.)
4. Sign the claim form and record the date the bill was sent out in the patient account ledger.

5. Mail the claim right away.
6. Review all patient accounts at the end of every month to detect any delays in payment by the insurance company.

Claim forms (HCFA 1500s) can be obtained through professional associations and medical supply companies. I like to get the duplicate version that provides a tear-off copy of the claim for your own records. I order them with certain boxes (25, 32, and 33) preprinted. This costs a bit more money but saves time and reduces errors when typing claims. Have your procedure code sheet and diagnostic codes handy for billing time.

Certain data must be obtained from the patient at the beginning of the first session. This includes the patient's name, date of birth, address, phone number, and social security number. After obtaining this information, ask to see the patient's insurance card. Copy the name and insurance ID number off the card. If the name on the card is not the patient's, ask how that person (the insured) is related: spouse, parent, ex-spouse. Copy the name of the insurance company, the plan name (because many insurance companies underwrite several kinds of plans for the same employer), and the group or plan number. From the back of the card, copy the claims address and phone number of the insurance company. If you have a copy machine, you can simply copy both sides of the card when the patient presents it. Social security and some other insurance companies recommend having patients present a photo ID to verify that the card does indeed belong to the person in front of you.

After you obtain all the insurance information, have the patient sign sections 12 and 13 on the HCFA 1500 form. The signature in Box 12 allows you to release the data necessary for payment. The signature in Box 13 allows the payment to be sent to you, rather than to the patient. Confidentiality rules have changed. It is best to explain to patients that the insurance company will need to know the diagnosis, the type of service provided, and the dates of service in order to pay any claims. If they are using a managed care company, explain that more detailed information will often be required for authorization for payment. Managed or not, all insurance companies retain the right to look at the patient's record to verify that treatment is being given and to confirm medical necessity. Few insurance companies exercise that right unless there is a serious question of fraud or the cost of care is unusually high. In theory, HIPAA rules allow providers to give any information necessary for insurance payment without the patient's authorization. In practice, some insurance companies still will not process the claim without a patient signature on the initial claim form. Once the initial claim form is processed correctly, subsequent claim forms do not need any signature. Simply type "SIGNATURE ON FILE" in Boxes 12 and 13.

Some providers and consultants (Goldsmith, 2000) recommend calling the insurance company of every new patient to verify coverage, obtain the deductible amount, and delineate limitations on mental health benefits so that all of this is known by the provider in advance. I feel this is the patient's responsibility and provide information in my introductory packet (see Appendix B) to help them check out the limitations. While calling the insurance company yourself may prevent a few problems, it takes a lot of time and the information given over the phone is not always accurate. Large-volume practices may find calling insurance companies more efficient, since nonclinical staff is available to make the calls and inquiries about several new patients can be made at once.

Filling Out Insurance Claim Forms

It usually takes only three to five minutes to fill out a claim form once you become experienced. Often it takes less time, depending on the number of services on the claim and your writing or typing speed. Handwritten paper claims are accepted for all small providers, but typewritten claims are preferable because they can be optically scanned and turn around more quickly with fewer errors. Use the pica setting on the typewriter and try to line up the boxes. *Medicare claims require the use of all capital letters* (CMS, 2004), and private insurance carriers like Blue Cross are following suit (Blue Cross Blue Shield of Massachusetts, 1989), because they scan better and are easier on the eyes of claims personnel. Medicare requires the use of eight-digit date codes for all dates (CMS, 2004), and many other insurers do the same. Get in the habit of using the MMDD-CCYY format (month month, day day, century century, year year), which looks like this: 01312004. Information about a secondary payer will often allow Medicare to electronically submit the claim to that payer for you. This process is called "automatic crossover." It saves a lot of time when you can get a claim to cross over automatically.

FIGURE 4.1
The HCFA 1500 form

PLEASE DO NOT STAPLE IN THIS AREA

CARRIER

PICA **HEALTH INSURANCE CLAIM FORM** PICA

1. MEDICARE (Medicare #) MEDICAID (Medicaid #) CHAMPUS (Sponsor's SSN) CHAMPVA (VA File #) GROUP HEALTH PLAN (SSN or ID) FECA BLK LUNG (SSN) OTHER (ID)
1a. INSURED'S I.D. NUMBER (FOR PROGRAM IN ITEM 1)

2. PATIENT'S NAME (Last Name, First Name, Middle Initial)
3. PATIENT'S BIRTH DATE MM DD YY SEX M F
4. INSURED'S NAME (Last Name, First Name, Middle Initial)

5. PATIENT'S ADDRESS (No., Street)
6. PATIENT RELATIONSHIP TO INSURED Self Spouse Child Other
7. INSURED'S ADDRESS (No., Street)

CITY STATE
8. PATIENT STATUS Single Married Other
CITY STATE

ZIP CODE TELEPHONE (Include Area Code) ( )
Employed Full-Time Student Part-Time Student
ZIP CODE TELEPHONE (INCLUDE AREA CODE) ( )

9. OTHER INSURED'S NAME (Last Name, First Name, Middle Initial)
10. IS PATIENT'S CONDITION RELATED TO:
11. INSURED'S POLICY GROUP OR FECA NUMBER

a. OTHER INSURED'S POLICY OR GROUP NUMBER
a. EMPLOYMENT? (CURRENT OR PREVIOUS) YES NO
a. INSURED'S DATE OF BIRTH MM DD YY SEX M F

b. OTHER INSURED'S DATE OF BIRTH MM DD YY SEX M F
b. AUTO ACCIDENT? PLACE (State) YES NO
b. EMPLOYER'S NAME OR SCHOOL NAME

c. EMPLOYER'S NAME OR SCHOOL NAME
c. OTHER ACCIDENT? YES NO
c. INSURANCE PLAN NAME OR PROGRAM NAME

d. INSURANCE PLAN NAME OR PROGRAM NAME
10d. RESERVED FOR LOCAL USE
d. IS THERE ANOTHER HEALTH BENEFIT PLAN? YES NO *If yes*, return to and complete item 9 a-d.

READ BACK OF FORM BEFORE COMPLETING & SIGNING THIS FORM.
12. PATIENT'S OR AUTHORIZED PERSON'S SIGNATURE I authorize the release of any medical or other information necessary to process this claim. I also request payment of government benefits either to myself or to the party who accepts assignment below.
SIGNED ________ DATE ________
13. INSURED'S OR AUTHORIZED PERSON'S SIGNATURE I authorize payment of medical benefits to the undersigned physician or supplier for services described below.
SIGNED ________

PATIENT AND INSURED INFORMATION

14. DATE OF CURRENT: MM DD YY ILLNESS (First symptom) OR INJURY (Accident) OR PREGNANCY (LMP)
15. IF PATIENT HAS HAD SAME OR SIMILAR ILLNESS. GIVE FIRST DATE MM DD YY
16. DATES PATIENT UNABLE TO WORK IN CURRENT OCCUPATION FROM MM DD YY TO MM DD YY

17. NAME OF REFERRING PHYSICIAN OR OTHER SOURCE
17a. I.D. NUMBER OF REFERRING PHYSICIAN
18. HOSPITALIZATION DATES RELATED TO CURRENT SERVICES FROM MM DD YY TO MM DD YY

19. RESERVED FOR LOCAL USE
20. OUTSIDE LAB? YES NO $ CHARGES

21. DIAGNOSIS OR NATURE OF ILLNESS OR INJURY. (RELATE ITEMS 1,2,3 OR 4 TO ITEM 24E BY LINE)
1. ___ . __ 3. ___ . __
2. ___ . __ 4. ___ . __
22. MEDICAID RESUBMISSION CODE ORIGINAL REF. NO.
23. PRIOR AUTHORIZATION NUMBER

24. A DATE(S) OF SERVICE From MM DD YY To MM DD YY	B Place of Service	C Type of Service	D PROCEDURES, SERVICES, OR SUPPLIES (Explain Unusual Circumstances) CPT/HCPCS MODIFIER	E DIAGNOSIS CODE	F $ CHARGES	G DAYS OR UNITS	H EPSDT Family Plan	I EMG	J COB	K RESERVED FOR LOCAL USE
1										
2										
3										
4										
5										
6										

25. FEDERAL TAX I.D. NUMBER SSN EIN
052607418 [X] EIN
26. PATIENT'S ACCOUNT NO.
27. ACCEPT ASSIGNMENT? (For govt. claims, see back) YES NO
28. TOTAL CHARGE $
29. AMOUNT PAID $
30. BALANCE DUE $

31. SIGNATURE OF PHYSICIAN OR SUPPLIER INCLUDING DEGREES OR CREDENTIALS (I certify that the statements on the reverse apply to this bill and are made a part thereof.)
SIGNED DATE
32. NAME AND ADDRESS OF FACILITY WHERE SERVICES WERE RENDERED (If other than home or office)
CECILIA MIKALAC, M.D.
57 CEDAR STREET
WORCESTER, MA 01609
33. PHYSICIAN'S, SUPPLIER'S BILLING NAME, ADDRESS, ZIP CODE & PHONE #
CECILIA MIKALAC, M.D.
57 CEDAR STREET
WORCESTER, MA 01609
(508) 752-7529
PIN# **MI J08334** GRP#

PHYSICIAN OR SUPPLIER INFORMATION

(APPROVED BY AMA COUNCIL ON MEDICAL SERVICE 8/88) ***PLEASE PRINT OR TYPE*** APPROVED OMB-0938-0008 FORM CMS-1500 (12-90), FORM RRB-1500, APPROVED OMB-1215-0055 FORM OWCP-1500, APPROVED OMB-0720-0001 (CHAMPUS)
ITEM 063-8502/9144 **006953**

The HCFA 1500 is a nearly universal claim form (Goldsmith, 2000). Although it looks imposing (see Figure 4.1), most of the boxes are not filled out. The instructions given below are not perfect. There are subtle variations with some health plans. If you plan to bill insurance companies,

I recommend that you download (or obtain by mail) the claim form instructions from Medicare,* Blue Cross, and any private insurers. The instructions are updated often. In general, changes in filling out the form will continue as providers, insurers, software engineers, and the government strive for more consistency, simplicity, security, and fraud prevention. I refer to each step by the box number on the claim form.

1. Mark "X" in the box indicating if the claim is Medicare, Medicaid, or a Group Health Plan. Champus and ChampusVA are military insurance plans.
1a. Fill out the insured's insurance ID number as obtained from the insurance card. Remember that the insured won't always be the patient. Do not include dashes but do include any letters.
2. Using capital letters, type the patient's name, last name first, exactly as it appears on the card. Include middle initials and abbreviations like SR or JR.
3. Type the patient's date of birth. Use four digits for the year of birth. Check the appropriate sex box.
4. If there is an insurance primary to the one you are sending, type the insured's name *only* if the insured is not the patient. If the patient and the insured are the same, type "SAME." If there is no insurance primary to the one you are sending the claim to, leave this space blank.
5. Type the patient's address.
6. Mark "X" in the box for the relationship of the patient to the insured.
7. Type the address of the insured only if Box 4 is filled out and the address is not the same as the patient. If the address is the same, type "SAME."
8. Mark "X" in the box for the patient's marital status.
9. If the patient has another insurance that is secondary to the claim you are sending, write in the name of the insured for the secondary policy. If the insured of the secondary policy is the patient, simply type "SAME."
9a. If there is a secondary insurance, write in the policy number or identification number. For Medicare claims you want to cross

* These instructions are available to providers for downloading at http://www.medicarenhic.com.

over automatically to a Medigap policy, type "MG" followed by the policy number. If you have already gotten reimbursement from the primary and this claim is to the secondary insurer, write "EOB ENCLOSED" in this space and attach a copy of the EOB from the primary insurance company.

9b. Fill out only if the secondary insured is not the patient.

9c. Leave blank if you filled out 9d. If you don't have the Medigap policy identification number, write the Medigap claims address here.

9d. Enter the 9-digit payer identification number of the Medigap insurer. If no payer identification number exists, enter the insurance program or plan name. (A list of Medigap payer identification codes can be obtained from your local Medicare carrier's Web site.)

NOTE: Within the next few years, Medicare intends to simplify crossover claims by assigning numbers to all secondary payers. Much of the information listed in 9a–d might not be required after this change takes place.

10a–c. Check the appropriate boxes. Insurance companies will not pay health-related claims that are covered by worker's compensation or accident liability because payment by these entities is always primary to the health insurer.

10d. This item is used to identify Medicaid recipients on Medicare claims. Type "MCD" followed by the Medicaid ID number and the claim will automatically crossover.

11. For private insurance companies, type in the Group Insurance Policy number, available from the insurance card. If there is no group number on the card, leave this box blank. For Medicare claims, fill this box out only if there is insurance primary to Medicare. Otherwise type "NONE."

11a–c. This is where you fill out the primary insurance information. Put the policy or group number in only if it is on the card, then the employer and the individual insurance ID number. Leave all these boxes blank for Medicare claims unless there is insurance primary to Medicare.

11d. Check the appropriate box. Leave blank for Medicare claims.

12 and 13. The first claim submitted for each patient must have signatures and dates in both of these boxes. After that, simply
type "SIGNATURE ON FILE" in both of these areas.

14 through 20. Leave blank because they are not relevant for most
outpatient psychiatric providers.

21. List the diagnoses for which the patient is being seen in the
order of priority. Use *DSM IV* or *ICD 9* diagnostic codes up to
the highest level of specificity.

22. Leave blank.

23. Fill out only if a prior authorization number is necessary.
Leave blank for Medicare.

24A. Fill in one date of service on each line of the claim form. For
non-Medicare claims, use the MMDDYY format (032904). For
Medicare claims, use the MMDDCCYY format (03292004).
Do not use slashes, dots, or dashes to separate the month, day,
and year.

24B. Place of service codes are becoming more universal, but
check your provider manual to verify the place of service
codes for each insurance company. For most private insurances, 3 or 03 is the place of service code for an outpatient office and 4 or 04 is the place of service code for a home visit.
For Medicare and most Medicaid carriers, 11 designates an office location and 12 is for home visits.

24C. This can be left blank for most insurances due to the parity
laws. The insurance provider manual will give instructions if
this code needs to be filled in.

24D. This is where you type the procedure code. If you use an unlisted procedure code, you must include a narrative explaining
the nature of the work and attach it.

24E. Type the one-digit number that refers to the correct diagnosis listed in Box 21. Usually this will be 1, but sometimes
2 if the second diagnosis was the reason for the service provision.

24F. Enter the charge for the service. Do not use dollar signs or
decimal points, but you can leave a blank between the dollars
and cents portions of the charge.

24G. Enter a 1, because in mental health each service represents
one unit.

24H. Leave blank.

24I. Leave blank.

24J. Leave blank.

24K. For Medicare claims, type in the servicing provider's number. Use the individual number of the provider in a group practice. For other insurance companies, type in the servicing provider's number only if different from the billing provider. Otherwise leave it blank.

25. Federal Tax ID number (TIN) or social security number. Often this can be preprinted on the claim form when you order it. Check the EIN box if your TIN is not your social security number.

26. Patient account number if you assign one, otherwise leave it blank.

27. Leave blank.

28. Leave blank.

29. Leave blank.

30. Leave blank.

31. Sign the claim form including your professional degree. *Do not initial.* Type in the date. Use the eight-digit format for Medicare.

32. Now has to be completed for Medicare claims, even if it is the same as 33. Get it preprinted.

33. Name and address of the provider with individual or group provider number (can also be preprinted).

In some cases, one provider performs the service (the *servicing provider*) but another provider bills and is paid for the service (the *billing provider*). This may happen when the servicing provider is a supervisee or employee of the billed provider. The claim form must clearly indicate which provider performed the service (ApA, 2001b) and which provider billed the service. The "local use" Box 24K on the HCFA 1500 is often used by insurance companies to differentiate the servicing provider from the supervising or attending provider.

The billing provider can't simply be a figurehead (ApA, 2001b), receiving payment for the services of many other providers while off the premises or doing other work of their own. As a result, insurers do not allow supervisors to bill for the services of trainees unless they actually see the patient face to face for some part of the visit or are on the premises and accessible at the time of the service. They also will not reimburse the clinician of record (the "attending" clinician) for services provided by a covering clinician while the attending was away, since no service was provided.

An attending clinician can bill the patient or another party for services provided by a covering provider (ApA, 2001b) as long as the patient is aware this will happen and the bill indicates which person actually provided the service. Any fee received may not be split between the attending and covering providers because this violates anti-kickback laws. However, if an attending sends a bill for services provided by a covering practitioner, then a partnership or supervisory relationship could be inferred, making the attending liable for the actions of the covering provider. As a rule, it is better for covering practitioners to bill directly for services provided to a colleague's patients, unless the two providers are partners in the same enterprise or an established supervisory relationship is already present between them.

Submitting Secondary Insurance Claims

The original HCFA 1500 is submitted to the primary insurer and the practitioner retains a copy. If the primary insurance is Medicare and the secondary is Medicaid or another plan and you provided the necessary information, often Medicare will send the claim electronically to the secondary insurer for you. Such claims are referred to as "automatic crossover claims." The EOB you receive from Medicare will indicate if the claim was sent on to the secondary insurer.

If the claim does not automatically cross over or if the primary insurer is not Medicare, you need to submit a claim to the secondary insurance after you receive the EOB and payment from the primary insurer. In many cases the secondary insurer only needs a copy of the original claim form sent to the primary insurer (especially if it has the secondary insurance information on it), but sometimes the secondary payer will want a new claim form. Call to ask. A copy of the EOB from the primary insurance company always has to accompany the claim form sent to the secondary payer. If you lose an EOB, you can obtain another copy by calling the provider services at the insurance company.

Telephone Billing

Using a telephone for billing is an option for some Blue Cross plans. Called the Info-Dial® system, data entry follows the HCFA 1500 form and is cued by phone instructions. The only tricky part is the numeric codes for the letters used in the provider number and the patient insurance number. The numeric codes for letters are easy to figure out using the instruction booklet. Telephone billing allows for more rapid payment. The system detects some input errors, like incorrect patient identification numbers or incompatible codes, but it can't detect all errors. A confirmation number is given at the end of each entry. Multiple lines can be entered for a single patient and several patient claims can be done at one time.

Computer or Electronic Billing

Electronic billing is not required for small providers and probably will not be for many years. Before it becomes required, there will likely be a long period (years) where providers pay a small fee for each paper claim submission. Many insurance companies prefer electronic submission and will provide free software and technical assistance for using it. The problem is that the software is not universal and a different one is needed for each insurer. For providers accepting many insurance plans, it simply isn't feasible to download and install all of them. There are universal or comprehensive electronic claims filing software packages but they are too expensive for small provider use. The updates and servicing also cost money. Small- and medium-sized groups may hire a billing service to submit electronically for them. Billing services do enough volume that they can afford to purchase and maintain the comprehensive electronic billing software packages.

Basically, electronic submissions follow the same pattern of data entry as the HCFA 1500 form. The programs can detect many errors prior to submission and the software is HIPAA compliant for privacy and security. The main advantage of electronic claims submission is that it speeds up payment. Turnaround time is about two weeks. Denials and other problems can also be picked up more quickly.

However, electronic claims submission systems are not perfect. They aren't paperless, because a hard copy of the electronic claim has to be generated and saved to verify the submission. Attachments, like notes about special services or copies of EOBs, still have to be submitted on paper. Some insurance companies are still not equipped to accept electronic claims. Most importantly, computer programs do nothing to forward the patient end of billing and payment, which in this day and age is a growing portion of practice revenue.

Common Claim Submission Errors

The most common errors that result in denied claims are listed below:

1. Typos in the patient ID number.
2. Typos in the procedure code.
3. Dating errors:
   - An incorrect year on the date of service, especially in January of a new year.
   - The date at the bottom of the claim occurs before the date of service listed on the claim.
4. The provider forgot to sign the claim form or only initialed it.
5. There is no provider identification number in Box 33 (have this preprinted).
6. There is no prior authorization number for the service codes or dates of service listed on the claim.
7. The patient forgot to tell you that their insurance plan changed.

Always record the date the claim was sent on the patient account page for easy tracking. Payments should never take longer than six weeks. Immediately call the insurance company to inquire about a claim if there has been no payment in six weeks. Recording claim submission dates also allows you to anticipate cash flow in the next few weeks or months.

BILLING PATIENTS

The sooner the patient is billed, the better. When the bill comes soon after the treatment it is easier for the patient to keep up with payment, and with the services freshly in mind, the patient is more receptive to paying. Prompt billing also minimizes avoidance on the part of the provider in asking for payment. If a patient is self-pay or if the co-payment is a fixed dollar amount, say $25 per visit, bill the patient as soon as possible. That said, if the patient has an insurance company where there is a yearly deductible that has not been met or the co-payment is a percent of the fee rather than a fixed dollar amount, it is generally better to bill the insurance company first and wait for the EOB and payment before billing the patient for the remainder since the balance of the deductible and the exact amount of the co-payment can't be known until this information is received. The patient will get their EOB from the insurance company around the same time you do, so they will be primed for your bill if you send it promptly. Some insurance plans (Blue Cross and Blue Shield, for example, Blue Shield of Massachusetts, 1989) do not allow contracted providers to bill patients until the insurance company has paid their part.

If possible, give the bill to the patient in person at the beginning of a visit, either by hand or by leaving it on a table by their chair in full view so they can pick it up themselves when they are ready. Presenting the bill in a session in person maximizes communication. The patient can immediately comment on the cost, note any errors, and ask questions about deductibles, co-payments, or the timing of payment. Giving the bill in a session also clarifies the nature of the treatment relationship, especially for therapy patients. ("This is not a friendship.") Patients who are seen often usually respond to billing in-session by paying in-session, usually with a prewritten check, providing one more opportunity to discuss potential payment problems.

In terms of the actual bill itself, always print patient invoices on something with your professional letterhead. Include the date the bill was written up, a description of the service or services provided, the fee for each type of service, the dates of service, the amount paid by the insurance company and the co-payment for each visit, if applicable. Beneath this information, clearly state the amount due with a due date if that has not been made clear some other way. If there was an outstanding balance at the time the bill was written up, place that at the top (perhaps labeled *past due* or *previous balance*), before the current bill. Add it to the current charges and show as *total due*.

If you do not accept insurance payment, you are still obligated to give patients all the information they need to submit the claim (ApA, 2001b). For patients who submit to the insurance company themselves, this means an invoice including all of the above, with the procedure code written after the description of service and the diagnostic code somewhere on the invoice. See Figures 4.2 through 4.4 and 4.6 for examples of patient bills.

Billing for No-Shows, Late Cancellations, and Services Not Covered by Insurance

No-shows and late cancellations cannot be billed to the insurance company; they must be billed to the patient. The policy of charging for either must be made clear to the patient ahead of time. Bills must clearly indicate which charges are for late cancellations or no-shows (see Figure 4.5).

Some psychiatric services are not covered by insurance (telephone calls, legal reports, and sometimes family meetings without the patient). As with charging for no shows, the patient must be informed before the service is rendered (Woody, 1989) that insurance won't cover the fee and the patient will be billed. Opinions are split on billing patients for psychiatric

FIGURE 4.2	FIGURE 4.3
Sample Patient Bill with No Past Balance	Sample Patient Bill With a Deductible

Your Name *Address and Phone Number Here* 　　　　　　　Date of Bill Your Patient's Address Here Individual psychotherapy × 50 min @ $125/visit Dates: June 7, 14, 21, 28, 2004 Co-payment is $25/visit Amount Due: $100.00 *Please pay by the end of the month.* *Thank you.*	*Your Name* *Address and Phone Number Here* Patient's Name And Address 　　　　　　　Date of Bill Psychiatric Evaluation @ $170/visit Date: June 7, 2003 (Applied to yearly insurance deductible.) Individual therapy x 50 min @ $100/visit Dates: June 14 (Partially applied to deductible.) 　　Your Co-payment is $80. 　　June 21, 28, 2003 　　Co-payment is $20/visit Total Due: $170 + 80 + 40 = $290.00 *Please pay by the end of the month.* *Thank you.*

FIGURE 4.4   FIGURE 4.5
Sample Bill to a Patient With a   Sample Bill to a Patient With a No
Balance   Show

Your Name
Address and Phone Number Here
 	
Patient's Name
And Address
 	
                            Date of Bill
 	
Previous balance = $100 (May visits)
 	
Individual therapy × 50 min @ $100/visit
Co-payment is $25/visit
New Date: June 7, 14, 21, 28, 2004
 	
Total Due: $200.00
 	
Please pay by the end of the month.
Thank you.
	Your Name
	Address and Phone Number Here
	
	Patient's Name
	And Address
	
	                            Date of Bill
	
	Individual therapy × 50 min @ $100/visit
	Copayment is $25/visit
	New Dates: June 7, 14, 28, 2004
	June 21, no show @ $100
	
	Total Due: $175.00
	
	Please pay by the end of the month.
	Thank you.

telephone services. On the one hand, brief calls can be considered part of the pre- or post-service work for psychotherapy or psychopharmacological management (Schmidt et al., 2004). It can also be argued that although time is spent on the call, no real service is rendered because the patient is not examined. On the other hand, calls are sometimes not brief and multiple calls can comprise a significant amount of direct patient care by the provider.

Woody (1989) used the following set of rules to determine if a phone call is billable. If the phone communication:

1. relies on the expertise of the professional,
2. is intended to benefit the client, or
3. creates potential ethical, regulatory, or legal liability,

then the patient should be billed for the service. Note that using these rules, phone calls about changing appointments would not be billed, while phone calls about medication side effects, suicidality, or discussion of a family problem would be. Phone calls for simple refills may fit Woody's rules in that they certainly require a professional degree, benefit

FIGURE 4.6
Invoice for a Patient Who Submits
Claims Directly to Insurance Plan

Your Name
Address and Phone Number Here

Patient's Name
And Address

Date of Invoice

Psychiatric Evaluation (90801) × 50 minutes @ $170/visit
Date: June 7, 2003

Diagnosis: 296.20

Patient Billed: $170.00
Patient Paid: $170.00

Balance Due: 0.00

the client, and incur potential liability. However, as any physician or nurse can confirm, the act itself requires little skill and can be done by a receptionist with the medical person's authorization.

The other issue to consider is the local culture. If no one in the area charges for phone calls, be aware that the use of such codes could trigger an audit. If billing for phone calls is likely to be an essential part of your practice (because you have clients who go away for half the year or because you live in a rural area) include the charges and guidelines for phone calls in your patient information sheet. Do the same for any other services you expect to render regularly that are not reimbursed by insurance. The procedure codes for reviewing records, preparing reports, and unlisted procedures are at the end of the psychiatric section of the *CPT Manual.* Other miscellaneous service codes are listed in the 99xxx section of the manual. The codes and guidelines for telephone calls by physicians to patients are listed at the beginning of the E/M Section of the manual (codes 99371–99373; AMA, 2003).

Record Keeping

As with claims sent to insurers, be sure to record the date the patient bill was generated on the ledger page so you can keep track of it. This will enable you to see if payments from the patient are behind and how many notices you've given so far for a service.

BILLING SECOND-PARTY PAYERS

Who or what are second-party payers? Unlike insurance companies, which are third-party payers, second-party payers have a personal connection to the patient and a vested interest in seeing them get better. However, second-party payers are not without their own interests. The most common second-party payer is a parent, but employers occasionally pay for the treatment of an employee, especially a disgruntled or troublesome one. Occasionally, agencies will pay for services for a patient. An example is an adoption agency paying for the psychiatric treatment of an uninsured mother who is giving up her child. Parents or other family members, employers, and agencies may all fall into the category of second-party payer if they are paying directly for someone's psychiatric treatment.

Problems Specific to Second-Party Payers

The main problem with second-party payers is that they often stop paying for treatment midstream. Sometimes they stop because of the expense, sometimes because their goal has been accomplished (elimination of a specific behavior), or because their goals and those of the patients begin to diverge in some way during the course of treatment. Since the decision of a second party to pay for treatment is strictly voluntary, there is usually no recourse except to accept their decision. For this reason, when a patient enters into treatment with a second party paying the bill, there has to be a backup plan for continuation of the treatment should the second-party payer withdraw.

Another problem with second-party payers is that they may feel entitled to receive information about the patient's treatment, diagnosis, or progress. With parents of a young child in treatment, this is often not a problem, but it may be a problem for older teenagers and college-age children who have independence issues and their own privacy rights. Some providers feel concerned about the patient's motivation for treatment when a second-party payer is involved because the patient's financial investment in treatment is minimal and the second party obviously has enough interest to fork over the payments. Studies have shown that the degree of financial contribution to the treatment is not a reliable indicator of patient motivation (el-Guebaly,

1985a, 1985b; Manos, 1982; Pope, 1975; Yoken & Berman, 1987). However, nonpaying patients may not be conscious of the efficiency or progress of treatment the way a paying patient might. Patients may occasionally use second-party payment as a way of penalizing someone with whom they have a problematic relationship, say a parent or employer. Care must be taken that successful treatment remains the goal of the patient, not extracting financial retribution from the other party.

Invoicing Second-Party Payers

Whenever possible, give the invoice directly to the patient to pass on to the second party. If this isn't practical, then simply give a copy to the patient at the same time you send one to the second-party payer. This practice keeps the patient aware of the cost of treatment to the second party as well as any problems with nonpayment. It also promotes conversation about the payment situation in general and any potential negative effect on the treatment. The bill should include all the same information as a regular bill to a patient, but the addressee will be the second-party payer with a reference to the patient. (See Figure 4.7).

FIGURE 4.7
Sample Invoice to a Second-Party Payer

Your Name
Address and Phone Number Here

The Name
And Address of the
Second-Party Payer

Re: Name of Patient

Date of Bill

Individual psychotherapy x 50 min. @ $100/hour

Dates: June 7, 14, 21, 28, 2003

Amount Due: $100.00

Please make your payment by the end of the month. Thank you.

cc: Patient Name (if the patient will also be given a copy)

SECRETS TO STAYING ON TOP
OF YOUR BILLING

1. Obtain all the insurance information and the patient's signatures on the HCFA form on intake.
2. Store insurance and claims address information on the chart, preferably inside the front cover for easy access, and on the initial intake note.
3. Open and read all patient and insurance mail the day it is received.
4. As soon as you become aware of it, note any change in claims address or submission information with a post-it on the copy of the last claim form or a note in the billing log. For example, when an HMO changes the place of service code for an office visit from 03 to 11, post the change on the last claim sent for that patient, since it will be used as a template for the new one. When Medicare announces that Box 32 has to be filled out starting on a certain date, put a note on the calendar for when that practice must start.
5. Record all payments on the day received in both the patient ledger and the office accounting journal.
6. Keep the HCFA 1500s accessible in the closest drawer.
7. Get HCFA 1500s preprinted with as much provider information as possible.
8. Always keep a copy of the original claim form for your records.
9. Complete insurance claims for once-a-month patients on the day of service or by the end of that week. Complete insurance claims for patients seen more than once a month after their last date of service for the month so all the month's visits are included on one form. This saves time, errors, and postage.
10. At the end of each month, check all accounts to be sure payment has not been delayed longer than six weeks from the submission date. If no payment has been made, call the insurance company to find out what the problem is.
11. Immediately explore the insurance implications whenever a patient mentions:
    • birthdays of 18 or 65 years
    • graduation from high school or college
    • job changes or potential job loss

- insurance changes at work
- the cost of the insurance premium going up
- divorce

12. Always bill patients, even if you think they will not pay. Failure to bill may imply treatment irregularities. Not billing does not mean no service was rendered or that there was no treatment relationship (Woody, 1989). It does not protect you from liability.

RESOLVING PROBLEM BILLS

Problem bills are those that get hung up in some fashion and don't result in proper payment in the usual time period. The most common problem bill is an insurance denial of payment due to a mistake on the claim form. If the claim was sent to the correct address, the reason for the denial is stated on the EOB, sometimes with a code that is explained at the bottom or on the back of the EOB or in the provider manual. Almost always the denial is due to a provider mistake on the claim form: a typographic error, leaving a required box blank or forgetting to sign it. Find the error, correct it on a fresh claim form, and resubmit it, noting the date of resubmittal. Since most claims are read electronically, you can't just write over the error and send it in. White-out and other liquid correction methods are also not allowed. Don't worry about the time limit from the date of service. As long as you sent the original claim in on time, you won't be penalized if the resubmittal comes in a little after the 90-day limitation. But don't dawdle. Insurance companies are quite patient with resubmittals and corrections, but they do have their limits.

Less often, the error is due to insurance company mistakes, most often a key punch error made by the claims processor. If the error is theirs, most insurance companies will correct the error by phone, but some will require you to resubmit a new claim. Years ago, the error rate for Medicare payments was about 14%. Now it is less than half of that and falling (CMS, 2002).

Denials due to lack of authorization can't be corrected by calling the insurance company's claims department. These errors have to be corrected by calling the authorization department. The most common error is that the provider didn't know or missed the end date of the authorization and, although they have not exceeded the number of visits, the dates covered by the authorization have to be extended. Another common problem occurs when the authorization does not get transmitted to the claims department before the claim arrives. Send in the claim form after you have received authorization.

Denials due to lack of insurance coverage are rare now because most patients know exactly what is going on with their health insurance at all times. Health insurance never lapses unexpectedly. What usually happens is that the patient or spouse changes their health plan during the annual sign-up period at work and forgets to tell the provider. Whenever a denial occurs for lack of coverage, call the patient immediately. Only they can resolve this problem and usually they do it by simply giving you the new insurance information over the phone.

Crossover errors between Medicare and secondary insurer can be a headache. If there seems to be a problem, check the Medicare EOB to see if there is a code indicating the claim was electronically submitted to the secondary payer. If it was, call the secondary insurer to see if they received it. If Medicare did send the claim correctly to the secondary payer, the secondary will sometimes simply reprocess the claim by phone and you are all set. More often, the secondary insurance will require you to submit the claim manually to them by sending copies of both the original Medicare claim form and the Medicare EOB. This is either because Medicare sent incorrect information (possibly because you put the wrong information on the claim) or there is a system incompatibility that needs to be fixed between the two companies.

If the EOB from Medicare indicates that the claim was not automatically crossed over, this means that the secondary does not have the electronic capability or a contract to accept automatic crossovers from Medicare. You have to submit the claim to the secondary insurer manually. Sometimes a crossover problem means that you don't have the correct insurance policy number to allow Medicare to cross it over electronically. If you call the secondary insurer, they can tell you if they allow electronic crossovers with Medicare and what the proper number is. Medicare publishes a comprehensive list of insurance company numbers and is trying hard to get every major secondary insurer to accept automatic crossovers. It would be great if they all did.

Remember that most errors will be your mistakes, not the insurance company's, so your billing problems will diminish rapidly with experience. Make a separate pile for billing problems, because their resolution requires more time and patience than regular billing. They require phone calls, retrieving and making copies of EOBs or claim forms, and exploration of past records for previous payments and insurance information. Before sitting down to work on a billing problem get yourself a soothing drink and gather all the relevant billing and claim information for that patient. When you are ready and calm, make the call. Allow plenty of time (20–30 minutes) for being put on hold. A speaker option on your phone is great for allowing you to do other work while you wait.

Let me review a few "don'ts" to make the process of resolving problem claims easier. Don't try to resolve billing problems when you are in a bad mood. If there is a problem or the call becomes frustrating, you'll be driven to the brink of insanity or anger. Losing your civility will only compound the problem and make you feel like a heel afterward. Don't call on Mondays or first thing in the morning because telephone hold times are often extremely long at those times. Don't try to resolve any billing problem in one day. Break the task into pieces to be completed separately on different days. Gather the relevant information one day. Review the information another day. Call on the third. These short jobs are a good use of unexpectedly free hours during the work week.

USING A BILLING SERVICE

If all of this seems like too much for you, consider hiring a billing service. The direct cost is usually a percentage of collections, varying from 5–10% depending on the nature of the work, the local market, and the types of services you request. There are some indirect costs incurred by using a service. Patients may be less responsive to a billing service, so collections may fall off for some providers. The time and trouble of transmitting data to the biller creates a higher risk for submitting late claims. For providers already submitting late, inaccurately, or who are hesitant to collect payment, the indirect costs of using a professional service may be worth it. Remember that billers are only as good as the data they get from the provider. If you are so disorganized that you can't give the billing service good, timely data, then the biller will only be marginally effective.

Consider also how you will use the time not spent on billing. If the freed-up time will be used to generate income, it may be profitable to hire a billing service even with the additional expense. If the free time will not be used for income-generating pursuits, the cost of hiring a biller decreases profits. However, if visit volume is too high to allow time for billing, it may be worth the cost to hire a biller. Large psychopharmacological practices often have problems keeping up with billing because each visit results in a claim; unlike psychotherapy, where several visits per month are submitted on one claim. Sometimes profit margins and costs are not the primary consideration. You'd simply rather take the loss and use the time for other pursuits like spending time with family or friends. This is fine as long as costs are not exceeding income.

There are some liability issues with billing services. Because ultimately it is the provider who gives the data to the billing service, the Office of the Inspector General (OIG; 2003) stated on its Web site that "it is no defense for the physician if the . . . billing service improperly bills." The OIG is also becoming concerned about billing services being paid a percent of collections, which amounts to the same thing as a percent of service. The OIG feels this provides an incentive for billing services to collude in fraud with the billing provider, especially in terms of upgrading procedure codes or unbundling charges. Confidentiality is also an issue. HIPAA regulations outline the steps that must be taken to ensure that patient information given by the provider for billing purposes will not go beyond the billing service. This usually means co-signing the HIPPA-compliant trading partners agreement, which the billing service will provide to you. Make sure your billing service is HIPAA compliant.

Billing services have their limits. When the provider does not record service dates or obtain basic insurance information, the service cannot bill properly and claims will be denied, mispaid, or delayed. Insurance companies constantly change billing procedures, claims requirements, and benefits of a plan. Billing services may or may not keep up, depending on whether they are on the mailing list for the insurance company. Opening, reading, and implementing any changes is critical to billing, and this responsibility generally remains with the provider.

Billing services have slightly different interests in terms of collection. While both seek to maximize payments, the service generally has many providers competing for time with the service. Because time determines how much money any billing service can make, time-consuming accounts or providers are not as profitable. For a billing service, it makes more sense to take on many providers and send in a steady amount of routine claims than to spend a lot of time on one problematic case or provider.

Billing services do not receive payments directly and cannot bill under their own name (OIG, 2003). They are entirely dependent on feedback from the provider about delinquent accounts. With the extra middleman, a serious delay can occur between the time a claim is sent out and the time a billing service realizes it has not been paid. Passing the 90-day limit for claims submission can result in denial of payment.

The following are tips on getting the most out of your billing service, should you decide to use one.

1. Obtain all the insurance information the billing service requests from the patient directly.
2. Submit your data sheet promptly to the service. Write legibly.
3. Keep authorizations up to date.
4. Insist on a written contract with your billing service.
5. Obtain references from providers in practices similar to your own.

STORING BILLING INFORMATION

All billing information must be locked away at the end of the day for protection against theft or use by others. Obtaining the billing record can be as damaging as obtaining the psychiatric record because it confirms that the patient is in treatment, for what, and for how long. Billing information also contains personal information like the social security number and date of birth, as well as the patient's addresses and phone numbers, which can be exploited for financial or criminal ends. Computerized billing information must have limited access using passwords and all computers should be locked at the end of the day. The financial and billing information also needs to be backed up and the copied files locked up, again with limited access.

Explanations of benefits can be filed by insurance company if more than two patients are members and show up on EOBs together. When an insurance plan belongs to only one patient in the practice, as might be the case for a small psychotherapy practice, EOBs may be stored in the patient's record. Old closed accounts may be stored together in a file for closed cases or within the patient's medical record when it is closed. W-9s received from insurance companies, which show the year's payments to the provider, should be stored with the tax records for that year.

CHAPTER 5

Accepting Payment

The procedures, standards, and problems associated with accepting payment vary by the source (patient, family member, insurance company) and the form (cash, check, credit card) of payment. The first section of this chapter addressed issues related to the source of payment and the second section addresses topics related to the form of payment. The third section addresses some uncommon forms of payment.

SOURCES OF PAYMENT

Payers, the entities who issue payment to you, are grouped into three categories, commonly called *primary*, *secondary*, and *third party payers*. Primary payers are your patients who pay for their own treatment or at least part of it. Secondary payers are family members or other parties who have a vested interest in the well-being of the patient. Third-party payers are insurance companies. In this section I address the issues associated with accepting payment from each of these sources, beginning with insurance companies.

Since the procedures, problems, and standards associated with accepting payment vary by source and form, the following information is grouped first by the source and secondly by the form of payment.

Insurance Company Payments

Although most insurance companies can send payments for psychiatric services to either providers or patients, most prefer paying providers. The idea behind patient payment is to reimburse those who paid for services out of their own pocket. Medicare, Medicaid, many HMOs, and some Blue Cross plans will not send payments to patients because they do not allow contracted providers to accept prepayment from enrollees. When an insurance company does send a check to the patient, it is usually at the patient's request or because the provider failed to have the patient sign Box 13 on the HCFA 1500, which gives permission for the payment to be sent to the provider.

Patients sometimes don't report that they've been paid directly by insurance. They get the check in the mail and happily deposit it, often not reading the fine print or knowing what the check is for. The practitioner learns this when she calls the insurance company to find out why the payment hasn't arrived. When an insurance company says they sent the payment directly to the patient, find out why and correct the problem so it doesn't happen again. Then call the patient to ask if she received the payment. If she has deposited or cashed the check already, tell her you will send a bill for the services so she can pay you directly. If she didn't cash or deposit the check, she can sign it over to you. Make sure she brings the attached EOB as well, since you may need it for record-keeping and accounting purposes. If the patient says she didn't get the check, have her call the insurance company to see whether it has been cashed. If the patient denies getting the payment but the insurance company records show it was cashed by the patient, follow your usual procedures for nonpayment or theft.

Insurance companies mail checks out 2 to 6 weeks after claims are received. They rarely delay. If it takes longer, this usually means that they did not receive the claim or there was a problem with the claim. When the check arrives, post it to the patient's account and then add it into the practice ledger as income. If an employee will be depositing the checks, stamp or write on each check "For Deposit Only" so the check cannot be cashed. Deposit checks at least weekly so that they aren't lost and the businesses involved can keep their accounts up to date.

Patient Payments

The decision about whether to have patients pay each visit or monthly applies only to patient payments. Pressman (1979), Faustman (1982), and Freud (1913) all advocated for having patients pay each session; this keeps the patient's account current and avoids the accumulation of large bills. It also provides steadier cash flow if the daily receipts are substantial. Faustman's study in 1982 showed that nearly 20% of psychologists asked for payment at the time of service.

Before insurance payments were common for psychiatric services, the pay-as-you-go method made more sense because keeping accounts current was the main focus and daily cash flow was high. Now, with nearly universal insurance coverage and low co-payments, paying each and every session may not be efficient except in large practices, where nonclinical staff are available to accept and post payments. Patients have to remember to bring cash or a check every session and the provider has to make an accounting entry every visit, in addition to the entries for the insurance payments. Since it makes less sense fiscally to ask for payment each session in a small solo practice, doing so can cause some transference issues, perhaps making the therapist appear distrustful of the patient or in need of quick cash.

Paying monthly, especially for weekly therapy visits, saves time for the patient and the provider. It implies a certain amount of trust for payment between the two parties, which may enhance the alliance. Logistically, monthly payment runs more in sync with insurance payments (which occur monthly because most providers bill monthly) and patient's household budgets. You'll see that most patients calculate their ability to afford treatment by the month because most of their other important bills are monthly ones. There are problems with monthly payment, however. If the patient's portion of the payment is substantial, it's easy to accumulate a large bill if one payment is missed. And, with the longer interval between bills, the detection of nonpayment is delayed.

Given the pros and cons of both systems, it is up to individual practitioners to decide whether to ask for payment at every visit or at the end of every month. Also check with colleagues. The local culture is important, since your practice will inevitably be compared to others'.

Where to accept payment from the patient is another issue. In my experience, if you give the patient the bill in the session the patient generally pays you in the session, either the current one or the next if it is within 2 weeks. Billing and paying during the visit promotes good communication about the cost of treatment and affordability so that problems can be anticipated and dealt with early. In a similar fashion, mailing the bill is reciprocated by mailing the payment. Patients who are not seen often receive their bills by mail and pay by mail.

I'd like to mention the "Paradox of the Responsible Client" (Sommers, 1999), the one who pays on time, every time (even for missed sessions) for a long period of time without complaint. This kind of pattern indicates trouble and, for therapy patients, needs to be explored. Don't assume such patients have no concerns about money or the cost of treatment; often some kind of money neurosis or transference problem is at play. For example, a gambling client may pay on time to hide the debt load. A dependent client may idealize the provider so much that a wish not to pay can't be considered (Sommers). A flawless payment record conceals the money or transference issue and suspends exploration by presenting a perfect façade to the provider. Many a patient successfully avoids exploration of money topics by religiously paying on time.

Second-Party Payments

Second-party payers have a direct interest in the well-being of the patient (unlike a third-party payer), but also interests of their own that may contradict or oppose the patient's interests. Gedo (1962) reported that nonpayment is more common with second-party payment. Typical second-party payers include parents and other family members, employers, schools, and agencies. Let's look at some of the issues that occur with each of these sources of payment.

Parents are the most typical second-party payer, and the dynamics of the payment situation depend on the age of the patient. Adult children, 18 years or older, often pay themselves if they have a job, their own health insurance, or if their parents give them an allowance that they budget themselves. Taking over payment of the bill, even if the money in the bank ultimately comes from the parent, is a marker of independence, emancipation, and maturity in the adult child. If an adult child does not pay even a small co-payment, does not inquire about the cost, and does not express concern about the financial burden on the parent, this may indicate more than financial dependence on the parent, perhaps avoidance of responsibility, lack of confidence, a desire to extract retribution, or a simple sense of childlike entitlement. All are worthy of exploration if the child's adult development is to be encouraged.

The treatment goals of adult children are likely to be different from the parents'. Maybe the adult child doesn't want treatment but the parents are "making" him do it. Maybe the adult child wants more independence but the parents don't feel he is ready. Maybe the parents want the child to stop a behavior that the child feels is acceptable. And maybe the parents don't want the child to reveal any family problems but the child wants to tell all. On top of all this there is an obvious financial conflict: the adult child wants the parents to pay so he has more money for himself and the parents want the treatment to be short so they have more money as well. For this reason, parents who pay may want to know more about the treatment to see if it is "worth it." With all this conflict, it becomes a high-probability event that parents will stop paying for the psychiatric treatment of an older child prematurely or that an older child will drop out.

Payment by parents of children between the ages of 0 and about 13 is different. Any difference in goals between the child and the parents is either moot or minimal. Their financial goals are essentially the same because the child's money is the parents' money. It is rare for children to balk or complain about a parent's decision to end treatment. And unless there is a clear case for neglect, the provider can't do much about the parents' ending treatment beyond trying to convince them to continue.

Issues related to parental payment for children between 13 and 18 years old are somewhere in the middle. As with the adult child, at this age the goals for treatment may be different between parent and child. But like the young child, the patient still has no other means of payment. Treatment ends when the parent stops paying even though the child may wish to continue.

Sometimes other family members pay for a patient's psychiatric treatment. Adult children will sometimes pay for the psychiatric treatment of an elderly parent. The success of this arrangement depends on the relative independence of the elderly person and the cooperation and mutual agreement of the adult child. The payment arrangement should be discussed with the patient if possible, although it is not uncommon for a dependent or frail elderly person to refer everything to the child. Occasionally there may be a conflict in terms of the treatment goals of the two parties. Often this is less a matter of family dynamics than a generational matter, where the elderly person is skeptical of psychiatric treatment and the young family member is all for it. Occasionally, siblings will pay for the treatment of a disabled sister or brother. Payment by family members other than children and parents is often less conflicted because the expectations are not as powerful and the sense of obligation is not as strong. Since both parties are adults, disagreements about payment or treatment are usually discussed and worked out either before or during the treatment.

Let me say a word here about couples. Strictly speaking, a spouse is not a second-party payer, but a first-party payer. In other words, the couple is a unit financially and legally. Payment by one is the same as payment by the other. That said, we all know that couples manage their finances in many different ways and that many couples do not pool all of their monies. So it can sometimes seem as though second-party payments come from a spouse when the patient is not the one who writes the checks. In a good marriage, these payments can be treated as if they came directly from the patient out of the couples' joint property. When the marital relationship is not good, or is good except in the area of finances, problems can occur with payment.

The scenario often goes like this: The provider gives the patient the bill. Maybe she leaves the bill in her pocket accidentally and later blames her husband for not paying it. Or perhaps she takes it home and puts it in the large pile of bills to be paid by her husband. He goes through the pile at an undetermined time (or maybe at a scheduled time) and decides what bills should be paid. Maybe your bill is paid but maybe not, depending on how much money is in the account or how urgent he considers the bill. The point is that, with a couple, there is a lot of room for error. It is always interesting to learn how couples manage the complexities of bill payment.

Regardless of who pays the bills, the provider needs to communicate with the patient about payment, not the spouse, since the treatment agreement, which includes payment, is between the two of you. If the spouse is truly reluctant to pay, then that marital issue needs to be worked out. If it cannot be worked out, then arrangements must be made for the patient to pay herself. As a rule, it is best not to regard the spouse as a second-party payer.

Payment out of a trust fund can be considered a form of second-party payment, although it is somewhat unclear who is actually paying the bill because the trust is an incorporate entity. Is the payer the family member who put the money into the trust account for the patient, even though they may be deceased? Is it the trustee who releases the monies? Or is the patient paying himself out of money set aside for him? Patients with trusts are often unclear about this themselves. What is clear is that, while the money may look like the patient's, it is controlled and managed by the trustee(s).

In many cases, the patient is distant from the trustee, who may be a banker, lawyer, or corporate board. If the trust is controlled by several family members who disagree with each other (or the patient), or if the trust is part of an estate that is tied up legally, trustees may be reluctant to release funds until the disagreement or estate is settled. A refusal to release trust funds for the payment of psychiatric treatment is often beyond the patient's control. In these cases, the patient has to pay out of his own resources, without relying on the trust, and may or may not be reimbursed later by the fund. In this way, trusts really are a second-party payer.

Employers will sometimes pay for the psychiatric treatment of a troublesome employee when the Employee Assistance Program (EAP) strongly recommends treatment for a patient with limited means or no insurance. Occasionally, this is a condition of continued employment, a prelude to termination, or an attempt to limit liability in cases of temper outbursts or sexual harassment on the job. Sometimes an employer will request and pay for a psychiatric evaluation to substantiate (or refute) claims for disability or worker's compensation.

When employers are paying for an employee's psychiatric treatment, there is a conflict of interest of which the employee is usually well aware. The limits of confidentiality, the goals of the employer, and the fact that the employer may cease payment in the future should be discussed at the outset. If the case is likely to require treatment over some period of time, make alternate plans for payment with the patient so they can take over payment if the employer withdraws or if the patient wishes to assume control of the content and conditions of treatment.

Churches will sometimes pay for the psychiatric treatment of clergy who do not have their own salary or health insurance. Payment by religious organizations combines the issues involved in payment by employers with some of the issues entailed in payment by family members. The church has a vested interest in the clergy patient being well, but also has its own interests in terms of maintaining public image and retaining membership in the clerical order. Unlike parents and employers, church elders almost never intrude into the psychiatric treatment, perhaps because church personnel are familiar and comfortable with the necessity and benefits of confidentiality. Like older children whose treatment is paid for by parents, clergy patients may feel guilty about the financial burden lengthy psychiatric treatment places on the institution. They may also be relatively uneducated about financial matters if they are from a religious order in which all financial matters are delegated to outsiders or superiors. These dynamic issues can be addressed in therapy but will rarely be forced into the open by nonpayment.

Rarely, a social service agency will pay for the treatment of a patient. For example, an uninsured mother in an adoption program might need psychiatric services while she is waiting to deliver. The adoption agency may agree to pay for services so she is able to stick with the adoption program. Agencies clearly have their own goals, which may differ from the patient's. In the above example, the agency may stop treatment once the child has been given up for adoption and the mother seems stable because the agency's goal has been accomplished. The mother, on the other hand, may feel worse at this time and want more intensive treatment. As with other cases involving second-party payers for adults, be sure to have a backup plan for continuing treatment should the second-party payer withdraw.

Disability evaluations may be paid for by a patient, by an employer to contest or evaluate a patient's claim, or by a state or federal agency to evaluate eligibility for disability benefits. Disability evaluations are not psychiatric treatment and are not meant to be confidential because the report must be sent to another party. These evaluations may or may not benefit the patient. Be sure the patient is aware of these facts.

In these cases, it is unclear which party is the client. Is it the patient who is being evaluated, or is it the party requesting the evaluation? It might be most accurate to say that the client is the party who pays, which often is not the patient. For non-M.D. professionals, duty may lie with the payer when the patient and the payer (client) are not the same (APA, 2002). For physicians, fiduciary obligations to the patient supersede those of the payer, except if specifically discussed and agreed to by the patient.

Colleges sometimes pay for the psychiatric evaluation or treatment of a student who is uninsured or has no means to pay for treatment, often because there are potential liability or publicity issues (a student might commit suicide). Student counseling services may be limited and the student may be emancipated, have no parents nearby (if a foreign student), or be estranged from her family. When parents lack resources or insurance, public grammar schools will pay for evaluations required for funding special-needs children or facilitating transfer to a special school. In these cases, the treatment is clearly meant to benefit a patient and duty to the patient rises to the fore again. If payment by the second-party payer ceases, plans should be made to accommodate the continued treatment of the patient.

FORMS OF PAYMENT

Payments to you as a provider will come in many forms: cash, check, money order, credit card, or electronic transfer. The procedures for handling the payment vary by form and each payment type has unique benefits and problems.

Cash

Who still pays with cash and why? Patients with small co-payments often pay in cash just because it's easy. They'll need a cash receipt and will want one. Patients with no bank accounts pay in cash. These are new arrivals to town who haven't had time to open an account, patients who distrust banks, and undocumented workers who are unable to set up an account due to the lack of papers. They may want a cash receipt. Patients with confidentiality issues may pay with cash. They don't want to generate any piece of paper showing a payment to you and they don't want an employer or benefits office looking at their claims, no matter how anonymous and HIPAA-compliant. These patients will throw away or shred your receipt right after you give it to them. Some patients have a morbid fear of banks or view non-cash payment as "phony." They like cash payment and will accept a receipt. Patients who want to get out of treatment quickly without encumbrances will often pay with cash. This way they leave no balance, no tie, no debt. And patients who believe you want to avoid paying taxes (because they do), will often pay in cash. Needless to say, they think the generation of a cash receipt defeats the purpose.

Record cash payments immediately (at the very time of receipt, not at the end of the day) because once the cash is out of sight, it is too easy to lose to follow up. Cash can be stashed in the petty-cash box if there is a receptionist who accepts payments. Sole proprietors can put cash directly into their wallet or purse as long as it's been recorded. The petty-cash box can be used to make change or pay for small expenses, but it needs to have its own account record showing deposits and withdrawals. Ideally, the petty cash account is kept by someone other than the person who accepts and posts payments. On a schedule, or once a certain amount of cash accumulates, cash is withdrawn from the box to be deposited in the bank.

Always give cash receipts, even if the payer doesn't want one. This protects you, not them. Create two copies, one for the patient and one for the practice, so both of you have a record of the payment. Cash receipts with carbons are available at any office-supply store.

Checks

Insurance companies pay by check and most patients pay by personal check. Occasionally, a patient will pay with a check drawn off a business account. The first question is, are they charging their treatment to the business or are they drawing off a business medical account? The second question is, is it your affair? The answer to the second question depends partially on the nature of the treatment and the kinds of symptoms the patient is seeking treatment for. If the patient is in therapy for interpersonal, characterological, or financial problems, then it may become necessary to explore this issue. If the patient is in pastoral counseling where personal morality is a focus, again it may have to be pursued. If the patient is a pharmacology patient only, there may be no clinical reason to pursue monies paid to you from a business account.

Accepting personal checks from patients has many advantages. Nearly everyone has and uses a checking account and the overwhelming majority of personal checks are good. Checks also provide useful information about the patient. They give a full name, other names, maybe the name of the spouse. For older or disabled patients, the quality of handwriting can be observed over time. The dates and numbers on checks can provide some information about the patient's money management style if this is an issue in therapy.

The main drawback with personal checks is that, very rarely, they bounce. A bounced check is not necessarily a bad check in the sense that it was written for money the patient will never have. Most often bounced checks are simply "kited" checks written before the money was actually in the account. Many patients have overdraft protection so checks never bounce. In addition, most banks resubmit bounced checks within a few days when funds are available so you are never aware the check didn't clear the first time. Only the patient knows.

Practitioners can take steps to reduce the likelihood of bounced checks. Don't deposit checks, especially big checks, on the same day they were written. Give patients time to get the money into the account. New patients who are not familiar with your billing cycle are often too fearful to tell you to wait. Always obey patients who attach a little post-it to the check asking you not to cash it until Monday when their social security or work check is deposited. And don't cut your own finances so close that a single bounced check will cause your own checks to bounce. Some providers might feel such tactics coddle patients who kite checks. To them, I say that anything you can do to avoid bounced checks reduces stress in the practice and in the patient. The patient wanted to pay you, wrote out the check, and hoped you wouldn't cash it right away. Bouncing a check is (usually) not intentional.

If a check does bounce and is sent back to you, this means it didn't clear on resubmittal and something is wrong. Call the patient and tell them so they can clear up the problem. Most will send you another good check right away. There is no reason to assess a fee, since the problem didn't cost you any money. Discussing it is a more constructive response.

Patients with online banking services may pay via bank-generated checks. If they are not online regularly or if the spouse does all the entries, they are often unsure whether you've been paid or not until they get their bank statement.

Money Orders

Money orders are like cash in that they can't bounce, but like checks in that they have to be cashed first. Payment by money order is usually made by patients who don't have checking accounts: poor patients, undocumented workers, patients with paranoid ideation, and patients with poor banking histories due to repeated overdrafts. Record them the way you record a check.

Credit Cards

While most large group practices now accept credit card payment for psychiatric services, most independent contractors and small practices do not. Faustman's (1982) study in 1982 showed that only 7% of psychologists accepted credit card payments. There are some advantages to credit cards. Anxiety decreases all around, at least in the short term because practitioners don't need to rely on the patient for payment (Baker & Jimerson, 1992) and patients don't have to fumble with checks or jockey other bills in the budget. The long-term benefits of credit card payment are less clear and vary with the financial circumstances of the practice and the individual patient.

The biggest drawback to accepting credit card payment is cost. Credit card companies charge about 2% for each transaction and charge additional fees for the swiping machines and forms. The other problem is that you can't restrict credit card payment to those patients who would otherwise have trouble paying. Once you offer credit card services, you have to offer them to all customers. This means potentially losing 2% on most payments, so with credit card services a practice could actually lose money if the transaction fees amount to more than what would be lost by non-payment without credit card use. Do the math before signing up (or have your accountant do it) to be sure credit card services are worth the additional expense. Credit cards also cost patients more money if they don't pay the balance each month. In this way they could end up paying more for treatment than you actually charge for the services.

If you do choose a credit card service, put the logo up in your office so all patients know payment by credit card is available. In times past, many felt the posted credit card logos looked too mercenary for health care practices, but times have changed. Credit card payment is gaining acceptability in all branches of health care.

A second problem with credit card payment is that it dodges the cost-of-treatment issue. When the practitioner is always paid, there is no reason to broach the topic. The onus is now on the patient, who is even less likely than the provider to bring it up due to the power differential inherent in the treatment relationship and the fear of exposing any financial burden out of worry that treatment will be curtailed, transferred, or denied. Most households do not keep track of the expenses that are covered by the credit card, especially if there is a chronic balance. *Credit card payments* become the line item, not *groceries*, not *clothing*, and not *psychiatric treatment*. In this way, the costs of treatment (or illness) are hidden to the patient, subsumed in the morass of general debt.

Which brings us to the final problem: credit card debt. We all know people who run up credit cards to avoid dealing with a lack of funds when money is short or desire outpaces income. Credit cards cover up some of the serious financial problems that cause anxiety, depression, and stress-related physical complaints. It is hard enough for patients to reveal to a therapist that they are burdened with credit card debt, but when the psychiatric provider's services are also part of that load it is nearly impossible to mention. Practitioners who do not accept credit card payment are therefore in a better position to help patients with debt anxieties.

Electronic Payment

Insurance companies are now offering direct-deposit payment into practitioners' accounts because it is cheaper for them and reduces error. Payment is also faster for the provider. However, unless someone in the provider's office is online every day, tracking electronic payments is time-consuming. Unless all insurances are doing it (which they aren't), it does not save time. Statements are still sent out by mail and all the mail still has to be opened. The payments still have to be recorded and all the other checks and cash still have to be received, posted, and deposited. Going online to check for a few electronic deposits just adds one more task to the day.

ATYPICAL FORMS OF PAYMENT

In this section I address some atypical forms of payment: loans, barter, and art in lieu of payment. While these methods of payment are not standard practice and are frowned upon by ethicists and legal counsel, almost every practitioner will experience requests from patients to accept payment in one of these forms or be consulted by colleagues about the propriety of accepting payments of these types.

Loans

A loan allows a patient to afford treatment now and pay later. In times past, it was not uncommon for patients undergoing analysis or long-term psychotherapy to take out a loan to pay for treatment, especially if the patient was a mental health professional. The loan is taken out as a personal line of credit from the bank so the patient does not have to declare what it is for; confidentiality is maintained. As with credit cards, the interest charges mean that the patient ends up paying more than is actually charged for treatment. This may cause some resentment on the part of the patient, especially if the treatment was not particularly successful or if the loan payments become onerous.

It is not uncommon for mental health providers to extend credit to patients at no charge, as a kind of loan. This avoids interrupting treatment when a patient can't pay, but again it may prevent tackling the hard issues of cost and inadequate income. It also puts the therapist or psychiatrist in a second role, that of creditor or philanthropist or banker, creating a dual relationship that could affect the outcome of the treatment. And the extension of credit accentuates the difference in financial status between the treater and the patient when there is already a significant power differential set up by the treatment relationship.

In the mid-1980s Hofling and Rosenbaum (1986) studied the extension of credit in psychiatric treatment by mailing an anonymous survey to psychiatrists practicing psychodynamic or analytic therapy. Only about 63% returned the survey and the population was heavily male (94%), and so not representative of the mental health field as a whole. However, his survey found that 78% had extended credit to patients, usually to keep a patient from ending therapy. Many said they did it only early in their practices, because once they became experienced they dealt with the inability to pay as part of the therapeutic process. Regarding the effects on the transference phenomena, about a third said extending credit to the patient affected both the transference and countertransference, a quarter said it affected the transference but not the countertransference, and 4% said it affected them (countertransference) but not the patient. One third felt that extending credit to the patient did not affect the transference at all. As to whether the extension of credit was beneficial, 38% felt it had a favorable effect on treatment, 16% felt that it had a negative effect, and 17% felt it had no effect at all. Almost a third, however, said they were unsure of the effect on treatment. Regarding eventual payment for treatment, 62% of the patients eventually paid in full but 27% of patients repaid their bill only in part, and 11% did not pay at all. This data implies that extending credit to patients does not necessarily help them pay for treatment, since many do not eventually pay. It may not be beneficial to the practitioner or the patient, and may not forward the relationship or the treatment.

My own feeling is that credit should not be extended to patients, and that the main reason why practitioners do it is because they are inexperienced in dealing with the issues involved: the cost of treatment, inadequate patient income, and transference phenomena associated with payment. All of these will be dealt with in Part III, in the chapters on nonpayment, fee reductions, and monetary transferences. Once you become experienced with these topics, like the practitioners in Hofling and Rosenbaum's study, most likely you too will not extend credit to patients. It simply won't be necessary.

Barter

Barter has been around a long time and has some benefits (Davies, 1994). It still appears during financial crises, in informal or hidden economies, or where taxes are so high that people try to hide transactions. Barter fell out of favor because there are real problems with it (Parvin & Anderson, 1995), as we will see below.

The use of barter for payment in psychiatric practice is not uncommon for feminist therapists (Margolies, 1990), and providers who do use barter cite certain advantages. Barter provides a real alternative to insurance coverage (Hill, 1999), and so may increase access to psychiatric treatment for the uninsured or underinsured. By enabling patients to go outside their insurance, barter also keeps the treatment private. Hill (1999) and others (Baker & Jimerson, 1992) stated that barter personalizes the purchase, while money "disembeds" relationships. Hill (1999) also wrote that barter may be less shameful than fee reduction or waiver. Therapists who are committed to working with people with different social values and stations may find barter attractive (Parvin & Anderson, 1995).

Unfortunately, the problems with barter are myriad, which is why money reigns supreme. Barter requires what is called a "double coincidence" (Davies, 1994), meaning that a person has to find someone to trade with who has what is needed but who also wants what he has to trade. For example, a housepainter patient who wants therapy has to find a therapist who needs her house painted. The problem with barter in the therapy situation is that the cost of psychiatric treatment is so high that few clients have anything to exchange that can cover the costs (Hill, 1999). Most therapists and psychiatrists are well-off enough that they do not need goods and are more likely to need services, but exchanging services then creates the problem of a dual relationship in the treatment.

There are also problems establishing the relative value of the services to be bartered. The fair market value has to be established before making a transaction (Hall & Hare-Mustin, 1983), and setting charges for services is more problematic than for products. There is also the issue of the relative cost to each participant (Hill, 1999), especially when there is a distinct difference in income. For example, a housepainter may only be able to paint two houses at a time. If he paints the therapist's house in exchange for psychotherapy, his "payment" represents 50% of his income for that time period. That is exorbitant. The economic context of the barter situation is also critical. If the patient is much less well-off, the barter arrangement is potentially more exploitative. If the patient is well-off and barter is not necessary, then it becomes ethically dubious because of the dual relationship, and probably symbolically significant as well (Hill).

Barter adds other layers of power differential to the treatment relationship. If barter is being considered, the client is probably at a financial disadvantage relative to the therapist, which suggests a class difference as well. It creates a dual relationship in that the therapist becomes the patient's employer or an evaluator of the patient's work. The evaluation process adds to the power differential in treatment, and this second relationship is likely to heighten and distort any transference crunches in the treatment (Harrari, 1990; Hill).

The problem of compounding the power differential makes it hard to guarantee that any barter arrangement could be nonexploitative (Hill, 1999). A patient in treatment and in distress is not really in a position to say no if the barter arrangement is unfair or not advantageous, especially if the patient looks to the provider to set the rules about what is fair (Hill).

Money gives greater freedom, freedom to buy what you want (Baker & Jimerson, 1992) when you want it, from whomever you want. The lack of restrictions allows people to accept or reject the conditions under which a purchase is made. The process of calculating the worth of services using currency is more cognitive and less emotional (Baker & Jimerson) because there is no need to consider the other party's needs or desires. The other person can get whatever they want with the money you pay them. This depersonalized aspect of money is perhaps the beauty of it.

Some of the psychiatric professional codes address the use of barter for payment. While neither the *Principles of Medical Ethics* of the American Psychiatric Association (2001c) nor the *Ethics Primer of the American Psychiatric Association* (2001a) mention the ethics of barter, the Ethics Committee of the American Psychiatric Association (2001b) comments on a case in which the psychiatrist wished to accept construction services in lieu of payment for the treatment of both a father and son individually. The committee concluded that it was ethical to accept construction services for payment of the bill of the son, whose treatment had already been completed, but that it would be unethical to accept a barter arrangement for the father's current treatment because of the potentially negative effect on the therapeutic relationship.

Section 6.05 of the *Ethical Principles of Psychologists* (APA, 2002) states that "psychologists may barter only if (1) it is not clinically contraindicated, and (2) the resulting arrangement is not exploitative," but the *Code* does not elucidate the circumstances under which barter might be considered clinically contraindicated or exploitative. Section 1.13b of the *Code of Ethics of the National Association of Social Workers* (1999) recommends that social workers "avoid accepting goods or services from clients as payment for professional services." The *Code* goes on to clarify the occasional circumstances under which barter may be ethical and what conditions should be fulfilled first.

Many psychiatric professionals oppose the use of barter for payment in any circumstances. Gruenberg (1995) considered it exploitation. Lifson and Simon (1998), writing from a medicolegal viewpoint, found that nonmonetary forms of payment like barter are "problematic."

Barter exchanges, which link members in trading networks online, may remove some of the negative aspects of barter. Because they can have hundreds of members, it is not as hard to find the "double coincidence" of someone who has what you want and wants what you have. Exchanges may be indirect, eliminating the dual relationship problem. A practitioner member may provide services to another member for credit on the barter exchange. The credit points are then traded online for what is needed by the practitioner. Barter exchanges solve the freedom problem because credits can be used with other exchange members when, where, and for whatever you want (Van Yoder, 2002).

The disadvantage of a barter exchange is the cost. There is usually an initiation fee of $100–$500 in addition to annual dues of $200. Often the member is required to supply a minimum amount of trades per year and the exchange takes a 10–15% commission (Van Yoder, 2002). The other problem is that barter exchanges are still not in common use. Accounting can also be difficult. The exchanges provide monthly statements and issue 1099-B forms to members and the IRS to facilitate declarations. Practitioners must report barter income to the IRS.

For more information on barter exchanges, contact the National Association of Trade Exchanges at www.nate.org, the International Reciprocal Trade Associations at www.irta.net, Intagio at www.intagio.com, or Ubarter@www.ubarter.com.

Art in Lieu of Payment

Parvin and Anderson (1999) reported several cases of barter, all of which were for artwork. In each case, the value of the artwork was determined prior to the arrangement (presumably by the patient) and no negotiation was necessary. Parvin and Anderson seemed to imply that the acceptance of art for payment under these circumstances is okay, but I find payment with art problematic on several fronts.

As anyone directly involved in the art business can attest, establishing the value of artwork is extremely difficult. Art is not judged on technical merit alone (which is important but difficult for the uninitiated to assess), but also on subjective criteria like beauty and innovation. Personal taste and whether the artwork "matches" or fits in with the buyer's other possessions also play a role for those who are not professional collectors. This obviously places the buyer-therapist in a powerful position as evaluator of the worth of the work. Crafts run into many of the same dilemmas (Hall, 1983; Harrari, 1990).

Unlike other products, the absolute value (price) of artwork may vary greatly over time depending on local fads or fashions, relative availability, and the state of health or the death of the artist. Eissler reported that some physicians have made a lot of money by accepting as payment the artwork of a relatively unknown artist who later became famous (Eissler, 1974). Is this then payment in full or more than payment in full? It could be argued that, at the time, the medical services were worth the stated price of the painting, while the forthcoming value was simply the fortuitous rise of an investment. But is that investment tied in some way to the patient, continuing another (second) relationship?

Purchasing or trading services for the artwork of a patient establishes several parallel relationships that can contaminate the practitioner-patient relationship. In addition, it engages the fantasies of the patient on several powerful levels that can then lead to transference distortion (Eissler, 1974). If artwork is also an expression of the mind, the practitioner becomes an evaluator not only of the patient's work and creative ability but possibly of their mind's eye as well. As an owner or purchaser, does the provider also become a customer or sponsor of the patient-artist? If so, can the patient leave treatment freely? And if the therapist is a collector and the patient an excellent artist, how might this affect the course of treatment? Could retention of the patient become more important to the provider than the treatment? The complications are almost too numerous to count. My advice is to stay away from purchasing the artwork of your patients.

OVERPAYMENTS

Overpayments by insurance companies are almost more troublesome than underpayments because there is no standardized method of dealing with them. The first order of business is to clearly note the overpayment in the patient ledger and place the EOB and check in a separate pile, because it can take considerable time to sort out what has to be done. Check any written information you have from the insurance company about overpayments. Sometimes they provide overpayment or refund forms with specific directions. If the procedures are unknown or unclear, call the insurance company and follow their instructions.

Some insurance companies credit the overpayment to the next payment on the patient or, more commonly, on the next explanation of benefits, which may include other patients besides the one on whom the overpayment was made. For small practices using a cash method of accounting, this is the least desirable method because it makes things harder to track by patient. Many insurance companies allow you to mail a refund check with a copy of the relevant EOB and an insurance refund form. Occasionally they ask for a short letter in place of a form. The name of the patient, the insurance ID number, and the relevant date of service must be clearly indicated on the paperwork sent, as well as the provider's number.

Record the refund information (check number, amount, date sent) in the patient ledger and note the refund in the business accounts as a deduction from income. Make and store copies of any refund forms or letters sent with the refund check. If the overpayment occurred on a primary insurance, this then causes a mistake on the part of the secondary payer. Unfortunately, the mistake on the secondary payment cannot be corrected until the refund for the primary has been received, processed, and documented by a new EOB. Then the secondary payment can be reprocessed using the new (corrected) EOB from the first payer.

Overpayments by patients are much simpler to deal with. Immediately talk to the patient and find out if they want a credit or a refund. If they want a refund, send a check immediately. Note credits and refunds in the patient account. Refunds to second-party payers can be sent directly to the payer.

UNDERPAYMENTS

Underpayments by insurance companies are the result of some kind of error, usually on the provider's part (wrong procedure code), but are sometimes the result of a key-punch error in the claims processing department of the insurance company. Check the copy of the original claim for the error. If the claim seems correct, call the claims department to ask about the error. If it is theirs, they will usually make an adjustment over the phone and send a check for the balance right away. Your local Medicare carrier and some private insurance companies may require all adjustments be done in writing, which means sending copies of the original or a corrected claim form along with the EOB and an explanation to the Adjustments Department.

Underpayments by patients are usually dealt with simply by talking to the patient and correcting any misunderstanding.

LATE PAYMENTS

Late payments by insurance companies on clean claims will usually end up being treated as nonpayments since most insurance companies will deny receiving the claim. If you have documentation that you sent the claim to the correct address and a copy of it showing that it was without errors, you can petition for interest to be paid on the delayed payment. Usually they will simply deny the interest payment, saying it must have been lost in the mail and ask you to resubmit, but without any penalty for filing late. The documentation and process are so arduous, and the chances that they will pay interest are so low, that personally I do not think it is worth the aggravation. Only twice have I received interest on late payments for clean claims and I did not have to petition for them, they were sent spontaneously when the errors were corrected.

Late payments from patients are an entirely different matter. As soon as the payment is considered late (and there should be a clear delineation of what constitutes *late* on the fee sheet given to the patient at the start of treatment), make plans to talk to the patient as soon as possible. This means at the next session if the patient will be seen within the week, or sending a note home or calling if the patient won't be seen for a while. The purpose of the communication is to find out if the patient even knows the payment is late. Many don't, simply because they lost track of time, didn't know what your definition of *late* was, or because they assumed their spouse paid the bill. If they do know it is late, find out if there is a reason they are late. Usually I ask, "Is money tight at home?" or, "Are you behind on any other bills?" Patients see this as concern about their circumstances and readily respond. If the reason seems temporary, find out when they can pay. If the problem seems serious or long term, there needs to be a discussion about whether something further needs to be done, not only for the current bill but for future ones.

If you don't see the patient in person and are quite sure the patient can and will pay, it is fine to simply send a second bill with the previous month's charges on it and await payment. In most cases, the patient will pay all of the charges right away (Canter & Freudenberger, 1990). If the patient has left treatment and does not respond to either a note, a second or third bill, or a phone call, then follow your procedures for nonpayment.

Some practitioners wonder about charging interest on late payments. Charging interest on late payments enforces the expectation of timely payment, gives some (albeit minor) financial compensation for the effort of repeated billing, and provides a disincentive for paying late. Remember that accountants and financial advisors tell people with a lot of debt to pay only those bills that charge interest and pay those with the highest interest first. Since other service companies charge late fees (such as credit card, and utilities companies) and health care providers usually do not, charging interest keeps the psychiatric bill on top, or at least in the middle, of the pile.

However, charging for late payments is not standard practice among health care providers and may seem mercenary or "hard core." Since it is not standard practice (Canter & Freudenberger, 1990), charging interest could result in complaints against the practitioner. Accounting also becomes more difficult because the amount owed needs to be recalculated each month when the bill is generated and interest income has to be recorded separately. Charging interest is no substitute for asking about late payments directly. The practitioner can't simply wait and watch the interest accrue when a payment is overdue. This is not in the best interest of the patient or of the treatment relationship.

NONPAYMENT BY INSURANCE COMPANIES

The most important aspect to managing nonpayment by an insurance company is prevention. Timely claims submission, accurate typing, and obtaining authorization are critical and all within the provider's control. If all of these are done correctly, nonpayment will be rare and easily corrected. Late submission of a claim is hard to appeal. While occasionally an insurer will pay if the claim is submitted late in order to preserve goodwill, it is rare. Do not submit claims late. Authorization problems can usually be corrected, but the provider generally has to proceed through various time-consuming procedures, including a formal appeal. That said, providers are almost always paid eventually.

If an insurance company does not pay after all the necessary appeal procedures have been followed, and after the patient and perhaps the patient's employer have interceded on the practitioner's behalf, then the only resources left are usually the professional organizations and the state insurance commissioner. Some local professional organizations have committees that specifically compile data on problematic insurance companies. They then use the data to advocate with the insurance commission or directly with the insurance company to correct poor practices or clarify problems. State insurance commissions these days are overwhelmed with complaints from both patients and providers. In general, you or the patient will have to fill out a complaint form and the problem will then be investigated. This can take some time. If things have progressed to this point, it might be best to move on and forget about eventual payment on a specific claim. If payment does eventually arrive, that's a bonus.

TRENDS IN PAYMENT

Electronic payment (money direct-deposited via computer into the bank) accounts for 90% of transactions by value but only 10% of transactions by volume (Davies, 1994). This means that electronic payment methods have, until recently, been used mostly for very large transactions, such as the sale of a company, while most day-to-day purchases are still made by traditional methods. However, with the expansion of computers into accounting, more and more insurance companies are trying to entice providers to accept electronic payment. This saves the insurance company money on paper supplies, labor, and postage. For the same reasons, they actively encourage providers to submit claims electronically, often providing the necessary software.

For small providers, direct-deposit payments usually do not save time or money. Monitoring payments requires online capabilities and additional time on the Internet to verify and post the payments. Electronic billing also may not be cost-effective for small providers. Each insurer issues their own software package, cluttering up the computer and complicating the billing process. Universal systems are costly, often have bugs, can't be utilized by certain local insurers, and need constant updating. In addition, electronic billing does not leave the paper trail so essential for documentation of proper claims submission and exposes the provider to considerable risk when payments are denied, misrouted, or lost in virtual space. The larger the group, the more cost-effective electronic billing and payment may be, depending on the associated labor costs, but many groups still may find it cheaper to use a billing service than to try to bill and collect payment online themselves.

Intermittently, there is still talk of a universal payer, either a national health care system that would act as insurer for all citizens, or a national health care administration, through which all claims and payments would be routed while still maintaining individual insurance companies. Obviously, the use of one and only one payer would greatly simplify both billing and payment for providers while adding capabilities in terms of data collection on national health care trends. Billing and payment might be so simple that all providers could do their own billing. At the present time, however, any national system seems out of reach.

There are a few trends in payment by patients. Credit and debit card payments are accepted by many large groups, but whether plastic payments will ever extend to small groups and small providers remains to be seen, since collection is not as problematic for small groups and may not warrant the additional cost. As insurance companies increase premiums and employers shift those costs onto patients, the proportion of the bill paid for by patients will gradually increase. Saving for future health care costs used to be common, then declined, and now is beginning again in earnest. More employers are encouraging it through the use of medical savings accounts and many states allow tax breaks for medical accounts. Whether Americans, who haven't saved for years and are comfortable with debt, will change their savings habits remains to be seen.

The disparity between insurance coverage for psychiatric services and other medical services may decrease or increase over time. With more consumers accepting psychiatric treatment for various conditions, there will be continued pressure to eliminate any remaining differences on the grounds of discrimination. On the other hand, parity will likely drive up costs for insurance companies, costs that may then be passed on to consumers.

Medicare has had no current limitations on mental health coverage, except that treatment must be medically necessary. As the population ages, more and more patients will be using Medicare as their primary insurer and asking Medicare to cover psychiatric treatments. The increased cost could spur an introduction of limitations of psychiatric services or lower reimbursement rates to providers. Whatever the effect on fees, psychiatric providers who accept Medicare may find that the proportion of income coming from Medicare will increase as more of their patients obtain Medicare coverage. However, if a significant proportion of the elderly change into Medicare managed care plans like Blue 65, provider income from Medicare may decrease. Whatever the future holds, it is certain that any changes in the Medicare system will affect psychiatric providers of all types.

Returning to the issue of electronic payment, there is a question about the future of money altogether. Will the use of money eventually disappear? Barter exchanges, e-bay, and online shopping warehouses eliminate the need for travel and the use of money as a medium for transaction. The time required also decreases because the product can be shipped almost at the moment the money is electronically transferred from the buyer's bank or credit card. The process is simply reversed if the consumer is unhappy with the item.

Services like hair dressing and auto repair already accept electronic payment from customers (debit cards) and offer electronic deposit of paychecks for employees with payroll taxes and insurance premiums already withdrawn. It is only a short step to consolidating these into one transaction, in which the customer pays and the payment is automatically split up and delivered into the respective accounts of the service provider, the state payroll office, the employer, and the IRS. Rahn (1999) noted that money will disappear when the time interval between earning a wage, liquidation of an asset, and the acquisition of an asset or service also disappears. Perhaps this time is not too far off.

There are two major problems to be solved before all this can be fully implemented by providers, big and small: security and the reliability of the power grid. Security is needed for the protection of both personal health and payment information and for protection from theft or embezzlement by hackers, dishonest employees, or criminals. Structures to protect electronic claims and payment systems have to remain secure, as robbery shifts from the street to the computer terminal. Dependence on the power grid creates vulnerability. If a power outage occurs when the payment for all services is electronic, how will anyone pay, be paid, or even enter the data if the outage lasts for more than a day?

The use of money won't disappear overnight, but its use is gradually decreasing. The transition is occurring slowly in health care and may never occur for small mental health providers in our lifetime.

PART II

EXTERNAL FINANCIAL INFLUENCES

CHAPTER 6
Understanding Health Insurance

Health insurance is a pool of money used to pay for the health care services of its contributors. When health insurance is part of a benefits package, workers pay part of the cost and the employer pays the rest. People who are self-employed or unemployed can pay for individual plans or, in some states, band together as a group for cheaper rates. The money paid in (premiums) may go to a health insurance company that uses it to pay for the services outlined in the health plan contract. The premiums may also be given to a company that actually provides health care, like a health maintenance organization (HMO). Or, the premiums can be kept by a self-insured employer and used to pay the health care claims generated by its employees. Self-insured companies sometimes contract with an HMO for services or with an insurance company for administration of the claims and benefits.

WHY HAVE HEALTH INSURANCE?

We buy health insurance to avoid the financial consequences of illness. Medical costs are high enough that people don't have the money to cover a single episode of disease, especially if the illness also interferes with working. Since most ailments and injuries occur randomly and without warning, it's hard to prepare financially.

WHY DOES HEALTH INSURANCE WORK?

Most people are healthy most of the time, so the larger the pool of contributers, the lower the risk of draining the fund (Jenson & Morrisey,

1999a; Schnurr, 2000). Insurance companies can make a profit because workers are healthier than nonworkers, most services remain unused (Glasser, 2000), and people are willing to put more money in than the insurance company expects to pay out. Workers contribute to avoid financial catastrophe should they ever get ill (Jenson & Morrisey). Employers contribute because offering the benefit allows them to retain workers without increasing wages. Tax deductions save them some money, too.

A BRIEF HISTORY OF PAYMENT FOR MEDICAL SERVICES

Initially, medical care was fee-for-service or provided through charitable institutions. Religious organizations set up hospitals but they were only for the poor or insane (Porter, 1997; Ross, 2002). Outpatient care for the indigent was financed through Poor Laws or local taxes (Porter, 1997). Others paid privately and obtained their care at home. Since English law regarded medical care as philanthropic, physicians couldn't sue for fees (Starr, 1982) and many services went unpaid.

Medical expertise and care wasn't considered necessary because it usually didn't help. As a result, medicine operated more like an art or trade (Porter, 1997) and patient-doctor relationships were more businesslike. Patients changed treaters often to get a better deal, and physicians, surgeons, and apothecaries gave their customers what they wanted regardless of efficacy. There was no centralized medical authority and no body of knowledge that was consistently understood or practiced. Since anyone could practice medicine, the high level of competition drove prices down (Porter). Most care was provided on credit and collected quarterly. A large amount of income was lost through unpaid bills. As a result, nearly all physicians had a second occupation (Starr, 1982).

After the 1910 Flexner Report (Califano, 2000) exposed the poor training and lack of proficiency of most practitioners, medical schools were revamped (Porter, 1997) and states enacted statutes to restrict medical practice to licensed individuals who completed training. The quantity of doctors decreased and quality of service increased. Fees rose and more people became willing to pay for medical services (Califano; Porter).

Modern health insurance got its start in early service contracts under which physicians were paid a fixed yearly fee to provide all the medical services for a family, plantation, or the poor in a community (Porter, 1997;

Starr, 1982). After the Civil War, employers became interested in physician service contracts (Starr) as a way to minimize the productivity losses caused by ill workers. Costs were shared by employers and workers and the benefit provided a combination of sick pay, health care services, and funeral expenses.

When World War II wage controls prohibited pay raises, employers began to use health benefits to compete for workers (Cohn, 2000). Initially, these were also annual service contracts for doctors, clinics, or hospitals to provide health care to employees or labor union members (Glasser, 2000). Companies charged a prepaid fixed monthly rate per member regardless of service use. When service use and costs climbed, health maintenance organizations (HMOs) and the nonprofit Blue Cross and Blue Shield insurance companies entered the market (Porter, 1997). By the 1950s, most large corporations were offering some kind of health insurance benefit (Califano, 2000), and in the 1960s Medicare and Medicaid began to provide health care services for the elderly and poor. The medical industry benefited from the higher volume of patient visits, and for-profit private health insurance began to take hold (Porter). Health care costs climbed and managed care began to expand in the 1980s. After an initial decrease, health care costs continued to rise again.

THE CURRENT HEALTH
INSURANCE SITUATION

The 1990s ushered in several important health care reforms designed to close the gaps in health insurance coverage so more patients could seek services. The Health Insurance Portability and Accountability Act of 1996 (HIPAA) eliminated the preexisting condition clauses (Jenson & Morrisey, 1999) that forced many people to go without coverage for a chronic condition for as long as a year whenever they changed health plans. COBRA (The Consolidated Omnibus Budget Reconciliation Act of 1985) allowed most workers to buy and continue their group health insurance plan through their former employer for 18 months after leaving a job (Jenson & Morrisey), thus eliminating the harrowing waiting period for coverage whenever an individual changed jobs or was laid off. The Mental Health Parity Act was passed in 1996 (Jenson & Morrisey) and many states enacted parity acts as well, greatly increasing coverage for most psychiatric illnesses.

As of this writing, about 60% of Americans obtain group health insurance through work, 8% purchase their own individual plans, 25% are covered by the government through Medicare and Medicaid, and about 15% have no insurance at all (Jenson & Morrisey, 1999; Miles & Parker, 1997; Schorr, 1990; Short & Banthin, 1995; U.S. Census Bureau, 2003). (The numbers add up to more than 100% because many people have insurance from more than one source.) The numbers of uninsured are harder to establish because lack of health insurance is often seasonal or temporary due to lack of employment (Matthews & Goodman, 2000). Mental health practitioners who accept insurance payment will find roughly the same ratios in their practice, although as a rule they will see few uninsured patients. Lack of insurance is a major barrier to mental health treatment (Zuvekas, 1999).

Although more workers are now offered health insurance, more are declining coverage because their portion of the health insurance premium is too high. They forgo the health insurance benefit for increased wages (Pear, 2000) and take their chances on getting sick or injured, especially if they are young or have no children. Out-of-pocket costs are also climbing (Gabel et al., 2001) through higher deductibles and co-payments. Another trend is that HMO enrollments have been falling and PPO enrollments increasing (Gabel et al.). This is good news for mental health practitioners who prefer not to contract with HMOs.

INSURANCE AND PSYCHIATRIC PRACTICE

Probably the most profound effect of health insurance is that patients and providers now rely on insurance to pay (Englehardt & Rie, 2003; Parvin & Anderson, 1995), a fact that gives insurance companies considerable influence. Increasing deductibles and co-payments and limiting the number of paid visits per year decreases health care costs because patients who pay for part of their care use fewer services (Fuchs, 2002; Kralewski, 2000; Shapiro, Ware, & Sherbourne, 1986). Mental health services traditionally have been reimbursed at a lower rate, require higher co-payments from patients, and have more restrictions than general medical services. Studies show that the use of mental health services is more sensitive to price (Zuvekas, 1999), so higher co-payments drive psychiatric service use down. Most people do not use their coverage for psychiatric care, even if they have it, and fewer than 33% of people with psychiatric disorders get treatment in any given year (Zuvekas). This means that the number of claims paid is vastly lower than the estimated need for psychiatric services. Many believe that this is due to the differences between insurance coverage for psychiatry and coverage for general medical services.

As a result, there has been considerable effort aimed at equalizing the benefits paid for psychiatric and medical services (parity), most commonly in the form of *insurance mandate laws*. Insurance mandates are elements of coverage required by state or federal law. COBRA, HIPAA, and the Mental Health Parity Act are all Federal mandates. State mandates are usually more extensive than federal mandates, with most states requiring alcohol treatment, some mental health coverage, and some coverage for the services of non-physician psychiatric providers like psychologists (Jenson & Morrisey, 1997).

Mental health mandates and parity laws are supposed to increase access to mental health care where coverage is skimpy or nonexistent, but there are a lot of loopholes. The Mental Health Parity Act of 1996 does not mandate providing mental health coverage, only parity with medical coverage when mental health coverage is offered. It does not apply to firms with fewer than 50 workers, and it does not apply if firms can prove the mandate raises premiums by more than 1%. Since adding comprehensive psychiatric coverage tends to increase premiums by 9–13% (Jenson & Morrisey, 1997), many companies can opt out.

State mental health mandates tend to go further, but even these have limits. Conventional mandates require the inclusion of psychiatric services in all insurance packages (Jenson & Morrisey, 1997). The effect is that all insurance plans have mental health coverage. Mandate option laws require mental health to be offered in plans but employers do not have to purchase them. As a result, some work-based plans contain mental health coverage and others do not. Many state mandate laws have exemptions for firms with fewer than 25 employees, businesses not previously offering insurance (to encourage them to offer insurance), and those companies that are self-insured (Jenson & Morrisey).

Despite the loopholes and costs, mental health mandates are proliferating, and this improves the practice prospects for all psychiatric providers. Currently, 43 states have mandates for coverage of substance abuse treatment (27 mandatory and 16 as a mandated option) while 32 states have mental health mandates (18 mandatory and 14 as mandated option) (Jenson & Morrisey, 1997). This greatly improves access and affordability for most psychiatric outpatients: no more yearly maximums, no discrimination on the basis of brain disease, and much less managed care oversight. Psychologists and other non-M.D. psychiatric providers find their mental services reimbursed not only by private insurance plans but also by Medicare and Medicaid as well. This is good for business and good for patient care.

The other big effect of health insurance is that it changes the nature of the patient-provider relationship (Parvin & Anderson, 1995) by adding third parties with interests other than the patient's well-being (Englehardt & Rie, 2003). This means not only the insurance company itself but also the employer, and the government and tax payers if Medicare or Medicaid is involved. If the insurance plan is a capitated one, meaning that a lump sum is paid for the care of a population regardless of service use, the patient may also compete with other patients in the plan for resources (Parvin & Anderson; Rodwin, 1992).

THE RESPONSIBILITIES OF
INSURANCE COMPANIES

Fulfilling state and federal mandates is an important responsibility of insurance companies. Because states have no method for checking compliance, there is an estimated 10–15% noncompliance rate for mental health mandates (Jenson & Morrisey, 1997). If you or a patient believes that an insurance company is not complying with federal or state mandates, call the company first. They should be able to give you an explanation or correct the problem. If there is no response, have the patient file a formal complaint with the state insurance commission. (Practitioners may file complaints, but consumer complaints receive higher priority.) Providers can seek help from local legislators whose staff is able and willing to research compliance and take effective action.

Another insurance responsibility is to maintain an accurate provider list that reflects the diversity of the beneficiaries. Many mental health provider lists contain people who don't actually see patients, like administrators and researchers, or who see patients only on a limited basis because they are part-time, semi-retired, or highly specialized. To maintain the appearance of a large and varied provider base, many plans do not update the roster or delist practitioners who have left the plan. The result is that patients receive a huge list of providers in their area only to find that the majority can't or won't accept them as a patient. They may also find that the active panel is not diverse at all, with few women, minorities, or non-English speakers. Plans argue that it is too difficult to keep provider lists up to date, but in the age of computer technology, e-mail, and faxes, is it really harder to keep up with provider lists than it is to process all those claims?

A third obligation of insurance companies is to provide a clear explanation of the mental health benefits, either in a booklet or online. This explanation should include statements about the yearly deductible, co-payments, and any limits to mental health coverage by diagnosis or service code (Massachusetts Medical Society, 1996). Most booklets do an adequate job explaining deductibles and co-payments for medical services, but when it comes to defining the mental health benefit, they are much less clear. If the state has a mental health parity law, the benefits guidelines often do not clearly explain how it is applied. If the state has no parity law and there are limitations that apply only to mental health benefits, these are often not spelled out. Patients are left in the dark and feel too embarassed to ask for the details because of the stigma associated with seeking help for psychiatric illness. The general obfuscation and the differential coverage reinforce the attitude that psychiatric illness and treatment are illegitimate or not "real medicine." What the benefits booklet does not explain is left to the provider to clarify and often comes as a complete surprise to the patient.

On the positive side, most insurance companies fulfill their other obligations completely and accurately. Explanations of benefits (EOBs) are always sent to providers and are usually easy to read. They also usually send an EOB to the patient so the patient is primed about their portion of payment before they receive the invoice from the practitioner. Some Medicaid plans do not send patients EOBs, presumably to save money because the patients will not be paying any portion of the bill themselves. However, not sending EOBs to Medicaid recipients keeps patients unaware of the cost of treatment and the value of their benefits, information that could help them plan for when they are no longer on assistance. An EOB could help them detect mistakes and fraud as well.

Insurers are responsible for making timely payments and they almost always do, paying within four to six weeks for paper claims and within two weeks for electronic.

Insurers are responsible for providing no-hassle claims correction when they make errors, and most insurance companies have made great strides in this area. Good insurance companies correct claims quickly on the phone, simply by checking the EOB against your submitted claim. A few (including Medicare, although they rarely make mistakes) force you to re-submit the claim even if they made the error, delaying payment for six more weeks. That eventual payment is almost never accompanied by the required interest.

Insurance companies need to have a clear and consistent appeal process, and, to their credit, most do. Usually it involves talking to a clinical person at a higher level and then sending a letter outlining the relevent points. At this time, most appeals are adjudicated in the patient's favor.

THE INSURANCE RESPONSIBILITIES OF PROVIDERS

Psychiatrists who accept insurance payments are obligated to complete insurance forms, answer phone calls from managed care companies, and provide all the information needed for claims processing (ApA, 2001b). Practitioners who do not accept insurance payments are required to provide all the necessary documention for patients to submit a claim themselves to the insurance company. This usually means giving the patient a statement with the dates of service, service codes, diagnostic code, and fees, along with documentation of the patient's payment. Psychiatrists have a duty to appeal to the insurance company for the patient when necessary services are denied, whether or not they are contracted to that insurance or accept insurance payment (Behnke & Hilliard; Hilliard, 1998; MacBeth, 1994). Failure to appeal can lead to charges of abandonment if the treatment was medically necessary (Behnke & Hilliard).

Providers contracted to managed care companies must disclose any conflicts of interest or financial incentives that play a role in psychiatric treatment decisions. They must inform psychiatric patients of all appropriate treatment options regardless of cost or the extent of coverage under the insurance plan, and provide standard care regardless of any restrictions (Englehardt & Rie; MMS, 1996). The duty to provide standard care and the insurance company's choice about which treatments to pay for are entirely separate decisions and must not be linked (Behnke & Hilliard, 1998). An insurance plan's decision not to authorize payment does not in any way relieve the provider of the responsibity to provide care or liability should the patient sue for treatment (Hilliard, 1998; MMS, 2001). Sometimes providing the necessary care will not be in the provider's best financial interest.

Providers have an obligation to maintain confidentiality even if the insurance contract has a clause allowing release of records to them. Ultimately it is the patient's decision whether to release the records, even if refusal means the insurance company won't pay (Behnke & Hilliard, 1998; Hilliard, 1998). Some patients may choose to pay out of pocket for privacy reasons rather than have their record reviewed by the plan. When records are requested by an insurance company, the entire record is rarely needed. The provider should call and ask specifically what is needed because releasing the entire record may violate the patient's right to confidentiality. Such rights may trump the provider's contractual duty to provide information to the insurance company (Hilliard; MMS, 2001).

HIPAA regulations allow the release of only the information needed for billing or payment without patient authorization, meaning the dates of service, procedure codes, and diagnosis. HIPAA does not authorize release of the entire psychiatric record or psychotherapy notes, even if the insurance company makes payment contingent on that release.

EVALUATING AND NEGOTIATING MANAGED CARE AND INSURANCE CONTRACTS

Before requesting a contract with an insurance or managed care company, check out the company in the following ways. Verify that it is insured and what the limits are (MacBeth et al., 1994), because plans that conduct utilization and review risk being sued for malpractice. If the plan does not have its own malpractice insurance, you may be the only source of money for restitution should a claim arise (MMS, 2001). Find out if the insurance company is accredited by the Utilization Review Accreditation Commission and get evidence of state licensure. Obtain information about current enrollment, projected enrollment, and marketing plans so you can assess the future of the plan. Ask about the financial status of the company and if independent accounting has been performed. The company should be able to send you an annual report that you can review yourself or with a professional. Request all quality assurance (QA) and utilization review (UR) procedures and provider manuals before reviewing any contract (Macbeth; MMS). Find out who is on the provider list and talk to them. Find out if the practitioners listed are generally competent and if they are happy with their contracts. If the plan includes any salary withholds, penalties, or bonuses, ask participating providers how often these were applied.

Negotiating contracts can be done yourself, but few providers ever make the attempt. Marcinko (2000) devoted an entire chapter of his book to the details of the contract negotiation process, and I strongly urge those of you who are interested in contract negotiation to review his recommendations. The benefits of negotiation are considerable: gaining some control over the content of the contract, establishing a mutual long-term relationship with a managed care or insurance company, and getting maximum cooperation with fair prices for the services you render (Marcinko, 2000).

Examining Contract Content

California and Massachusetts provide excellent samples of model insurance and managed care contracts (MMS, 2001), which can be used for comparison to the ones you review. Before starting the review, make sure you have the provider manuals, appeal guidelines, and fee schedule, since these may be referred to directly in the contract or assumed to be part of it. All contracts should contain or make reference to the following elements:

1. *Malpractice insurance required for the provider.* Is the minimum required different from what you already have? (Macbeth et al., 1994) If you have to purchase additional coverage, this will add to the cost of accepting the contract. Make sure the company itself has adequate coverage against claims.
2. *Information about the patient panel.* This information should include facts about patient demographics as well as their general health status and will clue you into how much work is likely to be involved for each patient. There should be some information about the source of patients, whether they come only from within the health plan or from outside it as well. If some patients come from outside the plan, statements about in-plan members may

not apply to the rest of the patient population. For mental health providers it is especially important to find out whether psychiatric patients will have to see a primary care physician (PCP) before being referred to you. If so, ask whether the PCPs have incentives not to refer, and approximately how many patients you will be referred each year. Does that volume justify any proposed fee discount (Hogan et al., 2000)?

3. *Patient records and confidentiality.* Contracts often require providers to maintain confidentiality yet provide the managed care or insurance company with access to all the records, a seemingly conflictual position that should be explained to the patient. This section may also contain statements about medical-record security, both for the provider in terms of access and for the insurance company, which needs to have limited access for billing and authorization purposes (Marcinko, 2000). It is the duty of the provider to safeguard the confidentiality of patient records while still providing the minimum information needed to ascertain that treatment was medically necessary and actually took place so that reimbursement can proceed.

4. *Statements about standards of care or treatment guidelines.* Be sure to review these clauses, since deviation from them can expose the provider to liability that is not covered by malpractice insurance because it is a part of a contract (Hilliard, 1998; Marcinko, 2000).

5. *Fee or capitation rate issues.* The fee schedule should be attached to the document, but the contract should also contain statements about how often fees can be renegotiated (Hogan et al., 2000). There may be a clause that prohibits you from negotiating a fee that is higher than what you charge other companies or patients (Macbeth et al., 1994), which is one more reason to keep fees consistent. If the contract is a capitated one, it must include the capitation rate per patient and state whether the rate is fixed and if there is a minimum for low enrollment of patients. (For more details on calculating and evaluating the economics of capitated contracts, consult the excellent chapter in Marcinko's [2000] book.) This section may also have provisions about payment for supplies and on-call or coverage services (Hogan et al.).

6. *Financial incentives and penalties.* This section will list any bonuses, penalties, deductions, or salary witholds (Hogan et al.) and the terms under which they are applied. The amount of the salary withhold and the measures that determine whether the withold will be kept or returned to the provider should be stated precisely (Macbeth et al., 1994; MMS, 2001). The contract will also state whether the targets or measures apply to the provider alone or to a group. The larger the group, the less control the provider has in meeting the target. You might work very hard, but if other members of your group do not, your extra work may not result in any compensation.

   Beware of statements that salary withholds will be returned at the "sole and complete discretion" of the plan. This allows the plan to keep the withhold for almost any financial reason (MMS). The plan's history of returning witholds or administering penalties will not be included in the contract (Macbeth et al.). Research this by asking the plan for data or by discussing it with providers who have been in the plan for some time.

   Once you see the incentives outlined in the plan, think about how they will affect your decision making (Macbeth et al.). If the incentives are so compelling that it might be hard to do what is truly best for your patients, do not accept the contract. Some states have laws prohibiting incentives for care limitations. Other states place limitations on the size of the incentives. Review by a local attorney may be useful in assessing the legality of any offered financial incentive (MMS).

7. *Stop-loss protection clauses.* Stop-loss insurance protects the provider from the financial losses caused by very ill patients in a capitated contract. This insurance is usually paid for by a one-time, upfront charge to the provider (Marcinko, 2000) but sometimes it is paid for by the plan. The stop-loss insurance pays for the remaining health care costs of a patient who exceeds a certain maximum for either the individual provider or for the designated group of providers (Pearson et al., 1998).

8. *Payment and reimbursement issues.* This section of the contact will usually outline the turnaround time for payment of claims or the timing of disbursements if the contract is capitated (Macbeth et al., 1994). The longer the time interval between disbursements

the harder managing cash flow will be (Marcinko, 2000). Try to negotiate at least quarterly payments.

9. *Utilization/Review issues.* Be sure to request all QA and UR procedures before signing a contract (Macbeth et al., 1994; MMS, 2001). They are not secrets and you must understand the measures and philosophy behind the plan before signing on. The procedures should clearly state who makes decisions about quality of care and medical necessity for psychiatric treatments. If the reviewer is not a psychiatrist, there should be access to a psychiatrist if problems arise regarding mental health treatment. Beware of unrestricted utilization review policies like "the provider agrees to be bound by the utilization review policies of the PPO as now exist or may be adopted in the future." These kinds of statements expose you to a high level of risk because you are obligated to continue essential treatment for the patients in your care even if the insurance stops paying. Make sure the appeal procedures are attached to the contract if they are not contained within the body of the contract (Macbeth et al.).

This section often makes use of the phrase *medical necessity*. The definition of medical necessity is important because you, as the provider, will only be reimbursed for services that are considered medically necessary (MMS). Most plans and contracts use the following criteria (from Medicare) to determine medical necessity:

   (a) the service is the most appropriate available . . . for the insured
   (b) the service is known to be effective, based on scientific evidence, professional standards, and expert opinions
   (c) for services and interventions not in widespread use, there is some scientific evidence of potential efficacy

10. *Practice restrictions.* This section usually contains the so-called gag clause and any noncompete clauses. Gag clauses restrict communication between providers and patients about treatment options, especially those not covered by a plan (Jenson & Morrisey, 1999a). They are now uncommon in contracts because they restrict informed consent. Thirty-nine states (Jenson & Morrisey) prohibit them. Noncompete clauses are agreements that you

will not practice for a period of time within a certain geographical area (LaCava, 2000) after you end the contract. The idea is to keep a contracted provider from leaving the organization if the company has invested a substantial amount of money in attracting him or her.

Noncompete clauses occur in two basic circumstances: sale of a practice and as part of employment contracts (LaCava, 2000). In the case of sale of a practice, they are usually enforced by the courts because the reputation of the practitioner is part of what has been purchased. However, noncompete clauses in employment contracts are usually not enforced because they restrict the provider's right to practice and the public's ability to choose whom to see (LaCava).

Referral restrictions (Macbeth et al., 1994) may be included in this section or implied in the section on financial penalties. Referral restrictions increase your risk if consultation is needed from someone outside the insurance plan's network. If the network is very large, the risk is small. Restrictions on referrals are a basic part of most managed care contracts because they reduce costs. However, look for some leeway to refer out-of-plan if it is medically necessary or if there is no qualified consultant within the network (MMS, 2001).

11. *Service responsibilities.* These may be outlined in the contact or in the provider manual attached to the contract (Hogan et al., 2000; MMS, 2001). Be sure that all the services you provide are listed (Macbeth et al., 1994) and inquire about any services you provide that are not covered or mentioned (Hogan et al.). This is especially important for capitated contracts where you may be required to provide unlimited services for a fixed capitation amount (MMS). If you are a psychiatrist and the service contract limits you to provision of medications or evaluations, be wary. This usually implies that you will be acting as a consultant to nonmedical professionals, which will increase your medicolegal risk (ApA, 2001b). Negotiate out any "all products" clause that allows the plan to add services without your prior knowledge or agreement (MMS).

12. *Emergencies and coverage responsibilities.* Beware of contracts that require 24-hour coverage by beeper or phone (Macbeth

et al., 1994) or that require you to see patients within a specific time for emergencies (Behnke & Hilliard, 1998), because you may not always be able to fulfill these requirements. The definition of an "emergency" is important because providers are excused from waiting for prior authorization in emergency circumstances and reimbursement can proceed without it (MMS, 2001). Most plans use Medicare's *prudent layperson* (Jenson & Morrisey, 1999) standard, defining an emergency as any situation in which a prudent layperson would seek emergency treatment.

Coverage responsibilities should be outlined in some detail. Find out who you will be covering and who will cover for you when you are on vacation, and how you will be paid. If you are an independent contractor, find out if you can provide your own coverage and if the person can be an out-of-plan provider. Fee-for-service plans usually allow the covering person to bill at the same rate as the provider. If the contract is capitated, the provider usually must pay for coverage (MMS).

13. *Peer review or supervisory responsibilities.* There are defamation and malpractice risks inherent in any peer-review activity. Supervisors can be held accountable for the acts of clinicians under them (Weaver, 2003) if they delegate duties inappropriately or if the supervision is inadequate. Make sure that peer review and supervision are covered by your malpractice insurer (Macbeth et al., 1994). The procedures for credentialing (LaCava, 2000) become important if there will be coverage, supervision, consulting, or peer-review responsibilities. Find out how credentialing is done, for whom, and how often. Then find out how you will be reimbursed for this service.

14. *Dispute resolution* (Marcinko, 2000) *and grievance procedures* (Macbeth et al., 1994). Grievance procedures become important when either a patient files a complaint against the plan or the provider has a complaint about the plan or contract. Sometimes grievance procedures will require you to waive priviledges regarding the discoverability of information that apply during the defense of a malpractice action. This exposes you considerably should the complaint proceed legally. Some recommend having your malpractice carrier's legal department review a plan's grievance procedures first to make sure you will not be harmed in any

way should a case proceed to a lawsuit (MMS, 2001). Similarly, some arbitration clauses limit your ability to seek redress in court (Marcinko, 2000). Also make sure that the plan cannot agree to arbitrate malpractice claims without the prior consent of your malpractice insurer (Macbeth et al., 1994). Your malpractice insurer and the plan's malpractice insurer may have different interests when it comes to resolving a patient complaint.

15. *Indemnification clauses* (also called *hold harmless* clauses) (Macbeth et al., 1994). If the insurance plan is sued for any reason with respect to your treatment of a patient, an indemnification clause requires that you reimburse the plan for any financial loss it sustains, including attorney's fees, even if no negligence was found on your part (Behnke & Hilliard, 1998; Hilliard, 1998; Woody, 1989). Indemnification clauses are not covered by your malpractice insurance policy because they are a condition of the contract. You will be personally responsible for such monies (Behnke & Hilliard; Fenton, 2000; Hilliard). You may need to purchase an additional rider on your malpractice to cover any indemnity clauses (Fenton; Macbeth et al., 1994). Needless to say, it is best to take extreme care in agreeing to indemnify the plan.

The wording of indemnification clauses can be confusing; consultation with an attorney and your malpractice carrier is highly recommended (Macbeth et al.). Marcinko (2000) provided examples of the different indemnification clauses in his book, but a typical indemnification clause reads something like this:

> The provider agrees to indemnify and to hold harmless the plan, its officers, directors, shareholders, employees, and agents, from any claims or liabilities of any cause arising under this contract or from the provision of health care services. Any claims or liabilities . . . are the sole responsibility of the provider.

Sometimes the indemnification clause looks mutual, but this still places you at risk. A mutual indemnification clause is much like the one above, except that it begins, "Neither the provider nor the plan shall be held liable for defending or for the expense of defending the other party against any claims, suits, actions . . ." There are also contracts with "implied indemnification agreements" disguised as a simple sentence, such as, "The provider is solely liable for all patient care." These hidden indemnity clauses are another reason that all contracts should be evaluated by legal counsel and your malpractice carrier to see whether they are worth the risk, and, if they are, whether you need to purchase more extensive malpractice coverage (Macbeth et al.).

16. *Amendment or modification of agreement statements*: These allow the plan discretion to amend the fee schedule, policies, and procedures at any time without prior notice to you. Such clauses should be modified or eliminated from the contract. If the plan does provide advance notice of changes in fees or policies, find out how long you have to respond. You don't want to be rushed into anything or forced to end the contract precipitously if you can't agree to the change (Macbeth et al., 1994; MMS, 2001).

17. *Termination and renewal of contract.* The contract should contain a section about how the contract can be terminated by each party (Hogan et al., 2000). Often called *termination provisions*, these guidelines usually include a minimum of at least 90 days notice and may require notification in writing from either party (MMS, 2001). Appropriate causes of termination may also be listed. Contracts that allow the termination of providers "without cause" or by "subjective criteria" should be viewed with skepticism unless they are restricted to specific circumstances, such as loss of licensure. Beware also of immediate termination triggers, such as "failure to comply with plan rules and regulations" (MMS).

In some cases, your contractual duties to patients may extend beyond the termination date. Patients who are terminally ill, pregnant, or who require complicated care often can't be transferred or terminated with the contract because of issues of abandonment. If this is the case, make sure payment will be forthcoming even after the contract has ended (Macbeth et al., 1994). Single case agreements or restricted extensions of the contract through a specified date or until the patient is transferred often suffice, although the practitioner usually must accept the insurer's reimbursement rate. Note that continuing a capitation payment scheme may be risky when the group practice's patient population is dwindling. The practice should try to obtain fee-for-service compensation for services rendered after termination of a capitation contract (MMS).

Automatic contract renewal is convenient but may preclude negotiation if the deadline is too close (Marcinko, 2000). Although it is more work, it is better to review and renegotiate every contract up on renewal.

After Receiving the Contract

Read every managed care contract thoroughly, mark passages about which you have questions and concerns, then have an attorney and the legal department of your malpractice carrier review the contract (Behnke & Hilliard, 1998; Hilliard, 1998; Marcinko, 2000). Any legal fees should be small and more than outweighed by any potential losses (Fenton, 2000).

Do the math to verify the financial viability of any fee discounts or capitated contracts and then have a financial professional do the same. Most providers are not sure if their insurance contracts are profitable because only half actually get the data needed to run the numbers (Marcinko, 2000).

Be sure you understand the risks involved in signing an insurance contract. Remember that you will be an independent contractor, not an employee (MMS, 2001). Incorporation of the practice does not protect you from contract liability. Most plans credential you individually and require that you as an individual, not your corporation, sign the contract. This puts your personal assets at risk (Fenton, 2000). To bolster managed care and contain health care costs, state laws and ERISA (Employee Retirement Income Security Act of 1974) exempt managed care companies from liability relating to the treatment of patients or from malpractice committed by a health care provider on the panel (Fenton). As a result, the individual provider may be the only source of payment in a malpractice lawsuit. This increases the risk to the providers, even if they are employees.

After reviewing the contract with your lawyer and malpractice carrier, negotiate out any risks or clauses contrary to your interests (Behnke & Hilliard, 1998; Fenton, 2000). Plans are usually amenable to most reasonable requests. After the negotiation is complete, you must decide whether to sign (Davis, 2000). Always know your bottom line and be prepared to walk away (Marcinko, 2000) if you are unhappy with the terms of the contract, the fees, the risks, or any of the payment conditions. Never participate in an organization with a lower-than-normal standard of care (ANA, 2001; ApA, 2001a; MMS, 1996).

Because of the complexities and risks, don't take on too many insurance or managed care contracts, even good ones. It's hard to keep track of the details of different contracts and the hassle factor becomes stressful. Psychiatric providers are limited in how many patients they can carry at one time or see within a week. As a result, volume discounts are rarely worth the money. And there's another problem. The more managed care contracts you have, the fewer patients you'll have per plan; the fewer the patients, the less clout you'll have with each plan. Finally, remember that you may need to continue treatment with all of the patients in a plan, at least for a time, if the plan stops paying or bails out of the system.

Single-Case Agreements

Single-case agreements are contracts that pertain to only one patient. They are usually offered to a provider by a company with a limited provider panel when there is a confidentiality or clinical issue that requires the patient to go outside the plan. Since the responsibility to provide care is on the plan, a single-case agreement is almost always for the provider's usual fee and is not discounted. Single-case agreements are easier to negotiate and easier to break for both parties. There is also less risk because the provider is not included in all of the usual contract arrangements.

Ending Insurance or Managed Care Contracts

As a psychiatric provider, you can't simply stop the treatment of patients if you want to end an insurance contract, especially if it might be harmful to them (Behnke & Hilliard, 1998). Patients must be psychiatrically stable and given ample notice and time to change providers. If the patient is not stable enough to transfer, you must continue treatment at least until the patient's condition is stabilized enough that transfer can be effected without harm to the patient (Macbeth et al., 1994).

Before ending an insurance contract, review your patient list to see who will be affected. If ending the contract is likely to end your treatment relationship with a patient, assess any potential damage to future treatment relationships as well as the patient's response. Be prepared to discuss your decision and its effect on the patient at some length. Consider the availability of other providers who would be willing and able to pick up any patients. If you are in a group practice, or have an association with providers who remain on the contract, consider how they will be affected and whether they would be willing to continue with some of your patients. Some colleagues may be willing to pick up your entire panel. Others may worry about why you left the plan and reconsider their own involvement. Ending a contract also affects the insurance plan. While it may leave them with one less practitioner on the panel, it may also leave them with better-matched providers. Provider losses sometimes force the modification of contracts or procedures to encourage retention, so that the plan actually improves.

CHAPTER 7

Dealing with Managed Care

M uch of what has been said about insurance in the previous chapter also applies to managed care plans, but managed care has a few unique issues. These include the use of managed care "carve-outs" for mental health services, additional limitations on confidentiality, and all the topics related to authorization for payment: obtaining authorization, keeping track of renewals, coordination with billing, and managing denials.

Psychiatry is an area in which managed care use remains strong because adding comprehensive mental health and substance-abuse coverage generally increases costs by at least 10% (Jenson & Morrisey, 1999). Indemnity insurance plans may use managed care services for psychiatric services alone, a phenomenon called a mental health *carve-out*. As a result, patients who buy an indemnity plan are surprised to learn that the mental health portion may be managed in some way. In the future, parity laws may limit the use of mental health carve-outs if managed care is not also applied to general medical benefits.

The hassle factor for mental health providers dealing with managed care is generally decreasing. Denials and appeals cost insurance companies a lot of money in terms of time and labor. Complaints about denial of care cost money in legal fees and additional insurance premiums (because the plans need to insure themselves against lawsuits even with current prohibitions on suing HMOs). Many managed care companies have stopped denying reasonable claims because it is more cost effective to simply collect data on authorization forms and intervene only in cases falling outside of certain parameters. As a result, mental health providers who fill out authorization claims accurately and reasonably will find they are rarely denied payment for necessary services.

In addition, authorization processes are being streamlined: fewer pages, more check boxes, and less written narrative. Many companies have switched to telephone authorizations by appointment. The appeals process is more standardized and less haphazard, although still not very transparent. The nearly universal use of monitoring systems for telephone conversations has resulted in more consistent and satisfactory service and has eliminated much of the verbal contempt expressed on both sides.

The people who grant authorizations are now generally clinicians. In mental health, they are usually former social workers, nurses, or physicians familiar with psychiatric conditions and care. There is a specific hierarchy in terms of authorization and case management or review. A staff person who opens and sorts the authorizations generally returns or rejects incomplete authorization forms. A case manager collects the complete authorization forms and grants authorization to everything that seems reasonable according to the plan's guidelines. The case manager will automatically reject requests that obviously do not meet the plan's guidelines for medical necessity, usually because of a low-value diagnostic code (perhaps a V-code like V62.82 Bereavement) or a high global assessment of functioning (GAF) code. She can handle questionable cases in various ways: make her best guess about denial or authorization, call the provider for more details, or review it with her supervisor. If you want to talk to someone about a denial, the case manager is generally your first contact.

The case manager's supervisor will generally handle unusual situations, such as single-case agreements or circumstances requiring more privacy (perhaps an employee of the managed care company). In addition, she may handle difficult cases that require ongoing conversations with the provider. If you are having consistent problems with authorizations for a case despite the best efforts of the case manager, ask for the supervisor, who usually can and will help you, and may also act as a point person for a series of cases in a practice.

Above the supervisor is a medical director or physician advisor, usually an M.D. who may or may not be a psychiatrist. If a case is referred to her, it is generally because the plan really does not want to authorize the sessions. Hold your ground and follow the procedures outlined below for managing denials. In general, problems with managed care authorization rise through this hierarchy in an orderly and predictable fashion. Recurrent problems may bypass the case reviewer and go directly to an assigned supervisor or, very rarely, the medical director.

The contents of a typical authorization are fairly standard, showing the date it was granted, the dates of service covered, the authorization number, the kinds of services covered (usually listed by procedure code), and the number of visits (units of service) authorized within the designated dates. The letter may include a form for future authorization requests or indicate a number to call for authorization by phone.

Is managed care ethical? Managed care can be ethical as long as prospective patients and employers are informed and are willing participants in the contract. It is certainly ethical to make attempts to hold down health care costs, as long as no one is harmed or deceived in the process. To make an informed decision to participate in managed care, patients should understand the following principles. First, they should understand how managed care differs from other benefit options. This means knowing that there will be no payment to providers outside the plan and that the plan may deny payment for services that it does not think are efficacious or necessary. They should understand that PPOs and indemnity plans do not have the same limitations as managed care plans. Secondly, patients should understand the benefit limits, especially restrictions on access to specialists and any limitations peculiar to mental health, such as a yearly maximum number of visits. They should understand that before they can see a mental health professional, they may first need to obtain permission (authorization), or payment will be denied. Patients (and providers) should understand their right to appeal any denial and the process by which that appeal can be pursued. Finally, patients should understand that their medical and psychiatric records may be reviewed in more detail than other plans in order to fully consider whether the service is necessary or effective. The managed care plan should make no exaggerated claims of excellence. The care should be competent and the review process not too invasive. Reviewers should not be rewarded financially for denying care (ApA, 2001b).

It is not the responsibility of the provider to give all of this information to the patient. It is the plan's responsibility to make sure that the principles and policies of the plan are clearly presented to patients both before they sign on and while they maintain the coverage. It is the patient's responsibility to read and understand the information given before they sign up for a managed care benefit. That said, neither managed care companies nor employers explain the nature of managed care plans well, and patients who work at small companies often have no choice about whether they get a managed care plan or not. Patients usually don't check the details of the managed care benefits for outpatient psychiatric care and don't understand them when they do. They never expect to use the benefit. In order to prevent misunderstandings and problems, it then becomes the provider's de facto responsibility to explain the nature of managed care and its potential effect on the treatment given.

Providers have a few clear responsibilities when it comes to managed care. The most important is to read, understand, and adhere to the managed care contracts they sign. If a contract has provisions that the provider is uncomfortable with, it is the provider's responsibility to amend the contract or refuse to sign it. The second most important responsibility is to advocate for the patient against the managed care company if there is a denial of payment or abuse of confidentiality limits. All of the psychiatric professional codes specifically mention patient advocacy as a duty of the provider.

It is the practitioner's responsibility to fill out the paperwork for authorization regardless of his views about the utility of the information requested or personal philosophy about managed care. The practitioner should never deny access or refuse to supply the information needed for authorization. Make and return the phone calls necessary to facilitate authorization and submit forms on time. Never distort information by upgrading the diagnosis, amplifying suicidality, or exaggerating other symptoms, with or without the patient's permission.

It is also your responsibility to keep copies of authorization requests, authorizations granted, and authorizations denied. Document any phone conversations regarding authorization or requests for information clearly in the patient's chart. Keep the patient apprised of any problems and continue to see the patient if treatment is needed, even if authorization is denied. Never terminate a patient abruptly because of a denial of payment or authorization hassles.

CONFIDENTIALITY

Confidentiality issues are more of a problem with managed care than with regular insurance claims. HIPAA regulations state that no authorization from the patient is needed to transmit any information required for payment, but only necessary information can be given. In practice, HIPAA is still evolving. Many insurers and practices still require patients to sign a release of information for both insurance and managed care companies, mostly to protect themselves. Managed care companies often do not limit their request for information to that which is truly necessary. The most common abuse of confidentiality is to request a copy of the entire psychiatric chart for review. This is rarely necessary. Simply ask if you may send a summary instead and what specific information they need to be included. Discuss openly if and why you think the information they request is not necessary for review or can be obtained in a better way. In these cases, always consult the patient before releasing the entire record. You may also have to consult an attorney.

Requests for specific information about sensitive material like legal problems, criminal acts, child or elder abuse, professional impairment, AIDS, cancer, terminal illness, sexual abuse or harassment, and substance dependence require special care. Tell the managed care reviewer you feel uncomfortable discussing these symptoms over the phone without first talking to the patient. Talk to the patient about your concerns and then call the reviewer back to discuss further.

OBTAINING AUTHORIZATION

If you are a contracted provider with a managed care company and the patient is experienced, she may present with an authorization already in hand, compliments of the primary care doctor or a personal phone conversation with a case manager. The case has been "opened," and you can proceed with the visit already authorized. During the initial call, you can ask the patient to obtain authorization and book the appointment after she obtains it. However, if you are not a contracted provider, or in the case of managed care carve-outs, authorization will not occur before the initial visit.

The first item of business in obtaining authorization is to discuss it with the patient. Make sure they are aware of the process, and convey your concerns if you think the case is likely to be denied because of lack of medical necessity or other reasons. For example, payment for treatment of simple grief or adjustment reactions is unlikely to be authorized even if it might be helpful to the patient. Be sure to explain that denials are denials of payment, not of service. If you have had serious problems with the patient's managed care company in the past, it may be useful to convey this information to the patient in advance so that they are also prepared to take action.

If you think the case will be denied, make a backup plan. Make sure the patient understands what details will have to be communicated to the case manager. Discuss the appeals process if you believe a denial can and should be overturned. If you expect a denial will be legitimate, discuss having the patient pay for treatment. Patients in PPOs can opt for an out-of-plan provider to avoid authorization problems altogether, but make sure they understand that the deductible and co-payments will usually be higher than if they stay within the plan.

After discussing it with the patient, the second step is to call the managed care company to make sure authorization is necessary. In some states and for some companies, authorization for psychiatric services is not required for the initial evaluation or the first several visits (usually 5–8). The principle behind this exemption is to encourage both access and short-term treatment. You will need to call to find out how many visits are allowed before authorization is required. Ask them to mail you the authorization request form or explain the process of authorization if it will be done by phone. Even if authorization is not required immediately, the person receiving the call may take a fair amount of information and formally open the case to facilitate review when it does occur. Avoid calling on Mondays, if possible, because there will be a backlog from the weekend and hold times will be long and frustrating. Always make the call privately with the door closed, since specific and private information will have to be given aloud.

When you call the managed care company to open a case and obtain the initial authorization, have all of the patient and insurance information ready. Allow yourself plenty of time (20 to 30 minutes) and have the initial evaluation on hand. Try to be pleasant, even if the person taking the information isn't. Obtain the name of the person who is fielding your call. Note the date, time, duration, and contents of the call. After the reviewer obtains the information needed to authorize the first visits, you have to ask a few questions of your own. First, find out if claims should be sent to the insurance company or to the managed care company. In some cases, the managed care company only authorizes treatment and conveys that permission to the insurer, who then pays the claims. In other cases, the managed care company and the insurer are one and the same. Make sure you know both the claims address and the authorizations address. Ask if reviews will be done by phone or on paper and if the reviewer will always be the same person. If the review is done by mail, ask them to send you the forms needed for renewals of authorization. Find out how far in advance to apply for a renewal of authorization. Some companies like to do it two weeks in advance, others after the last session is used. Find out how they deal with new calendar years. Some companies allow a certain number of visits every year without authorization. Once that number is exceeded, authorization is required. Some companies require a new authorization every calendar year even if the old year's authorized visits are not used up.

RENEWALS OF AUTHORIZATION

When renewing by phone, anticipate any potential problems by reviewing the old authorization. Prepare your case if the situation is different than before. Make sure the old authorization, the initial evaluation, and the last few progress notes are before you and that you have plenty of time. Once you've gotten all of your stuff together and have prepared what you are going to say, call for the renewal.

Try to be pleasant and give the reviewers all the information they need. Case reviewers are not your enemy and you want them to like you. They need to check off boxes on their end in order to help you because they get paid for productivity. After you secure the authorization dates and the number, keep watch for the written confirmation in the mail, which usually arrives a few day later. Call back if you haven't received it within a week.

Written authorization renewals, the kind you have to fill out and mail in, are going the way of the dinosaur. In many ways, they are easier than phone reviews. You are not on the spot with the reviewer, like you are on the phone, and you have plenty of time to think and prepare. On the other hand, whether the authorization will be granted or denied may remain a mystery for a few weeks. Be sure to fill out the form completely and legibly, then date and sign it. Be accurate and honest and limit any narrative to the information needed to make a determination of necessity or efficacy. Refer to previous request forms for consistent terminology and documentation of progress or lack thereof. Mark the date you send it at the top, make a copy for the patient record, and mail it off. Note the date you sent the request in the patient record and watch for the authorization in the mail. It usually takes about two weeks for a company to respond to a written authorization. Call if it has not been received by then.

KEEPING TRACK OF AUTHORIZATIONS

From the directions above, it probably has become apparent that a big part of dealing with managed care involves keeping track of authorization dates, the number of visits used, and when to request a renewal. Every practice has to have a system for keeping track. In my opinion, this is best done through the chart, on the record of visits, and on the patient's account page. When an authorization is received, note the end date and place a reminder in your schedule two weeks before that end date to review the patient's authorization. Then enter the rest of the information on the patient's chart in the progress note under the heading "Managed Care," like this:

> *Managed Care*: Authorization (#129660) received for 10 visits of 90807 from 1/15/04 to 6/30/04. Send next renewal before last visit. 4/10 used as of today.

At the end of each progress note, write the number of visits used up as of that visit. Wherever the visit is recorded, whether on an index card or in the account ledger, it is helpful to indicate the visit number per authorization as a superscript. For example, if there are 10 visits allowed on the current authorization between April 1 and October 1 of 2004, three visits might be recorded as $3/29^{10}$ (^{10} indicating this was the tenth or last visit on the old authorization), $4/5^1$, $4/12^2$ (^{2} indicating that these two visits are the first two on the new authorization).

Patients who miss many appointments complicate authorization, since the end date of the authorization may occur before all of the visits are used. The entry in the schedule two weeks prior to the end date indicates that it is time to review the authorization regardless of how many visits have been used. Sometimes the plan will simply extend the dates on the old authorization if a patient hasn't used them all. Others will generate a new one.

Group practices with nonclinical staff may have a staff person dedicated to tracking authorizations, but that worker can only be as good as the information received. If a clinician does not inform that staff person about an extra visit or missed visit, the authorization schedule will be thrown off.

Nonclinical staff can neither fill out the forms nor make the phone calls for review. Only the provider can give the clinical information necessary for authorization. Never put off authorization requests. If it means staying late or going in early one day, so be it. Procrastination will only lead to further troubles.

COORDINATING BILLING AND AUTHORIZATIONS

When sending a claim to a managed care company, the authorization number goes on the HCFA 1500, in Box 23. Do not submit claims unless you have the authorization number for the dates of service on the claim. The only exception to this rule is when you expect such a delay in getting authorization that you risk going beyond the 60–90-day deadline for submitting claims. In this case, submit the claim without the authorization number, knowing it will be denied. Once authorization is received, resubmit the claim with the authorization number. In other words, always submit claims within the 60–90-day time frame, regardless of the state of authorization. Authorizations can be made retrospectively to accommodate previously submitted claims.

NONCLINICAL AUTHORIZATION DENIALS

Many authorization denials occur because of procedural or technical problems. For example, sometimes the provider did not know authorization was required because there was no mention of a managed care carveout for mental health on the insurance card. The provider and patient find out when a payment is denied for lack of authorization or a reviewer calls to open a case after a claim is received. If this is the situation, first call the patient and discuss the implications and requirements of managed care and the need for authorization. Point out that payment could be denied or, more commonly, be given retroactively for the visits already held.

Then call back the managed care company and explain that you and the patient were unaware that the case required authorization. The plan will almost always grant an authorization and make it retroactive to cover the dates of service that already occurred. Going forward, you now must comply with the plan's authorization procedures.

Sometimes the authorization for payment is denied simply because of an error in the contents, often with the dates or procedure codes, but sometimes from a data entry error. Call immediately to report the error and wait for the correction to come in the mail.

Missing the deadline for filing an authorization request usually results in denial of payment, not for clinical reasons but because of your failure to adhere to your part of the contract. If you miss the deadline for the authorization request by a few days, simply call and explain. Most managed companies and reviewers will let it slide the first time, especially if it is clear the patient needs care. Then review your system for keeping track of authorizations to find out why you missed the deadline. Make changes so it doesn't happen again.

If you missed the review date because the patient dropped out and then returned, call immediately and explain. The company will usually extend the date of the old authorization or generate a new one with retroactive coverage. If you sent the request on time but they never got it, call to explain. Be prepared to produce the copy of the original authorization sent. Occasionally, they will make you go through the appeals process if you can't produce a copy of the original request form.

If you have missed the time for review by a few weeks because you got hopelessly behind on your billing and paperwork, this is more of a problem. Even if it seems hopeless, call the managed care company, be contrite, and see if they'll still let you do it retroactively. If it's your first offense, they'll sometimes let it go. Sometimes your punishment is that you have to go through the appeals procedure. Do it. It'll give you experience in case you ever need to appeal again, and ultimately you are likely to get payment for the services. However, if you are a "repeat offender" (you miss the deadline often), the patient is no longer in treatment, or the case for medical necessity is weak, you may never get authorization for payment. You can't bill the patient for an error you made in fulfilling the contract. Going forward, your choices are basically three: make a more effective authorization tracking system, continue as you are knowing you won't be paid for some visits, or end your managed care contract.

CLINICAL AUTHORIZATION DENIALS

Clinical denials of authorization for payment are usually for *lack of medical necessity* or lack of severity and require more work on the part of the clinician. Usually the denial will not specify what element of the case did not meet the plan's criteria so a telephone call to the case manager will be necessary in order to clarify things if you want to go forward.

Anticipate what the problem might be by reviewing your last request and the patient's case. A typical problem is that the patient is better and the symptoms have improved to the point that they actually no longer meet the criteria for medical necessity. This is good! Don't try to hide this fact because it shows that your treatment was effective and that progress was being made. Patients do not have to be currently ill to meet criteria for medical necessity. Treatment to prevent relapse or recurrence is also medically necessary. If your patient needs continued treatment to prevent relapse, if they've been better for such a short time that the risk of relapse is still high, or a stress is looming in the near future that is likely to worsen the symptoms, these are bone fide reasons to continue treatment and should be mentioned to the reviewer.

On the flip side, there are also problems if the patient has shown no improvement at all. This may occur if the patient has been in treatment for more than six months and the requests for authorization show no improvement or change in symptomatology. The question the reviewer is asking (and the one you should be asking yourself) is why is this patient not improving? The answer to that question will dictate your approach to the reviewer. Perhaps the illness does not respond quickly to treatment, as is often the case with eating disorders. Maybe the diagnosis is inaccurate and further work-up or consultation is necessary. Maybe the current form of treatment is not very effective but the patient refuses another type of treatment. Perhaps the patient is not taking the medication or coming in regularly. Or, the patient could simply have a bad disease from which they may never fully recover. Sometimes one treatment has failed and a new one has to be tried. Complicating factors appear: you become aware that the patient is drinking or has a concurrent personality disorder. All of these are legitimate reasons for lack of progress with treatment and should be communicated to the reviewer.

Lack of severity of symptoms is another common reason for denial. In the old days, the patient had to be homicidal or suicidal or near hospitalization to get authorization. Times have changed. Treatment is considered medically necessary if it can control symptoms, return the patient to full functioning, preserve the patient's current functioning, or relieve suffering. Documentation of the patient's level of distress and level of functioning at home, work, and socially is essential. Make sure you comment on these factors in the progress notes and on requests for authorization.

Always include the GAF on Axis V in the diagnostic portion of your evaluation and on the review forms when asked. The numeric scale and descriptors are located near the front of the *DSM-IV*. Note the effect of the patient's symptoms at work or school, in relationships, and on activities of daily living, like shopping and driving. Be sure to record the patient's level of distress using their own words. The patient might feel out of control, afraid, or miserable. If the patient is not suicidal but has risk factors for suicide such as male sex, depression, social isolation, medical illness, impulsivity, or substance abuse, be sure to include the risk factors in your notes and on the review. Patients do not have to voice suicidal ideation to be at high risk for suicide.

Don't minimize the diagnostic code for the "protection" of the patient. This obviously could lead to authorization problems and is not good for patient care. If you fear the patient knowing the diagnosis, ask yourself why this is the case. Most patients ultimately want to know the truth and awareness of the diagnosis is usually necessary for consent, treatment, and cooperation. Probably the most difficult diagnoses to discuss are schizophrenia and some of the personality disorders. Once fully engaged in treatment almost every patient can deal with knowing the diagnosis and, with experience, almost every practitioner can learn to convey the diagnosis in a therapeutic way.

If there is a realistic concern about the patient knowing the diagnosis, perhaps because they are paranoid, actively suicidal, or at risk of fleeing treatment, and you can not put it on the form for fear the patient will request a copy, discuss this openly with the case reviewer. The reviewer has to put down an accurate diagnosis but may be able to arrange things so that the patient is less likely to obtain it. (Some states have laws prohibiting patient access to psychiatric records if it might be harmful to them.) That said, providers must always be prepared for patients to discover the diagnosis, either by asking you or another source directly, or through exploration on their own. If you fear the patient's employer will react negatively to a diagnosis, discuss this with both the patient and the reviewer.

Reviewers can often flag cases for confidential review. HIPAA regulations seriously restrict employer access to health information, even if the employer is self-insured.

Failure to be specific about treatment goals is another common reason for authorization denial. I find that psychiatrists in particular are weak in this area because their experience with treatment plans is often limited. Try to list goals, behaviors, or symptoms that can be roughly quantified during a course of treatment. This is a good practice in general because it prevents open-ended, drifting treatment. Failure to meet the goals or make gains is an opportunity for discussion with the patient: "I was filling out the review form for your insurance and I realized there doesn't seem to be much progress since last time. What do you think?"

Before you call to speak to the clinical reviewer about a denial, have on hand the patient information (date of birth, identification number), your provider number, the initial evaluation and last few progress notes, the previous authorizations, and the notes you have made about why authorization should be granted. Try to be relaxed. Don't call on the same day as receiving the denial, because your blood may still be boiling. Wait even longer if this is a repeated problem with the same managed care company, if a lot of money is involved, or if the case is especially difficult. You'll need more time to cool down after receiving the denial. Never call on a Monday or on a "bad day." Make sure you have plenty of time for the call so you don't rush through your arguments. Plan to appeal if the denial remains after the call. When the phone is ringing, remember that there is a person with feelings on the other end. If they have a bad time with the call, you will have a bad time.

If you discuss all the relevant facts and the reviewer still does not want to authorize the visits, ask to speak to the supervisor. This may require another phone call, often by appointment. Try to clarify your arguments and facts ahead of time so this call will be more effective. If authorization is still denied but you feel the patient needs continued treatment, ask for the appeals process and follow it.

Sometimes an authorization will be partial in that the visits will be approved but not at the frequency you requested. You can discuss this with the case reviewer or supervisor, but if no change results you have two options besides appeal. One is to continue the visits at the frequency you think is necessary and request another authorization when the visits run out early. You're on fairly solid ground here as long as the patient really needs to be seen often because partial authorization implies the criteria for medical necessity have been met. However, it is sometimes also the case that the patient actually can do just as well with a decrease in frequency. Discuss the pros and cons with the patient first and then decide how to proceed.

Valid Clinical Denials

Providing a psychiatric service to a patient does not in any way mean that you or the patient is entitled to payment by the managed care company. All insurance plans have limitations and it is the patient's responsibility to know those limitations. Many psychiatric services are not covered by insurance: grief counseling, pastoral counseling, therapy for adjustment disorders, couples' therapy if neither partner has a psychiatric illness, and any services for someone who has no psychiatric disorder. If you know or suspect that your services to a patient will not be covered under their benefit plan, explain this upfront. They may leave treatment because they don't want to self-pay, or they may opt to pay out of pocket. Occasionally you may decide to request authorization and see how far the plan is willing to go, but don't press too hard if the case is weak. Valid denials should not be pursued to appeal.

APPEALING AN AUTHORIZATION DENIAL

Always discuss an appeal with the patient before starting the process. The patient needs to know that this means there is a problem with payment to the provider and that they may have to pay themselves. This allows them to prepare for that. Secondly, appeals require the release of more psychiatric information. The patient needs to be made aware of this and consent to it. Don't assume release is okay because every patient wants insurance to pay. Some will opt to self-pay rather than expose more of the psychiatric record. Finally, the patient may need to participate directly in the appeals process either by talking with the reviewer or by contacting the benefits officer at work to inform him of the problem.

Obtain the details of the appeals process from the plan. You'll need the name and address to which the letter will be sent, a list of what information needs to be included in the letter, and how long it will take for a response. Carefully draft the letter on professional letterhead stationery.

Include the date, the patient's insurance identification number and date of birth, and your provider number. Indicate the names of the parties you spoke to and the dates you spoke to them. Explain clearly and concisely why you think authorization should be granted, specifically addressing the issues the reviewer and supervisor mentioned as reasons for denial. Use a bullet format if possible or summarize the information at the end. Write the letter in such a manner that the patient can read it. The tone should be neutral but committed. Indicate that you have discussed the situation with the patient. To facilitate the plan's compliance and minimize errors, state the precise number of visits you want and the dates you want the authorization to cover. Include copies of all supporting documentation. Make a copy of the appeal letter to keep in the patient's chart and send off the original.

Most denials are reversed on appeal if they are at all reasonable. Once the denial is reversed, you will eventually get paid all you are due. Continue to submit all claims as usual, without the authorization number, while the appeal is pending so you don't add late submission problems to the mix. When the claims are denied for lack of authorization, bill the patient (you've already discussed this with them) and have them pay for the services. Throughout the process continue the treatment as usual. Don't transfer the patient or indicate you want them to move on. Don't space out appointments unless you were planning to do it anyway. Once you obtain the authorization on appeal, resubmit the unpaid claims if you have to. Most appeals coordinators will offer to reprocess all the denied claims for you. Reimburse the patient immediately when you are paid by the managed care company.

WHEN MANAGED CARE BAILS OR FAILS

Educate patients about the pros and cons of managed care if they have a managed care plan. This helps them follow the process and anticipate problems. If a managed care company is having problems, most of the providers in the area will be experiencing delayed payments or denials. Tell the patients involved so they can plan and take action if they want to. Discuss whether the patient should change plans or complain to the benefits office at work. The latter option raises some confidentiality issues but most benefits officers are quite good about taking action without exposing the patient. Employers can be excellent advocates for employees (Peele,

2000) when it comes to insurance plans, and can often achieve the unachievable with managed care. As a rule, most employers are careful not to misuse employee information, but there is always a risk. Patients can also file formal complaints with the managed care company or the state insurance commissioner.

If you suspect that a managed care company is having problems, ask colleagues about their experience with the company. Then approach your local professional organization's committee on managed care. Professional committees may ask you for specific data on the problems you have had without asking for patient information. They then use the compiled data to talk to officers in the plan directly. If they get no response or no positive change occurs, they will take the data to local government officials and ask them to investigate the problems.

If you have a contract with a failing managed care company, reread the contract noting the conditions for termination. Most providers muddle through to the end of the contract and then don't renew. If you feel like you can't wait until the end of the contract, call the managed care company to see if they will agree to allow you to terminate early. If they don't and you are desperate to terminate the contact early, you can consult an attorney. Don't renew a truly problematic managed care contract no matter how dedicated you are to the patients affected. Ultimately you may grow to resent the patients involved, and that's not good for them *or* the psychiatric treatment. Non-renewal of the contract is how patients and employers learn about which managed care plans are good and which are not so good.

If you will be ending the contract with their managed care plan, give patients plenty of lead time to consider their options. They can transfer to another in-network provider, change insurance plans at the next opportunity, or pay out of pocket. If you offer fee reductions and the patient qualifies, that is another option.

CHAPTER 8

The Influence of the Pharmaceutical Industry on Psychiatric Practice

The purpose of this chapter is to help practitioners understand the competing financial interests in the pharmacological treatment of patients. Read this chapter if any of the following apply to you or your practice:

1. Prescribing medication is a major component of your practice.
2. You have managed care or insurance contracts with restrictive drug formularies.
3. Your patients complain about the cost of their psychiatric medications.
4. Patient compliance is affected by the high cost of drugs.
5. Your practice sees pharmaceutical representatives.
6. You give free drug samples to patients.
7. You defray practice expenses by attending industry-sponsored continuing education programs.

How are the financial interests of the provider, patient, and pharmaceutical companies competing when a patient is in treatment? The goal of patients is to keep their own costs down and obtain the medication necessary for treatment. When patients have one small co-payment no matter what the cost of the drug, there is no incentive for them to use cheaper medications. When insurance companies change to percentage or tiered co-payments (higher co-payments for more expensive drugs), patients begin to care about the cost of medications. Some patients are less interested in cost and more interested in trying something new. A few patients don't care about cost at all for themselves but do care about the rising cost of health care for others, especially parents. Generally, patients do not care about the psychiatrist's or nurse practitioner's financial interests and expect those to be set aside in favor of their own. They do not count the pharmaceutical industry's financial interests at all unless the patient or a family member is an employee of the industry.

Providers have direct financial interests in income from any source, whether the treatment of patients, providing services for the drug companies, or stock invested in drug companies. These interests may conflict with patients' financial interests when the acts that generate revenue for the provider are the very acts the patient must pay for. Providers have indirect financial interests in patient satisfaction and compliance in order to retain patients, grow the practice, and minimize liability. Patient and provider financial interests nicely coincide in these areas.

Drug company interests include generating revenue, improving market share, and researching existing and future products. They try to keep drug costs high to generate revenue, and in this they compete directly with patients, who want to keep drug costs low. Providers are not directly affected by the industry's drive for revenue because they usually are not on many medications and have the financial resources to pay for them. However, when medication costs are high, compliance suffers and this interferes with patient retention for the provider, which in turn drives down revenue.

The drive to improve market share is an area in which provider and industry financial goals may coincide. More patients taking medication means more patient visits for psychiatrists and nurse practitioners. Where patients want the least costly treatment and will forego pharmacological treatment when not strictly indicated (as in the treatment of personality disorders), both the industry and prescribers have a financial interest in promoting psychopharmacological treatment whenever possible.

As a psychiatric professional with fiduciary responsibilities to patients, you are obligated to put your own financial interests and the financial interests of the pharmaceutical industry beneath patients' financial interests.

HOW PRESCRIBING PRACTICES AFFECT
PROVIDER INCOME AND BUSINESS COSTS

For psychiatrists and nurse practitioners, increased prescribing means increased income simply because brief medication visits generate more money per hour than therapy visits. Studies show that giving a prescription in a psychiatric visit tends to shorten the duration of the visit (Olfson & Klerman, 1993), further increasing the number of patients that can be seen in a day. Prescribers who write many prescriptions per month are surveyed and pursued by the drug industry for marketing and research purposes because they have the most data and influence the most patients. As a result, practitioners who prescribe heavily may also receive compensation in the form of gifts, cash, or honoraria for participating in clinical research or speaking engagements.

However, there are costs associated with psychopharmacological practice. Liability risk increases with the volume of patients (Simon, 2001). Shorter visits also increase malpractice risk, presumably due to the decreased time for communication. Psychopharmacological practices may have more seriously ill patients, more overdoses, and more side effects. They also incur the risks of split-treatment with nonmedical therapists. High visit volume will increase office costs once the practitioner can no longer manage the scheduling or billing alone. Phone time is higher because of calls about side effects, drug interactions, and refills as well as the need to consult by phone for split treatment. None of these calls are reimbursed. However, the revenue generated from a high-volume psychopharmacological practice is often high enough to defray these costs.

THE MONETARY INFLUENCE OF DRUG
COMPANIES ON PATIENTS

Drug companies exert a certain amount of influence over patients. TV advertising of psychiatric medications is a new phenomenon but represents only a small portion of the pharmaceutical industry's advertising budget (although it is increasing; Oetgen, 2003; Rosenthal et al., 2002). Since the focus is on revenue and market share, TV advertisements target more expensive patented drugs (Rosenthal et al.). Consumer advertising does increase patient demand for certain drugs and it also increases the time spent with physicians and nurses (Oetgen) who have to explain in more detail the nature of the medications involved and their indications. Some believe that TV advertising contributes to inappropriate prescribing by practitioners who are uncomfortable declining patient requests for drugs (Lipsky & Taylor, 1997; Schwartz 1989).

On the flip side, TV advertising may have some benefits. It may create better-informed patients and decrease the stigma associated with present-ing for psychiatric treatment and accepting medication for treatment (Oetgen, 2003). If more patients present for psychiatric treatment, this improves the bottom line for all mental health providers as well as the pharmaceutical industry. It is not such a happy occurrence for insurers or employers who pay for treatment.

THE MONETARY INFLUENCE OF DRUG COMPANIES ON PROVIDERS

Pharmaceutical detailing (visits by sales representatives) and provision of samples are the main routes for promoting prescription drugs to providers (Oetgen, 2003; Rosenthal et al., 2002). Sales representatives focus on es-tablishing a personal relationship with the provider, a relationship that then becomes influential. The attention of an engaging, smart, and happy sales rep is just the right remedy on a difficult clinical day.

Many physicians do not believe their prescribing behaviors are influ-enced by pharmaceutical representatives (Avorn et al., 1982; McKinney et al., 1990; Orlowski & Wateska, 1992), but numerous prospective studies have proven that this is indeed the case. Marketing also causes prescribers to hold beliefs about medications that are not supported by scientific evi-dence (Avorn). Detailing, gifts, sponsored symposia (Orlowski & Wateska), and monetary payments from the pharmaceutical industry cause physi-cians to prescribe the targeted drugs more often, to lobby for placing them on the formulary (Chren & Landefield, 1994), and to write articles sup-porting the drug in journals (Stelfox et al., 1998).

Sales calls have other effects on the practice. The visits take up time and may interfere with the office schedule. Witnessing providers meeting with drug-company representatives can appear mercenary to staff and pa-tients who wonder if the provider can remain neutral when it comes to prescribing. On the other hand, engagement with the industry can seem positive. The provider appears up to date and well informed about the latest trends.

As medication and health care costs continue to rise, the issue of industry influence on prescribers has become more controversial and subject to scrutiny. Direct compensation from the industry may come in the form of gifts, free lunches, free industry-sponsored CME programs, honoraria for speaking to other providers, or for research. Since all have been shown to influence behavior, there are now efforts to minimize this effect. More and more clinics are banning sales-representative visits, removing industry-sponsored office paraphenalia (notepads, information posters, and mugs), and limiting the dollar value on gifts or honoraria that staff members can accept from drug companies and sales representatives.

Professional organizations are beginning to address this issue as well. The Ethics Committee of the ApA (2001b) wrote that modest meals with no honorarium are acceptable, as are low payments for completing questionnaires about drugs. The American Medical Association stated that gifts to physicians from the pharmaceutical industry are acceptable if they benefit patients, relate to the physician's work, and are of little value. Items for the personal benefit of the M.D., such as floral arrangements, tickets, and gift certificates, are therefore considered unacceptable while notepads, pens, office items, and modest meals are considered okay (AMA, 2002; PhRMA, 2002).

Financial compensation of providers for referring patients into a drug study is regarded as unethical. In a published opinion in 2001, the Ethics Committee of the Amercian Psychiatric Association wrote that it could be ethical for a psychiatric provider to accept payment for referrals only if the recruited patients presented themselves expressly for the study after seeing an advertisement, and if they were informed of the funding sources for the study. The committee did not consider recruitment of patients who present for treatment ethical, especially if the provider gets a referral fee (2001b).

The Ethics Committee (ApA, 2001b) expressed conflicting views about the use of drug-company funds to sponsor continuing education programs. While they considered such funding ethical "at this time," acceptance of funds could not be tied to advertising or mention of their companies or products. However, they also said that "because mandated continuing education involves a psychiatrist's license . . . , it would be proper if he or she assumed the full cost of such programs" (2001b, p. 63). Ownership of pharmaceutical stock can be considered either direct or indirect payment (this is addressed more fully in Chapter 9).

Whatever the standard is now, it is clearly moving in a direction toward minimizing or prohibiting compensation, gifts, and industry sponsorship of continuing education credit programs. Mental health practitioners would be well advised to move in this direction as well. Practitioners whose industry ties provide a significant portion of their income might consider increasing, rather than decreasing, that stream of revenue by making the pharmaceutical portion of their work the main portion, perhaps by dropping clinical work that is unrelated to the pharmaceutical studies, research, or education. In this way, the conflicts of interest are minimized and they become free to openly state their affiliation.

THE USE OF MEDICATION SAMPLES

There are many problems associated with the use of free drug samples in psychiataric practice. The first is that it obscures the cost of the treatment from both the patient and the provider. A second is that it promotes the use of the drug before there is evidence of improved efficacy or benefit over older, off-patent medications. Each success with a sample drug encourages the prescriber to expand its use to other patients and communicates this success to other providers. The use of free samples raises health care costs by committing the patient and provider to a more expensive course of therapy (because free samples are given only for more expensive, on-patent drugs). If it is successful, they are unlikely to abandon it no matter what the price. Free samples also increase office labor because of the record-keeping requirements (Sanchez & Fromson, 2002). Liability increases because the containers are not childproof, have no warning labels or directions, and are accessible to employees.

Free samples can be used appropriately for patients who are already on the medication but suddenly can't afford it because of a disruption in insurance coverage or a financial set back. Use of free samples can also be considered when the patient has failed trials of all the cheaper medications. If you do decide to use supplies of free samples on a trial basis, make sure you and the patient know the cost of the medication beforehand and make a realistic plan for when the free samples run out.

In December 1994, the Council on Ethical and Judicial Affairs issued a new clarification about dispensing drug samples for personal use or the use of a family member. The council's guidelines permit this activity in emergencies or when immediate use of the drug is indicated on a trial basis to assess tolerance and for the treatment of "acute conditions requiring short courses of inexpensive therapy." The use of free samples for the treatment of chronic conditions was deemed unacceptable (AMA, 2002). Some pharmaceutical companies have changed their policies as well, no longer honoring physician requests for drug samples for personal or family use (PhRMA, 2002; Smith Klein Beecham, personal communication, April 1995). One could postulate that if the use of free samples is not acceptable for health care providers except under certain conditions, then perhaps it is also not acceptable for patients.

MANAGING AND MINIMIZING DRUG COMPANY INFLUENCE

The goal in prescribing successfully is to use neutral, evidenced-based treatments and to minimize the influence of marketing on prescribing behavior. The achievement of this goal involves eliminating office visits of pharmaceutical representatives and relying more on mailed information that can be thoughtfully weighed without the influence of a relationship with the sales representative. It also means declining gifts, compensation, and honoraria from the pharmaceutical industry. Minimize the use of industry-sponsored continuing education credits and earn enough to cover payment for seminars and courses that are not industry sponsored.

To minimize marketing effects on yourself, patients, and staff, try to use generic names instead of brand names in the patients chart, on prescriptions (unless a brand name is medically necessary), and verbally with patients and colleagues. Always try to use the cheapest effective drug with attention to side effects for patients, and only prescribe medications if they are indicated. Follow the American Psychiatric Association practice guidelines regarding medication treatment. They summarize what drug and nondrug treatments are and are not supported by the literature. Be prepared to lose some patients who want what you do not think is indicated.

Read drug studies critically, taking note of which are sponsored by the pharmaceutical industry, even through an "unrestricted" grant. Note the disclosure statements following the article. These show which authors have financial ties to companies producing the medications mentioned in the article. Although there has been a recent push to exclude articles

written by authors with industry ties, many believe this move would so se-
verely limit publication that it is not possible (Stelfox et al., 1998). It is
concerning to think that the drug industry has become so deeply interwoven with prescribers that no one is able to publish or hold symposia
without that support.

There are many reasons why prescribers feel unable or unwilling to
give up industry ties. Professional isolation is one of them. When prescribers feel like cogs in a corporate machine rather than psychiatrists and
nurses practicing a profession, drug companies provide a large and effective support network. But professional isolation can be addressed in other
ways, like joining a peer supervision group, an action committee, or a professional organization. Many practitioners are reluctant to give up going
to free industry-sponsored continuing education symposia. CMEs and
CEUs are mandated for all licensed professionals and the yearly expense
can be considerable. If you truly need *free* continuing education credits,
then your income is either too low or your other expenses are too high.
Consult your accountant or supervisor about how to improve cash flow so
that obtaining CMEs or CEUs is relatively painless. Some people have a
psychological inability to turn down what's free. This can be addressed by
simple discussion with friends or a spouse, or, if severe, in consultation
with a therapist. If you or someone you know has an addiction that leads to
dependence on free samples, get help by confiding in a trusted colleague or
consulting with your local professional impairment committee.

If you need the money from the pharmaceutical industry to continue
your practice, re-evaluate your financial situation and your business. Do
you know where your money goes? Can you cut expenses or increase your
professional income in some other manner? Can you increase income
through other investments, like real estate? If you need the professional
recognition obtained from meeting with representatives or giving talks or
contracting for clincial research, can you get this kind of recognition in
some other way, such as teaching, supervising, writing, or through an independent research project?

WHEN THE GOAL IS NOT TO MINIMIZE
INDUSTRY INFLUENCE

Sometimes minimizing the influence of the pharmaceutical industry is
not a reasonable goal, despite the drawbacks. If your primary income is

from that industry, then neutrality is not an option; your work is part and parcel of the industry. Some administrative jobs, say for a hospital or research instituion, require interface with the industry. Members of formulary committees must have industry contacts for negotiating discounted payment for medications. Providers who are tertiary consultants, the psychopharmacologists of last resort, must have pharmaceutical contacts because their job is to be on the cutting edge and to try things other prescribers may be unwilling or unable to try.

If the prescriber has to or wants to maintain strong industry ties, then the process for taking care of patients becomes slightly different. The first responsibility is to be open about your bias and aware that it affects your prescribing practices. The second is to be open to any evidence that indicates that the medication to which the provider has committed him- or herself is in any way falling short. This means the prescriber must be willing and able to change beliefs if evidence of efficacy is not forthcoming, regardless of financial influences. Always fully disclose the extent of your ties, without shame or embarassment, to patients, colleagues, trainees, as well as journal editors.

CHAPTER 9

Monetary Incentives and Conflicts of Interest

While there is no way to entirely eliminate the influence of money on practice, it is important to minimize any negative effect on patient care by maintaining an awareness of that effect so bias can be corrected and balance restored. When the influence of money can not be detected, measures to protect the patient (or the provider) can not be taken and exploitation can result. Monetary incentives exist on a spectrum of transparency. The higher the level of transparency, the more acceptable the incentive is to all since patients and providers are free to act to correct any problem. This chapter reviews various types of monetary incentives with an eye to the level of transparency and the risk of patient exploitation.

PAYMENTS, INCENTIVES, KICKBACKS, AND BRIBES

Payments are made by previous agreement or contract as direct compensation for services or products with openly stated and fixed prices. Payments are legal and the income is declared to the government. Most of your income as a mental health provider will come in the form of a payment. Your patients and other payers are aware of the fees, what the compensation is for, and the terms of payment. The process is transparent and straightforward, and either party can choose whether to participate in the agreement.

Incentives are somewhat different from direct payment. Incentive agreements may be set up in advance or added to a contract if circumstances warrant a change. Incentives are not payment for services but rewards designed to promote or shape certain behaviors of either the providers who are being paid or the patients who have to pay. In general, incentive agreements are less open to scrutiny and may even be hidden. Patients are often unaware of the incentives paid to providers in return for some kind of behavioral goal. Incentive payments are usually legal and the income is usually declared by providers. Incentive payments are often not fixed amounts but vary depending on the desired goal, perhaps a percent of net profits or a tiered bonus based on productivity levels.

Kickbacks and fee-splitting are incentives paid by one provider to another for the referral of patients (Rodwin, 1992). Like other incentives, kickbacks are not payments for services but are designed to shape behavior, in this case to promote referrals. There are many kinds of kickback or fee-splitting arrangements. *Drumming* refers to payments made to nonmedical agents for referrals (Rodwin), people like clergy, resort workers, or barkeepers who are in a position to hear peoples' troubles and then make a referral. Fee-splitting is a type of kickback in which the referring provider and the receiving provider share the patient's payment for the service (Rodwin). Kickbacks and split fees are usually not discussed openly in contracts, with patients, or with colleagues. They are sometimes illegal and often unethical, so the income gleaned from them must be hidden or disguised in some way.

A bribe is a payment designed to influence the behavior of a person in a position of trust, perhaps a fiduciary. Legally, the term *bribery* is restricted to payments of government officials and is a felony in most jurisdictions (Garner, 1999). In countries where access is difficult, bribing medical providers for service is common (Colombotos, 1993) and may constitute a significant portion of physician income. It is not considered unethical since the bribes allow individuals to exert some influence where ordinarily they would have none (Field, 1993). Bribes are directed toward a single specific action; for example, the acceptance of a patient into an otherwise closed practice. The amount varies for each circumstance.

We can see that the factors differentiating payments, incentives, kickbacks, and bribes are whether the fees are fixed in advance, the degree of transparency, whether the payment is direct compensation for the service or designed to influence behavior, and how specific that targeted behavior is. Note that the influence of money increases as we progress from payments to incentives to kickbacks and finally to bribes, where the power of money is at its height.

FEE-FOR-SERVICE VERSUS
SALARY COMPENSATION

Direct compensation of psychiatric providers is either fee-for-service or salary, and the influence of money on the practitioner varies depending on the method of compensation. When payment is fee-for-service, practitioners generally try to increase both patient volume (the number of patient visits each week) and service intensity (the percentage of services giving higher compensation), because both of these increase income. This does not necessarily mean better treatment for each patient. When more income is desired, an unscrupulous practitioner may give more treatment than is indicated (prescribing psychotherapy when medication alone might suffice) or treatment that is less efficacious but better compensated (medication alone for personality disorders). Note that the financial incentive of fee-for-service practice decreases as the practice becomes full because there is a natural maximum of patients who can be seen and treated. Warbasse (1935) correctly pointed out that the financial incentives of fee-for-service could be reduced by separating the diagnostic and treatment services so that no provider is performing both for the same patient. The mental health provider who performs the diagnostic evaluation would have no incentive to skew the diagnosis one way or the other because another provider would provide the treatment. Accuracy in diagnosis becomes paramount and the patient is referred for the best treatment.

Some practitioners believe that they can avoid the financial conflicts of interest inherent in fee-for-service compensation by opting for a salary. However, while salaries decrease the financial incentive to overtreat, there is evidence that salaries promote undertreatment (Hemenway et al., 1990; Stone, 2000) because the incentive is to minimize the workload for any given compensation package. When salaries are only part of a compensation package (because bonuses or incentives form the other part) the opposite has been found to be true; the higher the proportion of the base salary, the higher the costs per patient (Kralewski et al., 2000) because the incentives to reduce costs are less influential. The take-home message is that there is no method of financial compensation for psychiatric care that is without financial influence. The best one can do is to be aware of the influences and try not to allow them to affect patient care.

FINANCIAL INCENTIVES
AND DISINCENTIVES

The purpose of the Health Maintenance Act of 1973 was to require health maintenance organizations (HMOs) to use incentives as a means of reducing health care costs (Englehardt & Rie, 2003). Where traditional fee-for-service payment provided incentives to do more, the new incentives were to do less (Stone, 2000). HMOs apply financial incentives to providers (Hillman et al., 1989) and other health institutions are following suit. Do these financial incentives work? Yes. Numerous studies have shown that monetary incentives influence physician behavior (Hemenway et al., 1990; Hillman et al.; Kralewski et al., 2000), and it is only a matter of time before studies show the same for other providers.

There are many types of incentives used (Hillman et al., 1989). *Capitation* is a payment method used by many HMOs (Gold et al., 1995) in which therapists or mental health agencies contract with an insurance company to provide mental health services for a defined population for one year for a certain amount per month (Parvin & Anderson, 1995) regardless of the number of visits used or patients seen. The psychiatric provider is therefore careful not to provide too much service. Capitation payments may be used in combination with salary withholds or fee-for-service, but in general pure capitation lowers costs the most (Kralewski, 2000). The risk to the mental health provider is bidding too low for the services needed by the population. The risk to the insurance company is paying too much for services not actually used by the insured population (Parvin & Anderson).

Bonuses are a familiar financial incentive but they have taken some unusual forms in mental health service. Bonuses are extra payments given to providers, not for services rendered, but for meeting certain goals or targets. Bonuses can be based on profit sharing, where a percentage (or all) of the profit is divided among the providers at the end of the fiscal year. This kind of bonus motivates participants to keep the practice profitable. Bonuses can also be based on patient satisfaction, quality of care, or other measures but most often bonuses are based on productivity. If productivity is measured in patient visits, there is a financial incentive for providers to increase the number of visits. If productivity is measured by billable hours, there is incentive to decrease the amount of free care delivered. If productivity is measured by the revenue generated by a provider, there is an incentive to perform high-paying procedures. Note that these productivity measures increase costs (Kralewski, 2000). To compensate for this effect, bonuses are sometimes provided for cost savings, perhaps based on revenues or resources not used (Kralewski). Contract-signing bonuses can be used to sweeten the pot when a group of providers agrees to join an HMO or an institution. Bonuses have also been given to providers for recruitment of patients into academic studies (Dresser, 2001), but this practice has come under serious scrutiny because patient interests are not often well served when this is the case.

Bonuses may be given to utilization reviewers of psychiatric services for managed care contracts. These bonuses can be ethical if they are tied to professionally developed criteria like medical necessity, or documentation of basic diagnostic criteria, as long as they don't conflict with the patient treatment or advocacy and aren't strictly based on decreasing the number of services provided to patients (Englehardt & Rie, 2003). Remember that licensed providers are obligated to advocate for all medically necessary psychiatric treatment, including psychotherapy, even when performing in a utilization and review (UR) role. In others words, taking a UR position does not limit professional obligation toward patients.

Gatekeeping incentives (Englehardt & Rie, 2003) are applied to primary care doctors to increase or decrease referrals to specialists, including mental health professionals. Positive gatekeeping incentives provide payment for increasing referrals. Negative gatekeeping incentives reward not referring, perhaps by prepayment of a fixed amount into a pool. When the referral pool money is used up, the specialist fees are deducted from the profits of the primary care group.

There are a few other financial incentives that deserve mention. Patient volume guarantees provide payment to the provider even when enrollment or utilization is low. They are used to induce a provider to agree to a contract for services at a discounted rate (Englehardt & Rie, 2003). Job promotion may be based on cost savings or performance measures and is a financial incentive as long as a promotion also means an increased salary. Profit-sharing means that any net revenue will be shared with eligible providers (Kralewski, 2000). Equity sharing (Englehardt & Rie) is when fulfillment of goals is rewarded with some amount of ownership in the company. This may or may not mean a bonus or profit-sharing at the end of the fiscal year because that depends on the fiscal health of the practice.

HMOs, insurers, and managed care companies use financial disincentives as well. Disincentives may be limits on the number of psychiatric visits compensated by insurance, limits on the dollar amount of psychiatric care provided per year (Englehardt & Rie, 2003), discounted fees, limits on admitting privileges if goals are not met, removal from an HMO panel, salary reduction, and of course termination of employment. There may also be financial penalities for running over the amount allotted for specialty referrals. Capitated contracts provide strong disincentives to provide service at the end of the contract period if the target amount is being approached (Pearson et al., 1998). They also encourage providers to eliminate the very ill from their practices, since they use up so many resources. For this reason, stop-loss insurance is an important component of any capitated contract. The insurance kicks in when the cost of caring for any patient goes way beyond normal, thus protecting the provider financially and hopefully discouraging him from ejecting seriously ill patients from the practice.

A salary withhold is when a percentage of a provider's salary is withheld until the end of the year. At that time, if certain productivity or financial goals are met by the group or the individual, the remainder of the salary is distributed. Salary withholds are an important component of many insurance contracts (Hillman, 1987) and have benefits to insurers and employers of psychiatric providers. Unlike a bonus system, which requires an additional pool of money, salary withholds use money set aside from the original salary. And unlike the bonus system, salary withholds demonstrate financial risk to provider-employees, qualifying institutions, and insurance companies for greater market share and size. Salary withholds allow initial salary quotes to seem higher. Instead of saying the provider will make $100,000 with a possible bonus at the end of the year, the contract states the salary as $110,000 with a 10% salary withhold. Providers are usually unaware that their participation in a salary withhold program increases the allowable market share of their employer.

Despite their pervasiveness, there are limitations on the use of financial incentives to decrease costs or utilization of psychiatric services. The magnitude of incentives can't be so large that it affects the provision of care (MMS, 1996), and even administrators and reviewers must advocate for medically necessary services (Englehardt & Rie, 2003). Most incentives are allotted by group (MMS), not to individual providers, so that any single patient-provider relationship can't be strongly affected. Productivity reviews can't be based on performance over short periods of time (MMS), again to mimize impact on single cases. Although this may change in the future, it is unfortunate that patient outcome is not considered in any scheme of incentives (Englehardt & Rie).

Certain incentive arrangements discouraged by the Office of the Inspector General (OIG) are common in psychiatric practice. One is the provision of free (or discounted) billing or staff services to other providers, because it looks like a kickback if referrals are also involved. Gifts and payments by pharmaceutical manufacturers and vendors are another area of concern to the OIG. Professional courtesy, payment of expenses for conferences, payment for administrative or consultative services with few real duties, income-guarantee supplements, and inducements from hospitals to reduce referrals of Medicare or Medicaid recipients are all frowned upon by the OIG. Patient incentives, like waiving the co-payment or deductible, are also regarded with suspicion by the agency (OIG, 2002).

As a rule, any business arrangements that involve referrals should be reviewed by legal counsel familiar with local anti-kickback and self-referral statutes. Any contracts containing incentives or penalties should also be examined carefully. Don't sign any contract in which the financial incentives or disincentives are so strong that they will inevitably influence how you deliver care.

Disclosure of incentives may or may not be required depending on state law and whether or not the patient asks about it (ApA, 2001a; Marcinko, 2000; MMS, 1996; NASW, 1999). However, the trend is increasingly toward disclosure in some form.

KICKBACKS AND SELF-REFERRAL

Kickback payments for referrals have been an issue for the medical profession for more than 100 years (Rodwin, 1992). Fee-splitting began in the 1890s, when apothecaries and medical-supply firms reimbursed physicians and surgeons for referrals. In 1899, G. Frank Lydston showed that 60% of physicians accepted the practice of paying fees for referrals. Usually the fees were paid by surgeons, pharmacists, and medical suppliers to primary care physicians who sent them patients. They were also paid by hospitals and psychiatric sanatoriums to physicians who admitted patients (Rodwin). By the 1900s, labs were paying physicians commissions for referrals for lab work, and in 1947 physicians were receiving rebates from optical companies. The American Medical Association waxed and waned on both position and enforcement (Rodwin).

Sometimes the payments for referrals were more indirect. Physicians were paid as associate directors in return for referrals rather than for the referral itself. Pressure then mounted to discontinue the practice. The IRS stopped allowing kickback payments as business deductions in the 1950s, but the practice continued despite professional regulation. Scandals led to federal legislation prohibiting kickbacks in the 1970s, and when this was not effective legal prohibitions were expanded in the 1980s (Rodwin, 1992).

Despite increased state and federal prohibitions against fee-splitting and kickbacks, the 1980 American Medical Association *Principles* dropped the injunction against fee-splitting (Rodwin). There is still no statement against kickbacks or fee-splitting in the 2001 *Principles*, although there is an allusion to fee-splitting not being acceptable in the *Principles of Medical Ethics with Annotations for Psychiatry* (ApA, 2001c). The *Code of Ethics for Nurses* (ANA, 2001) makes no comment on fee-splitting. The *Ethical Principles of Psychologists* (APA, 2002, Section 6.07) seems to discourage payment for referrals, but the wording seems to allow payment under certain circumstances. The *Code of Ethics of the National Association of Social Workers* (1999) is clear in its prohibition of payment for referrals.

Why is fee-splitting and remuneration for referrals illegal and unethical? The main reasons have to do with the effect of payment on medical decision making. Payment for referrals causes overutilization of services, increases the costs of federal health care programs, creates unfair competition by shutting out those unwilling to pay the fees, and decreases the quality of care because referrals become based on profit, not quality (OIG, 2002; Rodwin, 1992). Proponents of referral payments have argued that the practice does not affect their recommendations of whom to refer to, and payers of kickbacks argue that without the inducement they would never get the referrals they need because the public does not understand the value of their services. Federal anti-kickback laws prohibit payment or acceptance of "anything of value" for referrals of Medicare or Medicaid patients. Violations are criminally prosecuted as felonies (SS Act 42 U.S.C. 1320a–7b).

To avoid the kickback laws, providers are sometimes offered limited partnerships with the other providers. Self-referral is more subtle than receiving a direct kickback for a referral (Rodwin, 1992). Federal Stark Laws (SS Act 42 U.S.C. 1395nn) prohibit self-referral, eliminating profits derived from referral to companies in which the provider has a financial interest. Stark Amendment I prohibits physicians from referring patients to laboratories in which they or a family member has any financial interests. Stark II extends the prohibition to any designated health service. Medicare law also prohibits physicians from referring Medicare patients to any health care entity with which the physician or a member of the physician's family has a financial relationship (CMS, 2002). Many studies have documented the fact that physician ownership affects referrals (Hemenway et al., 1990; Hillman, 1987; Rodwin, 1992). The Ethics Committee of the American Psychiatric Association published an opinion in 2001 that stated that self-referral to a day hospital owned and managed by a psychiatrist would not represent a conflict of interest if the referral is clinically appropriate and patients are informed in advance of the psychiatrist's financial interests. The psychiatrist must make other arrangements if the patient objects to going to that facility (ApA, 2001b).

There are a few circumstances in which self-referral may be allowed or tolerated (OIG, 1999). There are some exceptions for rural providers (Kusserow, 1989; Marcinko, 2000) who have no one else to refer to. Practitioners can also refer to members of their own group practice and to large publically held corporations in which the provider has some investment funds (Kusserow; Marcinko; OIG, 1999). Incentives or disincentives for referrals listed in contracts or as part of incentive plans are allowed (Marcinko). Recruitment incentives are technically allowed, but the OIG believed that these are thinly disguised referral inducements (OIG, 2002). Referrals to bona fide employees are also allowed (Marcinko). Unlike violations of the federal kickback laws, violations of self-referral laws are prosecuted civilly.

States also have anti-kickback and self-referral laws. Between 1914 and 1953, 22 states passed laws making fee-splitting illegal (Rodwin, 1992). Now 36 states have laws against giving or receiving payments for referrals (Kusserow, 1989). Idaho's law includes gifts. No states have a ban on physician ownership of a health care entity, but Michigan completely prohibits referrals by physicians to entities in which they have financial interests (Kusserow). Many states* require disclosure of those financial interests to patients prior to referral. That said, enforcement of these laws by the states

---

* Arizona, California, Delaware, Florida, Massachusetts, Minnesota, Nevada, New York, Pennsylvania, Virginia, Washington, and West Virginia (Kusserow, 1989).

has proven to be difficult because most states have no method of monitoring compliance and have to rely on patient complaint to detect violations (Kusserow).

Since payments between providers for the rental of space or equipment are allowed (Marcinko, 2000), they can be used to disguise kickback arrangements to a provider-landlord (OIG, 2002). As a result, some state laws specifically address rental arrangements between providers. This practice is particularly relevant to psychiatry, where it is common for a psychiatrist or psychologist landlord to refer patients to mental health providers who are tenants within the building. The rental agreement may include a "percent of collections" fee, but suspicions arise when that percentage is not clearly used only to defray office expenses (ApA, 2001b; Macbeth et al., 1994). This practice is so common in mental health that the New York State law specifically exempts mental health practices from rental restrictions. Percent-of-collections fees are allowed by Medicare law if there is a bona fide employee relationship with a nonmedical therapist, but not for independent contractors (Macbeth et al.). The Ethics Committee of the ApA (2001b) urged providers not to pay or accept payment for rent, supervision, billing services, or secretarial services on a percent-of-fees basis because this is a form of fee-splitting.

The OIG has issued guidelines for providers wishing to set up rental agreements that include fees based on the collections of tenant-providers. The rent must be fair and within the current market range and cannot be based mainly on patient or service volume. The rental agreement should be in writing, with specific mention of the space used, the schedule for rental, and the exact rent amount. The contact term should be for at least one year and be signed by both parties.

FINANCIAL CONFLICTS OF INTEREST

There are two components to a conflict of interest situation: an obligation or duty on the part of one individual to another, and a conflict of interest that could undermine the fulfillment of the obligation (Rodwin, 1992). It is important to remember that conflicts of interest are not acts themselves but situations that influence acts or clinical decision making in the case of psychiatric providers (Rodwin). Influence based on a power dynamic (from high to low in the context of a hierarchy), like in the clinician-patient relationship, is also referred to as undue influence or exploitation.

Note that undue influence and patient exploitation can occur whether or not harm comes to the patient (Gruenberg, 1995). Studies have shown that physician ownership is extensive and does affect referrals (Hemenway et al., 1990; Hillman, 1987, 1989; Kusserow, 1989; Rodwin), and that conflict of interest situations were common among all groups of mental health providers (Borys & Pope, 1989). Largely because of the effects on cost, conflict of interest situations are being proscribed, described, or limited through various regulatory and legislative means. Insurers, including the government as a payer for Medicare and Medicaid, have become increasingly active in studying the effects of conflicts of interest and minimizing negative financial effects (Rodwin).

Providers themselves have not been as interested in this subject and often do not regard conflict of interest situations as unethical. Borys and Pope (1989), in their national survey, found that male respondents and psychologists were both more likely to see conflict of interest situations as ethical, while psychiatrists and female respondents were more likely to see them as unethical. Four defaced the questionnaire with hostile comments, showing that willingness to explore and mitigate such situations may be difficult. Nevertheless, because of increasing scrutiny by payers and the risk of patient complaint (Borys & Pope), participation in conflict of interest situations has serious drawbacks for all mental health providers that far outweigh potential financial gains. Lifson and Simon (1998) advised psychiatrists to avoid all and every business relationship with clients.

Rodwin (1992) defined two types of conflict of interest situations: conflicts between the personal or financial interests of the provider and the patient, and conflicts that divide the provider's loyalty. Let's examine the financial conflicts between patients and providers first. The most common financial conflict situation is that an increased number of procedures increases the income of the provider, but that situation is obvious to the patient, who can take action against the situation. I will focus instead on conflict situations that are either hidden from the patient or unobvious, like dual relationships.

Dual relationship conflicts refer to situations in which the provider has a relationship with the patient outside the practitioner-client relationship. Sometimes the other relationship explicitly involves the exchange of money, as when the provider sells other products or services to a patient (Lifson & Simon, 1998), buying and selling property to a client, and employing clients. The ethics committee of the American Psychiatric Association (2001b) specifically recommended avoiding these practices because of exploitation of the patient. Borys and Pope (1989) noted that living in a small town or rural area was a predisposing factor in establishing dual relationships with patients, and, in fact, dual relationships may be impossible to avoid in rural areas. The best solution in these cases is full disclosure, so that both the patient and the provider can monitor any negative effect on the treatment.

Sometimes, the involvement of money in a dual relationship is not explicit because no money changes hands. Providers using patients to raise money, perhaps for a book or for advertising, or advising patients to make an investment for which the provider receives a finder's fee, are both considered patient exploitation by the American Psychiatric Association (2001b).

The treatment of wealthy patients creates one financial conflict situation that may not be obvious to either the patient or provider, where an unconscious desire to increase income can lead to unconscious retention or failure to terminate the patient when it is clinically indicated (Gruenberg, 1995). Hitting up wealthy patients for donations to an institution or cause of the provider's is more obviously an exploitation based on a dual relationship, the second being one of donor-recipient.

Leaving the area of dual relationships, conflicts that divide providers' loyalty are also potentially problematic. The tug-of-war may be between two or more patients, as in the case of capitated contracts; between a private practice and the provider's employer, as when the provider transfers patients between the two practices depending on their ability to pay (Pressman, 1979); or between a patient and a third party, usually the insurance company, as when provider compensation causes clinicians to increase or decrease delivery of care (Rodwin, 1992).

Minimizing conflicts of interest should be the goal of all mental health practitioners. This can be accomplished by avoiding all dual relationships and by establishing standards and procedures for your practice regarding fee-splitting, kickbacks, and self-referrals. Evaluate employment and managed care contracts carefully, avoiding those based more heavily on exerting financial influence on the provider. Pass up contracts where more than 20% of your income is at risk (perhaps as a salary withhold), capitation contracts with no per-patient stop-loss insurance, contracts where bonuses and withholds are calculated often and paid as lump sums, contracts where providers are evaluated individually rather than as a group, plans with small numbers of patients, and plans with incentives narrowly targeted to reduce specific services like psychotherapy (Pearson et al., 1998).

Remember that your patients' interests must come first. Don't prescribe, refer, hospitalize, or give unnecessary treatment for your own financial benefit (MMS, 1996). Don't offer financial inducements to patients, such as waivers for co-payments or deductibles. If you have a financial conflict of interest, full disclosure is the best policy (American Nurses Association, 2001; MMS) and is sometimes required by state law.

CHAPTER 10
Gifts

In the previous chapter, we examined monetary incentives and financial conflicts of interest. A patient's gift could be considered an incentive and accepting it a conflict of interest, but patient gifts have attributes that require special attention. In this chapter, I will address some of the problems associated with gifts in psychiatric practice, review various policy options for dealing with gifts, and wind up with suggestions for declining gifts in a therapeutic, kind, and consistent way.

Unlike monetary rewards, there is usually a lack of clarity about both the meaning and value of a gift (Guilder, 1981), since a price tag is not attached. Explanation about the intent may be forthcoming, but often there are unconscious components to the act that are out of the awareness of both the giver and the recipient. Another difference is the apparent lack of freedom of choice (Guilder) in terms of acceptance. Gifts are meant to be accepted, no matter what, and it is hard to decline a gift even when clearly indicated.

There are particular problems with gifts in professional settings. There may be confusion about whether a gift can be considered part of the payment (Zelizer, 1994), a kickback for a referral, or a means of exerting influence. While a provider may never consider a gift, especially a small one, as part of payment, the patient might if they are behind on their bill or seeking a barter arrangement. A gift from a provider to a lawyer for a referral is clearly a kickback (ApA, 2001b). Sharing a patient gift with the referring psychiatrist might be considered fee-splitting (Kusserow, 1989). Gifts from providers to patients can be seen as an attempt at influence (Davies, 1994), which is especially problematic in fiduciary relationships.

So we see that the effect and meaning of gifts is much less clear than with purely monetary transactions.

Gifts occurring in the context of a psychiatric treatment obscure the nature of the professional relationship and create other therapeutic problems. Gifts are never a component of treatment. Claims that acceptance of gifts is therapeutic are usually rationalizations on the part of a provider who misunderstands the nature of psychiatric treatment. Remember that words are the tools of the profession, not actions (Behnke & Hilliard, 1998). If an ethics complaint arises from a gift, the burden is therefore on the treater to show what therapeutic role the gift played. Practitioners will be hardpressed to demonstrate that acceptance of a gift is the only means of forwarding treatment.

With the legal and ethical risks involved, why do some providers still accept gifts? In my experience, there are two main reasons: they believe they deserve the gifts or feel unable to decline the gifts therapeutically and gracefully. While we all, as practitioners, sometimes feel we deserve something extra for our work, there is a fundamental difference between wanting a gift and actually accepting one. Practitioners who accept gifts are acting on their feelings or desires at the expense of the patient. Professionals are at the highest risk for accepting gifts when the case is hard, the pay is low, and when they receive few gifts in their personal life. The solution is to treat the underlying problem in the provider if it is known, or for the provider to obtain supervision or therapy if it is unknown.

Federal Medicare and Medicaid laws specifically prohibit the acceptance and receipt of gifts from patients and referring providers because gifts can be viewed as added remuneration for services or as kickbacks. This is not to say that providers who accept cupcakes from patients and Christmas presents from a referral source will be prosecuted, but that if a complaint arises, gifts of all types will be regarded with suspicion. The relevant statute does not contain the word *gift*, and this confuses the issue. It says, "Whoever knowingly . . . receives any remuneration . . . directly or indirectly, overtly or covertly, in cash or in kind . . . in return for referring an individual . . . or in return for purchasing . . . [any] service . . . for which payment may be made in whole or in part . . . shall be guilty of a felony. . . . (Social Security Act [42 USC 1320a-7b])" State laws are generally more specific, but only Idaho and New Jersey actually use the word *gift* in the relevant statutes. The rest use vague terminology, which may or may not include gifts. Some insurance contracts specifically prohibit accepting gifts from patients, so be sure to check before implementing a policy of acceptance.

The ethical codes of the psychiatric professions are not helpful; none mentions the issue. The *Ethics Primer* of the Amercian Psychiatric Association (2001a) has a chapter on gifts that should be read by all psychiatrists, and several of the published opinions of the Ethics Committee (ApA, 2001b) make specific reference to gifts from patients. It is certainly unethical to encourage patients to give gifts (Polster, 2001). This leads to the question of whether displaying gifts in the office, where other patients might ask about them, a common enough practice, could be construed as encouraging gifts. Or whether a policy sheet stating that only gifts of less than $10 are accepted implies that inexpensive gifts are expected. Polster (2001), writing for the *Ethics Primer*, stated that extravagent gifts, gifts that place any financial burden on the patient, intimate gifts such as lingerie, and money for the physician's personal use are all unethical.

Borys and Pope (1989) studied psychiatric professionals' beliefs and practices regarding gifts. Since opinions about the ethical nature of gifts seem to vary with monetary value, they questioned psychiatrists, psychologists, and social workers about whether it is ethical to accept gifts worth less than $10 from patients. Three percent said it was never ethical, 40% said it was ethical under some conditions, 40% that it was ethical under most conditions, and only 5% felt it was always ethical. Regarding whether they actually accepted such gifts, 14% had never accepted such a gift from a client, 56% had accepted them from a few clients, 11% from some clients, and 17% from most or all clients who offered such a gift. As expected, both beliefs and practices changed when the value of the gift was increased to more that $50. In response to the question of whether it is ethical to accept gifts worth more than $50 from patients, 45% said never and 37% said rarely. Only 1% said it was always ethical. Regarding whether they had actually accepted such gifts, 92% said they had never accepted a gift worth more than $50. Many believe, and I agree, that accepting gifts of high monetary value is always unethical (Behnke & Hilliard, 1998; Lifson & Simon, 1998).

THE GIFT RELATIONSHIP

Gift behaviors follow social rules determined by the nature of the relationship between the two parties. Gifts are not part of professional relationships but of personal relationships. Breaking the gift-giving rules redefines or dissolves the professional relationship. When gift-giving occurs within the context of psychiatric treatment, a social or personal relationship is implied. Acceptance of the gift confirms the formation of a new, nonprofessional relationship. The relative status of the two parties is critical. If the two parties are peers, reciprocity is the rule; both parties give gifts. This is clearly not the situation between the provider and the client. If the giver is of lower status than the recipient, as is the case when a patient gives to a provider or a child gives to an adult, then there is no expectation of reciprocity beyond a gracious thank-you in acknowledgment. Providers who accept gifts unconsciously follow this rule. If the giver is of high status and the recipient of low status, say from a wealthy CEO to a "poor" psychiatrist, there is no expectation of reciprocity, yet the recipient often feels he or she owes the donor and are diminished in some fashion.

There are significant gender issues with gifts. Men rarely give tangible presents to unrelated men, except through their wives. Although not formally studied, men patients rarely give gifts to men providers. That occurrence may indicate a paternal or fraternal transference is at work, like when a boy gives a gift to his father or brother. When a man wants to give to another man, the gift is more likely to occur in the form of advice or a tip. Gifts between men may occur in the context of establishing rank or status, especially regarding wealth. For example, a wealthy patient with narcissistic features may present a gift to his male therapist, not as an act of generosity or thanks, but as a means of expressing his higher status.

By contrast, woman-to-woman gift-giving is widespread. Between women, resisting gift exchange, even within a professional setting, sometimes seems like swimming against the tide. The function of giving between women is usually to establish reciprocity and mitigate power differentials, almost the opposite of men. The grateful woman patient will present a personal gift to a therapist not for payment but to show appreciation and bring them together as equals, however temporarily. The content of women's gifts is different as well: flowers, food, crafts, or personal-care products, items that reflect the nonmonetary and personal quality of the exchange. Equality is achieved because the gift demonstrates skill, taste, or caring, attributes by which women judge and are judged. To deny a gift is to deny that equalizing effect in some respects.

Cross-gender gifts carry the highest risk in professional relationships because of the sexual overtones. Because men do not habitually give, gifts from a man to a women almost always imply sexual or personal interest. The big exception to the sexual-interest rule (although Oedipally this is no exception at all) is a child-mother transference in which a man patient bestows a gift on the woman provider acting out a desire to please. A gift from a man patient to a woman provider is more easily managed in a treatment relationship because the power differential favors the woman provider. However, a gift from a man provider to a woman patient is more readily seen as exploitation because it parallels and amplifies the power differential in the treatment relationship. As a result, the woman patient feels less able to decline such a gift if she feels uncomfortable with the man provider's interest in her.

Because societal norms about women's seduction of men are still changing, it is much harder to characterize the motivation behind a gift from a woman to a man without exploration. While gifts from a woman to a man occasionally imply sexual interest, often they convey maternal interest (the man as child) or personal interest (getting to know you). The power differential between provider and patient remains, so that the woman-to-man gift exchange with higher risk is the one that parallels it, in this case a woman provider giving to a man patient.

There has been little study of boundary violations and gifting patterns within gay and lesbian provider-patient dyads, and the transference issues have not been fully described. The rule is to pay close attention to the power differential between provider and patient and avoid any exchange that parallels it. Explore the act and its meaning in some detail with the patient if it occurs within the context of psychotherapy.

There are situations in which presenting a gift is so compulsary that it may be acceptable within the context of psychiatric treatment, as long as the social norms are followed. Elderly patients give gifts as they approach the end of life as a sign of attachment to those they will leave behind. To decline the gift is to deny mortality and perhaps the attachment as well. End-of-life giving is also a manifestation of the final passage on which all material possessions are left behind. It is a sign of adaptation and acceptance. The nearer the end of life, the more appropriate the giving away of goods and money. Socially isolated elderly persons may have no one on whom to bestow their leave-taking and the final bearer may well be the psychiatric provider. Acceptance of such a gift may not only affirm the relationship, but symbolize the acceptance of loss and death. What the provider accepts, the patient can also accept.

There have been cases where a patient has left some of their estate to their psychiatrist. This kind of gift was addressed in two opinions rendered by the Ethics Committee of the American Psychiatric Association (2001b). The first stated that it is unethical for a psychiatrist to knowingly allow a patient to bequeath them part of their estate. The second opinion on the same topic stated that acceptance is appropriate if the psychiatrist didn't know about it ahead of time, but also advised the psychiatrist-heir to ask questions about the value of the gift compared to the inheritence of other family members and the family's feelings about whether there was any perceived coercion on the part of the psychiatrist. Knowing the power of the therapeutic relationship, I am unsure myself about the propriety of accepting such a gift even if these criteria are met. The opinion did not give a recommendation for disposal if the psychiatrist feels the willed gift is improper. Perhaps such a gift could be re-gifted to a charitable organization or returned to the family if they need or want it.

Children spontaneously give gifts for many reasons. Since acceptance of the gift implies acceptance of the child, all gifts from children below the age of 15 or so should probably be accepted by the provider. Once a child becomes a teenager and has integrated the complications of gift-giving in terms of reciprocity, status, owing, and seduction, as well as the idea that they can be loved in the absence of a gift, then acceptance of gifts becomes less beneficial and perhaps even countertherapeutic. The other caution with gifts from child patients is to make sure the gift is from the child and not from the parent. Gifts that are clearly not made or purchased by the child are really gifts from the parent presented by the child. Acceptance of such gifts can create problems in the child's perception of both himself, ("my gifts aren't good enough" or "I have no gift") and his perception of the provider's connection to him ("He likes my parents better than me," "I should give him something too.")

For women, pregnancy sets into motion powerful gift-giving urges from the nonpregnant woman to the pregnant woman because pregnancy confers status. The pregnant patient, because of the power differential, will almost never expect a gift from a nonpregnant psychiatric provider. However, the woman provider's impulse to give something to a pregnant patient may be very powerful, especially if she has been pregnant herself, and may prevent her from considering that the patient may not be comfortable with the act. When the provider is pregnant, the impulse of women patients to provide a gift is even more powerful because the status differential parallels that of the treatment relationship. If the patient becomes aware of feelings of competition with the therapist's unborn child (now there in the room) for the therapist's love or attention, the woman patient may feel inclined to erase thoughts of competition by providing a gift.

Some feel that pregnant therapists should accept gifts from their patients even when it is their regular policy not to accept gifts. They feel that acceptance of the gift repairs the damage caused by the intrusion of the pregnancy, both in terms of the relationship but also in terms of actual disruption of treatment for maternity leave (Rapoport et al., 1990). I do not agree. Again the work of therapy takes place in verbal discussion and thought, not in action. Accepting a gift does not change the reality that has always been true and should be true, that the therapist's family members will always be foremost in her mind and her patients second. It also does nothing to change the fact that a maternity leave has profound effects on both the treatment and the patient. Gift acceptance smooths over what cannot be changed and may represent some accomodation on the part of the patient, but the goal of treatment is to explore negative feelings and use them to grow, not to avoid them. Feelings of loss, competition, and lack of control can and should be dealt with verbally and with compassion, especially in psychotherapy.

There is a general reluctance on the part of providers to acknowledge and manage the negative feelings of patients regarding pregnancy and maternity leave. Guilt and fear may conspire to cause therapists who ordinarily never accept gifts and who always explore the actions of their patients verbally to just take the gift and drop the subject. As men and women, adult and child, friend and colleague, we have all been "abandoned" temporarily by a pregnant woman preoccupied with the coming child and birth, encumbered physically and psychologically by the huge physical changes. Sometimes the timing is not always the best for us, but this is life and procreation in the human race. Perhaps open discussion brings up our own past disappointments, leading to avoidance of meaningful discussion with patients. Many also fear that discussing the feelings associated with pregnancy will lead back to the whole issue of whether women belong in the workforce in general, or limitations on their commitment to patient care specifically. Yet these are also issues that can and should be discussed without threatening the right of women to practice whatever profession they feel is best.

Patients who are ending treatment represent another group for which the gift relationship is slightly different. One consideration is the finality of the impending termination. The more absolute the ending, the more appropriate gift-giving and acceptance might be. The likelihood of returning may be moderately high with certain patients and specific psychiatric disorders and is not unlikely for most other patients. Although many patients prefer to return to a previous mental health provider who was successful and knew them well, it is often not so easy to go back because of feelings of embarassment, failure, or dependence. If the patient underlined the final visit with a gift, this can make it even more difficult. Unless the patient's return is extraordinarily unlikely, I feel the acceptance of a goodbye gift is risky because it may impede return should the disorder recur or new problems arise.

In psychotherapy, the verbal expression of feelings and thoughts is the primary therapeutic tool. Acting out feelings or thoughts in treatment is discouraged. Consistency then requires that gift exchanges be avoided. The feelings that inspire the gift and that follow the refusal of the gift can be discussed in the session to the benefit of the patient. Patients who understand the nature of the treatment readily, although uncomfortably, go along. For psychopharmacology patients, there is neither the theraputic contract to translate behaviors and feelings into words, nor the forum in which such things can be discussed at length. In such cases, it becomes hard to decline a gift.

Let me say a brief word about gifts given by a mental health provider either to another provider or to a patient. Caution needs to be taken when giving to providers in a position to refer to you. Woody wrote that a "small but relevant gift . . . is appropriate and motivates another professional to make a referral" (1989, p. 82), but this may look like a kickback and probably should be avoided. There is almost no circumstance under which it is totally safe to give a gift to a patient. Patients may be suspicious of the provider's intent because of the power differential in treatment. Perhaps the provider is trying to get them to stay in therapy or accept medication (Sand & Davis, 1999). Perhaps the provider sees them as inferior or in need of charity (Zelizer, 1994). Any suspicion could interfere with the alliance.

Lifson and Simon (1998) stated that it is appropriate for providers to give gifts to adolescents or regressed adults in order to establish an alliance or mark major events like a birthday, as long as the gift is not "extremely valuable" or of an intimate nature. I disagree. Adolescents, in their quest for separation and individuation, are rightly suspicious of any act that smacks of coercion, and gifts are high on the list, especially from parental stand-ins like therapists. The task for regressed adults is verbalization, not acting out, with the provider as an important role model. Gift-giving and acceptance counters that process. Regarding the establishment of an alliance with a difficult or suspicious client, any alliance that has to be supported with a gift is not yet an alliance; more work still needs to be done. Trust must be earned, not purchased, bribed, or bought. As far as a marker for life events, for most patients sincere verbal congratulations and expressions of joy or sadness are all they really need. People crave understanding and connection at major events, not gifts.

The most fundamental component of an effective psychiatric treatment is the maintenance of boundaries. Without boundaries, there is no safety for the patient, no frame to contain the ups and downs of the alliance, and no limit on the actions generated by a transference. Gift behaviors inherently alter the boundaries of the provider-patient relationship by introducing relational components that are not part of the treatment. They must be understood and avoided if at all possible. Policies are the guides that help providers guage and manage their countertransferential impulses that arise during treatment.

I believe it is useful to think of gift-giving as an act that takes the place of an important communication. The goal of psychotherapy is to bring meaning to action, to understand the purpose and consequence of behavior, and to verbalize thoughts where communication or purpose is unconscious. Once the logic behind the action is made apparent and is consciously conceptualized through language, the patient gains personal freedom and choice in relation to others and the self. Acceptance of a gift can then be seen as nontherapeutic or even antitherapeutic (Behnke & Hilliard, 1998), since the provider's act forestalls exploration and runs counter to the model of self-control, analysis, and thoughtful restraint.

THE NATURE OF THE GIFT

Gifts of cut flowers have some unique properties. If homegrown by the patient, flowers are hard to decline even if your policy is not to accept gifts. Flowers are transient so they do not stick around to prompt you into thinking about their meaning or the patient, but they are highly visible to other patients who may see and ask about them. For allergic providers, the presentation of flowers is an unintended curse, with the subsequent difficulties of getting rid of them as soon as possible and fielding questions from the patient about how they liked them. Plants, flowering and otherwise, are in some ways more difficult than cut flowers because patients often hope you will keep and grow them in the office. How well you care for your plants can carry a lot of meaning for the patients you care for. Don't keep plants around if you are likely to kill them. It sends the wrong message.

Food gifts that are homemade or homegrown are also productions of the patient and should be treated with appropriate respect. Store-bought food gifts can be treated like other store-bought gifts, unless there are issues related to eating or weight. Food gifts from difficult or scary patients often elicit from the provider fears of being poisoned. This isn't a bad thing, as long as the provider realizes the cause and does not convey it to the patient. When the "poisoned" food gift can't be declined, it is often transferred to staff, friends, or colleagues who don't have the same reaction and will happily eat it. This still leaves the problem of fielding questions from the patient about how the provider liked it.

I have mentioned that intimate gifts are not acceptable (Behnke & Hilliard, 1998; Lifson & Simon, 1998), but what exactly are they and why are they so unacceptable? Jewelry and clothing are examples of intimate gifts because they are worn on the person, sized to the person, and usually only given by family members and close friends. As a result, acceptance of such a gift within the context of psychiatric treatment establishes the existence of an intimate relationship in addition to, or as a substitute for, the professional relationship. Whenever a patient offers such a gift, the ideas that led the patient to believe that this would be acceptable need to be carefully explored. Was there something the provider said or did that led to this conclusion, or is the patient confused in general about the nature of the treatment relationship?

Charitable gifts from patients for a foundation or institution the provider has established or supports have been addressed in published opinions of the Ethics Committee of the American Psychiatric Association (2001b) and the *Ethics Primer* (ApA, 2001a). The opinions stated that solicitation of donations is an exploitation of the provider-patient relationship and that donations offered by patients cannot be accepted because they are not therapeutic. In addition, psychiatrists may not give the names of any current or former patients to charitable foundations as potential donors.

The *Ethics Primer* of the American Psychiatric Association does not go so far. Polster (2001) felt that such donations are okay as long as they don't change the way the psychiatrist treats the patient. If the donation is large, he felt that it should be publically acknowledged. In my opinion, the acceptance of such donations always changes the nature of the provider-patient relationship because it adds a second relationship. If the patient feels the need to donate to an institution, there is no reason why it needs to be done during the treatment or through the treating provider.

I divide art and handmade gifts into two groups: those with low economic value, commonly called crafts, and those of high economic value, commonly called art. There are three problems unique to such gifts. One is that the value of such gifts varies by taste. What the patient regards as beautiful may not be what the provider recipient thinks of as beautiful. Questions like, "Do you like it?" and, "Where did you hang it?" lead to obvious difficulties when it comes to art and crafts. The second problem is that the monetary value of works by professional artisans or artists may grow considerably over time. What starts as an inexpensive gift may become a valuable collector's piece. Finally, like all homemade gifts, art and crafts are more difficult to decline without offending the patient (Kudirka, 1977).

I also want to say something about "good" gifts versus "bad" gifts. Good gifts are based on an understanding of the needs and desires of the other (Guilder, 1981). As a result, they elicit a positive response and are hard to decline. An observant patient, especially one who has been in treatment for a long time, may intuit such a gift. After declining, careful examination of the unmet need or desire which the patient perceived correctly can be explored by the provider in private.

Bad gifts are off the mark in terms of what the recipient needs or wants. They are offensive because they communicate a lack of understanding or connection to the recipient. Exploration may reveal what led the patient to such a conclusion and to whether such mistakes are happening in relationships outside the treatment. Another type of "bad" gift is one that establishes a debt the recipient has to repay in some way (Guilder, 1981). Gifts of high monetary value often have this effect, especially when unsolicited or unexpected. "Bad" gifts may force or mistake the nature of a relationship (Zelizer, 1994), such as when a man patient presents a woman therapist with flowers and chocolate. Such gifts are almost always offensive or annoying, and must be declined to preserve the recipient's

integrity. Finally, good gifts maintain the relative rank of the people involved (Backhouse, 2004; Zelizer). The gift of a handmade pot from a
child to a psychologist maintains both persons' ranks. A "graduation" gift
of an ice cream for a child leaving treatment maintains relative rank. A
gift of money from a child to a psychologist does not maintain rank. The
gift of a book on therapy from a patient to a therapist also does not maintain rank.

OPTIONS FOR GIFT POLICIES

It is best to establish policy against acceptance of gifts, unless you are a
geriatrician or child practitioner. A no-gift policy is the most therapeutic
because it maintains the boundaries of the treatment relationship, allows
no distortion in the quality of the alliance, and requires psychotherapeutic exploration in the act of declining. Regardless of your own views, there
should be a formal gift policy in place to avoid inconsistencies, make it
easy on patients and other members of the practice, and avert misinter-
pretation by colleagues and third-party payers. If a provider plans to accept some gifts under certain circumstances, conditions of acceptance
obviously can't be mentioned in policy sheets without sounding as if there
is an expectation for gifts. Before you write a policy, be sure to note any
prohibition against acceptance of gifts in your state laws and insurance
contracts.

There are various ways to implement a policy of no acceptance of
gifts. One is openly stating this in the preliminary information given to
new patients or on signs in the office. The policy can be reinforced
through additional reminders at high-risk times, such as during holidays,
when the provider is pregnant, or when a staff member is out ill. For example, a sign in the waiting area may state: "We are grateful for all wishes
of holiday cheer, but no gifts of any kind can be accepted." A letter to patients about a staff member's maternity leave could specifically address
the gift situation: "Cards and messages are appreciated and will be conveyed to Dr. X, but please do not send gifts. They will be respectfully returned. Thanks."

Unannounced no-gift policies are useful for psychotherapy practices
where transference, insight, and exploration of interpersonal relationships
issues are critical to success. They are good for experienced therapists who
can handle awkward situations to good effect with patients, thus modeling

how to handle embarrassing situations while preserving and deepening the relationship. The beauty of an unannounced policy is that it allows patients to be themselves and make mistakes. Each situation can be discussed at length. Unannounced no-gift policies are harder for inexperienced therapists to manage. Therapists who are new to practice may start with an announced policy and change to an unannounced one a few years later. A supervisor can also help an inexperienced practitioner manage a no-gift policy well, even from the start.

For those who wish to accept gifts under certain circumstances, the risks of acceptance can be assessed on a spectrum, with high-risk gift situations at one end and low-risk situations at the other. High-risk gifts are given cross-gender, are worth more than $50, have high symbolic value or sexual connotations, and have a high personal value to either the patient or the provider. Gift acceptance is also higher risk if the patient is new, in the throws of a transference, or if the patient is a compulsive gift-giver. Lower-risk gift situations are those where the participants are both the same gender, the gift has low economic value, and the gift is practical with low symbolic value. Gifts from children, elderly, or terminating patients are generally of lower risk.

DECLINING GIFTS THERAPEUTICALLY

In psychopharmacological or consultation practices where meetings with the patient are infrequent and short, the use of signs and policy sheets to discourage gift-giving is useful and beneficial. They are also useful for practitioners of psychotherapy who don't want to get into involved discussions about gift-giving and who do not do transference work. Despite your best efforts to be clear in your policies, there will always be some patients who still attempt to give a gift. If a gift occurs, acknowledge the kindness of the giver and refer to the policy or signs to see if the patient had indeed missed the information. "You must not have noticed our signs . . ." or "I'm sorry if you were not aware that. . . ." Emphasize the need not to make exceptions. Most patients understand and agree with the concept of treating everyone equally. You may also mention applicable state laws or insurance rules. Acknowledge the diffculty of the situation you are both in: "I know this is awkward, but I really can't accept this gift"; "It may seem embarrassing to have me decline this, but I realize you didn't know the policy."

If time allows, you may explore further by asking what the gift is or why the patient wanted to bring a gift. If the patient is truly upset about it, which is rare, offer to make another appointment to talk about it or send a note home to the patient expressing your apologies for declining. If the patient sees a therapist, call them to see if they can intercede on your behalf. After the discussion, make sure the patient leaves with the gift and doesn't give it to office staff. Make sure your staff is totally on board with the gift policy. Some staff members may feel that because their relationship to the patient is different, they can accept gifts when the provider cannot. They may also feel entitled to accept gifts to the provider because of lower pay.

If the patient is new but stable, simply but kindly state that you don't accept gifts of any kind and why this is the case. This is an opportinuty to discuss the nature of psychiatric treatment and how the therapeutic relationship is different from other relationships. For example, a practioner might say in response to a gift, "What a kind thought this is. But I have to tell you that I cannot accept it and why." Some practitioners focus on the boundary issues, others on the need to explore or analyze acts, others on the distinction between feeling and acting, and some may mention all three. After presenting your case, if the patient seems confused (or even if they don't) acknowledge that while declining the gift may seem crazy now, later in therapy, when they have more experience, it will make more sense to them.

For new patients who are unstable or at high risk for quitting, thank them for the gift and save it for the first session when discussion of it seems tolerable. Have the gift in view when the patient comes in so they know it will be a topic in the day's discussion. Talk about your hesitancy to discuss it, knowing their feelings might be hurt, but explain the policy and any other issues related to it. Acknowledge that while this may seem insulting now, as they become familiar with therapy, declining the gift will seem more in keeping with the nature of the treatment. If the patient seems to have survived the discussion and understands it, give the gift back. If the patient's ability to withstand taking the gift back is unclear, ask, "How would you feel about taking the gift home today?" If they can't, save it for another session, again keeping it in view for each session. I rarely have had to keep a gift in view for as long as a month before the patient was comfortable taking it home. If the patient has given something that cannot be saved, such as fresh produce or flowers, this tactic can't be used.

Acceptance of transient gifts are lower risk and sometimes you just have to let it go. However, later in the therapy process the gift might come up again and you can say, "Remember when you brought me those flowers in the second session?"

For experienced new patients or patients who are fully engaged in the therapy process when the gift is presented, explain the policy and begin the analyzation process. Since gifts are an important component of all relationships, interpretation (Gruenberg, 1995) of the giving act is crucial for forwarding the treatment. Discuss the elements of the gift in some detail, the type of gift, its meaning, and what it says about the nature of the provider-patient relationship. Gifts are a useful segue into discussions about the nature of transference and how it can be used in therapy to make the patient better. Return gifts with thanks and appreciation, acknowledge the awkwardness of the situation, and always remember the gift, the giver, and the intent, since that is the purpose of the gift anyway.

PART III

MANAGING MONEY
WITH PATIENTS

CHAPTER 11

Patients and Insurance

We reviewed provider rights and responsibilities regarding insurance payment in Chapter 4. Now let's review patient rights and responsibilities regarding health insurance.

PATIENT RIGHTS CONCERNING COST
AND PAYMENT

Whether access to psychiatric treatment is a right is still in dispute, and I will not review the debate here. At this time, access to treatment is determined by insurance and income level. In rural areas, it may also be determined by the availability of skilled providers.

To Understand the Potential Cost
of Treatment

Upon accessing psychiatric treatment, it is the right of all psychiatric patients to hear about the potential cost of treatment as part of the informed consent process. This usually involves educating the patient about the nature of the disorder as well as the possible outcomes with and without treatment. All effective treatments for the disorder in question should be mentioned, including psychotherapy (long-term or short-term), medication, a combination of treatment modalities, and methods for self-help. The relative costs of each treatment should be discussed the same way with each patient, regardless of insurance coverage and apparent ability to pay.

To Understand What Insurance Will and
Will Not Pay For

The information about insurance coverage should be clear and accessible to patients. The amount of the yearly deductible, any yearly maximum on visits or by dollar amount should be stated clearly, along with the percentage of the fee paid for the service. Most insurance companies are fairly accurate, if not totally clear, on the above cost parameters. Limitations on coverage by diagnosis (such as the V-codes, the relational, behavioral, or phase of life problems listed in *DSM-IV* whose codes begin with a V instead of a number) or whether coverage is unlimited for certain biological conditions (because of a state parity law) are very infrequently mentioned. Limitations by service type are not usually mentioned, like when couples' therapy is not covered or under what conditions psychological testing is covered.

To Receive Clear and Timely Bills
and Statements

Patients have a right to receive clear and timely bills from both their insurance companies and from psychiatric providers. Most insurance companies now provide EOBs (explanations of benefits), which clearly show the dates of service, the provider's name, the charged fee, and any reductions due to discounts or deductibles. Most still do not describe the type of service or procedure, perhaps for confidentiality reasons. The patient's portion is also clearly shown. A few insurance companies still do not provide good statements and patients may turn to the provider for an explanation or call the insurance company directly.

Providers need to take the same care with their own bills. Patient bills should clearly show the dates of service, the kind of service provided, the fee charged, and any balance due from the patient. Patient bills should be sent on time, either right after the service if no insurance is used, or as soon as possible after payment by the insurance company is received. This keeps patients current and attentive to their accounts and allows them to manage their budgets efficiently.

To Know When and Why Services Are Denied

Patients have a right to know when and why service payment is denied by managed care or an insurance company. Remember that psychiatric services are never actually denied, only payment for services. Patients can continue to receive and providers can continue to give psychiatric services even though payment is denied. Confusing a denial for payment with a denial of service needlessly heightens the emotionality of denials, and that emotion may cloud the ability of both patients and providers to proceed with either an appeal or an alternative payment plan.

Historically, denials of payment by managed care companies are usually not communicated directly to the patient, unlike denials of payment on explanations of benefits for deductibles or for the yearly maximum being reached. Instead, the authorization denial is usually sent to the provider alone. Not only does this exclude the patient from the process, it poses the provider as the bearer of bad news when the denial is conveyed to the patient. The provider seems both complicit and responsible when this occurs. Complicating the situation, the exact reasons for denial are often not given to the provider, making it harder to pursue corrective action. The provider usually has to call to obtain the specifics. Managed care companies are reluctant to put the reasons for denial in writing, although practitioners who intend to appeal should ask that they do so.

It is unclear why this cumbersome process has come about. It would be easier if denials of authorization were complete, detailed, and sent to both providers and patients simultaneously. Many practitioners believe that managed care companies make the process difficult in order to cut down on costs, hoping that neither party will take the time or effort to pursue an appeal. Or it may be that managed care companies are fearful of liability when the details of denial are clear and in writing. Whatever the reason, if the case is legitimate and the treatment typical and indicated for the patient, denials of authorization are most often overturned on appeal when the appeal process is correctly followed. As a result, managed care companies find denials costly and are less likely to deny services when documentation is adequate. That said, it is still better for the patient to know when authorization for payment has been denied.

To Appeal Denials

Since patients often have to participate in the appeals process and since their records are exposed in more detail, the appeals process should be made clear, along with the patient's responsibility for payment until the appeal is adjudicated.

PATIENT PAYMENT RESPONSIBILITIES

While patients have many rights concerning payment for psychiatric treatment, they also have several important responsibilities, which are listed below.

To Pay What They Owe on Time

Patients are responsible for paying what they owe the provider on time. Fulfillment of this responsibility implies several other responsibilities. One is to anticipate and communicate any potential payment problems to the provider in advance. This means letting psychiatric providers know when they are getting behind on their bills or if the cost of treatment is too high. It is also the patient's responsibility to pay the insurance premium and communicate any loss of coverage or potential loss of coverage to the provider so plans can be made to continue the treatment.

To Research Their Insurance Coverage

Patients pay for their insurance coverage and are responsible for knowing the benefits they pay for. They should read the benefits package for outpatient mental health coverage. When the extent of coverage is unclear, it is the patient's responsibility to ask the insurance company questions about coverage and the exact portion of the costs that will be borne by them. Patients should research the choices in the plans made available to them by their employer and report any problems with their choice to their employer so changes can be made or problems corrected.

Common types of problems patients report to their benefits officer include lack of clarity in the extent of mental health benefits, paperwork or payment problems, and an inaccurate or too-limited provider list, if there is an in-network panel for psychiatric services. Insurance companies often get behind on their provider lists. They do not drop providers who are not taking new patients and do not make notations about providers who have limitations on practice, for example those who don't see children or adolescents. Many providers do not have evening hours or have their evening hours full. Some conditions, like many of the sexual disorders, are treated only by specialists, and it is not uncommon for no one on the panel to treat such a condition. If the patient obtains their insurance through a family member who does not live close by, it is possible that there is no provider available close to the patient's home or work. Often in-network provider panels are not as diverse as they appear. Women psychiatrists, psychiatrists who can do therapy and medications for patients with personality disorders or complicated medical problems, African American providers, providers who speak Spanish, and sometimes child psychiatrists are all in short supply in many areas.

Confidentiality is sometimes a problem when the in-network mental health panel is limited. Patients who are well known in their community may need to go outside their local area. Employees of the main medical institution or the main psychiatric provider group in a network have to be seen outside their place of employment in order to maintain confidentiality. Most managed care and insurance companies will make accommodations for problems due to the limitations of their in-network panel, but unless they are made aware of the problems by the patient, there is little they can do.

Patients can report insurance problems directly to their employer's benefits office or to their insurer directly. Serious problems that are unresolved can be reported to the state insurance commission.

To Manage Their Money Responsibly

It is the patient's responsibility to manage his money well, and providers should respect their patients' choices. Patients have other financial obligations that must be met before psychiatric treatment such as rent or mortgage, utilities, and costs of transportation. All patients should have some savings for emergencies and car repairs. They must buy food, clothing, and health insurance. They must pay off their other debts. All of these bills legitimately compete with psychiatric treatment in the budget.

Let me say something about patient payments for entertainment and vacation, because providers often feel upset when they learn that their patient is regularly paying his cable bill while paying his therapy bill late. A certain amount of entertainment and leisure is needed for stress management and a healthy social life. To a limited extent, fulfillment of some of the entertainment desires of their children is also essential for patients who are parents.

That said, every provider and patient needs to clarify in their own mind the line between what is really necessary and what is simply desired when items in a limited budget compete with paying for psychiatric care. Choices to forgo treatment to pay for better vacations, private school, college education, a nicer car, or a better home are simply that—choices. Remember that patients have important connections to other people in their lives who may make demands on their money: parents, children, spouses, and ex-spouses, as well as other needy relatives. When the maintenance of those connections is more important than the treatment or treatment relationship, paying for treatment may fall to the bottom of the list in terms of financial obligations.

To summarize, both patients and providers should be aware of the patient's rights and responsibilities in terms of payment for treatment. Providers must do their best to protect their patients' financial rights. Patients must do their part in carrying out their responsibilities.

PATIENT INSURANCE RESPONSIBILITIES

It is the patient's responsibility to understand what managed care is and how it applies to him and his treatment. As mentioned above, this usually requires some discussion with the provider. Probably the most important points to hit upon are the limitations to coverage if the treatment is not authorized and the patient's responsibility to pay for uncovered services. It is also important to discuss the reduction in confidentiality that goes with managed care. For some patients, it is critical to know that not only their diagnosis will be released but often specific behaviors related to the diagnosis.

The patient also has some responsibility in facilitating payment when there are problems, just as with any other insurance problem. This may be as simple as a phone call to the managed care company or it may mean having to visit the benefits office at their place of employment to fix a serious roadblock. The latter may mean discussing problems with personnel at work, which often doesn't feel too good to patients, although in my experience, benefits personnel are quite sensitive and only require or record information that is absolutely essential to fixing the problem.

PATIENT CHOICE OF INSURANCE PLANS

Whether a patient even has a choice in health insurance plans depends largely on the size of the company that employs them; smaller companies give fewer choices (or no choice at all) and larger companies give more choices. Job status or rank also influence the degree of choice. Part-time and full-time workers in high-turnover jobs (like retail and food service) may not be eligible for insurance at all. Professional and management staff are usually given more or better choices in plans than other workers.

Patients who have choices usually can change plans once a year during the open-enrollment period. Once that choice is made, the patient has to stick with it until the next enrollment period. To make a good choice, patients have to understand the options in the plans they are offered and do the math to see which one will benefit them the most. Sometimes it is cheaper to get a more restrictive managed care plan and pay out of pocket for a psychiatric provider outside the plan than to enroll in a health plan that has no access restrictions.

Employers frequently change the health plans offered, dropping expensive or problematic plans and adding less expensive or hassle-free plans. They depend heavily on the feedback of employees about the quality of service a plan provides, while also considering the bottom line in terms of the expense.

Patients are often unaware of the limitations in the coverage they chose, especially for mental health services. This is especially true for young or healthy people who never expect to use their coverage and have no experience with it. Education about insurance usually has to be done by the mental health provider, either in the introductory sheets given to the patient or verbally in the first visit when discussing the patient's insurance information.

HOW INSURANCE OPTIONS INFLUENCE
PATIENT CHOICE

Until patients start using medical or psychiatric services and gain experience, they generally pick the least expensive plan or the one most of their friends or co-workers choose. In this way, the cost of premiums to workers influences their choice of plan. Deductibles also play an influential role in patient choice. High-deductible plans ($1,000 and up) are less expensive to purchase because when patients are responsible for the first $1,000 or more of outpatient services, they will limit spurious or nonserious use. For patients who do not have $1,000 in the bank or a medical savings account, high-deductible plans may deter access to outpatient psychiatric services. Most deductibles are in the $200 to $250 range, large enough to prevent casual use but small enough to allow easy access for anyone who believes they may need services.

Yearly maximums on psychiatric-service use limit the costs of insurance companies. They may cause patients to drop treatment when the maximum is reached because they don't want to pay that much out of their own pocket. There are no limits on the use of outpatient medical services, leading many to charge that the use of yearly maximums for psychiatric services alone discriminates against people with psychiatric disorders. Many states are passing parity laws to limit insurance companies' ability to discourage use of psychiatric services through yearly maximums.

Co-payments also influence patients. The lower the co-payment, the easier it is for patients to pay for and stay in treatment. If the co-payment is too low, patients may present for problems in living rather than waiting for more serious symptoms to emerge. There is also little financial incentive to leave treatment if the patient is dependent by nature or has an undeveloped social life. While psychotherapy can be extraordinarily effective for many psychiatric problems, it is also highly gratifying. The cost should be significant enough that patients have an incentive to end treatment when they are finished. My own opinion is that co-payments should be means-tested in some way, higher for higher-income patients and lower for lower-income patients.

THE UNDERINSURED

What is underinsurance? There are many ways a patient can have insurance but still be "underinsured." If a health insurance plan's yearly maximum for psychiatric treatment is low (let's say less than 10 visits or less than $500 each year), access to treatment for patient subscribers is essentially nil. If the provider list is very limited, with either no women psychiatrists, no foreign-language speakers, or no providers at all in a rural area, again access is essentially denied to some subscribers. Plans that restrict referrals to psychiatric providers, or provide such high incentives for primary care physicians to treat rather than refer, also restrict access to psychiatric treatment.

High out-of-pocket costs for psychiatric services restrict access to care even when health insurance coverage is present. Fifty-percent co-payments are often too high for patients of lower incomes, especially if the treatment requires weekly psychotherapy meetings. If several family members are in treatment simultaneously, as may be the case with a child victim of sexual abuse, or when a family member is diagnosed with a serious psychiatric illness like Alzheimer's or schizophrenia for which the other members will need support in order to care for her, fifty-percent co-payments can really add up. We can see that even among patients with health insurance, coverage for psychiatric services may be inadequate.

Potential solutions often involve looking for an alternative health plan. For example, can the patient obtain better coverage through a spouse's plan? Can the patient change their insurance plan during the period of open enrollment at work? Are they eligible for a medical savings plan either through their state or through work? Can or should they change jobs to improve their insurance benefits? Unfortunately, inadequate coverage is often part of a larger problem, like a low-income or low-educational background. Often that problem will need to be improved before the patient can obtain better coverage.

WHEN INSURANCE CHANGES DURING TREATMENT

Certain logistical actions are necessary whenever a patient changes insurance. Make sure patients understand that they need to let you know if and when they believe their insurance coverage will change. You will need to see the new insurance card for the new information. Patients will have to check on any new parameters for deductibles, co-payments, and yearly maximums for psychiatric services.

When patients initiate a change in plan by switching at work, usually they are doing so to improve their coverage. This kind of change of insurance is less of a problem because it is not a surprise to the patient. However, when an employer initiates a change of insurance by dropping the patient's old plan from the options, it often comes as a surprise to the patient. The new options may not be as beneficial for the patient as the old option was, although sometimes they are better. Sometimes a parent or a spouse initiates a change of insurance. They may or may not consult with the patient family member beforehand, depending on whether they wish the decision to be a joint one or not. Occasionally, a patient will initiate an insurance change when they want to end treatment but are afraid to say so. Insurance change is a polite but concrete tactic.

The most typical serious problem caused by a change in insurance coverage is when the current psychiatric provider is not on the in-plan list of the new HMO. Note that this problem is prevented when the provider does not have *any* contracts with HMOs or is on *every* HMO panel in the area. In other words, providers who contract with one or two HMOs in an area are at higher risk. What are the options if this occurs? If the provider has many patients undergoing the same change, the new plan is a reasonable one likely to stay in the area, and the fees are acceptable, the provider may try to become an in-plan provider.

Another option is to transition the patient to a new in-plan provider. Have the patient obtain the provider list and review it together to see if there is someone you can in good faith recommend. The patient should also find out about any transitional period allowed for a changeover. Most plans will allow an out-of-plan provider to continue to treat the patient for a short number of visits to effect a transition to the new provider. With the patient's permission, contact the new provider and at a predetermined date terminate with the patient.

Sometimes a patient will want to continue with their current provider as a self-pay client rather than transitioning to someone within the plan. If this is the case, discuss the potential costs openly. The out-of-pocket costs of treatment may not be high for some patients, like those on quarterly medication visits, monthly meetings, or patients in the process of finishing up treatment. Some patients have the income and means to afford more costly treatments, especially if their health insurance premium is lower. If the patient's employer changes insurance policies often, it may not be practical for the patient to change providers, since they are likely to have to change again the following year.

Some patients should not be or cannot be transitioned to a new provider. Patients in the middle of a serious transference crisis in psychotherapy, patients who have had problems sustaining psychiatric treatment in the past, and patients in the middle of a complicated medication trial should probably not be transitioned until they are stabilized. Again, the costs must be discussed. If the patient requires it and the provider is willing and able to see the patient at a reduced fee, that is one option (see Chapter 13).

Another option is to obtain a single-case agreement with the new insurance company. If it would be potentially harmful to change providers or if there is no one suitable on the new plan, health insurance plans will often be willing to set up a temporary contract with the current provider (at the provider's usual fee) for services of a certain duration in order to minimize their liability should the patient not do well with a new provider. Remember that they do not want unstable or seriously ill patients transitioning haphazardly because they will cost money. It is also their responsibility to provide services. If they don't currently have a signed provider who can treat the patient, they are quite willing to enlist a provider by single-case agreement to fill the void. Single-case agreements are also common when there are special diagnostic, language, or confidentiality issues or when a new provider would have a hard time integrating all the medical and psychiatric data.

Single-case agreements usually are not full contracts but simple documents outlining the fees to be paid and the duration of the contract. Usually a date for review of the case is set in advance.

The other big problem with insurance changes is a switch to managed care from a non-managed care plan. For patients, this is a major change in terms of paperwork and hassle factor, even if they do like the lower premiums and co-payments. The potential for limitations or denial of services does not usually enter the patient's mind until it happens, and the limitations on confidentiality caused by the need for periodic review are also not obvious to most patients.

With any change of insurance there may be new limitations: a higher deductible, a lower or higher yearly maximum, or a change in co-payments. Discuss the costs with the patient as they occur. The patient can then decide what is best for them to do.

CHAPTER 12

Talking Money with Patients

While it is hard enough to face accounting, payroll duties, taxes and budgets, none of these is as tricky as talking to patients about money. Financial talk includes not only insurance issues, which most clinicians quickly dispatch, but fees, billing and sometimes the patient's financial situation if affordability of treatment becomes an issue. The difficulty lies in keeping money issues openly on the table without giving the impression that payment is all the provider cares about. This chapter provides suggestions about inoffensive openings to financial topics during the most common phases in treatment when money issues should be discussed.

THE FIRST PHONE CONTACT

Affordability of treatment is an issue even before the patient makes the first contact with a psychiatric provider because it determines access to the mental health system. Depending on how they handle money in their private lives, patients fall into two camps: those who manage their money and those who don't. People who manage money well in their private lives call clinicians covered by their plan, apply to clinics where they know they can get a sliding fee if it is necessary, or ask about fees on the phone. People who do not manage their money will simply book an appointment with the best provider they can get and hope it will work out. The evaluating clinician finds herself sitting opposite an upset and symptomatic patient who either can not afford to pay for treatment or whose insurance plan mandates that she see another provider. The patient is dismayed to find she has to "start all over" with another provider. Avoiding this situation should be the first goal of treatment. This means the topic of affordability has to be addressed in the first phone contact.

Questions the Patient Asks

Most patients begin their call by simply asking for an appointment or describing what they are seeking help with. The issue of payment, either with or without insurance, arises later on or not at all. More and more patients, however, begin the phone call with a question about whether the provider "accepts" their insurance. What they mean is: will their insurance pay for the services of the provider? The peculiar phrasing is a holdover from times long past when providers chose if they would accept insurance payments and from which insurance companies. Now the insurance companies choose who they will reimburse and for what services, not providers, but the public is still unaware of the switch.

If they deal with insurance at all, most psychiatric providers accept insurance payment from any company who will pay them. The huge number of insurance plans makes the patient question "What insurances do you take?" nearly impossible to answer. The provider is forced to turn the question around and ask the patient, "What insurance do you have?" in order to expedite the inquiry. Patients who have made more than one call quickly learn to lead with the name of their insurance plan: "Do you take X HMO?" For members of HMOs or PPOs who want to stay within their plan, answers to questions about insurance may end the first contact abruptly if the provider is not on the panel. Try not to feel offended. It is the patient's responsibility to search out a provider within her plan. A negative response from you allows her to move on and makes things more efficient.

Sometimes a patient will ask about fees over the phone. Be clear about the charges. Patients are usually unaware that the fee for the initial evaluation is different from the fee for an hour therapy visit. I usually state that the initial evaluation visit is the most expensive and quote the fee. Then I tell them the fees for hour visits, half-hour visits, and brief medication visits, since those are the services I provide most often. Offering to mail a fee sheet is also acceptable practice.

Some patients ask if a sliding-scale fee is available. The provider must be prepared to state their policy in clear but simple terms without determining eligibility on the phone. The details of the policy and the determination of need are best done in person after the initial evaluation is complete. Never guarantee or indicate for certain that a patient might be eligible for a reduced fee. Assessing eligibility and negotiating a fee reduction are complicated processes that are, to some extent, dependent on the intensity of treatment. Since the plan can't be known until the evaluation is complete and the treatment options reviewed with the patient, there is no way to accomplish a determination of eligibility over the phone. If the caller refuses to make an appointment unless they are assured of a fee reduction, my advice is to refer them on. They want a guarantee where none can be given.

Some providers don't like to get into insurance, payment, and fees on the phone, but it is in the best interest of the patient and the future treatment relationship to do so. The initial conversations are important in several respects. They establish that insurance, fees, and costs are acceptable topics of concern and conversation within the treatment. They demonstrate the provider's concern about the patient's situation despite their conflicting financial interests. They also show how the business relationship runs parallel to the treatment relationship and that both can and will be dealt with as the treatment proceeds. And they are the first foray into the shared work of solving problems. It is important not to cut these conversations short.

Questions the Provider Asks

The provider should ask every caller about the problem they are seeking treatment for to make sure it is something he or she can and will treat. Try not to book evaluations for patients you have no intention of treating or keeping; this wastes time, money, and resources. Inquiries about the problem may also give an indication about the possible duration and intensity of treatment in case the issue of cost comes up right away. For example, the treatment of obsessive-compulsive disorder is generally more difficult and of longer duration than the treatment of panic disorder. The treatment of borderline personality disorder is generally longer than the treatment of an uncomplicated major depression. It may be better for patients needing longer treatments to go within their plan's network of providers because the cost could be high.

If the patient does not mention insurance, the provider may want to find out what kind of insurance the patient has so there are no unnecessary surprises. The direct approach, asking, "What insurance do you have?" is quick but can sound as if insurance payment is the only consideration. The phrasing of the question also contributes to the public belief that providers control what insurances to accept, not the other way around. I use an indirect approach by asking, "Is insurance an issue?" Almost all patients respond by volunteering their insurance information and are generally relieved the provider brought it up. A few patients reply with a "no" and give some kind of explanation, such as, "I have an indemnity plan," or, "I'll be paying out of pocket."

Occasionally, a patient will answer, "Insurance is not an issue," but then give no explanation at all. This can mean the patient knows the appointment will be covered by insurance and is too anxious to elaborate. Or it can mean the patient thinks she's covered but really isn't sure. Or it may mean that it really doesn't matter because she has a means to pay. This is a bit of an awkward moment. Should the practitioner press on at the risk of seeming mercenary or intrusive, or should the practitioner let it drop and find out more on intake?

Providers who are comfortable with risk or who deal with a population that is generally well off and able to pay out of pocket might feel fine about not inquiring further. If the patient comes in and insurance really is an issue, that is dealt with at the time. Practitioners whose community is of mixed income or who see many insurance-naïve patients may not want to risk having a patient come to the first appointment only to find out they can't or won't continue because of the cost or lack of insurance coverage. This is awkward for both the patient and the provider. If the provider prefers not to be surprised and the caller has stated that insurance is not an issue, the provider can simply ask, "You won't be using insurance?" Patients almost always provide more detail and you'll find out for sure why insurance coverage is not a concern.

It can be disconcerting to realize that a caller has no idea what insurance plan she has. While this seems impossible, it is quite common among young adults, people who have had never used medical services, and people whose spouse handles all the bills and paperwork. Even if a patient knows the name of her insurance, she is often unclear about the type of plan, since most insurance companies offer HMO, PPO, and indemnity products. If the patient doesn't know whether she has an HMO or PPO plan, ask her to look at the card in her wallet. It is also common for people who have never used their insurance to have no idea that an HMO requires that they must see someone on the plan's list.

For patients who are unfamiliar with their insurance plans, their phone call to you is a learning experience. Politely advising them about their options allows them to pursue their next call with more knowledge and they will greatly appreciate it. You are helping them access the treatment they need.

THE INITIAL INTERVIEWS

On first sitting down with the patient, obtain the relevant personal and insurance information so the appointment can be billed. Address any immediate problems, especially if the insurance information reveals that the patient's appointment will not be covered. Most commonly the patient didn't realize they had an HMO and the provider is not on the panel. This difficult situation is usually prevented by telephone screening, but occasionally mistakes are made. If the appointment won't be covered, give the patient the option of continuing and paying out of pocket (in which case they will ask the fee) or ending the appointment. If the patient chooses not to go forward, I do not charge the patient because no service has been provided. Mistakes are made; there's no need for punishment or compensation.

A few other topics require some exploration during the initial interviews. If the insurance is through a different insured, for example an ex-spouse, the provider might ask how that has been working out. When the evaluation is completed, this can be discussed further if the patient indicates there might be a problem. If the insurance is through a parent and the patient is nearing an age when coverage might be terminated, the provider might have to bring up this possibility. Sometimes patients forget their insurance card and no information can be collected. Have the patient bring it next time but be on alert. If the patient does not return, send a letter with the bill but explain that you'd be happy to bill the insurance company if they fill out and sign the enclosed claim form.

Sometimes the first few sessions are not the best times to get into fees, insurance coverage, or payment, especially if the patient is very depressed or suicidal (Canter & Freudenberger, 1990). In this case, obtain only the information needed to submit the claim and address the other issues once the treatment has begun or the patient had been stabilized. If the patient gives permission and there are serious concerns about payment, a family member's help can be elicited.

After the initial evaluation is complete, the treatment plan and recommendations are discussed. If there are insurance, payment, or financial problems that have become apparent, this is the time to discuss the costs of treatment and the options. Financial problems such as gambling, debt, low income, or unemployment should be explored just like any other symptom or problem. Obtain the history and explore its current severity. Find out how the patient has tried to correct the problem and add it to the problem list. Potential insurance problems, like an end to coverage, can also be addressed around the time the treatment plan is discussed.

It is not necessary to resolve every financial, payment, or insurance problem before moving on to treatment, but there has to be an agreement to address and work on the problem as treatment proceeds.

ANTICIPATING FINANCIAL TROUBLE

Managing money in psychiatric practice is highly dependent on the ability of the provider to anticipate problems before they become severe enough to interrupt treatment. The following indicators may signal potential money trouble and should be explored.

College Students

College students who are covered by their parents or by a school plan are often subject to termination at a certain age or if their student status changes. For example, students who reach their 26th birthday while still in college may be terminated from coverage regardless of their dependent status. Students who drop out of school for academic or medical reasons, or who cut down to part-time, may also have their insurance coverage terminated. Ask college-age patients for whom this might happen to talk to their parents about this potential problem rather than talking to the parents directly. This makes the patient a party in the process and greatly aids joint problem solving should insurance coverage end. Children who are not in school but are about to turn either 18 or 21 face the same issue of termination from a parent's plan. The process is no different for them.

Patients at Risk for Unemployment

Losing a job is one of the most serious stresses people face and the potential loss of insurance only compounds the anxiety. The temptation to avoid adding another worry may cause both patients and providers to ignore the obvious health insurance implications. It is the provider's job to deal with unpleasant business, and a forewarned patient is a forearmed patient. Ask patients if they have thought about what will happen with their health insurance if they lose their job. Many already have a contingency plan, such as coverage through a spouse or using COBRA (which allows patient's to continue their health insurance coverage at the group rate for 18 months after ending their job). In some states, health insurance is available through the unemployment office or through state plans for low-income residents. Occasionally, a family will be eligible for Medicaid. Some patients will not have COBRA available to them because their term of employment was too short or their employer too small. Some will simply be unable to afford the premium, since they now have to pay the full premium rather than split it with the employer. Patients who are already unemployed on intake have fewer options because the COBRA application time period may have expired.

Sometimes the risk of being laid off is nonspecific, like when the economy is bad and the patient is in a high-risk job, like middle management or manufacturing. Be alert for any signs of change or problems in employment status.

The Patient Appears to Be Disabled

Occasionally, patients present so ill that they appear to be disabled. Such patients are at risk psychiatrically but may also be at risk for losing their job. Assess their level of functioning at work. Have they been calling in a lot? Have they been completing their work? Has anyone asked any questions or taken them aside? Find out how much sick time they have left and what medical leave options are available. Taking medical leave protects the patient from the loss of health insurance and their job while they are recovering and getting treatment. The extended time off allows time for a more comprehensive assessment of the nature of their illness and the prognosis. For patients whose condition is either permanent or likely to last for more than a year, steps can be taken to apply for Medicare or disability, thus obtaining health insurance that is not tied to work should the patient be unable to return.

The Patient Has a Gambling Problem

Gambling problems can remain hidden for a long time, even in individual therapy. They most commonly are exposed when, during the exploration of other financial problems, the provider directly asks about gambling. Gambling must be treated directly. Refer the patient to GA (Gamblers Anonymous) and institute treatment. Explore the patient's current financial situation and make whatever changes are necessary to allow the patient to continue in treatment.

The Patient Complains of Financial Stress

Financial stress usually comes in one of four forms: high debt, low income, poor money management, or what I call the "high in–high out" problem. The high in–high out problem is when a family has a high combined income due to two wage earners, but expenses are also extraordinarily high because of child care and keeping up appearances. These families have enough money but always feel tired and afraid, aware that slowing down will cause financial problems.

Whether these problems can and will be treated by the provider as part of therapy is really up to the practitioner, since there are other professional sources of help. The Consumer's Union and other nonprofit organizations help patients manage debt. Consultation with a fee-only financial advisor or a bankruptcy lawyer may also be useful. There are many excellent self-help books for patients with high debt and poor money management skills. The important thing is not who helps the patient, but that the problem is identified as serious, in need of correction, and that someone helps the patient pursue it.

HOW PATIENTS BRING UP
MONEY PROBLEMS

While many patients will directly name financial stress as a problem causing anxiety, most will not be this open. Instead, money anxieties will come up indirectly, usually through a comment that they can't afford treatment or a request to decrease the frequency of visits. Whenever a patient wants to decrease the frequency of appointments, I always ask if the cost of sessions is a consideration, freeing them up to answer in the affirmative. Likewise, if a patient is canceling often or paying late, I ask if money is tight at home. This opens up the issue for discussion. Dropping out of treatment is the most indirect and problematic way to communicate financial problems. Again I will ask patients if they have left treatment because of the cost. If they answer yes, then I make an attempt to deal with the financial problem so they return to treatment, either with me or with someone else.

DISCUSSING TREATMENT AFFORDABILITY

Discussions about whether the patient can or cannot afford treatment often get bogged down, confusing, or difficult. Money has value on several levels, and the debate changes subtly from one to the other almost without awareness. The only signal is a vague feeling of discomfort and uncertainty. Successful talk about affordability requires separation of the arguments caused by the distinct values of money. The arguments are first resolved individually and then are brought together into a final understanding.

Three Values of Money

Money has many values, but for our purposes here I am going to address only three: mathematical, purchasing, and symbolic. Mathematical value refers to the numbers involved, that is, the fee for the service and the dollar value printed on the currency. This doesn't change (or shouldn't) and so we refer to it as "fixed." It is also not subjective. Ten dollars is ten dollars.

The purchasing value of money is not fixed. Purchasing value refers to the "worth" of a service or product or the value that money can buy. Unlike the mathematical value of money, judgments about worth *are* subjective, and are subject to change over time depending on supply and demand, fashion and fad, quality and quantity.

Symbolic values of money are those that exist in the realm of the imagination, beliefs, social organization, and culture. Money's connections to power, morality, status, and intelligence are all symbolic. This is not to say that they aren't real, but that they require the participation of belief in order to maintain that value. For example, possessing a nice home in an expensive neighborhood might bring a person respect and admiration because the belief is that the person who earned the money to buy it must be competent or intelligent. However, if the owner is discovered to have inherited the wealth or to have obtained it illicitly, that respect quickly disappears.

The Changing Argument

During a discussion about whether the patient can or cannot afford treatment, patients and providers change from talking about one value of money to another. For example, the patient often begins with the mathematical value, stating that there is not enough money in the budget to cover the cost of treatment. The provider pursues this in an effort to assess the patient's actual financial need. They go over the patient's income and expenses to see how they compare and add up. During this accounting it may be discovered that the patient's car payment is extraordinarily high for his level of income.

Exploration reveals that he has purchased a very expensive car, and if the car payments were "normal" for his income there would be no trouble at all affording the co-payments for his treatment. The therapist thinks to himself, this patient values his car more than his health. In this thought, the therapist is changing the argument from one of mathematics to one of evaluating worth and value, or the purchasing value of money. When he points this out to the patient and opens it up for discussion, the patient feels on the defensive because the debate is no longer one of mathematical fact, but about his behavior or money management.

Let's say the exploration and discussion of affordability continues between them, with some discomfort around the issue of the large car payment versus paying for treatment. The patient's eyes light upon the therapist's medical degree hanging on the wall or the expensively cut suit or mahogany desk. He is filled with awareness that he cannot afford both the car and therapy on his income and strong feelings emerge. He finds himself yelling that all doctors think about is money and angrily motions as if to leave the session. The argument has now changed from the realm of purchasing value to the realm of the symbolic in the very real associations of money to status.

The psychiatrist feels attacked and on the defensive. All he is aware of in the moment is that what had started as a simple exercise to see if the patient could afford treatment progressed to an uncomfortable confrontation about the car and then to an angry accusation about his relative wealth compared to that of the patient. Without careful preparation, this progression will happen all in one session, condensed and intense, a tight knot of interwoven arguments.

Separate the Arguments

The best therapeutic technique is to separate the arguments both intellectually and in time, marking each transition openly for both parties to see. For example, in the case described above, when the psychiatrist notes the high car payment during the mathematical discussion and the patient tells about the car, instead of exploring it further the psychiatrist allows the issue to lie exposed for a time. He relaxes after his comment about the high car payment and listens to what the patient has to say on the subject.

After some time, perhaps even at the next session, he brings up the car issue again, not in the mathematical sense but strictly in the *worth* sense, commenting that this is a completely different line of discussion. He begins by mentioning the car, perhaps by saying that the car must be important to the patient. And he separates any confusion with the previous discussion by commenting that, while the budget shows that the patient cannot afford treatment as it is, the importance and value of the car are another matter altogether. This validates the patient's desire to have a nice car while noting that it also makes the budget tight.

Discussions about nice cars present an easy segue into the symbolic value of money. The therapist can mark the transition by saying something like, "I know this car is important to you, and I also know a lot of people judge others by the car they drive. Cars have a lot of meaning to people." Again, this part of the discussion can be saved for another session or delayed to emphasize the separateness of the symbolic issues. This part of the discussion allows the patient to comment on the psychiatrist's car, issues of status, and, hopefully, to voice any concerns about the status differential between treater and patient, an important transference the resolution of which might be permanently helpful to the patient.

Go Back to Resolve the Affordability Issue

Once the three discussions have occurred, the therapist can return to the original issue. "You know, we looked at your budget and saw that it was tight. We saw that the car payments are high but that the car is important to you. Not only do you like the car, but you feel like it bolsters your self-esteem. Should we be working on your self-esteem more?" At this point, the discussion may or may not return to affording treatment but going forward will now be easier. Any decision on the part of either the therapist (not to reduce the fee) or the patient (to cut back to every other week) becomes a real choice and an agreement between the two based on mutual understanding, even if they don't actually agree. Treatment moves forward.

PARTICIPATORY DECISION MAKING

Participatory decision making refers to the process of including the patient in decisions about treatment. It does not mean relinquishing professional judgment but providing patients with the information they need to make a decision about treatment based on their values and circumstances. This may mean a decision not to get treatment. Participatory decision making in psychiatric treatment usually requires that the provider be upfront about the diagnosis and all the options for treatment, regardless of insurance or ability to pay, including the potential costs. Listen to the patient's explanations of what they want and why they want it. Remember to ask the patient for recommendations or solutions when there is a problem.

For patients, participating in treatment decisions means they have to be upfront about payment and insurance problems, as well as their values and judgments about the worth of treatment and the seriousness of their symptoms.

For any treatment condition, or when negotiating a payment plan or fee reduction, be consistent and follow your policies. Document the patient's participation in the discussion and any problems that were raised, resolved, or left standing. Note the reason for any deviations from your usual practice.

WHEN THE TALK GOES BADLY

Sometimes money discussions go badly because the patient is angry. The anger may be related to their illness, its cost to them, or about health care in general. Sometimes a patient gets angry because the provider won't agree to a fee reduction. Often anger in money discussions is a cover for fear—fear of humiliation, fear of not having enough, fear of being exposed or vulnerable. Addressing the anger or fear may allow the talk to go forward, but if the anger or fear is too great, the patient may quit or drop out.

Sometimes the money talk goes poorly because the patient doesn't participate. Perhaps they don't provide any of their own thoughts, or maybe they agree with the therapist but then don't follow through. Bringing up the lack of participation is sometimes useful. "I feel like you are not really engaged in this subject." If it isn't, it can be dropped as long as the patient continues to pay. When the patient is further moved by the cost, an attempt can be made again to talk things over.

Rarely, a patient will just disappear or drop out after a money discussion. The options are either to pursue or allow the patient to drop out. If you decide to pursue the patient, say that you wondered whether it was because of the money discussion and indicate that, if it was, you think the problem can be worked out. Acknowledge any contribution to the problem. If the patient responds, then treatment moves forward. If the patient does not respond, that's okay. Patients drop out for many reasons and have the right to do so. Treat them as you would any terminating patient. If they have left an unpaid balance, allow some time for cooling off before sending the final bill.

Sometimes a provider will decide not to pursue the patient, either because the patient was too difficult to work with, or the financial disagreement was too fundamental to work out.

WHEN THE TALK GETS STUCK

Sometimes the patient is coming in despite the money issue but the problem isn't getting resolved, even with consistent discussion. Review the case and then your policy sheets to make sure you are following them to the letter. If so, are you following them too rigidly? Are the policies unreasonable, either for this patient or for others? Should they be changed?

If the policies don't seem to be at the root of the problem, are there transference or countertransference problems regarding money? Discuss the case with a supervisor or colleague, paying attention to your feelings, your policies, and any patient feelings you may be missing. Ask the patient for feelings or insights about the situation. Patients often have professional opinions that they keep to themselves for fear of disturbing the traditional balance of power in treatment. Review the specific monetary transferences mentioned in Chapter 15 to see if any apply to the case.

CHAPTER 13

Fee Reductions and Increases

More than a third of private practitioners lower their fees if a client is unable to pay (Faustman, 1982; Tryon, 1983a), but many still find fee reductions difficult to deal with. Why is this practice so challenging? First of all, the act has to do with money, a topic laden with anxiety in its own right. Secondly, it is hard to obtain realistic, useful information about fee discounts in actual practice. While there are a few reports from private practice, collected information about the fee discounts of clinics, institutions, and large groups remain unknown. Professional schools and educators have not really begun to tackle the business end of psychiatric practice so the effect of fee reductions on income is not discussed. Finally, as new practitioners quickly discover, it is a delicate matter to get concrete information about fee-reduction policies from other professionals, even (and sometimes especially) close colleagues.

What can ease the discussion about how and whether to implement a fee-reduction policy? There are many fee-reduction policy options. Understanding the benefits and risks of each one and the impact on practice and patients makes it easier to choose an approach that fits the practice and the philosophy of the owner. The idea that different practices need different policies softens judgmental attitudes about which policies are "good" or "bad." A nonjudgmental approach allows colleagues to discuss their fee-reduction policies and learn from each other. The tests of a good fee-reduction policy are whether the practitioner can explain it clearly, consistently, and without regret to both patients and colleagues, and implement it without undue concession, anxiety, or guilt. The ability to accept commentary and criticism about your policy is important because it facilitates modification of the policy over the years, advancing the practice and increasing satisfaction for the practitioner over time.

THE IMPORTANCE OF
FEE-REDUCTION POLICIES

Ideally, setting up your fee-reduction policy is best done before starting practice but after the general plan and philosophy of the practice have been defined. This is to make sure that the policy fits with the goals and mission of the practitioner. If the main goal of the practitioner is to maximize income, a policy that leads to a high percentage of reduced-fee clients would not be consistent with this goal. If a practitioner is committed to providing service to all socio-economic levels, a strict "no fee reduction" policy would not be consistent with this goal. Failure to make the fee-reduction policy consistent with the goals of the practice may lead to confused implementation, problems explaining the policy to others, or unhappiness with the practice.

Making the fee-reduction policy consistent with the goals of the practice can take some creative thinking. For example, if a practitioner is committed to providing some work at a reduced fee but also does not want to engage in lengthy personal negotiations with patients, a contract with Medicaid can fulfill both goals. Because the fee discount for Medicaid is set by contract ahead of time, there is no individual negotiation with patients.

The main purpose of establishing fee-reduction guidelines is to minimize inconsistencies in the practice, especially over time. Let's consider a common example. Early in his practice (perhaps even in residency), Dr. Green took on patients at reduced fees in order to build his practice. Several years later, he changed to a no-fee-reduction policy because his practice was extremely full and he no longer needed to reduce fees to attract patients. He never made a written fee sheet so he did not generate a written notice when he made the change. Instead, he spoke to the affected patients in person. He privately decided to keep one patient whom he had picked up as a resident at a very reduced fee because he was a good patient and needed chronic treatment. He did not mention the change to him because the change did not affect the patient directly.

Over time, the practice gradually changed to all full-fee patients except for this one patient. One day, an established patient in financial straits asked Dr. Green for a reduced fee, which he denied according to his policy. After that visit, Dr. Green began to feel uncomfortable about the one patient with a very low fee. Did the patient know his exclusive position? Could he hear about it from other patients? If he knew, would he be comfortable with it or would he feel ashamed? Could he bring it up now or is it too late?

A written fee sheet and established fee-reduction guidelines might have forced Dr. Green to consider the implications of the policy change on established patients. Informing all patients of the policy changes by distribution of new information sheets allows mutual and therapeutic discussion of the implications with every patient, relieving the practitioner of exclusive control over the consequences and allowing patients some say in the destiny of their treatment. In this case, failure to notify all patients left one patient in a "special" category of which he was unaware. The effect of that exclusive position on Dr. Green lay dormant until a subsequent patient requested the same fee.

Clear guidelines also allow practitioners to say no comfortably to patients. "I don't reduce the fees for any of my patients because I have never felt comfortable I could be totally fair in the negotiation process." With consistent guidelines, the dialogues you have with patients over fee reductions are repeated over and over. The right way to say things is well learned so there is less avoidance of potential problems. "I looked over the information you gave me and I don't think you qualify for a fee reduction because your current income is too high. Let's think of what else we can do to make treatment easier to afford."

Of course, most practitioners do not start out with written guidelines; instead, they let their fee-reduction system evolve over time. For example, a new practitioner may initially accept a lot of fee-reduction cases but then find it cumbersome and switch to a stricter system. Or an experienced practitioner who initially did not take any reduced-fee cases because she had a lot of contracted fee reductions from HMOs may decide to offer fee reductions after she phases out her HMO contracts. Change is fine, as long as the policies remain clear to both the practitioner and the patients.

Other general principles of fee reduction have to do with timing. Fee negotiation should always be avoided during an emergency. Emergencies give an unfair advantage to the practitioner and neither party is in the proper frame of mind to be objective or reasonable. Simply tell yourself and the patient or patient's family that the fee will be discussed after the emergency is over and that you are sure something can and will be worked out. When the emergency is over, evaluate the situation and discuss the treatment, cost, and fees with the patient and decide what to do.

One must also be careful negotiating fee reductions after bad outcomes, even if the patient qualifies. To an outside observer, a fee reduction in such cases may look like an attempt to influence the patient or an acknowledgement that the treatment was substandard. The other problem is that, after a bad outcome, guilty or anxious feelings may bias your decision. Careful implementation of your guidelines and documentation in the patient's chart are essential at these times.

TYPES OF FEE-REDUCTION SYSTEMS

I describe below three basic types of fee-reduction systems, which I call *loose, tight,* and *combined.* Each has various subtypes.

The Loose Fee-Reduction System

A *loose* fee-reduction policy refers to any system with a great deal of flexibility, either in the criteria for deciding who is eligible or in choosing the exact amount of the fee. Examples include considering a fee reduction whenever a patient asks, basing the new fee only on loose parameters of income, or, looser still, on whether "it seems like they need it." Factors other than financial need may also be considered, such as patient likeability, professional interest, or an important referral source. To avoid being flooded with trivial or pro forma requests for discounts, practitioners with loose systems usually do not mention the availability of fee reductions in the initial interview or written information for new patients.

There are many advantages to the loose fee-reduction system. Because it requires individual negotiation, there is an opportunity to learn about human monetary behaviors and develop a scheme of normal and abnormal financial behavior for an entire patient population. Loose systems also encourage patients to come forward with financial problems, like poverty, gambling, or substance abuse. For psychotherapists, fee-reduction discussions are a goldmine of transference issues, especially those having to do with status. Fee negotiations elicit feedback from patients about the business aspect of your practice that can be useful for making improvements as well as learning about which of your own neurotic conflicts over money may be impeding your success (Schonbar, 1967). The loose fee-reduction system improves case mix by accommodating a wider range of people, including un- or underinsured patients. Fee-reduction policies may increase the volume of patients in a practice because new patients will generally choose the practitioner with the cheapest rates. However, one must also be careful not to appear "too cheap."

What are the disadvantages of the loose fee-reduction system? The most important is that it is easy for the practitioner to manipulate. Fee reductions can be used to reward good patients, punish bad ones, or to keep someone in therapy. There is also the problem of bias, for example, giving more fee reductions to black patients or single mothers "because they need it more." The loose fee-reduction system is also easier for patients to manipulate. With no ceiling or floor and no clear requirements, it is easy for patients to make a case for need that is difficult to disprove. The loose system is also biased toward "askers," usually women and experienced patients.

Application of a loose fee-reduction system may lead others to suspect that you are arbitrary or can't say no. Patients or colleagues may even verbalize these thoughts to you. The solution is not to change your system but understand it well enough that you can discuss these perceptions comfortably in detail. For example, a supervisee, on reviewing a list of your patients and their various fees, may comment that it seems arbitrary. You don't disagree that it may be somewhat arbitrary but go on to discuss how you manage that. The point is that no matter what your system is, if you truly understand it and remain open there is almost no question or criticism you can't deal with gracefully and therapeutically.

The Tight Fee-Reduction System

In contrast to the *loose* system, a *tight* system is one where there are strict controls or limits on the reduction of fees. The most rigorous example is a policy of no fee reductions. Let's take a look at this type of policy before moving on to other examples of tight systems.

Practitioners used to advocate for the no-fee-reduction system based on the belief that fee reductions decreased the efficacy of therapy by undermining its "worth" to the patient or by providing motivation where there really was none. Studies of treatment efficacy do not support this theory (Herron & Sitkowski, 1986). What has not been studied is whether fee reductions increase the duration of therapy or whether fee reductions interfere with expressions of discontent with the treatment enough that compliance or efficacy is affected. Since this philosophy was common years ago, some practitioners today have no-fee-reduction policies simply because they were unable to obtain reduced fees as patients themselves. This represents a countertransferential fee policy that will be difficult to defend in the face of rational challenges by patients or colleagues.

However, there are good reasons for instituting a no-fee-reduction policy. If a practitioner is concerned about fee reductions acting as an incentive to stay in treatment or "be a good patient," then a policy of no fee reductions makes sense and is easy to explain and understand. Another valid reason for allowing no fee reductions is that "the fee is the fee is the fee." The point of this argument is, if the fee can be reduced, what is the real economic value of the service? (The effect of fee reductions on the value of psychiatric services will be discussed later in the chapter.) Another good reason for instituting a no-fee-reduction policy is when the goal of the practitioner is to reach a certain income target within the least hours worked. This is harder to discuss with patients but perhaps not so hard to explain to colleagues.

In order for a no-fee-reduction policy to work well, however, certain conditions must be met. The practice must be able to fill without trouble, and the practitioner must be comfortable with doing no charitable work and at ease with transferring patients who can not afford the full fee. A period of discounted fees may be necessary until the transfer of care takes place in order to avoid exploiting or abandoning a patient who can't afford to pay.

Other examples of tight systems include using strict income guidelines for consideration of fee reductions, using a scale where the fee is based on income, or simply setting one minimum fee. All of these systems have established rules that limit the application of fee reductions.

What are the advantages of a tight fee-reduction system? The tight system is harder for the practitioner to manipulate, and is a useful protection against feelings that drive therapists to give inappropriate fee reductions, such as wanting to be liked by patients (Schonbar, 1967). The tight system is also harder for patients to manipulate because there are clear income guidelines and documentation is required for wages and expenses. This is not to say that tight fee systems can't be manifestations of countertransference (Schonbar). Practitioner conflicts associated with a tight fee system include fears of losing in negotiation with patients and guilt about income differences.

Tight systems also have their disadvantages. The bias risk is now in the system itself rather than in negotiation. Tight systems restrict access, narrowing the case mix of the practice, and may lead to charges of elitism from patients or colleagues. They also allow more avoidance of money issues because there is no need to bring them up. Money problems like gambling or poor financial management are not forced forward and not addressed. This is not to say that practitioners who choose a tight system can't or won't discuss money issues with patients, but without the easy and early segue of asking for a fee reduction, they must be vigilant to pursue any hint of money problems.

The Combined System

A *combined* system has elements of both the loose and tight fee-reduction plans. It may have tight requirements for qualification, for example, no fee reductions for incomes greater than $40,000, but looser parameters regarding the actual charge. The fee reduction may be decided on a case-by-case basis by going over expenses, estimated cost of treatment, and other factors. Another combination system is when a practitioner does not allow fee reductions for new patients but will allow them for current and former patients if they meet certain requirements. A third example is a practitioner who uses a loose system only until a certain percentage of patients is at a reduced fee and then stops granting any fee reductions at all, saying, "All my reduced-fee slots are full." Finally, Blanck and Blanck (1974) varied the strictness of the fee-reduction guidelines with the level of ego development. The idea is that strong egos can withstand the frustrations and fears associated with a tight fee policy, while a lower-functioning patient may need a more flexible approach.

The advantage of combined fee-reduction systems is that they allow practitioners to tailor their systems to meet individual goals and philosophies. Practitioners whose time is tight will generally want to see fewer reduced-fee patients but may also want to maintain case mix. A new practitioner needs to set limits on fee reductions to allow for turnover in the practice, since reduced-fee patients may not leave treatment as readily. Note that the combined system is still a policy. The guidelines are written out and still consulted. And there is still the risk of bias in either the setup or the negotiation phase.

Let me make an aside on the routine waiver of co-payments as a method of administering fee reductions. This is a combined approach. It is loose in that there are no barriers as to who may have the reduction, but it is tight regarding the amount. Medicare specifically disallows this practice and considers it fraud (CMS, 2003a), and for good reason. The act of routinely waiving co-payments raises the question about what the fee really is. If all co-payments are waived, is the fee still $125, or is it more like $100? This is especially true if there is no documentation of financial need. The fee distortion caused by routine co-payment waivers affects all insurances, not just Medicare, and should be avoided.

ANNUAL MONITORING OF
FEE REDUCTIONS

No matter what guidelines are used, it's necessary to monitor the fee-reduction policy and its effects. At the end of each year, make a list of all the patients seen that year, the fee they were charged, and some basic demographics like age, sex, race, insurance status, and diagnosis. Note the distribution and range of fees. Compare the demographics of the reduced-fee clients (including the contracted fee reductions of Medicare or HMOs) to those of the full-fee clients. How are they different?

Note the effect of the fee reductions on the annual practice income — it may or may not be significant. This is not so easy to figure out. The simplest method is to mark the number of visits that year next to each of the reduced-fee patients' names. Note the income from this group and then calculate what the yearly income would have been if they had paid full fee. This gives an overestimate, since the number of visits per patient probably would have decreased if the patient had to pay full fee, or they may have dropped out altogether. Another way of estimating is to replace each of those clients with full-fee patients, if indeed that is a realistic possibility, and then compare the income. The fiscal significance of fee-reduction patients really depends on whether the practice could be full or not without them. If the reduced-fee patients would not have been replaced by full-fee patients, then the net effect of fee reductions on income is to increase it, by increasing visit volume.

In the annual review, note who dropped out of treatment prematurely. Of these people, who probably dropped out due to an inability to pay? Do you have any regrets about this? Who might have stayed in treatment if a fee reduction had been given? Are your fee-reductions policies still compatible with the goals and vision of your practice? Did this year's policy seem fair and easy to implement ? Did it add any undue financial or psychological burden? Did the fee reductions force you to take more patients or work more hours to make up the income? These are big questions for the practice because they assess whether the fee reductions were worth it, not just in terms of money, but in the time spent in negotiation, the knowledge gained, and the effect on the treatment.

If you are a woman, be extra sure to monitor your fee reductions and their effects. Studies show that women consistently reduce their fees more than men (Lasky, 1999). The reasons for this have not been closely examined, but I will offer some possibilities. One is that the goals of practice may be different for women. Women set lower income targets, prefer to spend more time with patients, and are weaker in negotiating for money (Callahan-Levy & Meese, 1979; Heatherington, 1993; Mikula, 1974; Nadler & Nadler, 1987).

Check your local median income and expenses every 3–5 years by using either the most recent *Statistical Abstract of the U.S.* (U.S. Census Bureau) or local publications available in the reference section of your library. These guides provide useful information about average rents and mortgages, as well as other expenses by which you can judge if your patients' lists of expenditures are "normal." Stay aware of the local economy, the insurance situation in your area, and the unemployment numbers. Any or all may influence your decision about how to proceed next year.

THE TWO TYPES OF FEE REDUCTIONS

Contracted fee reductions are the discounts you agree to accept from a particular insurer. If you contract with Medicare, you agree to accept their allowed amounts as full fee for all the Medicare beneficiaries you see as patients. Contracts with HMOs also include negotiated (or unnegotiated) fee discounts. Generally these fee reductions are fixed for one year and are applied to every patient with that insurance plan. *Patient fee reductions* are negotiated directly with the patient depending on the estimated cost of treatment and the patient's financial circumstances. They are not permanent (this is addressed later in the chapter) and are not applied to other patients. It is possible for one patient to have both a contacted fee reduction, perhaps because of Medicare, and an individually negotiated patient discount, perhaps for the copayment after Medicare.

Contracted Fee Reductions

When evaluating your practice, contracted fee discounts should be considered fee reductions. If you are a contracted Medicare or HMO provider but do not slide your fee in other circumstances, the proper response to an inquiry about fee reductions may run something like this:

"I don't slide my fee individually but I see Medicare patients at the contracted discount."

"About 10% of my practice is reduced fee, but those are all fee discounts through insurance."

Try not to minimize or underrate these fee reductions. They are meaningful both psychologically and financially, especially when patient volume is high.

What are some of the advantages of contracted fee reductions? Acceptance of reduced-fee contracts may increase case mix. Contracting with Medicare usually adds elderly patients, some low income, and some disabled patients. Acceptance of an HMO contract may add younger and healthier working patients. Acceptance of contracted fee reductions may increase patient volume because you are now on the referral list for other in-network providers. More potential patients may hear about you, and the decreased cost may increase patients' access to you. With contracted fee reductions, however, an increase in volume does not always translate into an increase in income. At the end of the year, it is important to assess if the contracted fee reduction was worth it in terms of volume, income, hassle factor (filling out forms or getting authorization), and case mix. If it was, continue the contract. If not, reconsider or renegotiate the contract with the insurer.

There are some disadvantages unique to contracted fee reductions. The first has to do with the perception of the fee. As a contracted provider, you view the patient as a reduced-fee client, while the patient sees himself as a full-fee client. Another is that one difficult patient becomes the representative of every patient on that contract, tempting the practitioner to cancel the contract in toto because of the bad case. This is especially true in practices that have so many contracts or so few patients that only one or two have any one insurance plan. In these cases, there aren't the numbers necessary to dispel the notion that "all the patients with this plan are bad." A third problem stems from the opposite situation, when a practice has too high a percentage of cases on one contract, let's say an HMO. This significantly increases the risk to the practice if and when the HMO changes its policies or fees or loses a major contract with an employer. Even though the contract ends, you are still responsible for those patients and must make adjustments to care for them or transfer them in a therapeutic, professional way.

Patient Fee Reductions

A data-entry clerk comes to you for medication management of depression that is fully covered by her insurance. You see her for four years and she has a nearly complete but not full response. She has always been reliable. One day, during a brief medication visit, she reveals a serious personal problem. She needs and wants individual therapy, preferably from you since you have an established relationship. Her insurance will only pay for 15 visits a year and it is clear she will need more. A full assessment of her financial situation reveals she fits your requirements for fee reduction. A reduced fee is negotiated for the visits after her insurance maximum for the year is met and treatment proceeds with good effect. She experiences complete remission of depression for the first time ever.

There are many therapeutic situations that can be resolved by an ability to reduce the patient's fee, but what are those situations, and is a fee reduction the best way to move forward? What is the actual process for thinking about it and then discussing this with the patient? Are there any disadvantages to reducing the fee for either the patient or the practice? Let's first review the advantages of fee reductions to individual patients and the practice.

Reducing the fee may allow patients who could otherwise not afford treatment to get it, as in the example above. Continuity of care can be maintained because a patient may not have to change providers if the insurance plan, treatment modality, or financial situation changes. Fee reductions permit patients to continue treatment during rough financial times when they need it most, such as periods of unemployment, sick leave, or divorce. Financial extensions to patients can be therapeutic in and of themselves. The patient may experience a boost in self-esteem. A wavering therapeutic alliance may solidify. Or reduced stress over payment is translated into energy for solving problems. The improvement that sometimes occurs with fee reductions can be rewarding and surprising for the practitioner, renewing flagging hopes or feelings of generosity and caring. Fee reductions can have practical advantages for the practice. They can increase case mix by allowing less wealthy patients to stay in treatment. They may increase volume where there is stiff competition for patients at full fee.

The advantages of individually negotiated fee reductions with patients can be compelling, but the list of disadvantages is discouragingly long. If these disadvantages are understood in advance and the process is carefully thought out, most of these problems are easily addressed. I'll divide the disadvantages into three groups: problems for the practice, problems for the practitioner, and problems for the individual patient.

In terms of disadvantages for the practice, one might think that the reduction in income caused by fee discounts would be the most important. This is not the case, simply because no practice should have fee-reduction guidelines that allow the income of the practice to decline. If practice income is substantially reduced by fee reductions, then there is something wrong with the structure of the fee-reduction policy, not the fee reductions, and the guidelines need to be revamped.

Another problem with fee reductions is that they may imply to some (patients, insurers, colleagues) that the service you provide is not actually worth the full fee. This is especially problematic if the percentage of fee reductions in a practice is high, let's say more than 10%. When fee reductions begin to approach one in five patients (20%), suspicions begin to arise about what the value of the service really is. A related question is whether the charged fee (the one on paper) is artificially inflated to compensate for fee reductions.

A final negative effect on the practice is that once fee reductions are given, an expectation for future fee reductions is created. The more fee reductions are given, the more they are considered routine by both practitioner and patient. High desire coupled with a strong expectation for obtaining a discount can elicit anger, distortion, or lying in some patients in an attempt to secure what they believe everybody else gets. There may be threats to leave treatment, refusal to comply with requests for documentation of income or expenses or misrepresentation of the financial situation. Be sure to document these behaviors carefully in the patient chart. A climate of frequent fee reductions generates this type of response. Avoid creating that climate.

Fee reductions can also cause changes in the attitude of the practitioner. The treater may experience resentment with problematic cases, especially if the fee reduction was impulsive (DiBella, 1980). For this reason, it is important to assess the potential difficulty of a patient's treatment before reducing the fee (Citron-Bagget & Kempler, 1991). Carefully document the reasons for extending the fee reduction, because at some difficult juncture with a patient in the future the well-thought-out note you wrote at the time of the reduction may provide enough perspective to carry you through.

Practitioners can also feel resentment about the decrease in income caused by a fee reduction. Good guidelines will prevent any significant decrease from occurring, but resentment can still appear. For example, you may feel like a dupe if the fee reduction turns out to be unwarranted (Citron-Bagget & Kempler) or if the patient leaves treatment anyway. Positive feelings of being charitable or generous can become a liability if you begin to expect reciprocation in some form (more consistent work or compliance or appreciation from the patient) and get none. Remember that genuine feelings of generosity should not depend on the response of the recipient. If they do, then the fee reduction was not a gift but an exchange.

Finally, fee reductions can have negative effects on patients, even if they really wanted and needed them at the time. Negatives attitudes occurring after implementation of a fee reduction may reflect feelings about self-worth. The patient might feel diminished, dependent, or humiliated and act on those feelings. Langs (1973) and others (Borneman, 1976; Haak, 1957) noted that the fee is one area where a patient can really hurt or frustrate the psychiatric provider. Fee reductions can impede treatment by inhibiting this expression of aggression. Patients often feel a mixture of both positive and negative feelings after fee reduction, appearing simply labile or confused.

Initially, there was some talk that fee reduction might decrease the efficacy of treatment, but studies have not borne this out. There is no evidence that a low fee or no fee reduces the success of psychotherapy (Herron & Sitkowski, 1986).

To summarize, most of the negative effects of individually negotiated fee reductions on the practice can be eliminated by careful application of the fee-reduction policy or by restructuring the policy to minimize problems. The negative effects on the practitioner can be minimized again by diligent recourse to the guidelines, careful consideration, and discussion with colleagues or a supervisor. Intractable negative feelings in the provider about fee reductions indicate that a no-fee-reduction policy should be considered.

Negative repercussions for the patient can be discussed openly at the initiation of the fee reduction, at the time of review (see "Conducting Regular Reviews of Fee Reductions"), or if there is an impasse in treatment or threat of premature termination. The therapist must be open to discussing the philosophy behind and the practical application of the policy in some detail with patients who experience difficulty. Remember that your fee-reduction guidelines are neither a secret nor a personal matter but a policy that impacts patient care.

Let's say that the practitioner has guidelines, is comfortable using them, and understands the potential negative effects of fee reductions and wishes to proceed further. What is the actual process by which the fee reduction is negotiated with the patient?

NEGOTIATING PATIENT FEE REDUCTIONS

This is the how-to section and many of you jumped directly here on purchasing this book. Negotiating fee reductions is probably one of the most dreaded tasks of clinicians. Some avoid it by not offering fee reductions at all but many more avoid it by haphazardly agreeing to discounts without careful thought or discussion. Female clinicians especially avoid negotiation despite giving fee discounts more often (Burnside, 1986). I strongly urge women psychiatric professionals to read the gender studies on negotiation and reward allocation listed in the recommended reading list (Appendix C). Awareness of our own gender bias mitigates many of the conflicts we feel negotiating fees.

Consideration of Nonfinancial Factors

This step is usually a private matter of the practitioner and seldom, if ever, revealed to the patient, because it involves the question, "Do I want to continue with this patient?" At this point, the patient has already raised the issue of affording treatment and the possibility that the patient might leave treatment because of the cost arises. Other nonfinancial considerations are whether you like the patient, want to continue the work, or improve the patient's motivation, or encourage a certain referral source (Chessick, 1968; Citron-Bagget & Kempler, 1991; DiBella, 1980). Most practitioners are more comfortable with this initial psychological sorting process than with the subsequent financial assessment, and some use only these factors in determining whether to give fee reductions. But this can lead to inconsistency and may not support the goals of the practice over the long term.

While they have to be considered, use of nonfinancial factors in determining fee reductions should be treated with caution because they are financial incentives and can be used to manipulate the patient. For example, giving professional courtesy is an added incentive to stay in treatment. Trying to accelerate the therapy by keeping the fee high (Chessick, 1968) is a disincentive.

Providers sometimes use a fee reduction to improve a patient's level of motivation or keep a scared patient in treatment (Citron-Bagget & Kempler, 1991). If the patient remains in treatment after the fee reduction, then the fee reduction is retrospectively considered the correct therapeutic action and causal. If the patient subsequently drops out, "nothing was lost" because the patient would have dropped out anyway. But is this a good use of a fee reduction? Can it be seen as coercive?

While using the fee to influence patients to stay in treatment is not ideal, it is hard for practitioners to resist "doing good" in this way. The moral reasoning is a form of "the ends justify the means" philosophy, which many people espouse. However, the experienced practitioner has other techniques to use in this situation, one of which is to clarify this problem to the patient by pointing out the dilemma, perhaps even before the financial assessment has begun. For example, a clinician may say:

> Although you technically qualify for a fee reduction, I find myself worrying about giving it. I know you are not really sure you want treatment and I

don't want this fee reduction to act as an incentive for you to do something you don't really want to do. Should we wait until you are more sure that you want treatment?

Occasionally, a practitioner feels tempted to give a fee reduction when the patient comes from an important referral source. This is particularly difficult if the referral source, say an internist, is on salary and has little understanding of the business end of practice. If a colleague refers you a patient who doesn't stay in treatment due to failure to meet the fee reduction requirements, this can and should be explained in the routine response to the referral. For example, in a written letter:

> I met with Mr. X and agree with you that he needs treatment for his depression. He requested a reduced fee but does not meet the guidelines for a fee reduction. I therefore referred him to the X clinic for treatment where they may be able to accommodate his request. Please feel free to call me if you have any further questions regarding this patient. Thank you for the referral.

Sometimes a practitioner wants to decrease the fee because the patient is interesting (Harrari, 1990). For new practitioners who need to expand their experience, this can sometimes be considered, but in general one must be careful not to "collect" patients or "buy" them using the incentive of a fee reduction. DiBella (1980) also wondered how much sacrifice should be made for an interesting patient. There must be limits that prevent any serious effect on the financial health of the practice or the patient.

Determining Financial Need

The best reason for considering a fee reduction for a patient is their financial need, but how is this determined? First, consider the annual amount of the bill. A patient who comes in once every three months for a medication visit and has a $15 co-payment does not need a fee reduction even if their income is low, because the cost of treatment is only $60 a year. A patient who makes $2,000 a month and comes in for only a one-hour consultation may think the $170 consultation fee is high, but he does not need a fee reduction because he can pay it in installments of $60 a month over three months. It is important not to give fee reductions to patients for whom the cost of treatment is low; they can afford treatment.

The next thing to consider is the income of the patient's household. You may take the patient's word for it or you can ask for a pay stub. Mean local incomes as well as the distribution of income can be obtained in publications in the reference section of the library. Each practitioner should have an upper limit of household income above which there will be no fee reduction no matter what the circumstances of the patient. If your upper limit is $60,000 per household, then even if that patient is in debt, being chased by the IRS, and in danger of losing their home, you will not slide the fee. People in this position usually still have considerable means and options at their disposal, which naturally will be kept from you as well as other creditors. Once they actually lose their house, declare bankruptcy, and are in a low-income job, their need for a fee reduction can be reassessed. Maintaining an upper limit basically provides protection against being a dupe, feeling like a dupe, and looking like a dupe.

If the patient's income seems to be in a range where consideration of a fee reduction is reasonable, then it is time to assess the patient's necessary expenses, like rent or mortgage, utilities, and childcare. You may request documentation of expenses, usually via a tax form or a handwritten statement, whatever your guidelines dictate. The advantages of requesting documentation are to show seriousness of intent on the part of both parties and eliminate any misunderstandings in the initial phase of negotiation. For example, the patient may state a certain take-home pay, but review of the pay stub reveals $100 a month going into a savings account. The patient doesn't count this as take-home pay but the provider may wish to. Good documentation is also important for documenting progress, renegotiating the fee when financial circumstances change, or when a discrepancy is discovered later in treatment, such as the existence of another savings account or supplementary income from a rental property.

Critical to the early phase of negotiation is a clear understanding of what you personally consider necessary expenses. What people consider to be *necessary* varies considerably with the local culture and individual belief systems. There are many people who consider cable television a necessary expense, while others consider cable a luxury. Many patients do not count clothing as a necessary expense and leave it out of the budget. Some of your patients will consider private education, lawn-care service, cigarettes, or remodeling the kitchen necessary expenses. It's not essential that you and your patients agree on what is necessary; in fact, that won't be possible. What is important is for you to decide what you are willing to consider a necessary expense and make your fee-reduction decisions based on that. Needless to say, this part of the negotiation can lead to very interesting discussions with patients.

To take this one step further, let's consider vacation and entertainment expenses. It is true that for human beings to be reasonably content and have good mental health, they must have some vacation time and some allotment of money for entertainment, however small. If a patient has a budget that does not include either vacations or an amount per month for entertainment, this is an issue that needs to be addressed. Even the best psychiatric treatment cannot succeed if the patient does not have some rest, relaxation, and stimulation.

However, it is also true that within the budgets for vacations and entertainment, there are ranges of acceptability. While almost everyone needs a car to get to and from good jobs, everyone does not need one that costs $400 a month. While everyone needs a vacation, not everyone needs to spend $2,000 a year for it. Practitioners who wish to give individual fee reductions must know the normal and reasonable costs of expenses within each budget category: for vacations, for phone bills, for rent. Only then can a list of expenses brought in by the patient be assessed accurately.

It is perfectly reasonable to deny a fee reduction to a patient who would rather spend their money on an expensive car than pay for psychiatric treatment, but how do you say that to the patient?

> We discussed that your treatment is going to cost you about $250 a month after your insurance. I looked over your budget and it is tight. However, I also noticed that you are paying $400 a month on your car, which is unusual for a person of your income. I don't want or expect you to get rid of your car, but I'd really feel strange giving you a fee reduction on your health expenses when you are paying so much for this car.

The patient can respond to this statement in any way he chooses and this may lead to important revelations about how he spends his money and why. Having a nice car may be extremely important to him, and if he can give you a good enough reason, perhaps you'll relent. Or, he may quit treatment over it, but that is his choice. Patients have their own priorities and, realistically, psychiatric treatment may not be high on their list. That freedom to choose is a basic tenet of our society.

Once you decide that the patient does qualify for a fee reduction, the amount can be decided upon based on the cost of treatment per month and the patient's monthly budget. At this point, any minimum fee you have set may come into play. You may ask the patient what they think they can afford and accept that amount if it seems reasonable. Or, you can pick a fee and discuss it with the patient. In general, with a nervous, new, or shy patient, it is better to have the patient pick a number because the power of the practitioner makes it difficult for many patients to argue against a certain amount, even if they know they can't afford it.

Often a compromise can be negotiated that requires the patient to improve his financial circumstances for the future as a condition of fee reduction. For example, the practitioner might say, "I will lower the fee to what you request if you give up cable for the duration of treatment." Or, the practitioner might say, "I will set the fee at $70 if you put $25 into a savings account each pay period to set up a cushion in case your car breaks down again." Such agreements identify the patient's money problems as an obstacle that must be addressed and give the patient a sense of empowerment despite the fee reduction and his current need.

After the fee is set, attention is drawn to logistical matters such as payment for missed appointments, timing of payment if your guidelines require payment each visit for reduced fees, and a future date for review of the fee reduction.

ALTERNATIVES TO FEE REDUCTION

What are the alternatives to reducing the fee if a patient does not qualify for a fee reduction (or even if they do)? One is transfer or termination of treatment. It is certainly acceptable to transfer a patient to another provider because she cannot afford your care. It is also acceptable for a patient to quit treatment because you will not give her a fee reduction. If it is simply a policy issue, as in you don't give fee reductions at all or your low-fee slots are full, she may easily find another treater who can accommodate her request. If a patient wants a fee reduction but is unlikely to get one from any other provider because her income is too high to qualify or because her case is difficult, she may only become convinced this is the case if she is given a chance to shop around. Such patients are unlikely to return to you even if they are unsuccessful in their quest, so don't hold out hope that you will be proven correct. When a patient leaves over the cost of treatment, you will most likely never know if you did the right thing. All you can do is follow your guidelines and try your best.

Another alternative to fee reduction is decreasing the frequency of appointments, say from once a week to once every two weeks or from once a month to once every two months. This works well for therapy patients who work hard between sessions and arrive prepared. It also works well for medication patients who come equipped with a list of questions, side effects, or symptoms and can start right in. Decreasing frequency is also therapeutic for patients with dependent traits who understand the work but need to try flying solo. Of course, one shouldn't wait for the cost of treatment to prompt such an intervention if it is indicated, but cost does spur many patients to think about becoming independent from the practitioner.

For some patients, reducing the frequency of visits reduces the intensity of treatment, to the point where it is much less effective. This can be dealt with by an *on–off regimen*, where the therapist sees the patient at the recommended frequency for a certain time, let's say eight weeks, and then not at all or infrequently for another period of time, during which the patient tries flying solo or accomplishes certain assignments.

Psychopharmacologists often vary the frequency of appointments. The frequency of appointments is high when the medication is started and a lot of education must be done. Frequency is then decreased once the patient has improved, the side effects are under control, and the patient has a firm grasp on understanding the medication. For medication patients who take a long time to warm up enough to ask questions or generally have a lot to say, the duration of appointments may have to be increased when the frequency is decreased. The frequency of appointments can always be increased again if there is a problem or a rough period for the patient. The use of homework assignments, journals, or coming with lists of things to discuss can be useful for patients who tend to "seal over" too much between sessions when they are further apart.

The duration of appointments can also be changed to decrease cost. A highly verbal and prepared client may be able to do excellent work in half the time an average patient takes. Half-hour visits for that type of client may work just fine.

Whenever a decrease in frequency or duration of appointments is considered, the potential benefits and risks should be discussed with the patient. A trial period should ensue after which both of you will reevaluate the treatment for effectiveness. If the new plan is working, it can be made permanent.

A final alternative to decreasing the fee is to allow the patient to carry a balance and have them repay the debt gradually after they leave treatment. This is no longer considered standard practice in psychiatry, and for that reason alone it should be avoided. If the patient's debt becomes too large to pay off easily, both the patient and the treater are likely to get nervous, something which can only have a negative impact on the treatment. With so many other options available to reduce costs for patients, there is little need to use this one. A related practice is to allow patients to pay by loan, barter, or credit card if they don't qualify for a fee reduction. These issues are addressed separately in Chapter 5.

DEALING WITH PATIENT DISTORTION

How does a clinician deal with patient distortion about income, assets, or expenses during fee negotiation? The first principle is to expect some distortion. As humans we have a natural desire to hide income and assets. Patients fail to mention income from family sources, investments, and trust funds. Expenses can be exaggerated to present a very tight budget or to cover undeclared expenses, like a mistress or a sailboat.

It has long been known that this type of data is falsified even in anonymous national surveys. "Disclosures of total expenditures could provoke suspicions about various frowned-on activities, such as gambling, alcohol and tobacco consumption and secret support of nonhousehold members" (Bloom, 1998, p. 847). If this kind of distortion occurs in anonymous surveys where there is no motivation to twist the answers, how can we expect complete honesty when the payoff of a fee reduction is explicit?

Doren (1987) gave useful advice about how to deal with lying or distortion in patients. He noted that:

1. Lies are usually simple but may be intricate.
2. You will not usually be able to demonstrate that the patient is lying.
3. You do not need to trust the patient (the patient needs to trust you).
4. Lying is simply patient pathology, not a sign of your incompetence. (p. 207)

When you grant a fee reduction to a patient, it is best to assume that there is some misrepresentation of the facts. Often you will never know the truth, but it is sometimes the case that the patient will accidentally or purposefully confide that they have other assets or expenditures that they did not disclose during the fee negotiation process and that would have affected the outcome of that negotiation. Once a significant distortion is discovered, then what? When the new information is obtained, the fee must be renegotiated. If the patient is in therapy, the distortion can be visited as an issue. If the patient is a medication patient, then renegotiating the fee may be therapeutic enough.

CONDUCTING REGULAR REVIEWS OF
FEE REDUCTIONS

This brings us to the final, and possibly most important, principle of any fee-reduction policy, and that is to make the agreement temporary and to set a date for review. The practitioner simply says to the patient, "This agreement is based on your current situation. Let's review it in 12 months." The scheduled review can be anywhere from 3 to 12 months after the negotiation, depending on the stability of the patient's financial situation and on your level of confidence in the information given. If you feel something is amiss about the patient's presentation but have been unable to put your finger on it during the initial discussions, in six months you may know more.

The scheduled review may also be mentioned at relevant times in the treatment, for example, when the patient reports a raise or a new job. The practitioner may say, "That's great. I don't want to adjust your fee now, but we can discuss it when the fee review comes up in two months." This gives the patient and the practitioner some time to adjust and makes the discussion seem less like a punishment for good deeds.

Scheduling a time for review in advance saves face both for the patient and the practitioner. The review allows for incorporation of new data and renegotiation of the fee without the patient or practitioner having to purposefully bring it up in the middle of unrelated psychiatric issues. It allows for confrontation outside of the negotiation so that the pressure on both parties is less. The treater may say, "I know we are not going to reevaluate your fee until July, but I want to ask about paying for this cruise when you have complained that your budget is tight." Knowing renegotiation is not taking place now allows the patient to fully discuss the conflict without the simultaneous task of trying to hold onto a reduced fee. It also frees the practitioner from trying to extract the money from the patient when they wish to explore what is happening between them. When July comes around, both you and the patient can then reference previous discussions and use the content to decide whether to continue the reduced fee or change it.

FEE REDUCTIONS BY
INTERNS AND RESIDENTS

Residents and interns slide fees too readily and too low. The reasons are many: they consider their work second-rate, they want patients to like them, and the fee reductions have no impact on their salary. Attendings sometimes collude with residents in sliding fees too low because it pulls indigent patients out of the attending pool and reaffirms their higher level of experience and training. Institutions often uphold this practice even though it decreases income. There are no productivity ratings on residents yet and perhaps institutions can use the low reimbursement numbers to their advantage. Whatever the reason, if everybody's happy, what's the problem?

The problem is the lack of education and supervision accompanying resident fee reductions. There is little or no discussion of the possible negative ramifications of the fee reduction on the patient, resident, or institution. Residents don't learn the monetary presentations of illnesses like mania, obsessive-compulsive disorder, gambling, and depression. The financial aspects of treatment are not discussed with the patient and not learned by the residents, who are then ill-prepared for the "real world" of practice. In the collusion over excessive or unquestioned fee reduction, the avoidance of dealing with money issues in the context of the patient relationship is perpetuated from one generation of physicians to the next. It is no wonder that insurance companies, managed care, employers, and patients complain that physicians are out of touch when it comes to money. We are.

INCREASING FEES

How does one decide when to increase fees? Some practitioners change their fees to parallel the national level of inflation (Harrari, 1990), usually about 3% a year, but it has been much lower the past few years. Many change their fees when they find they are below the market rate compared to colleagues with comparable experience or compared to insurance *allowed amounts*. It might seem that rising costs would be a common reason for increasing fees, but psychiatric providers have low overhead and practice costs generally do not vary much unless there is a major change, like hiring a biller or receptionist. Some practitioners never change their fees and eventually become such outlyers that both patients and insurers wonder what is going on. Try not to be the cheapest provider on the block. Be wary of increasing fees to increase revenue when the practice is not doing well. Usually, the problem is not the fee itself but low volume or excessive costs. The solution is to build the practice or reduce costs, not raise the fee.

What about the timing of fee increases? A supervisor once told me that spring is the best time, and I still consider this sound advice. Spring is after the holidays and before the annual insurance renewal cycle for many companies. Patients are usually doing better psychologically in the spring. January is the time of yearly deductibles, so any fee increase has a more drastic and immediate effect because it is not cushioned by insurance payments. January is also when the Christmas holiday bills come in. During the summer, many patients are away and many decide to leave treatment. They may use a fee increase as an excuse to jump ship at a time (in New England at least) when life seems good. Fall has the financial pressures of school and the impending holidays. Harrari (1990) wrote that she tries to make increases on the anniversary of beginning treatment with one month's notice.

What is the best way to notify patients of fee increases? It is important to give patients plenty of lead time, at least three months, so that they can plan and think carefully about the impact. Written notification is good but does not have to be in the form of a letter. A simple reissuing of the fee sheet is enough. If the practice is not too large or consists mostly of therapy patients, personal discussion and notification of the fee increase is extremely useful and greatly appreciated by patients. In a brief medication visit, the subject can be brought up by saying, "Did you get the notice about the fee increase?" Even a short discussion can give an indication of how it is being received by individual patients and lets patients know that you are aware of the impact on them. Be prepared to field questions if they think it's too much. And be prepared to accept some terminations with the fee increase. For those patients thinking of leaving or ambivalent about treatment, this may be a welcome opportunity for them to exit.

DOCUMENTATION

Be sure to keep the contracts and fee schedules of the insurance companies with which you have contracted fee reductions. For individual fee reductions, keep copies of any supporting documentation, such as W-2s, bills, or handwritten expense lists from the patient in his or her chart for future reference. In the progress notes, document requests for fee reductions and the subsequent discussions, indicating why the fee reduction was given or declined.

The purpose of documentation is for clarification if either party forgets the conditions or considerations of the fee reduction, and for legal purposes. The record also serves as reference for future fee reductions or increases as well as documentation of patient progress, financially and psychologically, over the course of treatment. For some patients, improved mental health leads to increased income through better money management, promotion, or a change to a better job. Such changes are important outcomes of treatment. The record will also serve as a baseline against which to measure any negative effects of the fee reduction, such as increased feelings of worthlessness.

ACCOUNTING TRICKERY WITH
FEE REDUCTIONS

I want to end this chapter with a short note about accounting trickery used with fee reductions. Fee reductions are not "losses" of income and cannot be declared as such for most individual practitioners. Money that is not collected is not income, is not taxed, and cannot be "expensed." Representation of fee reductions as "losses" is a distortion that obscures the financial status of the practice, which then leads to poor problem solving. Many practitioners speak of fee reductions as losses even though they don't actually declare them as losses on their taxes. This is often done to give a certain impression, for instance as a suffering mental health provider. A provider who feels such a loss so acutely probably should not be granting fee reductions.

CHAPTER 14

Managing Nonpayment

A voiding late payments is the best way to prevent nonpayment. The best ways to avoid late payments are to anticipate payment trouble before it starts (perhaps even before the patient mentions it) and use quick, simple communications to assess and mend the problem. Tell the patient, nicely, that the payment is late and why it is considered late. Address any issues the patient brings up and discuss when payment will occur, both this time and in the future. Less common practices for avoiding late payments are to have every patient pay each session or to accept credit card payment. These payment methods are pretty reliable for avoiding nonpayment but have other problems.

Nonpayment can be addressed on two levels: on a concrete level, as a breach of the patient-provider contract (Hall & Hare-Mustin, 1983), and on a psychological level, as resistance to treatment or a manifestation of a transference phenomenon. As far as the breach of contract aspect, since payment is part of the treatment agreement, nonpayment can be seen as the patient reneging on their part of the contract and not fulfilling their responsibility (Gedo, 1962). Because nonpayment breaches the contract, there is no legal duty to treat or continue to see patients who do not pay for services (Lifson & Simon, 1998; Simon, 2001). On the other hand, fiduciary duties are not contingent on payment (Lifson & Simon; Simon). Nonpayment does not give the treater permission to act unprofessionally, reveal confidences, or act in a way that might cause the patient harm.

As mentioned in the previous chapter, the fee is one area where a patient can really hurt or frustrate the psychiatric provider (Langs, 1973; Borneman, 1976; Haak, 1957). Analyzing this expression of aggression can move the patient forward. When nonpayment occurs as part of a transference reaction and the provider is in a position to treat such a reaction, the first task is to persuade the patient that understanding the psychology behind the nonpayment may forward the patient's personal growth (Hilles, 1971). Secondly, the patient must see parallels to nonpayment in other behaviors or relationships (Hilles). Finally, the patient is guided toward understanding nonpayment of the psychiatric treater as a repetition of this same pattern within the treatment relationship.

Sometimes nonpayment is a form of resistance to treatment (Hilles, 1971). Nonpayment allows, and even compels, the patient to end treatment. When the provider suspects this motive, it should be interpreted quickly and directly by asking the patient if he or she desires, on some level, to leave or end treatment. If the patient drops out or is terminated without this interpretation, nonpayment may cause repetitive treatment failures, leaving the patient to believe, erroneously, that he or she is untreatable.

NONPAYMENT POLICIES

It is critical for nonpayment policies to be set in advance, both in the mind of the provider and of the staff, as well as in any introductory sheets given to the patient. There are several points to address. After establishing the billing and payment cycle, choose a time after which a payment is considered late. This may be a set number of days or weeks after the bill is sent, a date mentioned on the bill, or the start of the next billing cycle. The actual time allotted is less important than consistency of practice. A system must be able to catch and monitor late payments and simple to implement. Once the parameters of late payment are established, the policy should include the steps taken to notify the patient and collect late payments. The steps may include a phone call, a note enclosed with the second bill, or a separate letter. Again, the form is less important than the consistency with which the steps are carried out.

The next step is to decide how and when a late payment turns into nonpayment. This can be determined by dates, by the number of billing cycles, or the number of patient notices. The procedures for following up on a nonpaying account should vary from the procedures for late payment, especially regarding the end point, which is termination. Late accounts end by being paid up or transformed into nonpaying accounts. Nonpaying accounts end in termination.

Once a patient's account moves into the nonpaying category, notify the patient according to the practice's standard procedures for nonpayment, which may include one, two, three, or more verbal or written communications to the patient about the overdue bill. At least one written communication should include information pertaining to ending the treatment relationship as well as any other actions that might be pursued, such as turning the account over to a collection agency or lawyer. Finally, the practice should have a policy about when pursuit of an unpaid account will be dropped as uncollectible and whether such patients will be allowed to return to the practice and under what conditions.

Firm policies and guidelines about the phases of nonpayment and the procedures for each help staff and billing services consistently apply the same measures to all patients. They also aid the provider should the case proceed to collection or small claims court, or if the patient files a complaint. Be sure both you and your staff are also comfortable with the policies and procedures before implementing them.

Nonpayment in Private Practice Is Rare

There is not a lot of data on collection rates for mental health practitioners. My own experience is that less than 2% and often less than 1% of accounts receivable end up unpaid. Morrison (1985) reported 1.3% of accounts unpaid. Gedo (1962) reported as high as 1 in 7, but that was before the widespread acceptance of insurance payments. Outstanding accounts receivables between 10–20% are considered acceptable in nonpsychiatric service sectors (Pressman, 1979). Larger clinics and hospitals generally have high rates of noncollection, but whether this is due to billing inefficiencies, the difference between the charged fees and discounted fees, or to actual patient refusal to pay is unclear. Most practices will try to run at 95% of collections. There will always be a few patients who refuse to pay their bill.

NONPAYMENT BY CURRENT PATIENTS

If a current patient's account is overdue and the patient's next visit is soon, bring the issue up and try to work it out in that session. Have a bill clearly showing the information on hand and present it to the patient, saying something like, "I notice you are behind on your bill." If the patient responds, address any of the issues that come up, documenting both the problems and the plan in the progress note. Stick to your policies regarding fee reductions and payment plans, discuss all of the available options. If the patient does not elaborate spontaneously on why the payment is late, further questioning may be necessary to assess the situation. "Is money tight at home?" and "Are you behind on other bills?" are common neutral inquiries.

If the patient still does not engage seriously in the discussion, it may be time to present your policy for dealing with late payments or outstanding accounts, as well as any consequences for nonpayment. I usually recommend that the patient think about the discussion and the issues at home for a time and then relay back any ideas either in another visit, if it is soon, or by phone if no subsequent visit is scheduled or the next visit is more than two weeks away.

As mentioned above, when nonpayment or late payment is part of a transference reaction or resistance to treatment, interpretation is indicated, especially for therapy patients. However, if the patient is new or inexperienced with therapy, interpretation may have to wait until the nature of transference and how interpretation permits change can be explained. For patients not yet able to incorporate this aspect into their treatment, resolution by following practice policies for late and nonpayment may be the only alternative. If the patient leaves treatment, so be it.

Sometimes problems with money management or fulfillment of social responsibilities are the very reason the patient is in treatment. In these cases, dealing with nonpayment is an integral and potentially curative therapeutic process. Failure to engage the patient in the process will result in repetition of the problem within the treatment relationship. If the patient cannot grasp the situation or work hard enough to make a change, the treatment may end, but hopefully the patient will remember enough of the dialogue to prevent another failure along the same lines in the future.

When the patient's account is overdue but the next visit is a long time off, waiting for the next visit to discuss it compounds the problem by making the payment even more late. If the patient is well known by the provider and the alliance is good, it may be acceptable to call the patient at home. "I noticed you are behind on your bill and wondered if there is some problem?" Listen to what the patient says, document the call and the plan, and proceed according to your usual policy. If the patient is not well known or the alliance is not on firm footing, send a note home with the bill saying that you are aware that payment is overdue and asking them to call if there is a problem paying it.

If there is no response to your phone or written communications and a visit is coming up, address the problem in person. If the next visit is more than one month away or the patient misses the appointment, proceed as follows:

1. Continue to bill the patient monthly.
2. Number each bill in some fashion (second notice, third notice, etc.).
3. Perhaps enclose a note saying any of the following:
   • Please make at least partial payment.
   • Please call if there is a problem with paying this bill.
   • Please call to arrange a payment plan.

If there is no response after three billing cycles, then proceed to terminate the patient if they are not in crisis or there is not an emergency. If the patient is in crisis, stabilize the patient before moving through the termination process. Remember that ample notice—at least one month and sometimes more—must be given.

TERMINATING CURRENT PATIENTS FOR NONPAYMENT

Once you have carried out all of your procedures, attempted to collect the payment, and tried to resolve the issue with the patient, you should proceed to terminate the patient following your predetermined guidelines. Ideally, the policy of termination for nonpayment was noted in the introductory sheets given to the patient at the onset of treatment and mentioned again when nonpayment threatened the treatment. The requirements for terminating a patient for nonpayment are few. The patient cannot be in crisis or simply abandoned (Appelbaum & Gutheil, 1991; Simon, 2001). The termination must be done with care (Lifson & Simon, 1998) and discussed or communicated clearly to the patient. And the practitioner must follow their usual policies and procedures for termination.

Termination can be done during a visit, but it is often followed up with a letter. For patients who have dropped out of treatment or remained incommunicado, the letter home initiates the process. It mentions the outstanding bill, the lack of communication or action on the part of the patient, and that termination is occurring because of the nonpayment. It may or may not give one more opportunity for the patient to contact the provider to resolve the issue. The letter states the date on which termination from the practitioner's caseload will be effective. It may or may not contain a referral to another provider. If the account will be referred to a collection agency or to a lawyer, that should also be mentioned. Here is a sample termination letter:

Dear Ms. Jones,

I have not heard from you since you canceled your appointment of April 10, and have not received any communication to my inquiries by phone or by mail. Your account is still outstanding. As we discussed at our last meeting, I will be closing your case due to nonpayment as of June 30. If you wish to clear up your account and reopen your case, please contact me before that date.

Sincerely,
Dr. X

The referral issue is complicated. In the first place, most professionals are reluctant to refer nonpaying patients to colleagues. Secondly, nonpaying patients are unlikely to succeed with any provider, no matter how skilled. If the matter of nonpayment can be discussed with a colleague ahead of time and managed from the outset in the new treatment, it may be possible for a second treatment to succeed if the patient is willing to abide by new conditions. This requires the consent of the patient, admission that the treatment failure was caused by nonpayment, and a desire to overcome this obstacle in the next treatment. Sometimes a provider will simply refer the patient to a clinic, assuming that nonpayment is less of an issue there because free care is generally subsidized by the government or tolerated to an extreme. However, this does nothing to help the patient with the money problem and hurts clinics that are already in poor financial straits.

As far as documentation, include a copy of the termination letter in the patient chart. On the date of termination, close the case and decide how to proceed with billing for the outstanding balance.

NONPAYMENT AFTER TERMINATION

While termination with the patient ends the clinical aspect of the case, it may not end the accounting portion. Attempts to collect the outstanding balance may proceed for some time. Since the treatment relationship has ended, it is probably best not to call the patient at home to seek payment. This might be considered intrusive at best and harassment at worst because of the power differential of the treatment relationship. Although that relationship has ended, the provider is the holder of important documents and information that continue the power differential beyond termination.

Continue billing the patient by mail up to a predetermined date, noting the aging of the open account as it occurs. This time limit is important to be sure you are not overbilling out of anger about the unpaid bill (Harrari, 1990) and to facilitate moving on to the acceptance phase if no money is forthcoming. Again, small notes attached to the bills asking for a response, partial payment, or other communication are appropriate (Canter & Freudenberger, 1990; Pressman, 1979). Once the predetermined time limit for billing has been reached, a decision must be made about whether to write off the bill (Canter & Freudenberger) or proceed to collection, depending on the practice policy.

COLLECTION AGENCIES, LAWYERS, AND SMALL CLAIMS COURT

In terms of the ethics of using a collection agency, the American Psychological Association has determined that the use of a collection agency is ethical if the client knows about the policy in advance (Faustman, 1982; Hall & Hare-Mustin, 1983; Pope, 1988) and if the clinical material given to the agency is limited to that needed to collect the money. Faustman's 1982 study found that more than half of the psychologists responding to his survey did not obtain consent from the patient or discuss the collection policy ahead of time. Confidentiality issues have since been clarified by HIPPA regulations, which clearly state that authorization from the patient is not required for conveying information necessary for billing and collection. Remember that information that is not necessary to complete billing and collection may not be conveyed to the agency.

The parameters for which accounts will be sent to collection and after what time period must be established ahead of time. Indicators for collection may include the age of the open account, the amount owed, and whether the patient has made any communication or response at all (Canter & Freudenberger, 1990).

There are two general caveats regarding the use of collection agencies and small claims court: neither one guarantees payment, and their cost will almost always exceed the unpaid client bill (Behnke & Hilliard, 1998).

Collection Agencies

Faustman (1982), reported that 60% of psychologists had referred a delinquent patient account to a collection agency. Choosing an agency is a difficult matter. How the agency acts toward patients may reflect on you as the professional. Although it is easy enough to make recommendations, you cannot control an agency's actions (Harrari, 1990; Pressman, 1979). A referral from a colleague who has found an agency effective and respectful of clients is important.

The costs of using a collection agency can be considerable. Usually they charge 30–50% of the collected fees (Canter & Freudenberg, 1990; Harrari, 1990; Morrison, 1985), depending on the age of the account. Often the collected payment goes directly to the agency, which then issues a check for the remainder to you as the hiring provider. Occasionally, an agency recommends writing off an account as uncollectible, and, obviously, they should not charge for that. Rarely, an agency wants to pursue a client in court. Be sure that your contract with the collection agency requires your consent for a decision to proceed to court.

Collection Attorneys

The same study by Faustman (1982) reported that 35% of psychologists had referred an overdue account to an attorney rather than to a collection agency. Payment to the lawyer may be fee for service or on contingency (Harrari, 1990). Be sure to discuss the fees ahead of time and compare them to the amount likely to be collected. Attorneys often start with a simple demand letter (Harrari), but may proceed to court. If the process is likely to take time, the cost may not be worth it (Canter & Freudenberger, 1990; Morrison, 1985).

Small Claims Court

In most states, there is a ceiling on the amount that can be pursued in small claims court, sometimes less than $1,000 (Canter & Freudenberger, 1990), and usually you must pay a filing fee (Pressman, 1979). Proceeding through small claims court takes a lot of time and may not make sense financially. However, Canter (1990) said he once went through small claims court on the advice of a collection agency. Although he had not charged interest on the patient's outstanding balance, the judge demanded that interest be paid when the case was won.

The Litigation Risk of Aggressive Collection

Sometimes patients respond to aggressive collection practices by filing malpractice suits (Brodsky, 1990; Cohen, 1979; Faustman, 1982; Pope, 1988) for abandonment or harassment (Faustman), or by filing ethics complaints (Behnke & Hilliard, 1998) with the relevant professional boards. Remember that aggressive collection can cause harm to a patient by increasing his level of stress or breaching confidentiality. For this reason, it is probably unwise to pursue aggressive collection with clients who have been dissatisfied with treatment (Faustman). Since the decision to pursue collection through agencies, courts, or lawyers should be consistently applied to all patients, it is probably not a good idea to drop collection procedures for difficult patients while pursuing them for more compliant patients.

ACCEPTING LOSSES DUE TO NONPAYMENT

All practitioners have patients who never pay their bills and an occasional patient who does not pay a fairly large bill. It is important to analyze these losses, accept them, and move on in practice. In examining each case, pay particular attention to any clues that may have heralded a problem at a time when successful intervention would have been more likely. Review your own role (Harrari, 1990) in missing early indicators, not pursuing late payments, allowing balances to accrue, or avoiding the money issue altogether. Think about what measures you can take in the future to prevent or mitigate such a loss. If you think it might be helpful, review the case with a colleague or supervisor.

As far as the practice is concerned, does this nonpayment case indicate any need for policy changes? Not all cases that fail due to nonpayment are the fault of either the practitioner or the patient. Some are due to policies that are too lax or vague or a billing system that is not providing information on payment in a timely fashion. Don't hesitate to correct or amend procedures or policies if a nonpayment problem was even partially a systems issue. Note the amount of the unpaid bill compared to the income of the practice over all. In the course of a year, even a large unpaid bill usually represents only a fraction of practice income.

Managing the feelings associated with an unpaid bill can be difficult. My own recommendation is to file the paperwork, account sheet, and chart away soon after the account is written off. Seeing the unpaid account sheet, patient chart, or piles of bills can trigger feelings of anger, guilt, or shame, or lead to pointless obsessing over the case. Professional documentation of the collection-attempt process and the end result in the patient chart is helpful in managing the feelings.

Remember to include a note in the chart about the unpaid balance in case the patient reappears many years later. It is not uncommon for patients to completely forget an unpaid bill and call to resume treatment after a few years have passed. A decision has to be made about allowing such patients to return to treatment. Some providers allow it if the patient pays the old bill first and others allow it only if plans have been laid to prevent a recurrence. Some providers do not allow the patient to return under any circumstances because the negative effect on the relationship may be ongoing.

People don't like people who don't pay their bills. On some level, a patient who does not pay is asking you not to like them. Anger at, distrust of, and disrespect for patients who do not pay up are part and parcel of nonpayment. These feelings are not concerning as long as they do not become a preoccupation of the provider. What *is* concerning is when such feelings are *not* evoked by nonpayment. One might properly wonder about the defenses of a provider who successfully avoids dealing with nonpayment until a case has ended. When no negative feelings are elicited by nonpayment, the therapist remains unaware of the problem until after the treatment has failed.

You may wonder what a case of nonpayment says about you as the practitioner. Remember that not everything in therapy has to do with you. Much of it has to do with the patient alone. The patient may be sociopathic, a gambler, or have such serious money problems they simply could not pay the bill. But some issues of nonpayment may indeed have something to do with you or the treatment. Occasionally, nonpayment occurs because of lack of experience with certain issues: money problems, antisocial tendencies, patient dissatisfaction, or negative transference reactions. For this reason, it is important to review cases of nonpayment with other practitioners. While this is best done while the case is fresh in your mind, occasionally you are still too close to it to clearly see the issues. Reviewing the case a year later may provide additional insights. Once you can see where you went wrong (if you went wrong at all), you can take measures to correct the blind spot and move forward in your practice.

Sometimes practitioners find they do poorly with the payment end of treatment because their personal financial life is in disarray. Preoccupation with the payment of clients parallels the preoccupation with their own bills. Avoidance of dealing with the accumulating balances of patients mirrors denial of their own level of debt. The solution is this case is not to pursue patients for payment, but to straighten out the money management problems at home, either with a professional accountant or financial advisor, or in therapy if there are psychological underpinnings to the problem. Practitioners who manage their own money well tend to do well with patient accounts.

As a final note, you can not refuse to release copies of medical records because of nonpayment (Cooper & Winn, 2004; ProMutual, 2004).

CHAPTER 15
Money Transferences and Countertransferences

Transference occurs when feelings, attitudes, or beliefs from powerful relationships in the past are transferred to a relationship in the present (Greenson, 1967). Usually, the phenomenon is unconscious, but parts of it, or the irrationality of it, may be within a person's conscious awareness. Typically, a transference reaction is induced when something in the present triggers mobilization of those past feelings or responses (Basch, 1980). Transference may occur in any person in any situation, not just a clinical one. The term *countertransference* specifically refers to transference phenomena that develop in the therapist in response to the patient. I will often simply use the word *transference* to denote countertransference as well, since the transferences I describe below can occur in either party.

The identification of transference within the context of psychotherapy is critical to successful treatment. Recognition of unconscious transference processes is necessary for conscious control of unreasonable behaviors or feelings. For the patient, this creates an platform for change. For the therapist, recognition of countertransferential processes allows a change of treatment tactics. Hidden transference phenomena in either party can stall progress or precipitate premature termination, while resolution of transference phenomena often leads to comprehensive changes outside of therapy.

WHAT ARE MONEY TRANSFERENCES?

Unless we are fortunate enough to grow up in a household where money matters were talked about openly and in some detail, much of what we learn about money and money behavior has been incorporated unconsciously from early childhood through example or imitation, often without any discussion at all. Any talk that does accompany a transaction or the acquisition or loss of money is often rule-bound, shrouded in secrecy, or tied to morality. "Don't tell anyone what your father makes." "We don't discuss that." "Take off the price tag." "She has too much money for her own good." As a result, our internalized codebooks on money matters often have serious inconsistencies that can be revealed and corrected in the psychotherapy process.

I separate transferences involving money into three types. The first refers to a traditional transference acted out in the realm of financial behavior, for example when someone in the midst of a controlling transference attempts to manipulate someone else through money. Strictly speaking, this is not a "money transference" but a transference acted out or made manifest through money. The distinction is important because the focus of treatment in these cases must be on the transference, not on the money behavior itself, if resolution is to proceed. I will not address this type of transference reaction here.

While transference is usually associated with feelings about people, I use the term *transference to money* to connote unconscious attitudes and beliefs about money as an object. These transference reactions manifest themselves in irrational or ineffective financial behaviors that the patient feels may be outside their control or understanding. A belief that money will bring happiness is the most classic, but the belief that money corrupts is also a common money transference. These transference reactions affect human relationships, however the primary problem is not in those relationships but in the patient's relationship with money.

Bryan and Cameron (1992) addressed a myriad of transferences to money in their excellent book. To give a short but interesting taste, they mentioned "terminal vagueness" about money, money as respect, and money as evil. Transferences to money are fairly easy to address with clients because the therapist stands outside of the phenomenon. Although these transferences may manifest themselves in nonpayment, they often do not result in termination because the relationship with the therapist is not affected and the alliance remains strong enough to compel patients to work on the nonpayment behavior in order to stay in treatment.

I use the term *money transference* to refer specifically to interpersonal transferential phenomena in which a monetary component is essential to the dynamic. Transferences involving poverty and prostitution are examples. These transference problems are more difficult for therapists to resolve because the provider-patient relationship is often imbedded in them. Since payment for treatment is involved, failure to resolve these transferences (or countertransferences) will often lead to premature termination. The definitive book on money transferences remains to be written, and there are so many that the task of even listing them all is beyond this book. In the section following the next, I will review what I call *The Big Five*. These are the main categories of money transference that result in premature termination, largely because of the difficulty recognizing and discussing these topics with patients.

CLUES THAT A MONEY TRANSFERENCE MAY BE AT WORK

Because the cost of therapy is high, monetary transferences often manifest themselves in treatment. The following is a list of common behaviors that may indicate some type of money transference is active in the patient or the therapist. Prompt attention is needed to prevent premature termination or problems with the alliance.

1. The patient or therapist is canceling a lot.
2. The patient is not paying on time or at all despite adequate means to do so.
3. The patient often pays in advance.
4. Serious talks about payment or the affordability of treatment go nowhere.
5. The issue of cost does not come up on intake.
6. The issue of cost does not come up within a year of therapy.
7. The provider is not billing patients or insurance companies on time.
8. The provider avoids billing patients or touching money given by patients.

9. The provider sees a lot of patients but his or her income is low.
10. More than 30% of the provider's patients are seen at a reduced fee.

None of these behaviors indicates for sure that a money transference is the root cause. Exploration or experimentation is necessary to validate the hypothesis.

THE BIG FIVE

The Big Five—wealth, poverty, status, race, and prostitution—are the areas in which the most difficult money transferences develop because the exchange of money triggers a second interpersonal relationship that runs parallel to the treatment relationship. If the transference is mild to moderate in nature, it may simply affect the payment situation. If the transference is intense, it may distort or disrupt the treatment. Within each category there are a variety of subtypes. The subtype elicited largely depends on the culture, history, and character of the patient or therapist, but it may also be influenced by the practitioner's policies, the dynamics of the treatment relationship, or daily facts and circumstances such as unemployment or an economic downturn.

Wealth

The word *rich* refers to having a lot of money in the present. *Having means* or being *wealthy* refers not only to having money in the present but having the means to generate revenue in the future. *Rich* is a derogatory term, often implying the money involved was not earned or is undeserved. *Wealthy* is a term of admiration because it implies the opposite, that the money was earned and therefore deserved. The use of these terms by the patient or the provider provides valuable clues as to whether the monetary transference is positive or negative.

When the patient is rich, subtle and unconscious forces may shape the thoughts of the provider. The treater thinks, "If I had that much money I'd. . . ." This attitude may manifest itself in inattention to the patient's complaints or open dismissal of valid concerns or feelings. Positive transferences can also create problems in the treatment. If the therapist believes that the wealthy patient is smarter than she is, she may not feel comfortable directing the therapy or providing the necessary educational schpiels. Wealthy patients are entitled to and need to hear all the explanations that other patients receive.

Sometimes there is an unconscious belief that people with money should be healthy, as if health can be bought. Health cannot be purchased; it is determined by genetic factors, the nature of the disease process, and by environmental factors. Only health care services can be bought, not health itself. While the wealthy certainly have more access to treatment, most diseases (cancer, heart disease, schizophrenia) strike at any income level. A corollary belief is that because the affluent can afford the best care, they get the best care. The provider may ask, "Why are they seeing me?" Most people with plenty of money see regular providers and get regular care. A few, perhaps the extraordinarily wealthy or the famous, use a narrow group of providers or avoid care altogether because of confidentiality or status concerns.

Providers often fear lawsuits from wealthy patients, the irrational reasoning being that with means and education a person's natural inclination is to sue if things do not go well, or that the death or suicide of a wealthy patient is so egregious that a family would have to seek compensation in the form of a lawsuit. The belief that a death or loss in the wealthy is more unjust stems from fantasies that the wealthy are more indestructible, as well as the belief that health can be bought. If health does not follow, it is because the treatment or provider was inadequate, not because the disease process was bad. These irrational anxieties on the part of the mental health provider represent projections of commonly held false beliefs about money (technically a transference *to* money) and the well-to-do. Most people do not sue and no amount of money can rectify a personal loss, rich or poor. Once out of poverty range, increases in income, even large ones, do not improve subjective feelings of happiness (Deiner, 1993, Myers, 1993).

While not quite minimization, attitudes about substance abuse in the wealthy may also lead to inadequate treatment. Typical internalized beliefs are that "Rich people drink and drug too much" and "If they didn't have money they wouldn't be using." Rich patients drink and use drugs for the same reasons all patients do: to alter their emotional state. They need treatment and are not "too good" for AA (Alcoholics Anonymous.)

A therapist's belief that "money corrupts" could negatively impact the treatment of a wealthy patient by leading to an unnecessarily punitive, moralistic, or paternal stance toward the patient. Depression, flight, or feelings of unlikeability in the patient may follow. The nature of corruption is still not known, but current theory holds that corruption stems not from wealth but from power. While power and wealth are associated, they are not bound to each other. Great wealth can exist in a person who does not wield power, and great power can be wielded by a person of moderate financial means.

Unearned wealth triggers more negativity than earned wealth. Unearned wealth lowers status and may engender social disrespect. This can lead to serious psychological problems in lottery winners, heirs, and children of the wealthy. Depression, substance abuse, overspending, or profligacy are common manifestations of unconscious internalized denigration of unearned wealth.

Feelings of admiration, status by association, and curiosity are examples of positive countertransferences that can lead practitioners to retain wealthy patients in treatment beyond what is medically necessary. Casually mentioning high-status patients is a competitive ritual in medicine that undermines confidentiality. Retention usually occurs by simple failure to terminate when the patient is better. Other methods are to treat every symptom until it completely disappears or to provide supportive work without end.

Now I would like to turn to transference feelings aroused by wealth in the provider, especially physician providers because their earnings have been a target of public commentary for at least a hundred years. Because of their high income, patients and the public are less than sympathetic when physicians complain about insurance, reimbursement, and managed care. Patients think, "If I had that much money, I wouldn't care about $5 here or $10 there." The psychiatrists reading this now are thinking, Yes, but this does not apply to me. Think again.

Psychiatrists are both rich and wealthy by any definition. Mean psychiatrist income was about $125,000 in 1995 (sadly the latest data available) (U.S. Census Bureau, 2003) while mean income overall for a family of four in America is about $45,000. We psychiatrists prefer to see ourselves as middle class in order to avoid conflicted feelings about our wealth and protect ourselves against the fears provoked by others' envy. Patients and the public are not fooled by our protestations that we are middle class, and the facts support them.

How do we deceive ourselves? Most commonly, by pointing to all the people who are richer than us, either physicians in other specialties who earn much more than we do or richer people in our neighborhoods. The "bud-vase" economy (a term coined by Paul Solman) makes this easy. Only 5% of households in the population make more than $100,000 a year, and we are at the bottom of that long neck (see Figure 15.1). By nature, humans assess their position by looking up, not down. As we psychiatrists look up, we see a very long neck of people with higher incomes and are acutely aware of our position at the bottom. If we live in their neighborhoods, we are surrounded by people who have more than us. To make matters worse, the nature of our work puts an upper limit on our income, since only so many patients can be seen in a day. It is not really possible to make more than $400,000 per year providing direct patient care (seeing 24 psychopharmocology patients a day at $65 per visit, five days a week, 50 weeks a year with a 100% collection rate gives only $390,000 per year). This income ceiling may contribute to feelings of discontent.

Provider wealth affects patient payment. Patients feel comfortable asking for a discount ("my psychiatrist can afford it") or angry if the psychiatrist is chasing a small co-payment. Patients who believe in equality of opportunity may feel entitled to a reduced fee "to even things out." Visible signs of

FIGURE 15.1
The Bud Vase Economy

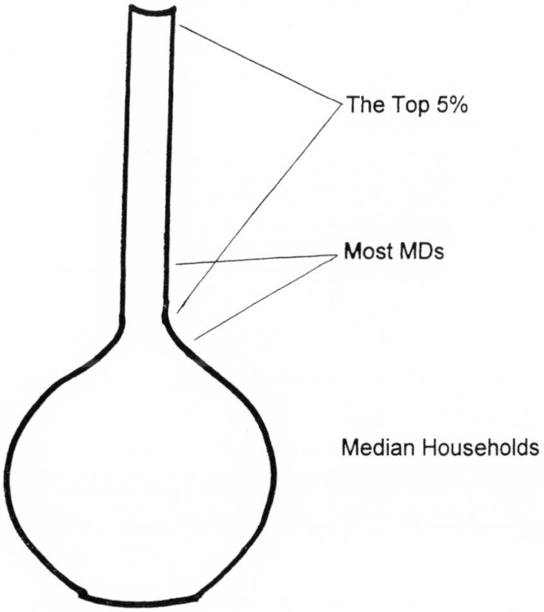

The Top 5%

Most MDs

Median Households

wealth in the provider become easy targets for ire when treatment is not going well, or when the patient is in the throes of a negative transference.

For some patients, the impact of provider wealth is positive. The richer the provider, the better he or she must be. And there is status by association. If the provider is high status, the patient by association is high status. "I see Dr. Famous. Oh, yes, she's very good. It's too bad for you she's not taking new patients." These patients pay promptly and in full because of their interest in maintaining the association to the provider.

Occasionally, wealth issues cause problems in split treatments, where a psychiatrist sees the patient for medication and a non-MD provides the psychotherapy. A patient and therapist who tacitly agree that the psychiatrist is too rich may collude to undermine the psychopharmacological end of treatment. A non-MD therapist unconsciously competing with an MD may compel a patient to choose sides or leave treatment.

Poverty

Definitions of poverty are tricky. Strict income definitions ignore the fact that almost all the poor in the United States have TVs, running water, phones, and access to education through high school. Sociologically and psychologically, relative income is sometimes more accurate. Comparing income to a local or national average allows us to say that, yes, someone with running water, a phone, two TVs, earning $10,000 a year may be considered "poor" even though technically they already have what the rest of the world considers essential.

I divide poor patients into four types: *those without money, the poor, the invisible poor,* and *those who believe they are poor but are not.* Considering which category of poor the patient falls into aids the analysis of money transferences and leads to better resolution of money problems in the treatment.

Those without money refers to people who are transiently poor or poor by choice—the temporarily unemployed, students, activists, missionaries, clergy, or Peace Corps volunteers. Members of this group have low incomes or token stipends but usually have benefits that include health insurance. They are usually educated and maintain hope, dignity, and status. They do not regard themselves as in poverty, nor do we regard them as part of The Poor.

The poor refers to people of longstanding or permanent low income, which may even be transgenerational. The condition of the poor is called *poverty*, and denotes hopelessness, resignation, powerlessness, and helplessness. Poverty is always a low-status condition. The poor may be idealized as children, either by religious tradition or by those unfamiliar with the real nature of poverty. Some even see altruism and poverty as synonymous (Goldberg, 1990; Walfish & Coovert, 1990). Assisting the poor brings status to the helper. People may engage in a sort of moral competition over who is helping the needy more; in psychiatry, those in public-sector work may disparage providers in the private sector. The poor do not idealize their own condition. They may even resent "do-gooder" clinicians because they feel like objects used by them to increase their moral status. As a result, members of the poor may sabotage treatment to assert individual status and control.

Members of the poor may possess credit cards, cell phones, and cable, which is often a source of irritation to providers, who feel the money would be better spent on other things or suspect that the patient has a secret source of income. These possessions, bought with credit cards or money earned under the table, give the appearance of being "normal," of having money. They render the owner visible, even though they are poor.

The *invisible poor* have even lower incomes and status than the poor. They have no credit cards, cable, cell phone, or health insurance. They may not register their children for school or apply for government assistance. They do not present for treatment and are rarely seen by psychiatric providers, except perhaps by those working in an outreach program. The invisible poor include the rural poor, illegal aliens, street people, migrant or itinerate workers, and the homeless. We don't see them, so we don't think of them. They remain invisible.

Those who believe they are poor but are not are a heterogeneous group. This includes people who remain attached or addicted to poverty even after their financial circumstances improve. It is important to avoid fee reductions in this population because discounts reinforce the fantasy of poverty. Discuss the patient's changed circumstances openly and factually, recognizing that they will struggle to keep their real situation hidden from you.

Another group of people who believe they are poor but are not are misers, hoarders, and pathological savers. There is some evidence that these traits are genetic or biological in origin and may not be amenable to change. However, this does not mean that the provider must also believe the patient does not have enough money. Affirm the need to save for the future, but also note the limit of what constitutes *enough*. Again, avoid fee reductions because they are reinforcing.

People who mismanage what should be adequate income often feel poor. Refer these clients to the many excellent self-help books on personal financial management or to professional fee-for-service financial advisors. With the patient, explore any psychological issues related to having or keeping money. Attend to any compulsive buying either for emotional release or to elicit a mood change. Stay on top of their account, perhaps having the patient pay each week. If they qualify for a fee reduction, be sure to schedule an increase over time so that mismanagement of funds is not consistently rewarded with a reduced fee.

Occasionally, you may run into clients who know they are not poor but want you to believe they are. They may hide their income or assets in order to obtain a fee reduction. These people may regard securing bargains as sport or believe that "all's fair in business." Problems erupt when the hidden assets are discovered by the clinician after a fee reduction has been given. Sometimes patients hide assets out of shame. They can't believe they have money (denial) or they can't accept that they have money (guilt). Discuss their feelings openly and do not reduce the fee.

Feelings related to poverty impact psychiatric treatment in various ways. Poor patients of any type are less likely to present for treatment because providers are high-status people whose presence accentuates the patient's low status. As a defense against exposing their condition, low-income patients present late in the course of their illness or at the time of a crisis, which angers the provider because the illness is harder to treat and poses higher risk. Poor patients may refrain from complaining or asking questions. They don't want to be seen as causing trouble, don't want to call attention to themselves, and don't want to appear ungrateful. The provider thinks the patient is satisfied and the patient pretends to be, but in reality the treatment may not be going well.

Because the poor experience shame and confusion about their impoverished condition, they won't bring it up. Yet, all the while, they are wondering what you think of them and their situation. They wonder themselves if their poverty is their fault, and if it is, what to do about it. Without a signal of interest or empathy from you, they may silently disappear from treatment, believing they can't be helped or that you can't relate to them.

Sometimes clinicians don't pursue the no-shows of poor patients as aggressively as they might for a paying client. They figure no-shows are due to problems at home or are a condition of poverty, not a reaction to it. Perhaps the therapist unconsciously wants the patient to drop out because she is feeling overwhelmed by the patient's poverty and the inability to alter that fact in treatment. Perhaps the clinician doesn't want to reduce the fee or doesn't know how to deal with poverty within the treatment.

There are ways of handling low income in treatment, but first the clinician has to know more about the patient's situation and how they view it themselves. Ask, "Is money tight at home? Has money always been tight? Have you ever thought of trying to make more money? How did you come to be on welfare?" Place "low income" on the problem list and discuss it like other stressful situations, with an eye to improvement.

Status

Status is recognition from others. It is a basic human drive and appears to be necessary for both survival and emotional health. Status is gained by demonstrating ability or knowledge, usually through work but sometimes through relationships. Money and status are connected, but high income is not necessary for high status. For example, students, clergy, and gifted artists are never low-status individuals even when their income is low. On the flip side, most wealthy people live anonymously in average neighborhoods, where only a few may be aware of their wealth (Stanley & Danko, 1996).

Status is connected to money through work. Wages allow the purchase of material goods and services, decreasing dependence on others. Work is where one's abilities, knowledge, and character are revealed to others. Work that does not allow the display of skill or intelligence is called *unrewarding*, even if wages are decent. Where work is rewarding, wages represent a numerical measure of respect and recognition from others, which is why labor disputes are often so heated. They may not be about the money per se, but about the respect given to workers by management or the corporation.

If money is not earned through work, the status conferred decreases. Many an heir will testify to the long rough road they ran attempting to gain the respect that their parents earned before them. Children of business owners struggle to gain control and respect within their own company when they take over; they have to prove themselves.

An unknown person's status will be judged by their income or possessions because of money's associations to work. They are assumed to have the level of ability reflected by their material goods. Big house = big skill. But disappointment, anger, and disdain will quickly follow if no commensurate ability is shown. Status, money, and education have equally complex ties. Education always confers status because knowledge is power. Education often leads to more rewarding work, although not necessarily the highest-paying work. Studies show that having more education actually decreases the likelihood of becoming a millionaire, and attendance at state universities is more highly correlated with business success than attendance at ivy league institutions (Stanley & Danko, 1996).

Mental health practitioners and patients avoid discussing status and power in treatment, probably because of discomfort with the status differential in the treatment relationship. Yet unconscious status situations are common causes for nonpayment and abrupt discontinuation of treatment. With practice and care, all practitioners can learn to address the negative and positive aspects of status differentials between themselves and patients. When equilibrium is restored, payment that has been withheld is often forthcoming.

Race

Money discussions across racial lines will have more emotionality. Status differences are exaggerated across racial lines and will implicitly include the concept of *privilege*. It is a basic American belief that if a person works hard and demonstrates ability, they will be rewarded monetarily and earn respect and recognition in direct proportion to their work or ability. However, what constitutes valuable work, ability, and knowledge is set by the majority in power, which up to the present time has been white and very much Anglo-European. Since status, recognition, and pay are given according to those majority values, people who are unlike the majority are less likely to agree with those values and meet the set requirements for recognition. A person is said to be privileged if they are a member of the group who sets the values and rules in a culture, because they automatically know, understand, adopt, and usually agree with those values and rules. They meet the standards set by their own group with less difficulty.

People in the majority don't have to learn the abilities, values, and knowledge base of the people who are not in power because their achievement is not dependent on it. As a result, they don't see or feel the problems of the others and feel upset when accused of bias, racism, or sexism. People in the minority group have to know and respect the system and values of the majority to get ahead, even if they don't agree with them. This dilemma leads to conflict, resentment, and confusion in members of minority groups who succeed or want to succeed.

Dealing with race in psychiatric treatment is always necessary, but especially if money needs to be discussed. If you are white, you should thoroughly learn and understand the concept of white privilege so that you will not be unprepared when the issue comes up. Avoidance of discussions about race, privilege, or status in therapy will almost always limit successful interpretation of transference reactions and will often lead to premature termination.

Prostitution

Prostitution transferences often occur when money is exchanged across gender lines, although they are not inevitable. The feelings may not be shared, but the transferences may be reciprocally reinforcing. Clues that a prostitution transference may be at work include sexual overtones or associations to conversations about payment, small boundary violations or deviations from policy, or the presentation of gifts. A third party, often the patient's spouse, may become anxious about the treatment relationship. Billing or payment may stop either as an attempt to resist development of the transference or as a manifestation of the actual transference.

The nature of a prostitution transference largely depends on the flow of payment across gender lines and the dynamics of the treatment relationship. Prostitution transferences and countertransferences generally occur when money is given by a man to a woman. When a male patient pays a female therapist, he is aware that he is "buying her services," and in fantasy these services may extend to more than psychotherapy. If he feels good about the therapist (positive transference) he may feel closer to her and believe the services rendered will make him happy. If he feels negatively about the therapist, he may feel she is "not putting out," is low status, or that she can be bought. He may see himself as a hopeless case (for seeking help from someone so low status) or feel relatively empowered.

A female therapist caught in a negative prostitution transference (triggered by the patient's payment for her services) may inexplicably feel he is disgusting or demanding in some way. She may wonder why he can't get what he needs in the usual way, like in his marriage. She may feel she has to prove her high status. She may fear sexual assault. Conversely, if the woman therapist enjoys her fantasied role of prostitute, she may try to seduce him by exploiting his vulnerability. She may try to keep him in treatment beyond what is indicated so that she can continue to collect his payment.

Returning to reality, the provision of psychiatric services by a female therapist to a paying male patient in no way represents prostitution. Her relationships, sexual and otherwise, occur outside of work and she never engages in a sexual relationship with a patient. The therapist is in the power position in the treatment relationship. She can and will terminate the relationship if it is indicated. He, as the patient, can buy psychiatric services only. He may have problems in his relationships with women, but those will be treated through the psychotherapy process, not by engaging in sex with the therapist.

Prostitution transferences are occasionally triggered when male therapists give female patients fee reductions. The woman reacts negatively, thinking he is trying to buy her cooperation. She may wonder what else he may want from her or feel that she owes him some kind of service. Conversely, if she is comfortable with using her seductive abilities, she may take a positive stance in reaction to this "payment," thinking he finds her attractive and wondering what else she can do to keep the relationship going.

The male therapist may find himself having positive feelings about the fee reduction "payment," hoping she'll do more work or put more effort into the work. Or he may have negative feelings toward the fee reduction, thinking he had to buy her cooperation or that he has been seduced.

The definitive book of money and transference has yet to be written. There are so many levels on which people relate to money and, with the numerous values and purposes to currency and countless cultural and demographic influences on financial behavior, such a book might indeed be a tome. Individual clinicians can play a role in the development of this important technical component by paying attention to and discussing the various transference and countertransference crunches that appear in treatment with trainees and colleagues. Good general financial management of the practice and thoughtful, consistent policies regarding payment provide the confidence necessary to introduce these difficult and sometimes embarrassing clinical situations.

It is my hope that all who read this book can put something in it to use for themselves, their trainees, and their patients. We set the standards of our professions. It is only a short step from practice to publication and only a few more steps from publication to general adoption and expansion of those ideas. Let us all be on the vanguard of managing money in psychiatric practice.

APPENDICES

Sample Introduction Sheet

B elow is a copy of a patient introduction sheet, which contains information about fees, services, and policies. It may or may not be applicable to your practice. Although it is not shown below, your letterhead should be placed at the top of the front page.

January 1, 2004

To My Patients:
    Please read the following information about my fees, appointment cancellations, and confidentiality. Feel free to bring up questions about these policies at any time.

Fees:		
	Initial Consultation (90801)	$170.00
	50-min medication/therapy visit (90807, 90806)	$125.00
	25-min medication/therapy visit (90805, 90804)	$85.00
	15-min medication visit (90862)	$65.00
	Practice Consultation	$125/hour

Insurance: Be sure to check your health insurance coverage for outpatient mental health care. Usually, there is a yearly deductible and a co-payment for each visit. Often, there is a yearly maximum on either the number of visits or the amount paid for psychiatric services, unless your plan has a parity clause. A parity clause means that psychiatric illnesses with a biological cause (most depressions, many anxiety disorders, bipolar disorder, and some other illnesses) are covered as long as medically necessary without a yearly maximum, just like other medical illnesses. Medicare has a 50% co-payment that is usually covered in full or in part by MassHealth or a Medigap policy. I am a contracted Blue Cross and Medicare provider, so my fees may be slightly lower for those insurances. Remember that you will be responsible for charges that are not covered by your insurance. Be sure to get the details. I will help you as best I can, but your insurance company or employer is the best source for information about actual coverage.

Cancellations: I will bill you for late cancellations and for no-shows unless you reschedule the appointment within the day or the week. A late cancellation is when you cancel on the same day as your appointment or after 5 P.M. on the day before your appointment. I allow one unbilled late cancellation or no-show per year if there is an emergency. If you cancel your appointments too often, I will bring this up with you. If you continue to cancel frequently, I may end the treatment.

Confidentiality: Anything you reveal in these sessions is confidential and can not be released to another person without your consent. Exceptions to the rules of confidentiality occur when there is an intent to harm yourself or another person, or if a judge requests information as part of a trial in which your mental health is an issue. If you believe there will be or might be any legal ramifications to your case, please let me know so we can discuss this before starting treatment.

If you are using your insurance to pay, the carrier requests the diagnostic code (a number), the dates of service, and the type of treatment (evaluation, therapy, or medication). If you have a managed care plan, that plan will sometimes request more detailed information about your symptoms and life situation in order to authorize treatment. If you would like to know exactly what they request and/or what I release, please let me know. Otherwise I will consult you only if the request seems too detailed, personal, or too comprehensive (like requesting the whole chart). Most parties will agree to a simple treatment summary.

I do not currently submit claims electronically. I submit some Blue Cross claims via an automated telephone system (no person) and I understand that this system is secure and HIPAA compliant. I do all my own billing and scheduling, so no other person has access to your information.

I sometimes obtain consultation for my cases. Specific information is exchanged in these meetings, but will not go beyond the consultants.

New Privacy Provisions and Changes

New HIPAA (Health Insurance Portability and Accountability Act) Privacy Standards were created to protect patients' health information when it is disclosed but also to facilitate the flow of medical information between treaters. With other medical treaters, billing, and for safety or security reasons, there is less protection of confidentiality than there used to be.

However, in other areas, such as releasing psychotherapy records, there is more privacy protection. Please read the following so that you understand your rights as a patient as well as the new rules about patient confidentiality. Feel free to ask me any questions about privacy, confidentiality, or your psychiatric record.

1. *Permission from the patient is no longer required for transfer of psychiatric and medical information between treaters as long as only the necessary information is supplied.* This means that if your primary care doctor, pharmacist, or an emergency room physician calls to find out if you are in treatment, what the diagnosis is, or what medications you are on, I can convey this information if it is medically relevant to your treatment with them. In practice, I will almost always discuss this with you personally before or after the fact, depending on the urgency and depth of the request. If you think this might present a problem for you, let me know ahead of time.

2. *Permission from the patient is no longer required for transfer of psychiatric information needed for business pertaining to insurance or payment as long as only the necessary information is supplied* (usually the diagnosis and type of treatment, but perhaps more). In practice, many insurance companies still require you to sign the first insurance sheet for authorization. In general, I do discuss any unusual requests for information from an insurance company with the patient first.

3. Remember that *if all the psychiatric records are requested, a treatment summary is usually given instead,* except if the treatment consists solely of psychopharmacological treatment or brief medication visits. While brief medication visits fall under HIPAA guidelines, psychotherapy visits are specifically excluded, meaning authorization from the patient is still required for release of the information in those notes and a summary is given in place of the record.

4. The *substance abuse records* from alcohol and drug programs are exempt from any disclosure without patient permission. If you are admitted to a treatment program for substance abuse, be sure to sign a release for me so I can talk to the treaters and obtain a discharge summary and lab data upon your discharge. Without this, I cannot obtain any information.

5. I may have to disclose some of your psychiatric information when required to do so by law. This includes mandated reporting of child abuse or elder abuse (this is not new).

6. *National security and public health issues.* I may be required to disclose certain information to military authorities or federal health officials if it is required for lawful intelligence, public health safety, or public security.

Individual (Patient) Rights

1. All patients have the right to inspect and copy their own protected health information (the medical record) on request, *except for mental health records*, which must be reviewed with a psychiatrist first (a Massachusetts state law). In cases where exposure to the record might be harmful to the patient, the psychiatrist may deny the request. If you request copy of your psychiatric record, I will generally review the record with you myself. I rarely have information in the chart that a patient should not or could not read, but much may require explanation.

2. Patients also have the right to amend or append their medical (or psychiatric) record. I, as your physician, have the right to deny such a request if I believe that the information in the medical record is accurate, but in that case the patient request must still be attached to the medical record.

3. Patients have the right to an accounting of all disclosures to other parties. This means that if you can ask me for a list of whom I have released psychiatric information to, I will supply it to you.

4. Patients have the right to have reasonable requests for confidential communications accommodated.

5. You can give written authorization for me to disclose your psychiatric information to anyone you choose, and you may revoke the authorization in writing at any time.

6. Patients can file a complaint with myself or with the Office of Civil Rights in the Department of Health and Human Services about any violation of the rights listed above. There will be no prejudice for filing such a complaint.

7. Patients have the right to receive a written notice of privacy practices from providers and health plans.

Phone Calls: I return *every* call by the end of my day at the office (which may be as late as 9 P.M.). I also call in for messages on weekends and holidays between 5 P.M. and 7:30 P.M. *If you do not hear from me by the end of the day, I did not get the message.* Please call again. Try not to use a cell phone, because the message is often disrupted. The [X] emergency room also has my home phone number if I need to be reached emergently.

Coverage: If I am out of town, the name and number of the covering psychiatrist will be on my answering machine. Usually the covering psychiatrist is [include your own coverage here]. She returns all calls by the end of the day.

Discontinuation of Treatment: I will usually discontinue treatment with a patient only after considerable discussion and usually for one of the following reasons: (1) not paying the bill, (2) canceling too often, or (3) not doing any work in treatment. If you foresee a problem in any of these areas, please let me know. If I see a difficulty in any of these areas, I will bring it up with you right away so we can discuss it and correct the problem.

You can discontinue with me at any time in person, by phone, or in writing. I am not easily offended if you want to quit or change providers. Transfer will be facilitated if we can first confer about ending. You can usually reopen your case simply by calling me if you ended the treatment in good standing or if you have made changes that will allow the treatment to go forward again.

Hopefully, these policies will make our interactions easier, but sometimes there are snags or unplanned issues. Please bring to my attention any questions about or difficulties with these policies. I try to be flexible but consistent. Thank you.

Sample Insurance Information Sheet for Patients

Understanding Insurance Coverage for
Outpatient Mental Health

Check the insurance booklet you were given for your health plan. If you filed it away, this is an opportunity to get it out and put it someplace for easy access in the future. Look for the section marked *outpatient mental health* in the table of contents or index. This section will list the yearly deductible, your co-payment for each visit, and the maximum number of visits allowed or the yearly dollar maximum.

Deductible: This is the amount you must pay before your insurance kicks in each year. Usually, it is about $250, but some plans (often HMOs) have no deductible or have deductibles as high as $2,000. If you have already seen other providers this year, your deductible may have been met.

In-Network: For HMO (health maintenance organizations) and PPO (preferred provider) plans, the term *in-network* refers to physicians who have contracts with the insurance company to see patients at a reduced fee. If you see someone within the plan or in-network, usually there is no deductible and your co-payments are lower. This is the cheapest option. For HMOs, you have to see someone in the plan. If you see someone in-network, the psychiatric care is usually managed in some way to keep costs low. This means that the treatment must be reviewed by the managed care company and that the visits must be authorized. The authorization process usually involves the provider giving the managed care company some details about your symptoms or illness. If the managed care plan does not authorize the visits, the insurance will not pay. **I am not an in-network provider for any HMO or PPO insurance plans.** Occasionally, an HMO will make a single-case agreement allowing me to treat someone because there are no other suitable providers in the area.

Out-of-Network: Usually, this means you can see any psychiatrist you want, even if they are not in the network. If you see a psychiatrist out of plan or out of network, usually you have to pay a yearly deductible and a larger co-payment. This is a more expensive option. Out-of-network psychiatric care is usually not managed, so there is more confidentiality going out of the plan.

Provider Lists: Preferred provider lists may be inaccurate or misleading, listing many providers who do not do clinical work or are not really available. Be sure to notify your insurance company if you are having problems obtaining a qualified provider on the list. They are obligated to provide care as part of the insurance contract.

Single-Case Agreements: If you have an HMO or PPO and no one on the preferred provider list can see you, it is possible to request a single-case agreement from the insurer to obtain treatment from someone outside of the plan.

Parity: In Massachusetts, insurers are required to offer the same limits of coverage for psychiatric illnesses of biological origin as they offer for regular medical illnesses, which means no limits as long as the treatment is medically necessary. Parity usually applies to most depressions, most anxiety disorders, bipolar disorder, all the schizophreniform disorders, and a few others. However, there are a few exceptions to the parity law. Be sure to check if parity will apply to you.

Allowed Amount: The fee (or *charged amount* on the billing statement) for each service is fixed and must be the same for every patient, but some insurance companies negotiate reduced fees with contracted providers. When a psychiatrist has such a contract, they agree to accept the *allowed amount* (the reduced fee) as payment in full and can not bill the patient for anything above that amount. **I currently have contracts with Medicare, Medicaid, and Blue Cross Blue Shield Indemnity plans,** so the fees charged to patients with those plans may be slightly lower than what is on my fee sheet. Please ask if you want to know the exact fee.

Some insurances set arbitrary allowed amounts that are not actually contract agreements, for example, $84 as the allowed amount for a 50-minute visit. They will pay 80% of that and state (or imply) that the patient pays 20% of that. What they do not clearly state is that this is *not a contracted fee reduction*, so that the physician *will* balance bill you for the *entire* amount that the insurance doesn't pay after the allowed amount. The allowed amount (sometimes called the *usual and customary fee*) is usually not stated in the insurance booklet because it changes each year, but you can call the insurer to ask if there is an allowed amount for a given psychiatric service and what it is.

Types of Psychiatric Visits (service codes for a psychiatrist): Useful in estimating cost or getting information from the insurer about what they will pay for a given visit.

90801 Initial Psychiatric Evaluation (1–2 hours)

90807 50-minute therapy and medical management (MDs only)

90805 25-minute therapy and medical management (MDs only)

90862 15-minute medication check (MDs only)

Estimating Costs: If you do not have your insurance booklet and cannot get one from the personnel office at work or the insurance company, your best bet is to call the insurance company and ask the following questions:

1. What is my yearly deductible for outpatient mental health?
2. What is my yearly maximum for outpatient mental health visits?
3. Can you send me a list of in-network providers or refer me to a psychiatrist within my plan?
4. What if I want to see someone out-of-plan?
5. What is my deductible and co-payment for an out-of-plan provider?
6. Is there an allowed amount, and what is it for each type of visit?
7. Can I be balance billed for the remainder past the allowed amount?
8. Does parity apply to me if I see Dr _____ and if my condition is _____ ?

Medicare: I am a contracted Medicare provider. Currently, Medicare has a yearly deductible for outpatient mental health visits (if you have a second insurance policy, this usually covers most, but not all, of the deductible).

After the deductible is paid, Medicare pays 50% of the allowed amount and you pay the remaining 50%. The allowed amounts for the year 2003 for Medicare are as follows (although they may have changed slightly):

90801 Initial Psychiatric Evaluation	$145.93
90807 50-minute visit	$100.05
90805 25-minute visit	$ 65.86
90862 15-minute visit	$ 49.75

If you have a secondary insurance after Medicare, they pay a percentage of what is leftover *after* Medicare pays. You are responsible for the amount left over after both insurances pay. Currently, there is no yearly maximum for Medicare, but there may be on your secondary insurance. If Medicare is your secondary insurance, not your first or primary insurance, then the allowed amounts for Medicare do not apply. Reimbursement will be based on my regular fees.

MassHealth: I can only take MassHealth recipients who have MassHealth as a secondary payer after Medicare because I am not a member of The Partnership, which manages the psychiatric part of MassHealth. There is usually no balance left for the patient to pay after both Medicare and MassHealth pay their parts.

Changing Insurances During the Course of Treatment

If your employer is going to change insurance plans or if you think you are going to change plans, be sure to check the outpatient mental health coverage for the plan and do the math. Sometimes it is cheaper to take an insurance plan for which I am not covered but that has very low premiums and pay out of pocket for my visits, rather than take an insurance plan that has high insurance premiums but covers more of your visits. Be sure to calculate your estimated costs both ways before making a decision.

Always let me know if you get a new plan, or a new card for the same plan, so I can submit the claims correctly.

APPENDIX C
Recommendations for Further Reading

Of General Interest on the Topic of Money

Davies, G. (1994). *A history of money: From ancient times to the present.* Cardiff, UK: University of Wales.

Hacker, A. (1997). *Money: Who has how much and why.* New York: Scribner.

Morreim, E. H. (1995). *Balancing act: The new medical ethics of medicine's new economics.* Washington DC: Georgetown University Press.

Starr, P. (1982). *The social transformation of American medicine.* New York: Basic.

For Deciding where Money Fits into
Life's Priorities

Covey, S. R. (1989). *7 habits of highly successful people.* New York: Simon & Schuster.

Dominguez, J., & Robin, V. (1993). *Your money or your life: Transforming your relationship with money and achieving financial independence.* New York: Penguin.

Menzel, P. (1994). *Material world: A global portrait.* San Francisco: Sierra Club Books.

For Understanding Status Issues

Frank, R. H. (1985). *Choosing the right pond: Human behavior and the quest for status*. New York: Oxford.

Ainsworth-Vaughn, N. (1998). *Claiming power in doctor-patient talk*. New York: Oxford.

For Women Who Struggle with Accepting Payment

Callahan-Levy, C. M., & Meese, L. A. (1979). Sex differences in the allocation of pay. *Journal of Personality and Social Psychology, 37*, 433–446.

Leventhal, G. S., & Anderson, D. (1970). Self-interest and the maintenance of equity. *Journal of Personality and Social Psychology, 15*, 57–62.

Leventhal, G. S., & Lane, D. W. (1970). Sex, age, and equity behavior. *Journal of Personality and Social Psychology, 15*, 312–316.

Liss-Levinson, N. (1990). Money matters and the woman analyst: In a different voice. *Psychoanalytic Psychology, 7*(Suppl.), 119–130.

Mikula, G. (1974). Nationality, performance, and sex as determinants of reward allocation. *Journal of Personality and Social Psychology, 29*, 435–440.

Nadler, M., & Nadler, L. (1987). The influence of gender on negotiation success in asymmetric power situations. In Nadler, LB, Nadler, M. K., and Todd-Mancillas, W. R. (Eds.), *Advances in gender and communication research* (pp. 189–218). Lanham, MD: University Press of America.

Tannen, D. (1995). *Talking 9 to 5: Women and men in the workplace: Language, sex and power*. New York: Avon.

Understanding Wealth and Poverty

Guilder, G. (1981). *Wealth and poverty*. New York: Basic.

Kiyosaki, R.T., & Lechter, S. (1998). *Rich dad, poor dad*. New York: Warner.

Stanley, T. J., & Danko, W.D. (1996). *The millionaire next door: The surprising secrets of America's wealthy*. New York: Pocket Books.

Wilson, W. J. (1987). *The truly disadvantaged: The inner city, the under-class, and public policy.* University of Chicago Press.

Wilson, W. J. (1996). *When work disappears: The world of the new urban poor.* New York: Knopf.

Personal and Business Finance

Bryan, M., & Cameron, C. (1992). *The money drunk: 90 days to financial freedom.* New York: Ballantine.

Marcinko, D.E. (2000). *The business of medical practice.* New York: Springer.

Racial Issues

Fine, M., Weis, L., Powell, L. C., & Wong, L. M. (Eds.), (1997). *Off white: readings on race, power, and society.* New York: Routledge.

Tatum, B. D. (1997). *Why are all the black kids sitting together in the cafeteria?* New York: Basic.

Professional Ethics Codes

Mental Health Counselors: The code of ethics of the American Mental Health Counselors' Association is available at www.amhca.org. Click on "code of ethics."

Nurses: Copies of the *Code of Ethics for Nurses and the Scope and Standards of Psychiatric-Mental Health Nursing Practice* can be obtained from the American Nurses Association, 600 Maryland Ave, SW, Suite 100 West, Washington D.C. 20024-2571. Phone: 800-274-4ANA. E-mail: www.nursingworld.org.

Psychiatrists: A copy of the *Principles of Medical Ethics of the American Medical Association with Annotations Especially Applicable to Psychiatry* are available from American Psychiatric Publishing, Inc., Attn: Order Department, 1400 K Street, NW, Suite 1101, Washington D.C. 20005; Phone 800-368-5777. E-mail: order@appi.org.

Psychoanalysts: A copy of the *Principles and Standards of Ethics for Psychoanalysts* is available at the Web site for the American Psychoanalytic Association at www.apsa.org/ethics901.

Psychologists: The *Ethical Principles of Psychologists and Code of Conduct 2002* is reprinted below, with permission of the American Psychological Association. A copy can also be downloaded from the Web site at www.apa.org.

Social Workers: The *Code of Ethics of the National Association of Social Workers 1999* is reprinted below, with permission of the NASW. Copies can be downloaded from the Web site at www.socialworkers.org/pubs/ code.

Other Mental Health Professionals: There are two other Web sites that collect and publish professional codes of ethics. One is www.kspope.com/ ethcodes. The other is www.iit.edu/department/csep. This second site is for the Center for the Study of Ethics in the Professions at the Illinois Institute of Technology.

References

Adams, D. B. (1990). Diversification in clinical practice: Primary- and tertiary-care considerations. In E. Margenau (Ed.), *Encyclopedic handbook of private practice* (pp. 250–259). New York: Gardner.

American Medical Association (AMA) (2002). Gifts to physicians from industry, Opinion 8.061 of the AMA's Council on Ethical and Judicial Affairs. Retrieved on 10/01/2004 from http://www.ama-assn.org/ama/pub/category/print/4001.html.

American Medical Association (AMA) (2003). *CPT®-Plus!: A comprehensive guide to current procedural terminology*. Los Angeles: Practice Management Information Corporation.

American Nurses Association (ANA). (2001). *Code of ethics for nurses with interpretive statements*. Washington, DC: Author.

American Nurses Association (ANA). (2002). *Scope and standards of psychiatric-mental health nursing practice*. Washington, DC: Author.

American Psychiatric Association (ApA). (2001a). *Ethics primer of the American Psychiatric Association*. Washington DC: Author.

American Psychiatric Association (ApA). (2001b). *Opinions of the Ethics Committee on The Principles of Medical Ethics with annotations especially applicable to psychiatry*. Washington, DC: Author.

American Psychiatric Association (ApA). (2001c). *Principles of medical ethics with annotations especially applicable to psychiatry*. Arlington, VA: Author.

American Psychoanalytic Association (2004). *Principles and standards of ethics for psychoanalysts*. Retrieved on 10/1/2004 from http://www.apsa.org.

American Psychological Association (APA). (2002). Ethical principles of psychologists and code of conduct. Washington, DC: Author.

Appelbaum, P. S., & Gutheil, T. G. (1991). *Clinical handbook of psychiatry and the law*. Baltimore, MD: Williams & Wilkins.

Avorn, J., Chen, M., & Hartley, R. (1982). Scientific versus commercial sources of influence on the prescribing behavior of physicians. *American Journal of Medicine, 73*, 4–8.

Backhouse, R. E. (2004). *The ordinary business of life: A history of economics from the ancient world to the twenty-first century*. Princeton, NJ: Princeton University Press.

Baker, W. E., & Jimerson, J. B. (1992). The sociology of money. *American Behavioral Scientist, 35*(6), 678–693.

Basch, M. F. (1980). *Doing psychotherapy*. New York: Basic.

Bass, A. (1999, October 14). Drug companies enrich Brown professor. *The Boston Globe*, p. A1.

Baurn, S. (1999). *Graduate and professional student borrowing: Are earnings high enough to support debt levels?* Quincy, MA: Nellie Mae Foundation.

Beahrs, J. O., & Gutheil, T. G. (2001). Informed consent in psychotherapy. *American Journal of Psychiatry, 158*(1), 4–10.

Behnke, S. H., & Hilliard, J. T. (1998). *The essentials of Massachusetts mental health law.* New York: Norton.

Benedict, J. G. (1990). Professional incorporation. In E. Margenau (Ed.), *Encyclopedic handbook of private practice.* (pp. 372–383). New York: Gardner.

Blanck, G., & Blanck, R. (1974). *Ego psychology: Theory and practice.* New York: Columbia University Press.

Bloom, D. E. (1998). Technology, experimentation, and the quality of survey data. *Science, 280,* 847.

Blue Cross Blue Shield of Massachusetts. (1989). *Update office guide* (vol. 2, No. 1). Author.

Borneman, E. (1976). *The psychoanalysis of money.* New York: Urizon.

Borys, D. S., & Pope, K. S. (1989). Dual relationships between therapist and client: A national study of psychologists, psychiatrists, and social workers. *Professional Psychology: Research & Practice, 20*(5), 283–293.

Brodsky, S. L., & Schumacher, J. E. (1990). The impact of litigation in psychotherapy practice. In E. Margenau (Ed.), *Encyclopedic handbook of private practice.* (pp. 664–676). New York: Gardner.

Bryan, M., & Cameron, C. (1992). *The money drunk: 90 days to financial freedom.* New York: Ballantine.

Burnside, M. A. (1986). Fee practices of male and female therapists. In D. W. Kreuger (Ed.), *The last taboo: Money as symbol and reality in psychotherapy and psychoanalysis* (pp. 48–54). New York: Brunner/Mazel.

Califano, J. A. (2000). America has the best health care system in the world. In J.D. Torr (Ed.), *Health care: Opposing views* (pp. 17–23). San Diego, CA: Greenhaven.

Callahan-Levy, C. M., & Meese, L. A. (1979). Sex differences in the allocation of pay. *Journal of Personality and Social Psychology, 37,* 433–446.

Canter, M., & Freudenberger, H. (1990). Fee scheduling and monitoring. In E. Margenau (Ed.), *Encyclopedic handbook of private practice.* (pp. 217–232). New York: Gardner.

Centers for Medicare & Medicaid Services (CMS). (2002). *Medicare and you: Physicians' edition.* Baltimore, MD: Author.

Centers for Medicare & Medicaid Services (CMS). (2003a). *Carriers manual* (Section 14002.4B). Baltimore, MD: Author.

Centers for Medicare & Medicaid Services (CMS). (2003b). *Medicare and other health benefits: Your guide to who pays first.* Baltimore, MD: Author.

Chapman, R. (1990). Sole proprietorship. In E. Margenau (Ed.), *Encyclopedic handbook of private practice.* (pp. 5–7). New York: Gardner.

Chessick, R. D. (1968). Ethical and psychodynamic aspects of payment for psychotherapy. *Voices,* Winter, 26–31.

Chren, M. M., & Landefeld, S. (1994). Physicians' behavior and their interaction with drug companies: A controlled study of physicians who requested additions to a hospital drug formulary. *Journal of the American Medical Association, 271*(9), 684–9.

Citron-Bagget, S., & Kempler, B. (1991). Fee setting: Dynamic issues for therapists in independent practice. *Psychotherapy in Private Practice, 9,* 45–60.

Cohn, J. (2000). Medical savings accounts will not improve the health care system. In J.D. Torr (Ed.), *Health care: Opposing* (pp. 173–177) San Diego, CA: Greenhaven.

Colombotos, J. & Fakiolas, N. P. (1993). The power of organized medicine in Greece. In F.W. Hafferty & J.B. MacKinlay (Eds.), *The changing medical profession: An international perspective* (pp. 138–149). New York: Oxford University Press.

Coonerty, S. (1990). Private practice: Promise and reality. In E. Margenau (Ed.), *Encyclopedic handbook of private practice* (pp. 453–460). New York: Gardner.

Cooper, D., & Winn, L. B. (2004). Fees for copying medical records. *Vital Signs,* September. Retrieved February 10, 2005, from http://www2.mms.org/vitalsigns/sept04/yp3.html

Covey, S. R. (1989). *7 habits of highly successful people.* New York: Simon & Schuster.

Davies, G. (1994). *A history of money: From ancient times to the present.* Cardiff, UK: University of Wales.

Davis, R. S. (2000). Ethical issues in managed care. In D.E. Marcinko (Ed.), *The business of medical practice* (pp. 351–365). New York: Springer.

Deiner, E., Sandvik, B., Seidlitz, L., & Deiner, M. (1993). The relationship between income and subjective well-being: relative or absolute. *Social Indicators Research, 28,* 195–223.

DiBella, G. A. W. (1980). Mastering money issues that complicate treatment: The last taboo. *American Journal of Psychotherapy, 24,* 510–522.

Dominguez, J., & Robin, V. (1993). *Your money or your life: Transforming your relationship with money and achieving financial independence.* New York: Penguin.

Doren, D. M. (1987). *Understanding and treating the psychopath.* New York: Wiley.

Dresser, R. (2001). Financial interests and research protections: Can they coexist? *Lahey Clinic Medical Ethics Newsletter, 4.* Retrieved February 10, 2005, from http://www.lahey.org/NewsPubs/Publications/EthicsJournalFall2001/Journal_Fall2001_Legal.asp

Duoba, J. L., & Gada, P. (Eds.). (2003). *Launching your first small business.* Chicago: CCH.

Durham, J. D., & Brosz-Hardin, S. (Eds.) (1986). *The nurse psychotherapist in private practice.* New York: Springer.

Eissler, K. R. (1974). On some theoretical and techinical problems regarding the payment of fees for psychoanalytic treatment. *International Review of Psychoanalysis, 1*(73), 74–101.

el-Guebaly, N., Prosen, H., & Bebchuk, W. (1985). On direct patient participation in the cost of their psychiatric care. Part I. A Review of the empirical and experimental evidence. *Canadian Journal of Psychiatry, 30,* 178–183.

el-Guebaly, N., Prosen, H., & Bebchuk, W. (1985). On direct patient participation in the cost of their psychiatric care. Part II. Access to services, impact on practice, and training implications. *Canadian Journal of Psychiatry, 30,* 184–189.

Engelhardt, H. T., and Rie, M. A. (2003). New financial incentives and disincentives in psychiatry. Retrieved August 2003.

Faustman, W. O. (1982). Legal and ethical issues in debt collection strategies of professional psychologists. *Professional Psychology, 13*(2), 208–214.

Fenton, C. F. (2000). Essentials of risk management. In D. E. Marcinko (Ed.), *The business of medical practice* (pp. 147–164). New York: Springer.

Ferrara, P. J. (2000). Medical savings accounts will improve the health care system. In J.D. Torr (Ed.), *Health care: Opposing views* (pp. 168–172). San Diego, CA: Greenhaven.

Field, M. (1993). The physician in the Commonwealth of Independent States [Russia]: The difficult passage from bureaucrat to professional. In F.W. Hafferty & J.B. MacKinlay (Eds.), *The changing medical profession: An international perspective* (pp. 162–171). New York: Oxford University Press.

Fox, J. (1995). *Accounting and recordkeeping made easy for the self-employed.* New York: Wiley.

Fromm-Reichman, F. (1950). *Principles of intensive psychotherapy.* Chicago: University of Chicago Press.

Fuchs, V. R. (2002). What's ahead for health insurance in the United States? *New England Journal of Medicine, 346*(23), 1822–24.

Gabel, J. et al. (2001). Job-based health insurance in 2001: Inflation hits double digits, managed care retreats. *Health Affairs, 20*(5), 180–186.

Galtress, E. (2000). Human resource options for the harried physician. In D.E. Marcinko (Ed.), *The business of medical practice* (pp. 39–62). New York: Springer.

Garner, B. (Ed.). (1999). *Black's law dictionary* (7th ed.). St. Paul, MN: West.

Gedo, J. (1962). A note on nonpayment of psychiatric fees. *International Journal of Psychoanalysis, 44*, 368–371.

Gigerenzer, G. (2002). *Calculated risks: How to know when numbers deceive you.* New York: Simon & Schuster.

Gilkerson, L. D., & Paauwe, T.M. (2003). *Self-employment: From dream to reality.* Indianapolis, IN: JIST Works.

Glasser, R. (2000). Managed care is unethical. In J.D. Torr (Ed.), *Health care: Opposing views* (pp. 70–77). San Diego, CA: Greenhaven.

Gold, M. R., Hurley, R., Lake, T., Ensor, T., & Berenson, R. (1995). A national survey of the arrangements managed-care plans make with physicians. *New England Journal of Medicine, 333*, 1678–83.

Goldberg, C. (1990). Typical mistakes of the beginning therapist. In E. Margenau (Ed.), *Encyclopedic handbook of private practice* (pp. 770–784). New York: Gardner.

Goldsmith, H. (2000). Effective insurance coding and billing guidelines. In D.E. Marcinko (Ed.), *The business of medical practice* (pp. 91–114). New York: Springer.

Granovetter, M. (1974). *Getting a job: A study of contacts and careers.* Cambridge, MA: Harvard University Press.

Granville, R. L., & Oshel, R. E. (2003). HIPDB: A tool to combat health care fraud (Part I). *Legal Medicine.* Washington, D.C.: Armed Forces Institute of Pathology.

Green, B. A. (1993). Psychotherapy with African-American women: Integrating feminist and psychodynamic models. *Journal of Training and Practice in Professional Psychology, 7*(1), 49–66.

Greenson, R. R. (1967). *The technique and practice of psychoanalysis* (Vol 1). Madison, CT: International Universities.

Grodzki, L. (2000). *Building your ideal practice.* New York: Norton.

Gruenberg, P. B. (1995). Nonsexual exploitation of patients: An ethical perspective. *Journal of American Academy of Psychoanalysis, 23*(3), 425–34.

Guadagnino, C. (2002). MDs challenged on disability insurance. *Physician's News Digest*, January. Retrieved February 10, 2005, from http://www.physiciansnews.com/cover/102.html

Guilder, G. (1981). *Wealth and poverty.* New York: Basic.

Haak, N. (1957). Comments on the analytic situation. *International Journal of Psychoanalysis, 38*, 183.

Haddrill, M. (2003, Nov./Dec.). Taking care of business: Employee fraud. *The Physician's Resource*, pp. 35–43.

Hafferty, F. W., & MacKinlay, J. B. (1993). *The changing medical profession: An international perspective.* New York: Oxford University Press.

Hall, J. E., & Hare-Mustin, R. T. (1983, June). Sanctions and diversity of ethical complaints against psychologists. *American Psychologist*, 714–729.

Harrari, C. (1990). Collections. In E. Margineau (Ed.), *Encyclopedic handbook of private practice* (pp. 243–249). New York: Gardner.

Heatherington, L., Daubman, KA, Bates, C., Ahn, A., Brown, H., & Preston, C. (1993). Two investigations of 'female modesty' in achievement situations. *Sex Roles, 29*(11/12), 739–754.

Hemenway, D., Killen, A., Chasman, S. B., Parks, C. L., & Bicknell, W. J. (1990). Physician responses to financial incentives: Evidence from a for-profit ambulatory center. *New England Journal of Medicine, 322*(15), 1059–63.

Hernreid, J., Binder, L., & Hernreid, P. (1990). Effect of student loan indebtedness and repayment on resident physicians' cash flow: An analytical model. *Journal of the American Medical Association, 263*, 1102–1105.

Herron, W. G., & Sitkowski, S. (1986). Effect of fees on psychotherapy: What is the evidence? *Professional Psychology: Research and Practice, 17*, 347–351.

Herron, W. G., & Welt, S. R. (1992). *Money matters: The fee in psychotherapy and psychoanalysis.* New York: Guilford Press.

Hill, M., & Kaschak, E. (Eds.) (1998). *For love and money: The fee in feminist therapy.* New York: Haworth.

Hill, M. (1999). Barter: Ethical considerations in psychotherapy. In M. Hill & E. Kaschak (Eds.), *For love and money: The fee in feminist therapy* (pp. 81–91). New York: Haworth.

Hilles, L. (1971). The clinical management of the nonpaying patient: A case study. *Bulletin of the Menninger Clinic, 35*, 98–112.

Hilliard, J. (1998). Liability issues with managed care. In L.E. Lifson & R.I. Simon (Eds.), *The mental health practitioner and the law* (pp. 44–53). Cambridge, MA: Harvard.

Hillman, A. L. (1987). Financial incentives for physicians in HMOs. *New England Journal of Medicine, 317*, 1743–1748.

Hillman, A. L., P., M. V. & Kerstein, J. J. (1989). How do financial incentives affect physicians, clinical decisions and the financial performance of HMOs? *New England Journal of Medicine, 321*, 86–92.

Hofling, C. K., & Rosenbaum, M. (1986). The extension of credit to patients in psychoanalysis and psychotherapy. In D.W. Kreuger (Ed.), *The last taboo* (pp. 202–217). New York: Brunner/Mazel.

Hogan, J., Gordon, A., & Herron, A. (2000). Basic capitation economics for internists and other specialists. In D.E. Marcinko (Ed.), *The business of medical practice.* New York: Springer.

Holden, C. (2000). Demanding less. *Science, 290*, 2065.

Holland, R. (1998). Planning against a business failure (ADC Info #24). The University of Tennessee Agricultural Extension Service. Retrieved October 1, 2004, from www. cpa.utk.edu/pdffiles/adc24.pdf

Hurd, M. J. (2000). Canada's health system is not a model for health care reform. In J.D. Torr (Ed.), *Health care: Opposing views* (pp. 162–167). San Diego, CA: Greenhaven.

Jenson, G. A., & Morrisey, M. A. (1999a). Employer-sponsored health insurance and mandated benefit laws. *Milbank Quarterly, 77*(4), 425–459.

Jenson, G. A., & Morrisey, M. A. (1999b). Small group reform and insurance provision by small firms, 1989–1995. *Inquiry, 36*, 176–187.

Kangas, S. (2000). Amercia does not have the best healthcare system in the world. In J.D. Torr (Ed.), *Health care: Opposing views* (pp. 24–30) San Diego, CA: Greenhaven.

Kaplan, S., Gandek, B., Greenfield, S., Rogers, W., & Ware, J. E. (1995). Patient and visit characteristics related to physicians' participatory decision-making style: Results from the medical outcomes study. *Medical Care, 33*(12), 1176–1187.

Kaplan, S., Greenfield, S., Gandek, B., Rogers, W. H., & Ware, J. E. (1996). Characteristics of physicians with participatory decision-making styles. *Annals of Internal Medicine, 124*, 497–504.

Kiyosaki, R. T., & Lechter, S. (1998). *Rich dad, poor dad.* New York: Warner.

Kotler, P., Hayes, T., & Bloom, P. (2002). *Marketing professional services.* New Jersey: Prentice Hall.

Kralewski, J. E., et al. (2000). The effects of medical group practice and physician payment methods on costs of care. *HSR: Health Services Research, 35*(3), 591–613.

Kreuger, D. W. (1986). *The last taboo: Money as symbol and reality in psychotherapy and psychoanalysis.* New York: Brunner/Mazel.

Kudirka, N. (1977). Trading therapy for art. *Voices, 14*, 51–54.

Kusserow, R. P. (1989). *Financial arrangements between physicians and health care businesses: State laws and regulations.* Washington, DC: Office of the Inspector General.

LaCava, F. W. (2000). Restrictive covenants and practice non-compete agreements. In D.E. Marcinko (Ed.), *The business of medical practice* (pp. 33–38). New York: Springer.

Langs, R. (1973). *The technique of psychoanalytic psychotherapy*, Vol. 1. New York: Aronson.

Lasky, E. (1984). Psychoanalysts' and psychotherapists' conflicts about setting fees. *Psychoanalytic Psychology*, 1(4), 289–300.

Lasky, E. (1999). Psychotherapists' ambivalence about fees: Male-female differences. In M. Hill & E. Kaschak (Eds.), *For love or money: The fee in feminist therapy* (pp. 5–13). New York: Haworth.

Leiter, R. A. (1993). *National survey of state laws*. Detroit, MI: Gale Research.

Leventhal, G. S., & Anderson, D. (1970). Self-interest and the maintenance of equity. *Journal of Personality and Social Psychology*, 15, 57–62.

Leventhal, G. S., & Lane, D. W. (1970). Sex, age, and equity behavior. *Journal of Personality and Social Psychology*, 15, 312–316.

Lifson, L. E., & Simon, R. I. (1998). *The mental health practitioner and the law*. Cambridge, MA: Harvard.

Light, D. W. (1993). Countervailing power: The changing character of the medical profession in the United States. In F.W. Hafferty & J.B. MacKinlay (Eds.), *The changing medical profession: An international perspective* (pp. 69–79). New York: Oxford University Press.

Lipsky, M. S., & Taylor, C. A. (1997). The opinions and experiences of family physicians regarding direct-to-consumer advertising. *Journal of Family Practice*, 45, 495–9.

Liss-Levinson, N. (1990). Money matters and the woman analyst: In a different voice. *Psychoanalytic Psychology*, 7(Suppl.), 119–130.

Lott, B. (1987). *Women's lives: Themes and variations in gender learning*. New York: Brooks/Cole.

Macbeth, J. E., Wheeler, A. M., Sither, J. W., & Onek, J. N. (1994). *Legal and risk management issues in psychiatry*. Washington, DC: Psychiatrists' Purchasing Group.

Manos, N. (1982). Free psychotherapy: The therapist's and the patient's view. *Psychotherapy and Psychosomatics*, 37, 137–143.

Marcinko, D. E. (Ed.) (2000). *The business of medical practice*. New York: Springer.

Marcinko, D. E. (2000). *The business of medical practice*. New York: Springer.

Marcinko, D. E., & Hetico, H. R. (2000). Health care economics in the United States: Evolution or revolution? In D.E. Marcinko (Ed.), *The business of medical practice*. New York: Springer.

Margenau, E., (1990). *The encyclopedia of private practice*. New York: Gardner.

Margolies, L. (1990). Cracks in the frame: Feminism and the boundaries of therapy. *Women & Therapy*, 9, 19–31.

Massachusetts Medical Society (MMS). (1996). *Ethical standards in managed care*. Waltham, MA: Author.

Massachusetts Medical Society (MMS). (2001). *Model managed care contract*. Waltham, MA: Author.

Matthews, M., & Goodman, J. C. (2000). The problems of the health care system are exaggerated. In J.D. Torr (Ed.), *Health care: Opposing views* (pp. 54–61). San Diego, CA: Greenhaven.

McKinney, W. P., et al. (1990). Attitudes of internal medicine faculty and residents toward professional interaction with pharmaceutical sales representatives. *Journal of the American Medical Association*, 264(13), 1693–97.

Mercado, O. K. (2000). Redefining the standard of care. In D.E. Marcinko (Ed.), *The business of medical practice* (pp. 343–350). New York: Springer.

Meyer, D. J., & Simon, R. I. (1999). Split treatment: Clarity between psychiatrists and psychotherapists. *Psychiatric Annals*, 29(5), 241–245.

Mikula, G. (1974). Nationality, performance, and sex as determinants of reward allocation. *Journal of Personality and Social Psychology*, 29, 435–440.

Miles, S., & Parker, K. (1997). Men, women and health insurance. *New England Journal of Medicine, 336*(3), 218–221.

Moody, E. F. (2004). Disability statistics. Retrieved October 1, 2004, from www. efmoody.com/insurance/disabilitystatistics.htm.

Morreim, E. H. (1995). *Balancing act: The new medical ethics of medicine's new economics.* Washington, DC: Georgetown University Press.

Morrisey, M. A., & Jensen, G. A. (1997). Switching to manage care in the small employer market. *Inquiry, 34,* 237–248.

Morrison, J. K. (1985). Settling 'delinquent' accounts in private practice: A five year review of the data. *Psychotherapy in Private Practice, 3,* 23–27.

Morrison, J., & Wickersham, P. (1998). Physicians disciplined by a state medical board. *Journal of the American Medical Association, 279*(23), 1889–1893.

Myers, D. C. (1993). *The pursuit of happiness.* New York: Avon.

Nadler, M., & Nadler, L. (1987). The influence of gender on negotiation success in asymmetric power situations. In LB Nadler, M. K., Nadler and W. R. Todd-Mancillas (Eds.), *Advances in gender and communication research* (pp. 189–218). Lanham, MD: University Press of America.

National Association of Social Workers (NASW). (1999). *Code of ethics of the National Association of Social Workers.* Washington DC: Author. Retrieved October 1, 2004, from http://www.naswdc.org/pubs/code/default.asp

Niemann, C. (1999). How much is enough? *Fast Company, 26,* 108–116.

Oetgen, S. (2003). DTC Advertising of prescription drugs: How does it impact patient behavior? *Legal Medicine* pp. 30–39. Washington D.C.: Armed Forces Institute of Pathology.

Office of the Inspector General (OIG) (1999). *Medicare and state health care programs: fraud and abuse; clarification of the initial OIG safe harbor provisions and establishments of additional safe harbor provisions under the anti-kickback statute.* Federal Register, 64, Doc. 99-29988 and Doc. 99-29989.

Office of the Inspector General (OIG) (2002). *Special fraud alert on rental of space in physician offices by persons or entities to which physicians refer.* Federal Register, 65, 9274–9277.

Olfson, M., & Klerman, G. L. (1993). Trends in the prescription of antidepressants by office-based psychiatrists. *American Journal of Psychiatry, 150,* 571–577.

Orlowski, J. P., & Wateska, L. (1992). The effects of pharmaceutical firm enticements on physicians prescribing patterns: There's no such thing as a free lunch. *Chest, 102,* 270–73.

Outka, G. (1976). Social justice and equal access to health care. In T. A. Shannon (Ed.), *Bioethics* (pp. 373–395). New York: Paulist Press.

Parvin, R., & Anderson, G. (1995). Monetary issues. In E.J. Rave & C.C. Larsen (Eds.), *Ethical decision making in therapy: Feminist perspectives* (pp. 57–87). New York: Guilford Press.

Parvin, R., & Anderson, G. (1999). What are we worth? Fee decisions of psychologists in private practice. In M. Hill & E. Kaschak (Eds.), *For love or money: The fee in feminist therapy* (pp. 15–25). New York: Haworth.

Pear, R. (2000). The uninsured are a serious problem. In J.D. Torr (Ed.), *Health care: Opposing views* (pp. 40–46). San Diego, CA: Greenhaven.

Pearson, S. D., Sabin, J. E., & Emanual, E. J. (1998). Ethical guidelines for physician compensation based on capitation. *New England Journal of Medicine, 339*(10), 689–693.

Peele, P. B. et al. (2000). Employer-Sponsored health insurance: Are employers good agents for their employees? *Milbank Quarterly, 78*(1), 5–21.

Perilstein, R. P. (2001). Physician's [sic] disability market. *Physician's News Digest,* May. Retrieved February 10, 2005 from http://www.physiciansnews.com/finance/501.html

Pharmaceutical Research and Manufacturers of America (PhRMA) (2002). PhRMA Code on interactions with health care professionals. April 19, 2004. Retrieved October 1, 2004, from www.phrma.org/publications.

Picker, L. A. (2003, Nov./Dec.). Computing compensation. *The Physician's Resource*, 26–33.

Polster, D. S. (2001). Gifts. In American Psychiatric Association, *Ethics primer* (pp. 45–50). Arlington, VA: Author.

Pope, K. S., Geller, J. D., & Wilkinson, L. (1975). Fee assessment and outpatient psychotherapy. *Journal of Consulting and Clinical Psychology*, 43, 835–841.

Pope, K. S. (1988). Fee policies and procedures: Causes of malpractice suits and ethics complaints. *Independent Practitioner*, 8(4), 24–29.

Porter, R. (1997). *The greatest benefit to mankind: A medical history of humanity*. New York: Norton.

Post, J. (1991) Medical discipline and licensing in the State of New York: A critical review. *Bulletin of the New York Academy of Medicine*, 67, 66–98.

Pressman, R. M. (1979). *Private practice: A handbook for the independent mental health practitioner*. New York: Gardner.

ProMutual Risk Management Group. (2002–2003). Who sues?: Patient satisfaction revisited. In *Perspectives on clinical risk management*, Winter, 1–7.

ProMutual Group & Massachusetts Medical Society (2004). *Closing a practice*. Perspectives on clinical risk management series. Boston: Authors. Retrieved February 10, 2005, from http://www.massmed.org/CME/Courses/007065/007065–P01.pdf

Rahn, R. (1999). *The end of money and the struggle for financial privacy*. Seattle, WA: Discovery Institute.

Rapoport, E., Phillips, S. S. & Fenster, S. (1990). The therapist's pregnancy. In E. Margenau (Ed.), *Encyclopedic handbook of private practice* (pp. 578–595). New York: Gardner.

Rappaport, E. J. (2000). Asset protection strategies for physicians. In D.E. Marcinko (Ed.), *The business of medical practice*. New York: Springer.

Reich, R. (2001). *The future of success*. New York: Knopf.

Rizzo, J. A., & Blumenthal, D. (1995). Physician income targets: New evidence on an old controversy. *Inquiry*, 31, 394–404.

Robbins, D. (1990). Taxes and investments. In E. Margenau (Ed.), *Encyclopedic handbook of private practice* (pp. 398–417). New York: Gardner.

Rodwin, M. A. (1992). The organized American medical profession's response to financial conflicts of interest: 1890–1992. *Millbank Quarterly*, 70(4), 718.

Rosenbaum, S. (2002). Medicaid. *New England Journal of Medicine*, 346(8), 635–640.

Rosenthal, M. B., Berndt, E. R., Donahue, J. M., Frank, R. G., & Epstein, A. M. (2002). Promotion of prescription drugs to consumers. *New England Journal of Medicine*, 346 (7), 498–505.

Ross, J. S. (2002). The committee on the costs of medical care and the history of health insurance in the United States. *Einstein Quarterly, Journal of Biological Medicine*, 19, 129–134.

Rundle, R. L. (2003, February 19). HMO Denial of crucial care is rare. *Wall Street Journal*.

Sanchez L. T., & Fromson, J. A. (2002). Handling of drug samples requires careful consideration. *Vital Signs*. May. Retrieved February 10, 2005, from http://www2.mms.org/vitalsigns/may02/pm2.html

Sand, H., & Davis, A. (1999). The price of talk in jail: Letters across the walls. In M. Hill & E. Kaschak (Eds.), *For love or money: The fee in feminist therapy* (pp. 93–105) New York: Haworth.

Scherer, H. (2000). Management information systems for the "wired" medical office. In D.E. Marcinko (Ed.), *The business of medical practice* (pp. 63–89). New York: Springer.

Schmidt, C. W., Yowell, R. K., & Jaffe, E. (2004). *CPT® handbook for psychiatrists*, 3rd edition. Washington, D. C.: American Psychiatric Publishing.

Schnurr, E. B. (2000). The federal employee health benefit program is a model for health care reform. In J.D. Torr (Ed.), *Health care: Opposing views* (pp. 187–195). San Diego, CA: Greenhaven.

Schonbar, R. A. (1967). The fee as focus for transference and countertransference. *Amercian Journal of Psychotherapy*, 21(2), 275–285.

Schorr, A. L. (1990). Job turnover: A problem with employer-based health care. *New England Journal of Medicine*, 323(8), 543–545.

Schwartz, R. K., Soumerai, S., & Avorn, J. (1989). Physician motivations for non-scientific drug prescribing. *Social Science Medicine*, 28, 577–582.

Shapiro, M. F., Ware, J. E., Sherbourne, C. D. (1986). Effects of cost charing on seeking care for serious and minor symptoms: Results of a randomized controlled trial. *Annals of Internal Medicine*, 104, 246–51.

Short, P. F., & Banthin, J. S. (1995). New estimates of the underinsured younger than 65 years. *Journal of the American Medical Association*, 274(16), 1302–1306.

Simon, R. (2001). *Concise guide to psychiatry and the law*. Washington, DC: American Psychiatric Association.

Smoller, J. W., McLean, R. Y. S., Otto, M. W., & Pollack, M. H. (1998). How do clinicians respond to patients who miss appointments? *Journal of Clinical Psychiatry*, 59, 330–338.

Social Security Act, 42 U. S. C. 1320a-7b.

Social Security Act, 42 U. S. C. 1395nn.

Sommers, E. (1999). Payment for missed sessions: Policy, countertransference, and other challenges. In M. Hill & E. Kaschak (Eds.), *For love or money: The fee in feminist therapy* (pp. 51–68). New York: Haworth.

Stanley, T. J., & Danko, W. D. (1996). *The millionaire next door: The surprising secrets of America's wealthy*. New York: Pocket.

Starr, P. (1982). *The social transformation of American medicine*. New York: Basic.

Steingold, F. (2001). *Legal guide for starting and running a small business*. Berkeley, CA: Nol.

Stelfox, H. T., Chua, G., O'Rourke, K., & Detsky, A. (1998). Conflicts of interest in the debate over calcium-channel antagonists. *New England Journal of Medicine*, 338(2), 101–6.

Stone, D. (2000). Managed care has harmed the health care system. In J.D. Torr (Ed.), *Health care: Opposing views* (pp. 78–86). San Diego, CA: Greenhaven.

Strom-Gottfried, K. (2003). Understanding adjudication: Origins, targets, and outcomes of ethics complaints. *Social Work*, 48(1), 85–94.

Sullivan, J. C., & Viglione, D. J. (1990). Public relations. In E. Margenau (Ed.), *The encyclopedia of private practice* (pp. 163–171). New York: Gardner.

Taragin, M., Wilczek, A. P., Karns, M. E., Trout, R., & Carson, J. L. (1992). Physician demographics and the risk of medical malpractice. *American Journal of Medicine*, 93, 537–42.

Torr, J. D. (Ed.) (2000). *Health care: opposing views*. San Diego, CA: Greenhaven.

Tryon, G. (1983). Full time private practice in the U. S.: Results of a national survey. *Professional Psychology: Research and Practice*, 14, 685–696.

United States Census Bureau (2000). *Statistical abstract of the United States*. Washington, D. C.: Government Printing Office.

U.S. Census Bureau. (2003). *Statistical abstract of the United States*. Washington, DC: Author.

U.S. Small Business Association, Massachusetts District Office. (2002). *Resource guide for small businesses*. Winterhaven, FL: RENI.

Van Yoder, S. (2002, Sept./Oct.). Cashing in on an old idea. *The Physician's Resource*.

Waitzkin, H. (1984). Doctor-Patient communication: Clinical implications of social scientific research. *Journal of the American Medical Association*, 252(17), 2441–6.

Walfish, S., & Coovert, D. L. (1990). Career as business. In E. Margineau (Ed.), *Encyclopedic handbook of private practice* (pp. 431–441). New York: Gardner.

Warbasse, J. P. (1935). *The doctor and the public: A study of sociology, economics, ethics and philosophy of medicine, based on medical history*. New York: Paul B. Hoeber.

Weaver, J. D. (2003). Levels of liability: It's not just the physician anymore. *Legal Medicine*. Retrieved February 10, 2005 from http://www.afip.org/Departments/legalmed/legalmed2003/Weaver.pdf

West's Encyclopedia of American Law. (1998). St. Paul, MN: West.

Woody, R. H. (1989). *Business success in mental health practice*. San Francisco: Jossey-Bass.

Yoken, C., & Berman, J. S. (1987). Third-party payment and the outcome of psychotherapy. *Journal of Consulting and Clinical Psychology, 55*, 571–576.

Zelizer, V. A. (1994). *The social meaning of money*. New York: Basic.

Zimmerman, R. (2003, February 26). Why trauma units seldom test patients for alcohol, drugs. *Wall Street Journal*, B1.

Zobel, J. (2000). *Minding her own business: The self-employed woman's guide to taxes and recordkeeping*. Holbrooke, MA: Adams Media.

Zobel, J. (2005). *Minding her own business: The self-employed women's essential guide to taxes and financial records* (Second edition). Napierville, IL: Sphinx Publishing.

Zuvekas, S. H. (1999). Health insurance, health reform, and outpatient mental health treatment: Who benefits? *Inquiry, 36*, 127–146.

Index